The Popular Culture Reader

The Popular Culture Reader

THE POPULAR CULTURE READER

Edited By

Jack Nachbar
Deborah Weiser
John L. Wright

Bowling Green University Popular Press
Bowling Green, Ohio 43403

 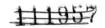

Library of Congress Card No.: 78-61077

ISBN: 0-87972-094-8 PB

Cover design by Tere Linn

CONTENTS

INTRODUCTION
WHAT IS
POPULAR CULTURE?

Introduction

I

Over ten billion dollars are being spent on advertising in the popular media in the United States each year. The average American is exposed to between 300 and 400 selling messages a day, from the toothpaste tube in the morning to the last television commercial at night. There are more radio and television sets than there are people in the United States — over 300 million. Ninety-eight percent of American homes have at least one television set, and that set is turned on an average of over six hours per day. More people watch even the lowest-rated program on television than would fill a Broadway theater in twenty years, even if it played to a full house every night. Two billion dollars a year are spent on phonograph records and tapes. *Reader's Digest* and *TV Guide,* the most popular magazines in the United States, have circulations over eighteen million.

What do these figures mean? Many people answer this question by arguing that popular culture is merely entertainment and that its lack of seriousness and depth makes it no more than trivial chewing gum for passive minds. Such an argument, however, too easily dismisses the obviously immense mass appeal of popular culture. Few people would deny that much of the content of the popular arts is poorly done, just as a great deal of the work of "serious" artists is also undoubtedly of rather minimum quality. Popular art is commercial; it is mainly produced for the purpose of turning a dollar. The popular arts are decidedly imitative and formulaic. Undoubtedly, a huge percentage of the popular arts is aesthetically inferior, judged by any standards. Nevertheless, popular culture products are so much with us, so much a part of the day to day lives of all Americans, that the values and beliefs both on the surface and hidden beneath these products inevitably have an important impact on all of us. On one hand, the products influence our thinking. In the morning our choice of deodorant, indeed the fact that we are convinced that we need a deodorant, might be based on last week's late show commercial or perhaps by the shape of the deodorant package itself. At lunch, our selection of food might well be determined by the latest diet-book best seller. And our decision of how to spend the evening—reading, dating, etc.—may have been determined by the hairstyle of a current movie star or by the guests on a talk show we heard on the car radio going to work this morning. On the other hand, we as consumers determine what is popular culture and what is not. Just a few less points in the audience figures of the Nielsen TV ratings, for example, and network program planners begin changing jobs, multi-million dollar shows are dumped, and entire new programming concepts begin to be planned. It is because mass consumption has such a powerful effect on popular products of all kinds that these products come to reflect the wishes, needs and desires of their buyers. The popular arts do equate popularity with quality: value is often measured in terms of millions of tickets or copies sold, and dollars of income. We may take this as a key in our understanding of the popular arts. Although choices may be at times limited, the very popularity of a work suggests that it has struck a chord in the public at large, that thousands or millions have found something in the work that is enormously appealing or stimulating. If we want to learn what Americans are thinking, their fears, fantasies, and desires, we should look at these most popular works for the reflection of the dreams of the multitude.

It is because popular culture has this two way relationship with our lives—both affecting the values we construct for ourselves and reflecting values we have already constructed—that popular culture taken as a whole is the most common part of our cultural heritage and our day to day present living environment. Ray Browne in his article defining popular culture does not exaggerate when he says that popular culture is such a pervasive part of our existence that popular culture surrounds us as water surrounds fish; even though we may be unaware of its presence, it is the environment in which we move and live.

The study of popular culture may begin with the question; why is this thing popular? Popularity is not, of course, a simple matter. People buy books, attend movies, and so forth, for a variety of reasons—to escape boredom and kill time, for social companionship, to be "in" on the latest thing and have a new topic for casual conversation, or because of an intense promotional campaign.

All of these reasons are important to the cultural analyst. But to stop here is to stop short, because we have to push on to the question: why are some things popular and others not? What is it about the detective novels of Agatha Christie, for instance, that accounts for their tremendous sales of more that 300 million books while many other mystery writers have toiled for years without achieving best-seller status? What is it about novels made into movies such as *Gone with the Wind, The Godfather,* or *Jaws* that makes these stories in both book and film forms major financial successes when so many other works fizzle as novels, movies or both? If you answer these kinds of questions, you are really getting at the essence of popular culture, which is that these works are perhaps not so much individual artistic expressions as they are expressions of mass taste and mass desire. People consume specific elements of popular culture mainly because they want to.

A second fundamental question is: what is popular culture. The answer to this question is the topic of the first two essays in this book. In the simplest terms, popular culture is best thought of as mainstream culture—the arts, artifacts, and beliefs shared by large segments of the society. We can't, of course, make a simple head count—that is, demand proof that 51% of the public likes this or that cultural product in order for the work to qualify as popular culture. There are perhaps some works that fall within the field even though they may not be popular at all. A detective novel no one bought or a Western that never manages to play at more than half a dozen sleazy drive-ins would be examples because they are both attempts to imitate more successful works in already popular genres.

In general, however, the definition of popular culture as mainstream or mass culture is a useful one for the serious study of what popular culture means to people. There is, after all, a logical pattern established by assuming a kind of formula for the study of popular culture in which the more popular a thing is, the more culturally significant it is likely to be. Thus, football is more culturally meaningful in the United States than rugby; pizza and hamburgers more a key to American life than escargot.

II

The term "popular culture" includes an almost countless variety of materials, and ideas both past and present. To more easily get a handle on this diverse subject matter, however, we may speak of four types or categories of popular culture. Furthermore, these four categories may be imagined as a house with a foundation and three rooms. It is around such an imaginary "house of popular culture" that the major sections of this book are organized after the initial general explanatory section.

The foundation of our house, like the foundations of most homes, is slightly underground—everyone knows it's there but it can't be seen. This foundation is called popular mythologies. Within this category we place those elements contained within the human mind: popular beliefs, values, superstitions and movements of thought. Popular mythologies such as American ideas of democracy, the American tendency to believe that Europeans are culturally superior to Americans and the American love-affair with mechanical gadgets, are usually accepted as true unquestionably by people and these same people proceed to lead their lives accordingly. But just as the basement holds up the visible parts of the house, popular mythologies are the basis upon which the other more obvious elements of popular culture are based. Specific items within the other three categories in other words, are constructed images representing the popular mythologies.

The first of these aboveground, visible rooms is popular objects including both things and people. Popular things, sometimes called artifacts, are the images produced by commercial packaging and advertising and three dimensional objects themselves, such as the architecture of suburban ranch style homes and fast-food restaurants. We may look at these images and artifacts as icons—objects that have special significance on both the individual and collective level. These icons are often surrounded by folklore; who has not heard stories of the powers of Coca-Cola?: what it will do to a nail left in it overnight? how to get high by putting a couple of aspirin in a bottle of Coke? doesn't it really have cocaine in it? Oftentimes these same icons reflect deeper, almost unconscious beliefs. Coke, for example, advertised for years that it was, "The pause that refreshes." Such a slogan suggests how work oriented American Coke drinkers are. To feel good about gulping down a Coke, that gulper should feel that his pleasure is only momentary and that its real purpose is to fortify himself for the greater labors that are to come immediately after the "pause." Drinking a soft drink for pure pleasure, is, apparently, sinful idleness.

People may also be considered popular objects and when they are, the student of popular culture finds it useful to consider these people in about the same way he or she would consider things. Popular stereotypes may be things but are usually a class of people. As the essays in the "Stereotype" section of the book demonstrate, a commonly expressed stereotype, whether it be racial, religious, sexual or vocational, tells us little about the people being stereotyped. After all, when individuals are depersonalized and mentally tossed into narrow groupings such as Indians, working women, or cops, the images that emerge of these individuals will surely be distorted. What we do learn from a stereotype, as we learn from icons, are certain ideas, both surface and hidden, that are held in common by those who believe in the stereotype. The other type of popular human object, popular heroes, functions for people in the same way as stereotypes. There is a major difference in that stereotypes often reveal the historic fears of American culture whereas popular heroes such as Daniel Boone, Abraham Lincoln and Martin Luther King, Jr. usually serve as images of the traditional ideals of our culture.

The second room in our house of popular culture is the popular arts, a vast field covering everything from popular fiction and poetry to popular theater, popular music, and the media—films, radio, and television. To enumerate some of the subdivisions of just one of these categories—popular fiction—we find sentimental and domestic fiction such as *Little Women;* inspirational literature such as the famous American bestseller, *Ben Hur*; historical romances such as *Gone with the Wind;* adventure stories like *Tarzan of the Apes;* modern Gothic romances, with heroines who find themselves in crime-ridden mansions; classic stories of detection by such writers as Ellery Queen and Rex Stout; the tough guy or hardboiled detective novels of Mickey Spillane and Ross Macdonald; the spy stories such as those about Ian Fleming's James Bond; Western fiction from its beginnings in James Fenimore Cooper to the works of Zane Grey and, more recently, Louis L'Amour; science fiction of all kinds, from gut-level "space opera" to serious speculation; big expose'and sex novels like *Peyton Place* and *Valley of the Dolls*; war stories such as *From Here to Eternity;* stories of the occult like *The Exorcist;* and, finally, those works that are enormous bestsellers but almost defy description, such as *Jonathan Livingston Seagull* and *Jaws.*

A list of the various kinds of popular music and television programs probably would be even longer. The important point is that the term popular arts covers a large area and their importance, as with objects, is that they reflect popular taste and, therefore, popular ideas. A primary means of studying popular art forms is through the concept of formula, based on the idea that a certain kind of popular art contains many elements which are familiar to both creator and audience. This shared familiarity of plots, characters, settings, etc., makes the popular arts accessible to the widest possible public.

The third room in the house is popular rituals—those events of our society that engage the interest of groups large and small. Like the popular arts, they employ a number of different popular elements often including icons, stereotypes and heroes. The difference between the popular arts and popular rituals is mainly that the popular arts tend to be imaginative creations produced for one of the mass media. Popular rituals are real events actually attended or participated in by those enjoying them. Here is a list of popular rituals: sports contests or public games of all sorts, from pie-eating contests to the Olympics; parades; group meals, such as church suppers; carnivals and circuses; fairs—county fairs, state fairs and world expositions; festivals—music festivals, town festivals, and ethnic festivals; reunions—family reunions, class reunions, war reunions; parties and dances; showers and weddings; funerals; holiday festivities; high school and college homecomings; and public gatherings and celebrations of every sort. These rituals serve a number of social purposes—to commemorate a link with the past, to affirm a sense of group solidarity, to show off one's products or, perhaps, just to have fun, to be there and to be a part of what's happening.

Popular events or rituals are probably the least-explored and least-understood area of popular culture. Of all the areas, they are most taken for granted. The serious student of popular culture, on the other hand, sees these rituals as also expressive of cultural and subcultural values. For example, Bowling Green, Ohio, is the site of an annual event called the National Tractor Pulling Championships. Each year over sixty thousand people gather for three days to watch one tractor after another pull a heavyweighted sled as far as possible down a 300-foot track. So what? Well, a closer look at what's going on shows that even a tractor pull is highly expressive. The largest tractors are super powered products of modern technology, but their useful purpose is agrarian. In short, the tractor pull celebrates a union of man and machine and reflects the American farmer in transition—from the simple life of the past to a complex, mechanized present and future.

None of the four major components in our "house of popular culture" stand isolated from the others. Corridors and hallways of shared popular experiences tie together all the rooms of the house. Many of the articles in this book discuss certain objects, heroes, etc. as isolated from other popular culture elements but it should be realized that the basis of almost all visible popular culture is popular beliefs and values and that each one of these beliefs and values is expressed in a large and complex variety of related ways. A brief examination of how one popular belief is reflected in various popular forms will hopefully illustrate this variety.

The belief to be discussed in some detail is the belief in perfect-ability—the idea that human beings, and by extension society, can achieve a state of perfection in which nothing more will be needed. We will rise above ourselves and acquire total fulfillment. Now the curious thing about our society, and here is where popular culture comes in, is that we think fulfillment can be achieved through secular means, instead of or in addition to traditional spiritual means. Oftentimes the crassest or most commonplace activities are motivated by the lofty desire to be perfect.

Someone once said that "The American dream is to pile up enough money and possessions to get to Heaven." This is rather crude, but it is not too bad as an oversimplified explanation as our multitudinous advertising messages hold out the promise of instant self-renewal. If we will only buy this deodorant or that new car, we will be transformed without further delay—not only will we smell good, we'll feel good and *be* good. No more worries, no more problems, our lives are fulfilled. Of course, we may intellectually refute this—we know it's not *really* going to happen, but these messages go deeper than the intellect. They appeal to a residuum of belief in magic, a belief in these products as talismans of modern life. In most cases it is possession of the product that is important: we buy ourselves, as a 1977 Buick TV ad stated "A little science. A little magic."

One of the best modern examples of the promise of salvation or self-renewal through consumption is the promotional campaign for Seven-Up. Through an intense advertising blitz over several years, Seven-Up moved from obscurity to a position competitive with Pepsi-Cola and Coca-Cola. This was done by means of the image of the Uncola, creating a picture of the Seven-Up drinker as something of a rebel against the establishment. The television commercials for Seven-Up became extremely psychedelic, consisting of bright and shifting hallucinogenic images backed by a soundtrack which sang, "See the light. See the light...of Seven-Up." The "light" referred to the light taste of the product, but it also suggested that drinking Seven-Up would bring about a sort of enlightenment. And the psychedelic pictures implied that Seven-Up was a mind-expanding drug. What was being promised was transcendence through a soft drink—sipping one's way to Paradise.

The popular arts are also expressive of the myth of perfectibility. The television private eye story, in its usual form at any rate, offers a good example. Even though the stories are often set in the grimmest realities of the lowlife sections of the city, the message nevertheless builds us a stairway to heaven. The method of telling the story is to rely on stereotyped characters who will immediately confirm our gut instincts. And the detective heroes are glamorous figures who are always tracking down dangerous criminals. The reality is that there are very few private investigators in the society, and most of the real ones earn their living by such activities as slinking around trying to catch adulterers. But we need hero figures, and if they don't exist they must be created. The heroes that television gives us are doctors, policemen, lawyers, private eyes, and comic book-like characters with wonderful powers. These heroes act as the representatives of the social order to bring health and justice for us all. This, too, is a temporary kind of perfection. For a moment, the case is wrapped up, the patient has found not only health but new life, and we can all rest easy with the knowledge that our heroes are still on the job.

Finally, the belief in perfectibility is expressed in many of our popular rituals. Beauty queen pageants are an obvious example. Typically, the contestants in beauty queen contests are as common as old shoes. We are told that they come from various ordinary American communities and are very often members of lower middle class families. But through the magical American combination of God given gifts (good looks), hard, diligent work (the demonstration of a talent) and a concern for other people (the personality test) an ordinary little nobody from nowhere is wrapped in a royal robe, receives a queenly crown and parades down a ramp to tearful applause. And each time we watch such a spectacle we have reaffirmed for us that *anyone* may, if enough dues are paid, become the worshipped image of human perfection. As students of popular culture we also might notice that part of the psychology of the contest has been to turn stereotyped female virtues into the essential qualities of queenly heroism, demonstrated with the icons of robe and crown and the "art" of the singing of a song of praise. Thus all of the major popular culture categories prove to be present at one popular culture event.

III

All three areas of objects, arts and rituals appeal to us in the same general way. They all impose structures upon experience that allow us to make sense of a world that often seems absurd and to find expression for ideas, beliefs and values that often seem inexpressible. Unfortunately, the danger for a student of popular culture is the possibility of experiencing an overabundance of structures—there is simply so much to do and read and hear and see that we can become confused and disoriented. The materials in this book of essays are intended to prevent or at least lessen such confusion.

Each section begins with an introductory essay that defines the area of popular culture under examination, and subdivides the subject into smaller categories. The essay also includes several examples of each topic or sub-topic. The last part of the introductory comments introduce the essays that follow it, explaining briefly how each essay illustrates the topics that have been defined and the approach each writer takes toward the topic. Also included in each section for those enthusiastic about the subject are a few additional suggested readings and a number of suggestions for further study.

The essays themselves were selected because the editors thought they were of high quality, because the editors liked the subject matter, and because they illustrated various approaches to the topics. Because the subject matter and approaches are so wide-ranging, you will undoubtedly find some essays much more rewarding than others. Such reactions may provide you with insights into what is popular with your personal tastes. And, more importantly, your like or dislike of particular essays will teach you ways you believe popular culture should and should not be studied. Is a highly serious, self-consciously scholarly approach in order? Or is an informal, personal and playful approach more appropriate for this type of subject matter? Hopefully, your reactions to the materials in this book will lead to your own research, discoveries and insights. The formal study of popular culture on the college level is only a few years old. Much popular culture material has never been analyzed at all. Your thinking and writing about popular culture can be pioneering work in an area crucial to our understanding of our culture and of ourselves.

Welcome to your new home.

Popular Culture — The World Around Us

By Ray B. Browne

Popular Culture, in its simplest definition, is the cultural world around us—our attitudes, habits and actions: how we act and why we act; what we eat, wear; our buildings, roads and means of travel, our entertainments, sports; our politics, religion, medical practices; our beliefs and activities and what shapes and controls them. It is, in other words, to us what water is to the fish: it is the world we live in.

Popular Culture is the culture of the people, of all the people, as distinguished from a select, small upper-class group. It is also the dominant culture of minorities—of ethnic, color, social, religious, of financial minorities. As the way of life of a people, popular culture has existed since the most primitive times. It has obviously become more complex and sophisticated as means of communicating have developed.

Although popular culture has existed as long as people have, the concentrated and widespread academic study of people's ways— even among anthropologists and sociologists—is a recent development. As such, today, of course, definitions differ somewhat about what Popular Culture really is. In the recent past many people have felt that popular culture is mass culture—that is, the common culture of the masses of people —and therefore it could develop only after the eighteenth century, when rapid means of producing the printed word came into being. Though this attitude has some validity and appeal, it may be too narrow in concept and too short in time span to be comprehensive. The development of rapid means of printing and distributing led to a faster way of disseminating people's culture than had existed before, to be sure, and the very

From *Popular Culture and Curricula,* Bowling Green University: by Popular Press. Reprinted by permission of the editors and the author.

means of distribution began to create its own culture. But before this phenomenon people had had much culture in common; nowadays we call that "folk culture."

Folk culture traditionally had to a certain extent been individual and community oriented. Individual artisans developed their own aspects of culture and folk community life evolved its own characteristics. Both aspects often were of necessity units unto themselves. After the eighteenth century, with the invention of rapid printing presses "folk culture" underwent some drastic changes. Wide and rapid dissemination of cultural phenomena made former folk communities become parts of a larger world, and mixing the cultures made them more similar. The development of machines to mass produce thousands or millions of copies of articles has had a dramatic and lasting influence. Means of dissemination always influence, or control, the material being disseminated. So, through the years, newspapers, magazines, radio, television and movies, as well as the numerous other means of communication, have demanded and worked best with a certain sameness in the material being communicated. This sameness created patterns of expectancy and understanding that appealed to a majority of the intended audience, all of which make dissemination easier and more profitable.

This is not to say that in this new mix of culture folk life has disappeared. On the contrary, folk culture is still important—though on a modified scale—and remains very much alive. Folklorists recognize that old definitions of the field of their interests were too narrow and inelastic in the past and needed to be broadened, as indeed they have been.

Another conventional way to define popular culture is to distinguish among three levels of society—the elite, the mass and the folk. In such an arrangement, generally speaking, the elite and the folk each constitute roughly ten per cent of society, each on opposite ends of the social and education line. Such a division leaves approximately 80 per cent of society for what many people call "mass" or "popular" culture. Such a distinction must be generalized and indeed might be somewhat artificial and arbitrary, since, in the anthropological sense of the term, virtually all people of a nation live in the same culture, are acted on by the same ways of behavior, experience the same buildings, use the same kinds of transportation, hear the same music on radio or in public performances, see the same movies and television programs, attend the same sports events, etc. To people who like to view mass and popular culture as one and the same and as the massive section lost between elite and folk cultures, this large field of phenomena was possible only after the development of rapid means of disseminating

14

culture such as the electronic media.

There is, of course, more to popular culture than that which is distributed by the electronic media, though they surely have a major impact. Popular culture consists of our patterns of thought and behavior, our educational system, what we study and why and how. Popular culture, in other words, is the world around us. As such it is more than mass culture. The term probably should include all three of the other terms—elite, folk and mass—and might in fact be a redundancy. Perhaps the term popular culture really equals culture.

A series of graphs might be useful at this time to show the interrelatedness among the various areas of culture. Traditionally cultures have been tiered according to degrees of sophistication (Fig.1), with elite being on top and folk on bottom. Folklore scholars, however, tiring of their field of interest always being relegated to the lowest echelon have properly insisted that all cultures drew from and fed into folk patterns (Fig.2). To a large extent, however, Figure 2 is false because it emphatically places elite culture above and therefore superior to popular culture, when in fact it ought to be designated merely as different. Perhaps the most revealing metaphor for culture is a flattened ellipsis or a lens (the CBS logo), with High and Folk cultures on either end, both looking fundamentally alike in many ways and both having some characteristics in common (Fig.3). In the center, largest in bulk by far is Mass culture. It must be remembered that lines separating the area are vague and indistinct—grey rather than sharply black and white. The overriding arch of all is Popular Culture.

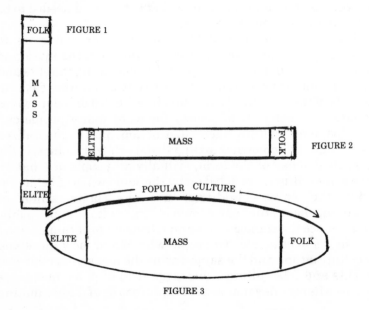

FIGURE 1

FIGURE 2

FIGURE 3

If people's popular culture consists of all the aspects that make up a way of life, it would seem obvious that it is necessary that we understand this culture if we are to understand the nation, its way of life, if we are to understand ourselves, if, in other words, we are to be "educated" in the full sense of the word. The controversy of what constitutes a proper education is old and is yet very much unsettled. Socrates held to the injunction "Know thyself." Plato, following hard on Socrates' counsel, was all for educating out of the context of life, for dealing only in the ideal, for despising the common people—whom he called the oxen of the world—and the materials of their lives. This same attitude was voiced in the eighteenth century by the Englishman Edmund Burke. Burke, as every student of American history remembers, had been a friend of the American Revolution, but he condemned the French—and all the masses—as the "swinish multitude" when they tried to throw off their Monarch's yoke. Burke's attitude was condemned by the American patriot Tom Paine and though it is still held by many has been gradually eroded away ever since. In fact, it seems obvious that the democratic way of life demands respect for and understanding of a people's popular culture. The Declaration of Independence proclaimed this fact and the Bill of Rights guaranteed it.

Americans generally have always been a practical people, and most realize that one must train for life as we lead it. It is not proper for people to be educated for life as it might have been or might become, or as we wish ideally it were. One makes more progress toward improving the conditions of life if he recognizes where reality begins and sets out working from that point, not from some idealized position where he is not and may never be. Many Americans therefore think that the old Socratic injunction of "Know thyself," must be modified to read "Know yourself in your surroundings."

Commenting on the change in people's attitudes toward popular culture, Irving Wallace, present-day author of half a dozen bestselling novels and co-editor of the popular *The People's Almanac* (1976) and *The Book Of Lists* (1977), observed "The relationship between the critical community and the popular author has changed in recent years. Some critics are honest enough to respect public taste, or at least be curious about it and treat it seriously." Concerning his own purposes in writing Wallace said, "I write to explore other human beings, the human condition, through my own psyche and within my limitations."

Ross Macdonald, contemporary creator of the great detective Lew Archer, commented, somewhat on the same subject as Wallace, on the value of popular culture in our society. "We learn to see reality through the popular arts we create and patronize. That's what they're for. That's why we love them." And Irving Wallace, again, attested to the power of the popular arts as model when he commented: "I was always going to be a writer. But if I ever faltered in my singleminded ambition, then surely there was popular art to influence me in my ambition and prop me up and carry me along."

The value of popular culture as a window to the human condition is timeless. Perhaps because it is less artful, less altered by the alchemy of the artist, popular culture is often a more truthful window of what the people were thinking and doing at any given time than artistic creations are. In other words, a catalogue of what Athenians in Socrates' time were wearing, eating, drinking, joking about, how they were reacting to sports, their sex habits, etc., might be more revealing of the real Athens than the philosophy of Socrates is. They surely would be important. Realizing the value of these documents of everyday life, Thomas Jefferson commented "...It is the duty of every good citizen to use all the opportunities which occur to him for preserving documents relating to the history of our country."

Jefferson might wisely have expanded his call to collect documents to include the preservation of all kinds of artifacts. If, for example, one wants to understand Shakespeare's plays fully, he studies outside the dramas, in what was going on in London at the time, the attitude of the people toward England's kings and queens, toward war, housing, poverty, foreigners, etc.

If one would understand eighteenth century America he should read the broadsides, sing the contemporary songs, investigate the wills, inventories of holdings, get as much into the lifestyle as possible, investigate all kinds of records.

In order to understand George Washington, for example, one needs to visit Mt. Vernon and while there study deeply the physical setting in which the man lived and worked: the house, the furniture, the geography of the surrounding houses, the slave culture, modes of transportation, distance, the music that was a part of the daily household, etc. And the visitor must visit and examine the artifacts in the museum—the clothing, the trinkets, items of daily living; why, for example, was the set of dental equipment used on slaves' teeth composed of five iron instruments, probably made by the local blacksmith and easily bent, while Mr. Washington's set was of eight stainless steel instruments that probably could easily be used by dentists today? These artifacts tell us much.

If a picture is worth a thousand words, a museum is worth a million, or a hundred books. And actually living the life—though the effort is to a large extent make-believe—is worth millions of words more.

So in order to understand present-day life, the place of the sports hero in our financial and cultural hierarchy, for example, obviously one must understand the setting.

Suzanne Sommers as sex goddess is a cultural pheonomenon who was created almost overnight by the media, and the questions that are immediately asked are How and Why? She was created because society cannot comfortably exist without heroes and heroines. The electronic media create and discard heroes so fast that they must always have new ones ready to be brought forward. She was available when needed. She is an example of one important aspect of our life that needs to be understood.

Such an attitude about the value of everyday things in the proper education is generally understood by the public, though often it is minimized by the academic, the so-called intellectual, because he, she is biased toward other things. For a long time intellectuals have been fond of quoting the old saying that one never went broke underestimating the intelligence of the American public. But is such a statement valid or is it the rankest snobbery? Is it pro or anti-democracy? The answer is of the greatest importance.

Regardless of its cultural error, the attitude is really beside the point. One should always make a distinction between studying some phenomenon in order to understand it and actually participating in it. For example, we do not have to engage in professional sports in order to be interested in them or to want to understand their place in society; one does not even have to own a set to realize that television has a great impact on our lives, and to realize that he or she needs to comprehend this phenomenon. In understanding one does not necessarily have to love—or to hate. **Understanding** is the goal. Then one can shape one's life accordingly. But understanding is or should be a prerequisite.

What is the role of the intelligent and educated citizen in society? How does one get to be educated? American education is, and perhaps always should be, in a state of crisis and consequently of great debate. This means that we should try to understand, then act; we should not be afraid. To this end, Raymond Williams, a noted British critic, has stated:

> The human crisis is always a crisis of understanding; what we genuinely understand we can do... There are ideas, and ways of thinking, with the seeds of life in them, and there are others, perhaps deep in our minds, with the seeds of general death. Our measure of success in recognizing these kinds, and in naming them making possible their common recognition, may be literally the measure of the future.

Toward better preparing the citizen for life, the critics Hall and

Whannell pointed out an important value of popular culture:

> Perhaps the most significant connection between popular
> art and high art is to be seen in the way popular work helps the
> serious artist to focus the actual world, to draw upon common
> types, to sharpen his observations and to detach the large but
> hidden movements of society. New art forms frequently arise
> when profound modifications are taking place in social life and
> in the 'structure of feeling' in the society. Often this change is
> first recorded in popular work, and new popular themes and
> conventions are devised to deal with them, or to express them.

Lewis Mumford, one of the keener minds of our day, observed
that education should be looked upon as a "lifelong transformation
of the human personality, in which every aspect of life plays a part."
In other words, these individuals, and many others like them, are
saying that a person owes it to himself to develop his learning as
much as possible, and this learning should include the popular
culture.

Perhaps a word of caution might be necessary. Educators who
insist that popular culture should be studied emphasize that it
should be a supplement not a substitute. Although for too long
popular culture was excluded from the ordinary fare of education
and should now be included, the more traditional materials—or at
least the genuinely valid ones—should be retained. Popular culture
should be studied to more nearly round out—to deepen and to
enrich—at least portions of the more conventional curriculum.
Education is too important to settle for anything less.

Bibliography

In the briefest bibliography possible, I suggest the following references:
Hall, Stuart and Paddy Whannel, **The Popular Arts** (N.Y., Pantheon Books, 1964).
Nye, Russel B. **The Unembarrassed Muse** (N.Y., Dial Press, 1970).
Toll, Robert C. **On With the Show** (N.Y., Oxford, 1976).
Williams, Raymond. **Culture and Society. 1780-1950** (London. Chatto & Windus.
1960) and **The Long Revolution** (N.Y., Columbia University Press, 1961).

Discussing "Popular Culture—The World Around Us"

1) For each of the following categories, give an example for elite, popular, and folk
culture: sports, food, clothing, entertainment.
2) How does the traditional hierarchical ordering of cultures promote prejudice and
snobbery?

Notes on a Rationale for Popular Culture

By Russel B. Nye

The term "popular culture" describes a cultural condition that could not have appeared in Western civilization before the late eighteenth century. People had always found pleasant ways of diversion, of course, but not until the appearance of mass society in the eighteenth century could popular culture, as one now uses the term, be said to exist. Though no one differentiated between folk and popular culture for another century, it was understood that both were distinct from elite, upper class culture. No one cared, however, about clearly distinguishing among them, for they all had much the same purpose insofar as the popular audience was concerned. Neither writers, performers, nor audiences bothered to separate the kinds of arts into cultural types; songbooks, for example, might contain half folk songs and half popular tunes—"Dearest May" or "Barbara Allen" appeared next to "Old Kentucky Home" or "Home, Sweet Home." But uncertain as its exact meaning may have been, the appearance of a truly *popular* culture was certainly one of the consequences of the Industrial and Democratic Revolutions. It was one of a number of responses to the new kinds of social, political, and intellectual relationships that these revolutions involved.

One of the conditions for the swift growth of popular culture in the later eighteenth century was a great explosion of population in Europe and the Americas, lasting well into the nineteenth, and its subsequent concentration into urban or semi-urban units which possessed unifying, common, social, economic, and cultural characteristics. As a result, there suddenly appeared a huge market with a tremendous desire for entertainment and the wealth to satisfy it. The origins of what is now called "the entertainment industry" can be recognized as early as 1750, when cultural goods

From pamphlet "Notes On A Rationale for Popular Culture." (Bowling Green, Ohio: Popular Culture Association, 1970). Reprinted by permission of the author.)

began to be manufactured and marketed in quantity as a response to the needs of this mass public.

Another factor in the rise of popular culture was the emergence, at about the same time, of a middle class, rapidly democratizing society. As the upper classes gradually lost control of cultural standards, the spread of education and literacy through the great middle class created a new kind of audience, predicated on the median tastes of the population at large. Control of the means of cultural production and transmission shifted from the aristocratic elite to the urban, democratized, essentially conservative middle class. By the middle of the nineteenth century nearly everyone in the United States (except slaves and Indians) was minimally literate; by the twentieth nearly three of every four American adults had received some kind of high school education. This mass society had leisure time, money, and cultural unity; it needed a new art—neither folk nor elite—to instruct and entertain it.

Popular culture was also, of course, the child of modern technology, wholly dependent for its extension on modern techniques of duplicating and multiplying materials (high speed presses, cheaper paper, new ways of graphic representation) along with much more effective and less costly methods of production and distribution. In nineteenth-century society, machines swiftly widened and cheapened the public's access to the printed page. Print was persuasive until the twentieth century opened other channels of cultural diffusion to even larger audiences with new methods of reproducing and transmitting sound and image— phonograph, film, radio, television.

The mass of today's population is accessible in such a variety of ways that print is no longer the chief means of contact between artist and public. The average American of today will by his sixty-fifth year have spent 3000 entire days (almost nine years of his life) watching television; by the time of the average five-year old of 1979 enters kindergarten he has spent more time before the family TV set than the average college student has spent in classrooms over a four-year span. Today's mass media have obliterated the boundaries between cultural classes; with the rapid growth of non-verbal, non-personal modes of communication, literacy is no longer a sole prerequisite for cultural diffusion.

The creation of this vast new popular audience, beginning in the eighteenth century, naturally elicited in response a new level of culture. Obviously, there had always been two artistic traditions— the high and low comedy of Greece, the drama and circuses of Rome, medieval cathedral plays and street-fairs, Renaissance court-drama and tavern farces—but the rise of a predominantly middle-class civilization, accompanied by a decrease in numbers and importance of the so-called "elite" and "lower" classes, drastically changed the cultural pattern. The eighteenth century established the outlines of a triple artistic tradition—the folk and high art of the past, plus a new *popular* level of art, although the lines which separated them were never precisely clear. Before the eighteenth century the serious artist created for a relatively small minority on whom his success and his support depended. But though Samuel Johnson looked for a patron, he prospered without one, for by his time the elite no longer held cultural control either of the powerful middle class or the great popular market.

The growth of this large popular audience, increasingly available for exploitation through the mass media, provided an unparalleled opportunity for artists who were willing to and could satisfy its culture needs. Success lay not in pleasing a rich patron and his small, aristocratic circle, but in gratifying the tastes of an increasingly larger "popular" audience. By the close of the eighteenth century a relatively large number of artists, particularly novelists and dramatists (whose work was most adaptable to mass consumption) wrote with this new popular market in mind. The popular artist made his own tradition by calculating what the public wanted and evolving ways and means (some adapted from folk art) for giving it to them. In other words, the artist who wrote for this audience turned professional (as Daniel Defoe did), creating for profit the kind of art that the public was willing to buy.

The *popular* artistic tradition as we know it, therefore derives from the shift—initiated in the eighteenth century and completed during the nineteenth—of control and support of the arts by a relatively small upper class, to that of a huge, growing middle class audience, during a period of great technological, social, and political change. Modern mass society was fully formed by the mid-nineteenth century; the mass media, in various stages of development, were already present to provide swift, cheap methods of communication.

Presently, the term "popular culture" has such broad meaning that it is difficult to describe it briefly or clearly. In most definitions there seems to be no consistent common denominator except that connoted by the word "popular" (occasionally used synonymously with "mass") as "reflecting a consensus, or a generally-approved set of attitudes." Extremes of meaning of the term "culture" range from the anthropologist's all-inclusive description of "culture" as "the total productions of a society," to the literary historian's restricted definition of it as "art on the printed page."

Nevertheless, whatever the difficulties of precisely defining the term, one must mark its boundaries—always with proper elasticity—in order to work with it. Most, though not all, of those in the field of popular culture today would probably agree that "popular culture" describes those productions, both artistic and commercial, designed for mass consumption, which appeal to and express the tastes and understanding of the majority of the public, free of control by minority standards. They reflect the values, convictions, and patterns of thought and feeling generally dispersed through and approved by American society.

Although it is not difficult to distinguish between popular and folk art on one hand, and high or "elite" art on the other, the line between the first two is not always clear. The folk artist often tends to prefer anonymity; he is less concerned with aesthetic context, and less with specifically aesthetic purpose—though he too hopes to satisfy his audience, of course, as much as the popular artist does. What he produces, however, tends to be thematically simple and technically uncomplicated; it is less likely to be influenced by technological factors—the folksong, the duck decoy, the tavern sign, the circus act.

Popular art is aimed at a wider audience, and it is a more calculated attempt to meet that audience's expectations. The popular artist is well aware of the need to sell the product, and more consciously adjusts to meeting the median taste. In folk and popular art the role of the performer is also recognizably different. The skill of the "name" or "known" performer (except in the limited circle of certain folk audiences) is less vital to the success of folk than of popular art, where it can often be of great importance.

High or "elite" art, on the other hand, is produced by known artists within a consciously aesthetic context under the authority of an accepted set of rules; its success or failure is judged in relation to an established, normative tradition which both artist and audience know and respect. The subjective element is vital to its effectiveness. High art is exclusive, particular, individualistic; its aim is the discovery of new ways of recording and interpreting experience. Technical and thematic complexity is of much greater value in elite than in folk or popular art; in high art, technique and execution may themselves become ends, as important as content or organization.

Popular art, on the contrary, is neither complicated nor profound—to understand and appreciate it ought to require neither specialized, technical, nor professional knowledge. It is relatively free of the corrective influence of minorities; its standards of comprehension and achievement are consensus-approved; it is "popular" in the sense that it does not deviate far from majority standards and conventions. More individualized than folk art, but less so than high art, popular art tends to be more dependent than either on the skill of the performer.

Popular art confirms the experience of the majority, in contrast to high art, which tends to explore the new. For this reason, the popular arts are sensitive and accurate reflectors of the attitudes and concerns of the society for which they are produced. The popular artist corroborates (occasionally with great skill and intensity) those things already familiar to his audience; his aim is less to provide a new experience than to verify an older one. To be effective, popular art should also be predictable. It deals with the known: the fulfillment of expectation, the pleasant shock of recognition, the validation of an experience already familiar—as in the detective story, the popular song, the Western movie.

Popular art must, of course, be adaptable to mass production and to diffusion through the mass media. It is irrevocably tied to the technology of duplication; for the popular artist the machinery of reproduction and distribution may be as important—or more so—to what he does as either technique or content. Popular art, therefore, must be produced in such a fashion as to reach the widest possible audience in the most efficient way, a fact of life which the popular artist must learn to accept as one of the stipulations of his craft.

The two most important characteristics of the popular audience are its size and its diversity—huge, heterogeneous, bewilderingly varied in its mixture of life styles, interest, tastes, containing a cross-section of economic and educational levels. This audience is much less self-conscious than an "elite" audience; its standards are less clearly defined, its expectations less consistent and integrated. The cultivated, elite audience and the elite artist hold common aesthetic and intellectual standards; they have their own specialized idiom of criticism and creation. But those who respond to the popular arts are not sure why; their standards are never precisely formulated, may swiftly change, and are much more flexible than those of a folk or "elite" art.

The relation of the popular artist to his audience is unique. The "elite" artist knows that his audience views his art in a context of an established tradition and that it comes to him with certain definable expectations; he knows that his success or failure occurs within an accepted framework of accepted theory and past achievements. His audience is acutely aware of him as an individual, knowing that he presents his particular interpretation of his own experience, and that he is deeply and personally involved with the content and technique of his product. The popular artist, however, works under no such set of rules, with a much less predictable audience, and for much less predictable rewards. His relationship with his public is neither direct nor critical, for between him and them stand editors, publishers, sponsors, directors, public relations and "A and R" men, wholesalers, exhibitors, and merchants who can and often do influence his product. No matter what else, what he does has to sell.

The elite artist works within the traditional conventions of genre and technique, and knows that he will be judged by them. Since his accomplishment is going to be measured by comparison with what others have done (or are doing) at his artistic level, he is always aware of the objectives and standards set for him by his critics. The popular artist, however, is always subject to the law of supply and demand; his primary objective is to win the largest possible audience in the marketplace. Neither what others *have* done, nor what critics say *must* be done, will necessarily guarantee success for what *he* does.

The criterion of the popular artist's success is contemporary, commercial, measured in terms of the size and response of his public. He competes not with his medium, nor with a preconceived set of critical standards, nor even sometimes with other popular artists, but always with the audience under whose control he must work—a notoriously capricious audience of unknown size and composition. And so too must he reach his audience through the mass media—with their constantly recurrent demands for materials, fixed publication deadlines, and yawning chasms of space and time to be filled. The novelist writing for the little magazine or the prestige publisher, and the mystery-story specialist writing for the mass-circulation weekly, stand at different ends of the pole in relation to their materials and audiences, because they reach their audiences in quite different ways, which in turn exert powerful influence on their products. Galleries, concerts, the quality press, the hardback book trade, classroom assignments, self-improvement book clubs and discussion groups are not for the popular artist; he finds his public via the newstand, the movie screen, the book-of-the-week list, the TV tube, the paperback. His audience sees him less as an individual than as its own representative; his personal vision takes on meaning and effectiveness only when it reflects a wider, majority experience. He expresses not only what he feels, but through what he feels he expresses what many others do.

These differences in elite and popular audiences, and in the artists' relationships with them, require corresponding differences in the aim and content of what they create. The popular audience is less inclined to accept the experimental or unusual. The popular artist deals with familiar, easily recognizable experiences with which large numbers of people can identify. The artist creating for an elite audience can assume that his readers, listeners, or viewers are willing to expend a good deal of effort to understand and appreciate what he does, but the popular artist can by no means expect either such attention or exertion from his public. Popular art cannot be novel, eccentric, esoteric, or unduly individualized; its audience will not sit still and concentrate for long.

The popular audience expects entertainment, instruction, or both, rather than aesthetic experience. To produce something for such an audience means that the popular artist cannot be primarily concerned with the preferences of minorities, unless they represent a significant market. Since they aim at the largest common denominator, the popular arts therefore tend to standardize at the median level of what the majority expects. The popular artist cannot disturb or offend any significant part of his public; though the elite artist may and should be a critic of his society, the popular artist cannot risk alienation. His success depends on as wide approval as he can attract.

The popular artist, then, hopes to do the very best he can within the rigorous limits set by his situation. His accomplishment must be measured by his skill and effectiveness in operating within the boundaries of the majority will and the requirements of the mass media, nor should he be expected to do otherwise. Since he hopes to make money, he aims at one thing—the largest possible audience—and whether it be a best-seller, a high program rating, a four-star feature, or a "golden disc," his talents (which may be considerable) are directed toward mass response.

This does not mean that what the popular artist does is not worth doing, or personally unsatisfying, or aesthetically bad, or commercially cheap. It merely means that he must develop certain kinds of specialized skills to accomplish it, for his program must pay the medium and show a profit. But it does mean that popular art, to be successful, has to be immediately popular; the mass public will not wait very long to be entertained, nor will it work hard at it. Therefore the popular artist must use those forms and media to which his audience has easiest access—movies, radio, television, the phonograph record, the magazine, the paper-back book, the popular song, the newspaper, the comic book, and so on—and which it can most easily comprehend.

The fact that the mass audience exists, and that the popular artist must create for it, are simply the elementary facts of life for the popular arts. Popular art can depend on no subsidy from state or patron; it has to pay its way by giving the public what it wants, which may not always agree with what the artist may feel to be the most aesthetically significant. Satisfying a large audience involves no less skill than pleasing a smaller or more sophisticated one; popular artists can and do develop tremendous expertise and real talent. Nor need popularity alone condemn what they do as useless or inferior. A best-selling paperback is not *ipso facto* bad; a song is not necessarily worthless because people hum it; a painting is neither bad because many look at it with pleasure nor good because few do.

With skill and talent alone, sometimes, a popular artist may transmute mediocre material into something much better than it is, or even good; the gradual improvement over the years of standards of performance in the popular arts provides sufficient proof of this. The technical virtuosity of a Tony Bennett or an Ella Fitzgerald, for example, can turn a routine show-tune into a polished piece of musicianship; Jack Benny's genius for timing a pause surely is a touch of artfulness rarely matched in comedy; how Ray Charles totally involves himself and his listeners in an uncomplicated gospel hymn can become a powerfully emotional audience experience. Furthermore, a brief glance at the almost unbelievable banalities and ineptitudes of early movies, radio, television, fiction, or popular theater, in comparison with today's product, makes it abundantly clear that contemporary popular artists have developed tremendous technical skill, and that their sophistication and subtleties of performance are much greater than their predecessors'. The distance between the movies of William S. Hart and Mary Pickford (and even some of Chaplin's); between the comedy of Gallagher and Shean or Amos and Andy; or between the music of The Wolverines or Paul Whiteman and today's equivalents, is incredibly wide. The simple literalness of Tom Mix and Edward G. Robinson has become the sophisticated, multileveled popular art of *High Noon, Bonnie and Clyde, or Star Wars.*

Whatever its manner of expression, popular culture and the arts included in that culture can no longer be treated with condescension nor merely dismissed as unworthy of study. Instead of the rigid divisions among high, mid-, and low-class art established by elitist critics over the past forty years, it is now much more reasonable— and useful—to view the arts as one long continuum, and to consider all levels of artistic accomplishment as related rather than disparate.

To erase the boundaries that have so long divided the arts means, in the long run, greater understanding of them. Aware today as never before of the potentials of this vast, unknown terrain of popular culture, critics and public alike may discover in it new knowledge of breadth, depth and variety of the American experience.

Discussing "Notes on a Rationale for Popular Culture"

1) Compare Nye's definition of popular culture with that of Herbert Gans, Leslie Fiedler, or David Manning White.

2) Some popular artifacts (song, movies, comics) are not supportive of the values of

the mainstream culture, yet they are endorsed by the population. How can the popular culture theorist account for these "subversive" aspects of American culture?

PART ONE
POPULAR MYTHS

Introduction

Many people, when they hear the term *Myth* think of marvelous Greek fantasies with gods wielding magic, and Greek heroes fighting one-eyed giants, or beasts half-man and half-bull. In the same way, American myths are John Henry in his deadly race against the steam-powered railroad spike driver or Paul Bunyan striding through the great North woods with his blue ox, Babe. With these images in mind, myths are taken to be monumental exaggerations and when people say, "that's a myth," they really mean that what is being referred to is untrue.

People who spend their lives studying myths have come to a different conclusion about them. While they agree that myth narratives do indeed stretch what could or does happen in real life, at the same time these stories tend to reveal the deepest beliefs of the people who share these stories. When the Greek hero Odysseus, for example, defeats the witch Circe, after Circe had sexually seduced Odysseus' crew of sailors and turned them into pigs, Homer was expressing a belief of the Greeks that reason should control sexual passion or mankind would be no better than swine. Myths, in other words, rather than being untruths, express basic truths a culture believes about the relationship of mankind to reality.

The *Random House Dictionary* has two definitions of myth that fit closely the idea of myth as cultural belief:

a) "a story or belief that attempts to express or explain a basic truth,"

b) "a belief or subject of belief whose truth or reality is accepted universally."

Three important ideas about myths are expressed in these

definitions. First, myths are *basic*. That is, they usually deal with essential beliefs about such crucial concepts as life, death, love, and hate. They deal with the bedrock issues of how and why we live or, as Richard Slotkin puts it in his essay, myths "define the total world—picture of a human culture, summing up the several ways men may relate to the cosmos. . . ." The second idea in the definitions is that myths are *universally accepted* beliefs. This means that myths really don't argue that certain ideas are true. Rather, they present in different forms ideas people already accept as true. The purpose of myths is not to debate beliefs within a culture but to re-affirm them.

The third idea is that myths are *beliefs*. What people believe is, of course, not necessarily true. The important thing about beliefs is that people accept them as true, whether they are or not, and conduct their lives on that basis. Myths are crucially important to a culture because they form the basis upon which that culture acts as it does, forming its traditions, customs, and values.

The stories used to express these essential cultural beliefs are called myth-narratives. Whether or not myth-narratives are realistic is not important. What is important about them is that they are expressions for the members of a culture of the very premises upon which the culture is based.

The four essays that follow discuss four popular American myths and their expression in various myth-narratives and other popular forms. Another popular myth, human perfectability, is discussed in the introduction. To illustrate the functions of myths in American life and how they are expressed in popular culture, three other popular myths will briefly be discussed here. It should be kept in mind, however, that we will by no means exhaust the subject here. There are dozens of myths in any culture. The perceptive student of American popular culture who begins searching will soon discover many more.

The myth of abundance tells us that we possess more than we can ever use. America is a land of such overwhelming natural resources and productive potential that we will never run out of anything essential to comfort and well-being. This concept was already in the minds of the earliest settlers, such as John Smith, who wrote that the new land was blessed with such abundance that to prosper a man only had to work four hours a day. Early explorers were so convinced of this myth that an intelligent man like Ponce de Leon struggled through Florida certain that he would find a fountain of youth. Francesco Coronado roamed the Southwest believing in seven cities of gold. Later, conspicuous waste expressed the belief that we could never run out of anything. Instead of using wood for building, forests were cleared by burning. The buffalo were annihilated largely for sport and luxury coats. In our day, the myth

"American Country." Smiling adults and fat, happy children. A Currier and Ives print illustrating the myth of rural simplicity.

"Preparing for Market." The rich productivity of the farm in this Currier and Ives print suggests the American myth of endless abundance.

is still, despite growing concerns about depleted energy resources, very much with us. We tend, for example, to gain status by buying new things. Cars are customarily traded every two or three years not because they are worn out, but because it makes us feel good to have a new one. The rise in popularity of disposable items—diapers, lighters, plates, razors, even dresses—reflects our faith that we can't ever run out of anything.

Cultural myths such as the myth of endless abundance are such elemental beliefs in a culture that they give rise to smaller but no less accepted concepts. Believing in endless abundance, for instance, encourages a related belief that convenience is a virtue. As a result we support gigantic companies who maintain themselves by selling appliances that will cut by a few seconds the time it takes to chop a carrot, or open a can, or cook a hot dog. Another related belief is that big is good. Prosperity is expressed through the purchase of a "full-sized" car. And the glutton at the ice-cream shop wins a medal if he can somehow force down a super-sized sundae.

A second important myth in America is the myth of rural simplicity. Articulated by Thomas Jefferson when he defined the true American as the yeoman farmer, this myth posits that true happiness and virtue are to be found by living close to the cultivated land. Television's brief history abounds with examples of highly successful shows who assume the truth of this myth from "Lassie" in the 1950's to "The Beverly Hillbillies" and "Green Acres" in the 1960's to "The Waltons" and "Little House on the Prairie" in the 1970's. Other types of popular culture have arisen from this myth. The contemporary popular ritual of leaving work and camping for a vacation is based on the idea of rural simplicity. And two related beliefs to be discussed in the section on stereotypes—that cities are by nature evil, and that farms and small towns are bastions of virtue—are also traceable to the rural simplicity myth.

A third myth at the heart of American culture is the myth of technology as a protector and savior. This may at first seem like a contradiction of the rural simplicity myth but, in effect, we generally believe that technology provides for and protects the continuing truth of the other myths. The mass production created by technology provides us, for example, with an endless abundance of affordable products. And, after all, don't such creations of technology as tractors and combines ease the drudgery of farm work and allow the life of leisurely communing with nature that Jefferson foresaw? The American space program is a concrete example of our fundamental faith in this myth. With only a few murmurs of dissent, billions of dollars were spent during the 1960's on the space program. Apparently, most people assume that such a remarkable technological triumph as landing on the moon inevitably would result in benefits worth the huge investment. A belief related to the myth of technology as savior is that efficiency is always a virtue. The omnipresence of vending machines in our lives and our passive acceptance of them testify to our faith in both technology and efficiency. The popularity of computers is based in part on believing that the efficiency of data processing will produce a higher quality of life for everybody.

The three myths just discussed may well be a part of the myths discussed in the four essays in this section. Neither myths nor less essential beliefs exist in isolation. Each of them modifies, corrects and reinforces the others in a complex set of perspectives we call a cultural worldview. Each of the four authors, using different subject matters and methods, do manage, however, to isolate and discuss other identifiable popular American myths.

Madonna Marsden uses a variety of popular literature from nineteenth century children's fiction to modern get-rich-quick manuals to demonstrate that from our Puritan forefathers to our present day business executives, Americans have always believed that wealth and success are synonomous with goodness and happiness. Marsden demonstrates that cultural myths invariably have origins buried far in the past and that myths persist in a culture through periods of immense economic and social change.

Richard Slotkin, in his essay "Dreams and Genocide," like Marsden, traces an American myth back to its colonial origins. Unlike Marsden, Slotkin's central focus, ultimately, is not the myth itself, but modes of conduct arising from belief in the myth. The fact that myths are not merely abstract ideas but powerful forces that lead directly to action has, in the case of "regeneration through violence," had tragic consequences.

In his article on the counter culture of the 1960's Harold Schechter analyzes a much narrower time span and employs a considerably different approach than either Marsden or Slotkin. As detailed in the first pages of his essay, Schechter's method of analysis relies directly on the psychological theories of Carl Jung. According to Jung the essence of myths are archetypes shared by all human cultures. The actions of the 60's flower children therefore do not reflect myths exclusively American, but follow a pattern recognizable in many cultures for thousands of years. Schechter's numerous examples are in themselves a good example of how a popular myth is infused in almost every aspect of popular culture. The essay also demonstrates how certain myths may attain popularity during certain periods within a culture in response to specific needs of that culture.

William Blake Tyrell works in the narrowest area of all of the four authors in this section. He concentrates on a single myth-narrative television series, "Star Trek." Through this procedure, Tyrell illustrates a theory of the famous anthropologist Claude Levi-Strauss that myths serve the valuable function of "mediators" between two conflicting ideas or values within the same culture. Myth-narratives resolve the tensions between the conflicting elements. Other ideas in this essay can also be related to myths discussed elsewhere in this book such as the myth of perfectability and the Western myth.

Selected Further Reading

Beane, Wendell C. and William Doty, eds. *Myths, Rites, Symbols: A Mircea Eliade Reader*. Harper and Row: New York. 1975.

Jung, Carl G. *Man and His Symbols*. Doubleday and Co., Inc.: Garden City, NY. 1964. A richly illustrated introduction to Jung's major ideas intended for the layman.

Marx, Leo. *The Machine in the Garden*. Oxford University Press: New York. 1964. Examines technology and the pastoral idea in America.

Nash, Roderick. *Wilderness and the American Mind*. Yale University Press: New Haven. 1973.

Rischin, Moses, ed. *The American Gospel of Success*. Quadrangle Books: Chicago. 1965. An anthology of primary and secondary sources.

Slotkin, Richard. *Regeneration Through Violence*. Wesleyan University Press: Middletown, CT. 1973.

The American Myth of Success: Visions and Revisions

By Madonna Marsden

Open almost any magazine and you'll find it—the lavish array of material objects which connote the comfort, the status and the security which are the components of The American Dream. For these are the cliches of the American good life—a chicken in every pot, a car in every garage, a place where even the person born into poverty can give a tug on his or her bootstraps and have a chance at the Presidency or a seat on the Stock Exchange. And it *has* happened here. Think of our great political and industrial heroes: Andrew Jackson, Abraham Lincoln, Andrew Carnegie, John D. Rockefeller. Though essentially simple men, they made the most of their native intelligence and natural spunk. They worked hard, rose through the ranks, and were rewarded by fame and/or fortune. And that is the American myth of success. With hard work comes achievement, and with achievement comes the material comforts of the American Dream and sometimes even great riches and a place in history.

Our mythology is not based upon invention and imagination, though it may not always be logical and is frequently heavily emotional. It is not merely the product of legend, or the result of fantasizing or wish-fulfillment, or even the effect of a primitive, pre-scientific mind trying to explain the ways of the world to itself (as we might be inclined to believe about the mythologies of Greece and Rome). On the contrary, our mythology derives from what is very real—our legal tradition, our history, and the biographies of our great men.

On the other hand, it would be a great mistake to say that because of this basis in reality, the American myth of success is therefore "true." We need only open the daily newspaper to find that a commitment to hard work does not always insure success. Consider, for example, the middle-aged executive "released" from his job after twenty years of devoted work for a company which suddenly decides it wants younger men. Or observe the changeovers in government personnel after an election and receive an eye-opening lesson about what kinds of allegiances America rewards.

Or consider less newsworthy cases even closer to home. An energetic and hard-working college student spends a total of seventy hours on a research paper only to receive a grade of *F*. Another spends a sleepless night studying for an exam only to discover that the test covers none of the material he has so carefully perused. These and hundreds of other documented examples stand in direct contradiction to the notion that it is only the lazy who can fail here in the U.S. of A.

But in the collective American mind this does not make the myth of hard work as a prelude to success equal to a lie. On the other hand, it should not be described as a truth, either. *Myth*, as when we speak of the American *myth* of success, means a deeply rooted cultural belief with no implied judgment as to whether that belief is true or false. *Myth* refers only to the existence of that belief and its persistence in a culture's artistic tradition despite whatever "logical" and "well-documented" evidence which there might be to contradict it.

The origins of the success myth can be traced back to the days of our country's first settlement. The private diaries and journals of some of the New World's first settlers as well as their public accounts for the folks back home can quickly confirm this. For a long time, Europeans had dreamed of a "brave new world" which would offer them freedom from the oppression of a largely feudal system where a few profited from the ownership of land while the many worked the land hard and reaped only minimal fruits for their labor. And because of the unified religious tradition in Europe at the time, these longings began to shape themselves around the Biblical story of the Garden of Eden, that paradise where man had been perfectly in tune because he was uncorrupted by sin and lived harmoniously with nature. Influenced by their economic and political longings as well as their Christian education, many of the first explorers and settlers of the new land sent back to Europe accounts which tended to confirm that the American continent might indeed be a New Eden.

Captain John Smith wrote of Virginia that "heaven and earth never agreed better to frame a place for man's habitation." His description of the topography made it indeed appear to be another Garden of Paradise: "The country is not mountainous nor yet so low but such pleasant plain hills and fertile valleys, one prettily crossing another, and watered so conveniently with their sweet brooks and crystal springs, as if art itself had devised them." [*A Map of Virginia,* 1612] And George Alsop promoted Maryland as a place so rich that crops grew "without the chargeable and laborious manuring of the Land with Dung," watered by rains which seemed to fall "by a natural instinct." [*A Character of the Province of Maryland,* 1666]

Others, however, particularly in the northern colonies, found the new land much less inviting. Those of our ancestors who landed at Plymouth Rock found the climate considerably less than ideal, the land rocky, and the Indians intimidating. Reports filtered back to Europe that the American natives were savage and hostile, "furious in their rage, and merciless where they overcome," beings who delighted "to torment men in the most bloody manner that may be; flaying some alive with the shells of fishes, cutting off the members and joints of others by piecemeal and broiling [them] on the coals." [William Bradford, *Of Plymouth Plantation,* first published in 1856] For them, America seemed much more like hell than heaven, inhabited as it was by demonic beings.

Not only those at Plymouth Plantation (who nearly starved during their first winter in America), but also the settlers in the warmer climates who found their ranks swelled by an increasing number of adventurers, vagabonds, ex-convicts and whores (lured there by the accounts of Virginia's sunshine!) suffered some second thoughts about this new "paradise." Yet both groups later came to agree that the great promise held out by America was not ease, but hard work. And the hope of freedom from want which America had to offer seemed equally as alluring as the promise of Eden.

Writing of the improved condition of life in Virginia, John Hammond noted that by paying more attention to the "planting and tending of ...quantities of Corn" and caring less about "that notorious manner of life they had formerly lived and wallowed in," the Virginians began to see the benefits of their labor and to understand that there is "nothing more pleasurable than profit." [*Leah and Rachel,* 1656] Not all of those who began the Plymouth Colony lived long enough to see that first sumptuous Thanksgiving feast, but those who did could easily agree with William Woods' assessment that "the diligent hand makes rich." [*New England's Prospects,* 1634] All seemed to concur that despite the obstacles in America, the work there offered rewards impossible in the Old World, and that the condition of even the lowest in America was far superior to the plight of the average man in England. For in America, at least, a man could directly reap the fruits of his own labors on his own piece of land. No overlord was around to take most of the profits away. Even the indentured servant here could hope to find himself (as George Alsop did at the end of his four year term) with "Cattle, Hogs, and Tobacco of his own..." because, wrote Alsop, "There is no Master almost but will allow his Servant a parcel of clear ground to plant some Tobacco in for himself...." In America, all were welcome to a piece of the action.

Thus quite early in our literary tradition was born the idea that in America a hard-working man was fated not to a life of drudgery and misery, but to one of material pleasure and comfort. Here, at least, a man could escape the fate of dying in poverty, though he may have been born into it. Even those whose migration was motivated more by religious than economic reasons soon began to absorb America's promise of success into their value systems. The Puritans, influenced by the theories of John Calvin, believed that at the moment of birth everyone was predestined by a rather whimsical God for either heaven or hell. One could never know until the day of private judgment whether one was among the "elect" (those chosen for heaven) or not. But, so the logic ran, it was possible to get some hint. If one had led a virtuous and industrious earthly life, it was quite likely that one had been predestined for heaven. Whether the good, hardworking life was a cause or an effect of predestination was never made quite clear, but the appearance of industry and outward success became an important part of the Puritan ethic since these were the tickets to the good life both now and later. For men like George Alsop, hard work was a means by which a man could change his fate. For the Puritans this was not possible, but that did not make the work ethic less venerable. Industry simply confirmed the inherent fate of a just man. As a corollary, sloth became quite easy to understand. One failed in this life because one had been predestined to fail in the next life, too. Or as the "Officer Krupke" song from the musical *West Side Story* puts it, "We're deprived on account o' we're depraved."

For the Puritans, success was a spiritual matter. Material success was only an accident of a much larger goal, and the pursuit of virtue was much more important than the pursuit of the dollar. But even for those of a less religious age, material success was still accidental to the pursuit of a larger end—in this case, an ideal community. For Benjamin Franklin, an eighteenth-century Rationalist who rejected most of the beliefs of institutionalized religion, fame, fortune, and world-reknown were certainly not the means to prove to the world that he was on his way to heaven. Franklin, an avowed Deist, believed that "the most acceptable service of God was the doing good to man." And as a consequence of this belief, he devoted himself to improving the earthly life in every way that he could. He started with himself, determined "to live without committing any fault at any time" in order to be a useful citizen. Industry was one of the moral virtues Franklin most prized, and he resolved to force himself to "Lose no time; be always employ'd in something useful; cut off all unnecessary actions." [All quotations are from *The Autobiography*, c. 1771.] Franklin's life is a testimonial to the American success myth, for by his self-discipline and his industry he proved that being the fifteenth child of a poor candlemaker was no obstacle to becoming a wealthy printer, publisher, writer, inventor and respected diplomat. The maxims that he popularized in his *Poor Richard's Almanac* (1758) have become the credo of the American cult of upward mobility: "God helps them that help themselves;" "The sleeping Fox catches no Poultry;" "Early to bed and early to rise makes a man healthy, wealthy and wise." His exhortation "Let us then be up and doing, and doing to the purpose" became the inspiration for a later generation of Americans who found themselves impatient and unwilling to wait for future spiritual payoffs and practical-minded enough to be convinced that the combination of the Industrial Revolution and America's natural resources might indeed make a heaven out of earth.

THE GOSPEL OF WEALTH
According to Poor Richard

Industriousness

Keep thy shop and thy shop will keep thee.
Industry pays debts, while despair increaseth them.
Never leave that till tomorrow which you can do today.

Frugality

A small leak will sink a great ship.
He that goes a borrowing goes a sorrowing.
Fools make feasts and wise men eat them.

Experience

If you will not hear reason, she will surely rap your knuckles.
Experience keeps a dear school, but fools will learn in no other.

The religious tradition of the seventeenth-century had attributed success to luck (some were born to succeed), while the secular eighteenth-century tradition attributed it entirely to pluck (anyone who put a mind to it could succeed). Though the two strains seemed entirely contradictory, one nineteenth-century man managed to reconcile them, and as a result,became one of the best-selling authors of all time and an American household word.

Horatio Alger (1832-1899) is more talked about than read by contemporary Americans. But in his own time, Alger's many novels were widely consumed by a working class who had found both some job security and some leisure time thanks to the Industrial Revolution. This increased prosperity gave Americans time to dream, and Horatio Alger provided them with the subject matter when he hit upon the story formula of the poor boy who rises to riches. The very titles of his books sound like abbreviated maxims from *Poor Richard's Almanac: Strive and Succeed, Bound to Rise, Helping Himself, Forging Ahead, From Farm to Fortune.* Once again, however, it is important to emphasize that just because Alger contributed to the success mythology, his works ought not to be considered idle fantasies. For in the nineteenth-century, enough self-made men existed to lend credence to Alger's theme. As Alger was writing, for instance, Henry Ford was laboring for $2.50 a week polishing steam engines, George Eastman was earning $3.00 a week in an insurance office, and John D. Rockefeller was unemployed.

Though each of Alger's many novels differs in its specifics, the basic pattern of all is the same. A poor boy (who is usually an orphan) is struggling to make ends meet as a bootblack, errand-runner, or some sort of street merchant. Though the hero is almost always on one of the lower rungs of the economic ladder, his personal moral code is quite high. He is always generous, self-sacrificing, honorable and gentlemanly. He has an innate sense of self-worth and a good deal of respect for others, especially those who are in positions of authority. Alger heroes are quite frequently fatherless, and consequently must shift for themselves at an early age. Because of this, they have a mature sense of responsibility and a devotion to work as the means of preserving the family unit. They are in general the kind of good, upright boys who would make model Boy Scouts. And it is this combination of innate moral goodness and a mature devotion to diligence which pays off for them in the end.

In the process of seeking his fortune, the Alger hero must often confront an assortment of thieves and confidence men who are seeking their own fortunes in unscrupulous ways. But the hero's common sense, which seems to derive from his innate sense of what is right and wrong, always saves him from ruin, and what he might lose in material gain by taking a moral stance is always compensated for later. In *Tom Thatcher's Fortune*, for example, Tom picks up $250 at a Wall Street firm as part of an errand for his

On the sidewalk lay the prostrate figure of a man. Over him, bludgeon in hand, bent a ruffian, whose purpose was only too clearly evident.

A new life about to begin for a typical Horatio Alger hero. The young man luckily happening upon a robbery, will apply his innate virtue and save his future benefactor.

employer. On the way back to his job, he meets a con man who offers to sell him a "solid gold" watch at a very low price. Tom is tempted, but his basic honesty about money and his common sense save him from closing the deal. Later on, a rich gentleman gives the shivering Tom his old overcoat, and when Tom discovers that the man has left some valuable securities in the pocket and very honestly returns them, the gentleman gives Tom a real gold watch as a reward. Similarly, the hero of *Shifting for Himself,* unemployed because he has been falsely accused of theft, gives his last dollar to a poor flower seller who has a sick father. In his magnanimity, the young man realizes that the girl's plight is much more wretched than his own. As luck would have it, the sick man turns out to be a former employee of the hero's dead father, and he knows that the young boy has been left a substantial fortune by his father's will. It has been usurped by an unscrupulous uncle, but it can be restored. In both cases (and in almost every other Alger book), the heroes reap riches due to an accidental good turn. But the financial success they achieve is never quite accidental, because in the Alger formula, virtue is the necessary antecedent to good fortune. It alone is the spring which triggers the lucky payoff.

For Alger, then, success was definitely a combination of Puritan luck and Ben Franklin's pluck. The repetition of his unvarying literary formula through at least seventy books raised the "luck plus pluck" hypothesis almost to the validity of a scientific law. The more clinical (though still hypothetical) observations of Charles Darwin were all that was needed to actually turn this unique blend of Puritanism and Pragmatism into a scientific rationale for the age of monopoly in American business.

Though Darwin wrote his *Origin of the Species* in 1859, it was not until the end of the Civil War that his ideas began to be widely promulgated in America. In some, Darwin inspired great fear because he undermined the Book of Genesis. No longer could humanity be seen as a special act of creation by a God who had carefully planned the universe. The creation of man was now seen as a kind of success story, an evolution from the bottom rung of life accomplished by an animal who made his way to the top not because this was his special destiny, but because he was the strongest and the fittest. Because "struggle for existence" and "survival of the fittest" were the most popular catchwords in Darwinian thought, his theories confirmed two old Puritan notions: 1) that hard work was an integral part of humanity's lot; and 2) that only "the elect" (Darwin rechristened them "the fittest") could ultimately succeed. For America's business elite, this theory served to reaffirm what Alger had implied—that for some, success was well-deserved, and that the business world was really a testing ground for the development and encouragement of an individual's personal character. In lectures and articles for the masses, the major industrialists of the time preached the gospel of self-improvement and individualism as the keys to upward mobility. Over and over again, they emphasized that success was earned only by aggression and constant work, and that one could rise only by starting very low.

Addressing students at a commercial college in Pittsburgh, Andrew Carnegie used the metaphor of a horse race to describe this struggle and said:

> I congratulate poor young men upon being born to that ancient and honorable degree which renders it necessary that they should devote themselves to hard work.... The [sons of rich men] will not trouble you much, but look out that some boys poorer, much poorer than yourselves...do not challenge you at the post and pass you at the grandstand. Look out for the boy who has to plunge into work direct from the common school and who begins by sweeping out the office. He is the probable dark horse that you had better watch. [*The Road to Business Success*, 1885]

In this same lecture, Carnegie counseled the students to cultivate practical virtues in order to advance in the race. "You all know," he said, "that there is no genuine, praiseworthy success in life if you are not honest, truthful, fair dealing." Above and beyond this, however, a man must be self-disciplined and do all things in moderation. "I beseech you avoid liquor, speculation, and indorsement [lending]," Carnegie counseled. Like Benjamin Franklin before him, Andrew Carnegie promoted temperance in all things because excess just didn't seem wise. It slowed a man down and made him less likely to succeed.

Given the influence of Darwin over him, Andrew Carnegie could not help but see life in terms of a continuing economic battle for survival that only the best could win. Both Carnegie and Alger were typical spokesmen for what the history books call the era of *rugged individualism:* an era which valued aggressive individual initiative, individual virtue, and individual goals. For in the nineteenth-century, these indeed were the marks of the thoroughbred.

It is an ironic turn of events that the year after the death of Horatio Alger saw the birth of the United States Steel Corporation. The trend toward industrial consolidation had begun in the 1870's, and by the dawn of the twentieth-century, the corporation had firmly entrenched itself as the successor to the individual entrepreneur. A study of the backgrounds of 190 of the top business executives in the first decade of the twentieth-century reveals that only three per cent were poor immigrants or farm boys. The average successful big businessman was profiled as white, Anglo-Saxon, Protestant, city-bred, well-educated, and from a family with high social status and a long-standing interest in business affairs. [William Miller, *Men in Business,* 1962] In Carnegie's race, that dark horse individualist had now become a nag. Since the odds were better than thirty to one that he could prove himself to be the "best" and therefore attain individual glory, the corporate structure called for yet another revision of the success myth, one which broadened the basic definition of what Americans had previously thought of as happiness.

Since the corporate mentality was essentially an update of the feudal mentality, it forever destroyed for Americans the unified dream of an ideal garden where fruit could be grown, picked, and eaten by any individual who made the effort. In fact, the whole American tradition of hard work and the struggle to the top was undermined by the two most essential features of the corporation. First, highly efficient and quick production methods made it unnecessary for people to work long hours each day, and work was therefore less of a social and cultural imperative. Between 1850 and 1950, for example, the average laborer lopped thirty hours a week off his work schedule with no loss in standard of living. Secondly, the principle of standardization which is the cardinal rule of modern business methods extended itself to employees, too, creating workers who were frequently divorced from the products they produced and the business that they did. The corporation's demand for conformity introduced the widespread use of heavy batteries of personality and preference tests to select highly "normal" people for its ranks. "Rugged individualists" were carefully screened out. Because of this, success today can only be defined by many people in terms of what they do *off* the job.

Thus though the new myth of the corporation offers the promise of material comfort and economic stability for all, it offers real profits to only a few and emotional riches to almost none. As a result, twentieth-century American success mythology fragments into a *series* of mythologies which define riches as a satisfaction of psychological rather than material needs. A scattershot look at some of the modern spokespersons for the revised myth of success will perhaps make this more clear.

One of the great best-selling books of our century is Dale Carnegie's *How to Win Friends and Influence People* (1936). It is a self-improvement handbook designed to make the reader a more pleasant and popular person by improving his or her skills in communication and human relationships. The book jacket urges: "Read it and improve your personality, secure your happiness, enhance your future and increase your income." Inside Carnegie glibly outlines "Six ways to make people like you," "Twelve ways to win people to your way of thinking," "Nine ways to change people without giving offense or arousing resentment," and "Seven rules for making your home life happier." This advice ranges from "Become genuinely interested in other people" to "Read a good book on the sexual side of marriage." His underlying assumption about the human condition seems to be much akin to that of Andrew Carnegie (who is no relation, incidentally)–that there is a jungle out there and that most people use animal instincts in order to survive. But his solution is quite different. Rather than joining the jungle, Dale outlines ways to: first, conquer aggressive tendencies which might make one abusive and abrasive to one's fellows; and second, disarm the aggressions in others. "Smile" (rule number two of the first six) is one sure-fire way to accomplish both these things.

Just as Alger's story formula achieved credence by its constant though varied repetition, Carnegie gives his advice the posture of truth by the inclusion of testimonials made by hundreds of graduates from his very popular Institutes. The book is filled with documentations intended to show that Carnegie's principles really work. One man, for example, whose spouse had typed him as a sourpuss, forced himself to smile at her every day for two months. He found that: "This changed attitude of mine has brought more happiness in our home during these two months than there was during the last year." And at the office, this principle seems to work even better, for says this same man: "I find that smiles are bringing me dollars, many dollars every day."

How to Win Friends . . . is filled with testimonials such as this. Dollars may flow in by heeding Dale's advice, but it is self-assurance and congeniality which replace big bucks as the definition of success here. The Ideal American is no longer the man who works *for* himself, but the one who works *on* himself.

And it is not just Dale Carnegie who has promoted non-material self-enrichment in this century. Over twenty years prior to the publication of *How to Win Friends* . . ., Russell H. Conwell, minister, writer, lawyer, schoolmaster and self-proclaimed "leader of men," had also seen that upward mobility was a concept which could be applied more broadly than just to the world of work and that the American Dream had very little to do with the land (now raped by the corporation) and everything to do with the self. In his famous lecture entitled "Acres of Diamonds" (published in book form in 1915) which he delivered nationwide, Conwell proclaimed that only blunderers seek riches in exotic places. "Your wealth is too near to you," he said. "You are looking right over it." For Conwell believed that each person had "acres of diamonds" in his or her own backyard. "The idea is that in this country of ours every man has the opportunity to make more of himself than he does in his own environment, with his own skill, with his own energy, and with his own friends." Each individual was a mine of untapped physical and mental resources which the powderkeg of will power could blast open and unleash. Once this process had taken place, material riches would probably follow. But the greatest reward lay in the construction of a better self.

This shift in emphasis from outward to inward riches is a major revision in American success mythology, but an even larger alteration is the inclusion of behavior ideals and courses of action aimed directly at women. Since women are at present considered the legitimate competitors of men, "How To..." handbooks now guide them on every topic from job competition to more aggressive sexual behavior.

However, one of the biggest selling contemporary success handbooks for women is an ironic reversal of the liberation movement's promotion of the aggressive success myth for women. In Marabel Morgan's *The Total Woman* (1973), no attempt is made to infringe upon a mythology which has been clearly male-oriented for more than two centuries. It avoids the world of business and concentrates instead on the traditional role of woman as wife and homemaker. Like Carnegie, Marabel Morgan believes that rewarding human relationships are worth more than dollars and cents. She is also convinced that the job of housewife is just as exciting a career as the job of an executive, and that it offers just as many opportunities for growth and advancement. The goal here is obviously not economic success, but emotional security, which has perpetually been listed by men as a woman's greatest need. The big payoff in this system is total adoration by a man. "I do believe it is possible," writes Mrs. Morgan, "for almost any wife to have her husband adore her in just a few weeks' time. She can revive romance, reestablish communication, break down barriers, and put sizzle back into her marriage. It is really up to her. She has the power."

Morgan is heavily indebted to Dale Carnegie both in content and in form. Like him, she believes that success occurs inside the self, and her procedure is very reminiscent of Carnegie in that she outlines simple and easy-to-remember maxims guaranteed to bring success. Her formula for making a happy husband is as easy as the measles to catch: "accept, admire, adapt, appreciate." And again like Carnegie, the testimonials of dozens of disciples are used to validate the truth of her messge and the value of her courses. Writes one graduate of the Total Woman course:

[I am] in heaven–a beautiful suite overlooking the Atlantic

> Ocean in the heart of San Juan–new, gorgeous luggage in my closet, with the sweetest guy in the world as my companion. That course is powerful stuff! "Nothing's too good for my honey!" Bob says. Those four A's are the keys to making my man come alive!

It is difficult to overlook the final parallel to Carnegie which the quotation implies—that sudden and almost magic accretion of material pleasures which seem to be a result of the purposeful inhibition of one's aggressions and self-interests and the unleashing of one's positive powers. Being a nice guy (or gal) brings double riches. Intrinsic rewards seem to magnetically attract extrinsic rewards.

The American myth of success, then, has undergone some transformations in its particulars and in its specifics, but the basic pattern of the success story remains very stable. Whether in fictional stories or in non-fictional guidebooks, whether aimed at male or female, the message is always the same—you need not be what you are; you need not live as you do; life can be better. This remains a constant even in the diversity of such apparently dissimilar messages as those of the Evelyn Wood School of Reading Dynamics, the Vic Tanny or Elaine Powers Health Clubs, the Fred Astaire School of Dance and the Ayds Reducing Plan. The hope of a new frontier is common to all, though that hope has shifted from the agricultural dream of our earliest ancestors to the industrial dream of our grandfathers and now resides in the last frontier available on this planet—ourselves.

It might be legitimately said that this message is truly a myth in the most negative sense of that term for a good proportion of our today—anyone who is not white, male, Anglo-Saxon and Protestant, for example. The decade of the sixties may have made us more cynical, less inclined to gobble up the philosphy of either of the Carnegies, less pacified by the stories of an Alger. But it seems to have made us more aware of the need for more broadly defined hopes in our time, hopes which can be documented by solid personal and social commitments to make this land the New Eden about which the W.A.S.P.'s, in their dark oppression, dreamed more than three hundred years ago.

Dr. Martin Luther King, Jr. provided the roots for that new and more broadly defined myth about the promise of a brave new world just as surely as Captain John Smith seeded the original myth when King said: "I have a dream—a dream of coming justice, when all Americans could join in brotherhood and sing free at last! Free at last! Thank God Almighty, we are free at last."

Our success mythology has often failed us as a nation and daily continues to fail us as individuals, but it has persisted in various forms since our earliest days. One can hazard a guess that it will continue to endure and to prevail, to adapt itself to the hopes of women and blacks and Latinos and Indians and others for whom in its present state it is often a lie. For a culture's mythology is a mirror of its hopes and aspirations. Without a mythology, a nation loses its sense of historical continuity, forgets why it is operating, and ceases to function at all because it lacks an understanding of why it came into being.

Discussing "The American Myth of Success"

1) How do contemporary self-help books such as *Your Erroneous Zones,* and *I Ain't Much But I'm All I've Got* compare with self help literature of the eighteenth century? Of the nineteenth century? What do major changes suggest about the evolution of American thought concerning this myth?

2) Cut out ten "Get Rich in Your Spare Time" ads from some recent issues of popular magazines. What is the appeal of these ads? To whom do they appeal? Would Benjamin Franklin and Horatio Alger, Jr. approve of these ads? Why?

3) Talk to a person who works for one of the companies that stress self-reliance in business sales such as Amway, Tupperware, or Avon Products. Bring up the American myth of success and ask them how important the myth is to them.

4) Examine how important the myth of success is in your own life. Would you be in school if you didn't believe it would help you get ahead? How pressured do you feel to succeed in your first job after college? How much of your life span do you plan to put into the aquisition of material goods?

5) How important is the myth of success in such 1970's hit movies as *Rocky, One on One, You Light Up My Life* and *Cabaret?*

Dreams and Genocide: The American Myth of Regeneration Through Violence

By Richard Slotkin

A myth is a story with peculiar powers: it defines the total world-picture of a human culture, summing up the several ways in which men may relate to the Cosmos in a single dramatic instance. It does more than define: it provides a scenario or prescription for action, and limits the possibilities for human response to the Universe. Myths reflect the life of Man, but they also can shape and direct it, for good or ill. They are made of words, concepts, images, and they can kill a man. Myth-narratives reflect and articulate the unconscious assumptions, the habits of thought, feeling and vision, which inform the "mind" of a culture. They draw on the content of individual and collective experience, on the deep structures of human psychology and the particularities of human history, establishing connections between the individual and the archetypal, the singular and the universal. Myth-narratives rarely occur in pure form, but rather are contained, perhaps hidden, in "ordinary" cultural phenomena like literary or journalistic narratives or in the stories people tell of themselves and the life around them—just as an individual psychological history is contained in the "narrative" of the dream and of the therapeutic confession. Myth is archetypal, and refers human consciousness to the universal, to the extent that there are universalities in the human condition and our consciousness of that condition. All men are born, live with parents or elders, are trained for participation in an economy, pass through puberty into adulthood, labor to survive, suffer deprivation or frustration, ambition and solitude, seek love

From the *Journal of Popular Culture*, 1971, 5(1), 38-59. Reprinted by permission of the editor and the author.

and power, fear death and dream of immortality, sicken or decline, and ultimately die. All men see in the world around them seasonal and natural patterns which conform to this life pattern, and pose the question of the human life's relatedness to something larger. At the same time, physical circumstances and peculiarities of social or historical conditions, give a special character to the ways in which men conceive and live their lives.[1]

The mythology of regeneration through violence developed in the colonial literature of the northern American colonies in the 17th Century, in response to the peculiar situation in which the Puritan colonists had placed themselves, on the frontier of an unchartable wilderness, rich in possibilities of terror and opulence, and haunted by a dark-skinned race whose Gods were so strange as to seem devils. Nor could the settlers confront the savages with entirely easy minds. In order to come to the New World they had first to uproot themselves from their traditional places in English society, breaking ties of love, kinship, filial obligation, legal duty and customary associations in order to recreate their lives in terms more suited to their personal ideals and ambitions. In a time of general social upheaval, of people rising and falling out of their appropriate spheres, these people committed the most outrageous act, by rising totally out of the sphere of English society itself. Their activities were Faustian—rather than submit to the world as God-given to them, they sought a new one, or rather, an opportunity to create one of their own. In this ambition they were opposed by their spiritual leaders and temporal rulers, their fellow congregants and business associates, and by the naggings of their own consciences. At a time when the English Church and Crown were shaken by Puritan and middle-class dissent, when the Puritanism they espoused was itself under persecution, these men were running off to a wilderness to do their thing in private. The government occasionally cried treason, the Puritan opposition cried desertion. The Colonists themselves doubted their own motives: were they going, as they said, to redeem the Satanic forest fot Jesus, or were they self-seekers, degenerate in virtue?

The moral problem was complicated by the character of their new environment. They came from Jacobean and Baroque England, the world of Elizabeth and Francis Bacon, of Newton and Handel, to live in a Stone Age wilderness, inhabited by beings whom they regarded as subhuman. As Puritans, they were convinced that the natural world was corrupt from its very roots, requiring total regeneration. In England they had attempted, and failed, in an effort to convert and regenerate church and society. Here their conflict could be conducted on a more elemental plane: in the Indian and the wilderness they confronted the extreme symbolic types of the corruption of nature and man. To convert the Indians into English Christians (or into nothing) and the wilderness into the clapboards of a New Jerusalem would be a triumph over the Devil incarnate—rather than over a devil whose nature was obscured by his kinship with the English saints, his Christian racial heritage and social graces.

For the New England Puritans, and to a lesser extent to the Puritanical Anglicans who settled the other colonies, the confrontation with the Indian American culture was a challenge to the premises of social psychology and organization. Moreover, it was a confrontation in which the English did not hold the position of strength. In the wilderness their technological superiority to the Indians was offset by the tendency of English cultural patterns to give way, to adapt to the requirements of life in the wilderness and thus become more like the ways of the Indians. Far from Anglicizing the wilderness, they feared that the wilderness was Americanizing and Indianizing them. They (and especially their children and grandchildren) adopted Indian styles of life, dress and polity in order to survive; and, horror of horrors, found that the Indian way and the wilderness life could be both enjoyable and profitable. Indian politics were democratic, leaders being chosen on an *ad hoc* basis, rather than because of their inherited position or wealth; and each man (and often woman) in the tribe had both personal liberty to improve his lot and enjoy it, and a claim on the communal wealth and care of the whole tribe. Not until the colonists learned to develop and use *ad hoc* leadership from the ranks of frontiersmen did they begin to succeed in developing their control over the wilderness; not until they democratized and individualized their economics did they begin to grow prosperous; and their failure to emulate Indian patterns of social welfare led predictably to an unnecessary augmenting of personal misery and hardship among the colonists. Institutional arrangements apart, the Indian and the Puritan minds had no common conceptual meeting-ground, as their myths reveal. The Christian Puritan conceived of the human race's genesis as the consequence of sinful disobedience, leading to exile from the Garden of Eden by an angered patriarchal God. For the Indian, genesis is a joyful event: a hunter, seduced by a goddess in the shape of a deer, follows her into the world; his people, similarly consumed by desire for her sweet flesh, follow. The world is populated as the result of a sexual or symbolically-sexual relationship joyfully entered between hero-man and goddess, not as the result of punishment. The consequences of this world-view can only be seen in a total consideration of American Indian cultures. But the consequence which most struck the Puritans was that the Indian had sexual freedom in youth, and could marry and divorce by mutual consent; and the Indian had freedom of affectional expression, especially towards children, which was not available to a people who saw the child as a little damned soul, in need of discipline and religious conversion.

For the Puritan the Indian represented the dark forces, both those in the external world and those in the Puritans' own souls: the force of sexuality, the desire for pleasure and comfort; the desire to be free of political and social restraints; the desire to be sensually at one with the Universe. Puritans were inclined to a Manichean conception of universal war between Good and Evil; in their frontier situation facing the Indians they found a correlative of that archetypal confrontation. Thus their world view itself became dependent on the concept of racial identity and racialized conceptions of the opposing forces that contended for America. Logically enough, the Puritan-Indian relationship finally resolved itself into one of overt race war—a war which lasted a century and a half and ended with the extermination of the New England tribes; then, extended westward, continued until the Sioux were massacred at Wounded Knee in 1890. At the same time that the race war began, the first recognizable myth-vision of Anglo-American history emerged in the literature of New England: the captivity narratives of 1680-1720. In the captivity narratives, American history is seen as a narrative of man's regeneration and purification from sin, through the suffering of an ordeal by captivity; the captivity occurs in the context of a universalized race war, in which the strife of Indians and Christians is identified with the warfare between the World and the Soul, the Devil and Christ. I will first recount the story, then attempt to justify my description of it as myth.

Figure 1

"Her child, an infant a few months old, she managed to conceal in her clothing, but on arriving at the place where the women were, it was discovered."

The first and best of the captivity narratives was that of Mary Rowlandson, wife of the minister of Lancaster, Massachusetts, and a rescued captive. Her narrative, one of the most popular American books ever published, set the pattern for a legion of imitators, but is superior to them in both style and insight, and therefore offers the best way into the subject. The tale begins with an image of pastoral peace and prosperity, and of familial solidarity binding men together. But this apparent Golden Age is in fact insecure, threatened by forces of darkness both within and without: Mrs. Rowlandson says she felt uneasy in her comforts, and almost prayed that God might send her some chastisement so that she could more clearly see how she stood with him. Suddenly, without warning, darkness and fire descend:

> On the tenth of February, 1675, Came the Indians with great numbers upon Lancaster: Their first coming was about Sunrising; hearing the noise of some Guns, we looked out; several Houses were burning, and the Smoke ascending to Heaven. There were five persons taken in one house, the Father, and the Mother and a sucking Child, they knockt on the head; the other two they took and carried away alive.[2]

The narrative begins when the family circle is broken, and the mother—embodiment of familial virtues and values—is carried captive into the wilderness by alien beings. These creatures immediately characterize themselves as devils by their immoderate sensuality, gluttony, and delight in cruelty:

> Oh the roaring, and singing and dancing, and yelling of those black creatures in the night...made the place a lifely resemblance of hell. And as miserable was the wast that was there made, of Horses, Cattle, Sheep, Swine, Calves, Roasting Pigs, and Fowl...some roasting, some lying and burning, and some boyling to feed our merciless enemies...I asked them whither I might not lodge in the house that night to which they answered, what will you love English men still?[3]

The father—symbol of the powers of the patriarchal deity Mrs. Rowlandson constantly invokes to aid her—is either absent from the catastrophe (like Mr. Rowlandson) or powerless to prevent it (like the murdered father in the first quotation). He has withdrawn as an agent in human affairs and given his human children over to the Devil. The family circle is increasingly fragmented as the mother and children are separated. The mother is carried deeper and deeper into the hellish forest: time is marked in the narrative not in days or hours, but in "Removes," a way of marking time in terms of spatial movement, of progressive states of alienation from the family church and society.

Although she is in physical bondage to devils, she tries to maintain her spiritual integrity by resisting temptations of the Indian lifeway. She refuses tobacco (to which she had formerly been addicted), repels sexual advances and offers of marriage, refuses to worship strange gods. But ultimately hunger wears down her resistance, the flesh's hunger for sustenance of its gross existence: like the worst, and unlike a great many of the Indians around her, she steals food from some captive English children after a kind Indian woman had given of her own store to save them. Thus the meaning of her ordeal is revealed to her: the Indians are not foreign devils, but rather the concretions of her own sins of pride, sensuality, complacency, selfishness and desire for prosperity and comfort. With this perception she perceives herself standing before the Judge as damned, her soul black and Indianized, racially and intrinsically unworthy of salvation. But resigning herself to the will of an angry God, the "base Indian" Mary Rowlandson achieves spiritual regeneration and conversion. God's arbitrary will rescued her from the Indians, both of the world and of the mind. Her blackness is exorcized—or is it? Although physically rescued and restored to the wounded bosom of her family, her mind remains possessed by the vision she has seen of her brotherhood with evil, her helplessness to resist it, her dependence on an incomprehensible, unworldly, inhuman God to redeem her from it. Mentally she relives the violent cycle of fall and rescue, her sense of the world defined from within by its terms:

> I can remember a time when I used to sleep quietly without workings in my thoughts, whole nights together, but now it is otherwise with me...When others are sleeping, mine eyes are weeping...My thoughts are upon things past, upon the awful dispensation of the Lord towards us...[4]

The incompleteness of her rescue is crucial to the mythology, since it implies the need for constantly recurring and expanding cycles of the myth, and seems to beget the expectation of further captivities and rescues, more complete exorcisms of Indian guilts, more total purgations of the soul and the world.

The problem with Mrs. Rowlandson's narrative and with its numerous imitators was that they did not sufficiently image the heroism which, despite its dark Faustian overtones, was a part of the common life of the colony: the bravery of the pioneer, the Indian fighter, the emigrant himself, and the growing prowess of the colonists, their increasing power over the New World. Jehovah is the hero of Mrs. Rowlandson's narrative, but he is transcendent, inhuman. To make the myth word-picture truly satisfying a respectable image of human heroism was required. This increasingly articulated need led to the development of what was at first a counter-stream of myth—the myth of the hunter—but which eventually merged with the mythic structure of the captivity narratives to produce figures like Daniel Boone, Leatherstocking and General Custer. The hunter myth involves a hero who goes into the wilderness willingly, and is the heroic master of his own and the wilderness' destiny. His hunt involves him closely with the dark forces of nature, the beasts, and the Indians; in fact, his experience is an initiation into the Indian life of the wilderness, and he comes to share some of the Indian's spirit through the very act of hunting the Indian to death. This quality is the source of his power; but it is also a defect in his virtue, since it compromises his racial purity. Thus the frontier hunter is often seen as low, coarse, rude-spoken, antisocial, outlawed or socially inferior. What redeems him finally for the American audience is his ability to maintain some degree of racial integrity—this is attested by his qualities of self-restraint, his racial pride, and his maintenance of celibacy; second by his service as an agent of pure white civilization; and finally, by his association with captivity, both by suffering captivity himself and by his rescuing of the Mary Rowlandsons from savage molestation. The most popular forms of these heroes began to develop in the 1720's, and culminated in a literary Trinity of Heroes: Daniel Boone, Leatherstocking, and Davy Crockett. The folksiness and the secular quality of these heroes were essential to their acceptance by later American audiences; but their mythic function can be more clearly seen if we set aside this folksy mask, and look at an earlier hero-narrative by Cotton Mather, in which the hero's place in the Universe is defined as that of savior of captives and exorcist of Indians.

The narrative, "A Brand Pluck'd Out of the Burning," recounts Mather's treatment of a possessed girl during the witchcraft hysteria of 1692. Mercy Short, a seventeen year old girl orphaned and captured in an Indian raid, and now living as a servant with kindly gentlefolk in Boston, has fallen into a fit of demonic possession, which seizes her suddenly in church. Mather, a professional exorcist and spiritual therapist, is called in to cast the demons out. As Mercy writhes in torment on her bed he subjects her to close questioning, taking copious notes for the work he intends to publish of this encounter with Satan. At the outset of the account, Mather invokes the framework of the captivity, reminding us that this narrative begins where Mrs. Rowlandson's left off, with the captive physically returned to Zion but mentally alienated by her wilderness experience:

Figure 2 This was followed by a faint moan; one of the savages had sunk his tomahawk in her brain. She was then scalped, her body mutilated in a shocking manner, and thrown warm and bleeding into the flames.

> Mercy Short had been taken Captive by our cruel and bloody
> Indians in the East, who at the same time horribly Butchered
> her Father, her Mother, her Brother, her Sister, and others of her
> Kindred and then carried her...unto Canada [after which she
> was ransomed]...But altho she had then already Born the Yoke
> in her youth, Yett God Almighty saw it Good for her to Bear more
> of that Yoke, before seventeen years of her Life had Rolled
> away.[5]

The whole pattern of the captivity is sketched here, from its
beginning in the destruction of the family to its conclusion in
incomplete restoration. Mather must now complete the rescue by
casting out the Indians from the jungle of her mind, ending what he
calls her "Captivity to Spectres." That he sees this ceremony of
psychic exorcism as part of the total universal race-war cannot be
doubted: he asks Mercy Short what color and shape her devils have,
and she replies that they are "Black" but of an "Indian" rather than
a "Negro" blackness.[6] Although he knows of her captivity to
Indians, her choice of imagery "surprises" him: where can the girl
have gotten the idea, if not from actually having seen the devils
themselves, as devils? The imagery suits his own notion about the
strategy behind the outbreak of witchcraft: it coincides with Indian
outbreaks on the near edge of the frontier, as close to Boston as
Gloucester. "This whole matter has been a prodigious piece of the
strange descent of the Invisible World...in the shape of Indians and
Frenchmen."[7]

Mercy Short's symptoms give shape to the invisible terrors of
the colonial mind, the elements in their own character which the
Puritans feared or despised, and projected onto Indians and
Negroes as the source of their darkness. Chief among these dark
forces is sexuality. Mercy Short is offered a black husband by her
demons; hot liquids are poured down her throat, and she is
continually pricked and prodded with pins, swords and clubs. In
addition, the child grows increasingly disrespectful of her elders,
and especially of her "father" Mather, ridiculing and mocking their
piety as a cloak for sensuality and Faustian ambitions. In Mather's
mind this is further evidence that the generation gap which divided
the Americanized younger generation from the pious English elders
was of a piece with the racial-diabolical struggle—that the spirit of
adolescent rebellion itself is an Indian spirit, racially compromised.

Two streams of development move the narrative to its
conclusion. The first of these is thematic: as the fit progresses the
captivity imagery becomes more and more concrete, until at last
Mercy sees herself as literally surrounded with "Indian Sagamores
and Frenchmen" as she had been during her physical (as opposed to

her metaphysical) captivity. Having thus polarized and clarified the racial character of the demons, Mather is able to exorcise them. The second stream is that of ritual: as her nightmare moves towards concretion, Mercy Short draws the adults in the room into participation in the dreamworld. The reader, his expectations aroused by the invocation of the captivity frame, finds himself finally convinced of the truth of Mather's world-vision by the fact that the citizens of note who observe Mercy's suffering share her experiences. They feel the demons rush about the room, feel the hot liquid as it slips down her throat. The girl makes them dance about the room, swinging swords at invisible devils: there they are! No! Over there! No, behind you! The devils hold a dance, and all assembled hear a trampling "as of barefooted people" on the floor.

Myth provides the framework in which experience can be understood, and by defining experience in its special terms it provides a limited scenario for responding to experiences. To the 20th Century reader, who has his own myths of psychoanalysis, Mercy's problem seems clear: she has survived her massacred family, experienced captivity among the Indians during the crisis of puberty; to the Indians she would have seemed a marriageable woman, and they would certainly have attracted her (although they would not, as Mather elsewhere asserts, have raped her). She returns to Boston, burdened with the guilt of having survived her family and been tempted sexually; instead of being dowered and married or adopted by new parents, as would have happened among the Indians, she is forced to earn bread as a servant in a wealthy family, and subjected to innuendoes because of her stay with the Indians. Guilty herself, and resentful of the elders who understand neither her guilt nor the sort of healing she longs for, she falls into her fit, earning sympathy and interest, and a license to strike back at the adult world, assert power over it, make Mather literally dance to her tune. Mather is incapable of helping her, because his mythology restricts his ability to interpret what he sees. What else can cause such impiety but devilish possession? What is the devil but the archetype of the Indian? What is the relation between white and Indian but that of captive and captor, Job and Satan? And what is the Church and its minister but an agent of Jehovah, rescuer of the captive, avenging destroyer of the demon? Thus Mather's response to Mercy is to foster her disease, help it to express itself more fully, in order to reveal the evil for purposes of exorcism. That the girl may be destroyed by the process seems not to occur to him, but in any case he would "destroy the city in order to save it"—he intends to use the purified Mercy as an instrument of further purgation, to make accusations against subversive Bostonians, in league with the red devils.

The structures and themes of the captivity myth can now be seen in completed form. The myth recounts the regeneration of the soul and the attainment of salvation through a complex experience of violent confrontation with the powers of nature, equated with the forces of darkness; the hero is either a captive or an avenging destroyer—or some combination of both. Men are either victims, avengers or devils. The cosmos consists of a world and an anti-world. The former is the commonday world of pastoral peace, a world which retains the memory and some of the attributes of a Golden Age, an Eden or Arcadia—but its landscape is dimmed by a nameless malaise, a fear of dark forces both inside and outside the world. The dark forces suddenly take form when the Indians leap out of the anti-world, shatter the family bonds that order the world, and carry its mothers from the hearth into captivity. Wrathfully the patriarchs pursue the enemy, compelled to live in the anti-world, on the enemy's terms and in his way, compelled to share the enemy's violence of spirit and life style. The captives too must eat the devil's bread and drink his wine, submit to his curses and caresses and the importunities of his priests. Both captives and hunters discover that the vicious qualities of the enemy—individual and collective—are extreme forms of the vices that have corrupted their own society and soul from within. The captivity and hunt apparently end with rescue, the consummation of vengeance and the exorcism of the Indian evil. But the exorcism is incomplete, the return to the family is compromised by the secrets learned in intimate contact with the Indian anti-world. Further exorcisms become necessary, to expel the guilt derived from the process of the first exorcism, each more intimate and profound than the last—the expulsion of demons from one's own society, one's family, one's own mind.

Is this structure in fact mythic? There are certain sorts of objective information which could be cited at length, but which are not interesting to listen to in this sort of setting. Let me summarize: the first sort of evidence relates to the popularity of the myth, determined by the number of editions and the variety of publication sites of captivity narratives; and (where known) the number of copies sold. Statistics of this kind indicate that such narratives were a staple of American popular journals and book-pamphlet presses up to 1850, and an important item until 1900. Between 1680 and 1776 captivities were the only American narrative works to contest for popularity with European fiction; between 1680 and 1720 they were the only narrative literature printed about the frontier; as late as 1824 a captivity pattern is frequently employed in rituals (especially conversion sermons and ceremonies) and in belletristic literature, serving as the source for political and sermon rhetoric and literary fiction.

The real test of myth is whether it is serviceable as a paradigm of the world-view of the people. Certainly the captivity expressed the Puritan world view accurately, and with some adjustments in imagery and emphasis also served Jacksonian America in the same way. But time tests the myth as well as popularity and relevance to an historical past, and the real test of the myth is whether it retains its power to express and shape the culture's world-view after a lapse of centuries. One can certainly find analogies between the 17th century context and our own in the prevalence of religious and nationalistic warfare, widespread social, political and economic upheaval; between the first Puritan emigrants and later generations of immigrants and socially mobile native-borns who experienced the "emigration trauma" of moving out of their home-place into an alien environment, to which they were simultaneously attracted and repelled; between the generation gap of Puritan and other mobile or emigrant groups and our own, which is the result of a rapidly-transforming social and political environment. Equally important is the fact that myths (if they are really functional as myths) draw on the content of the deepest levels of human psychology, restructuring external history to make it amenable to the requirements of that psychology. The myth of regeneration through violence is a variation on the archetypal myth and ritual of the "scapegoat," which is itself the reflection of a basic psychological mechanism for dealing with anxiety and guilt. That a myth-pattern conforming to the pattern of "scapegoating" should recur in times of stress—particularly in periods of extended stress following a series of economic and social transformations—is not extraordinary.

The myth of regeneration through violence defines one major component of the American mind, one stream of American consciousness, one major and characteristic conception of history and the cosmos held by Americans. Under certain conditions of stress, the myth emerges from our personal and social "unconscious" to define, motivate and rationalize behavior. It does not seem an evil thing, a state of mind similar to that of Nazi Germany, because it is an *American* myth: it carries with it images and associations which are beneficent, heroic, noble—Custer's Last Stand, Remember the Alamo, the cavalry rescuing the wagon train. Our power over the myth and the "scenario" it demands we live and think by, lies solely in our awareness of its existence, its sources and its powers, and our choosing to expose and criticize its character and its works.

NOTES

[1]The foregoing discussion of myth theory, and the discussion of Colonial history

which follows, are based on research detailed in a forthcoming book on the evolution of the American myth of regeneration through violence.

[2]M. Rowlandson, "Narrative of the Captivity...," in C. H. Lincoln, *Narratives of the Indian Wars* (N.Y., 1966), p.118.

[3]M. Rowlandson, p.121.

[4]M. Rowlandson, p.166.

[5]C. Mather, "A Brand Pluck'd Out of the Burning," in G. L. Burr, *Narratives of the Witchcraft Cases* (N.Y., 1966), p.259.

[6]C. Mather, p.261

[7]C. Mather, "Decennium Luctuosum," in C. H. Lincoln, *Narratives of the Indian Wars,* p.247.

[8]I. Mather, "An Earnest Exhortation...," in *A Brief History* (Boston, 1676), p.5.

[9]Quoted in *New Republic* (Nov. 15, 1969), p.18.

Discussing "Dreams and Genocide:"

1. How does the Captivity Narrative story parallel stories of Vietnam POW's of the 1960's? Of Americans held prisoner by the Japanese during World War II? Does the section in this book on stereotypes suggest any reasons why there are parallels between these stories?

2. America's Puritan heritage helped formulate the myth of success and the myth of regeneration through violence. What other American myths and beliefs may be traced back to American Puritan values and thought?

3. Name five specific instances in which during the last five years scapegoating was used in well known political instances, either national or international.

The Myth of the Eternal Child in Sixties America

By Harold Schechter

Except ye become as little children, ye shall in no wise enter the kingdom of heaven.
Matthew 18:3

> *I came upon a child of God*
> *He was walking along the road...*
> Joni Mitchell, **"Woodstock"**

Interest in the sixties is running high these days. Scholarly studies on the subject have begun to appear, Beatlemania is back, and many people, particularly those too young to have participated themselves, seem endlessly fascinated by the landmark events of the time: Woodstock, the peace protests, the Summer of Love. It's possible, I suppose, to interpret all this interest as just the next logical phase in the nostalgia boom; the fifties have been milked dry by the media. But it seems to me that there is a significant difference between the ways in which the fifties and sixties are perceived, for while the fifties have been transmuted into Happy Days, a prefabricated fairy tale,[1] the sixties are coming to seem more and more like a truly *mythic* age. Morris Dickstein, in his excellent study *Gates of Eden,* captures this sense of the sixties very well when he quotes two of the more common current responses to the era: "Was it that long ago? did all that really happen?"[2]

The interesting question, to my mind, is: How do we account for the legendary air which this period has taken on in the minds of so many people? And the answer, I believe, is that the sixties always *were* a mythic age, even while they were taking place, though no one could possibly perceive this at the time. We are never aware of the myths we are living out, or living within, while we are in the midst of them. But now that we have some distance from the decade, its mythic quality is becoming more clear. This essay, then, represents another attempt to make sense of the sixties. What I am interested in exploring, however, is not the social or political or economic significance of the time, but its mythological significance. What was the dominant myth of the sixties—the myth that gave them shape, direction, meaning?

I

Let me begin with a brief and necessarily oversimplified statement of the theoretical principles on which my discussion will be based. My starting point is the "archetypal theory" of C. G. Jung, the Swiss psychiatrist who began his career as a follower and friend of Sigmund Freud. Though very close for several years, the two men ultimately split over their differing concepts of the way in which the human mind, the psyche, is structured. Jung theorized that beneath what he called the personal unconscious—by which he meant basically what Freud meant by the unconscious, namely a repository of memories, desires, impulses, and fantasies relating back to our infantile experiences--there existed a deeper level of the mind which he called the *collective unconscious*. This part of our minds does not develop out of our personal experiences; its contents are not acquired during our lives. Rather, it is inborn and universal—the same in everybody. Just as we all share a common human anatomy over and above the particular variations of our individual bodies, so, says Jung, we all share, at the deepest, most fundamental level of our beings, a common human psyche. Or, to put it another way, just as we all possess an anatomical structure that makes us recognizable as human beings (not as Tom or Harry or Judy or Jane), so we all possess a basic psychic structure, a level of the mind which is the source of our *typically human* perceptions, responses, ways of behaving in and relating to the world. This level of the psyche is the collective unconscious.

Just as the personal unconscious expresses itself, among other ways, in dreams, which are symbolic statements or stories which relate to and reveal truths about our personal lives and situations, so the collective unconscious expresses *itself* in dreams, but dreams whose symbols are common to us, and meaningful to us, as a species. These dreams contain universal human truths—in other words, myths. Myths are the dreams of mankind, or, as Joseph Campbell puts it, "Dream is the personalized myth, myth the depersonalized dream; both dream and myth are symbolic in the same general way of the dynamics of the psyche. But in the dream the forms are quirked by the particular troubles of the dreamer, whereas in myth the problems and solutions shown are directly valid for all mankind."[3] These mythic symbols which emerge from the collective unconscious Jung called *archetypes,* and they appear in the imaginative products of the world, in all times and all cultures in religious mythologies, fairy tales, painting, "classic" literature, etc.

It was Jung's belief, moreover, that "the posture of the unconscious is compensatory to consciousness."[4] According to Jung, the psyche is self-regulating, and if consciousness—our consciously held attitudes and beliefs and our behavior—is one-sided or imbalanced or deviates too much from normalcy or health, the unconscious will actually attempt to correct the imbalance. How? By communicating a symbol (which is how the unconscious communicates, through symbols) to the conscious mind—the symbol of whatever is being overlooked or neglected or ignored in our lives. In the case of the individual who "so departs from the norms of the species that a pathological state of imbalance ensues, of neurosis or psychosis,"[5] the compensatory symbol will appear in his fantasies and dreams.

But according to Jung, it is not only individuals who suffer from this kind of imbalance and whose lives require a compensatory correction, but whole cultures, at different periods of time. As Jung says, "Every period has its bias, its particular prejudice, and its psychic malaise. An epoch is like an individual, it has its own limitations of conscious outlook and therefore requires a compensatory adjustment."[6] Where does this compensatory symbol appear? Just as, in the case of the individual, the symbol will appear in his dreams, so in the case of the culture, the symbol will appear in *its* dreams. But what do we mean by the dreams of a culture? Where are they to be found? As I indicated earlier, when we talk about collective dreams, we are really talking about myths. And in the modern world, the myths or collective dreams of a culture are found predominantly in its popular art.

Various critics and scholars have written about the mythic content of popular art, among them Northrup Frye, Leslie Fiedler, Alan McGlashan, Robert Jewett and John Shelton Lawrence, and even the religious historian Mircea Eliade. In his book *Myths, Dreams, and Mysteries,* Eliade asks, "What has become of myths in the modern world?"—and his answer is in part that they are to be found in our amusements. Noting that, through his participation in myth and ritual, primitive man is able to escape from the passage of time and enter a deathless, eternal world, Eliade argues that the "magico-religious" function is served in modern society by our entertainments, our diversions—by those things we do to "kill time." "It seems that a myth itself," he says, "never disappears...it only changes its aspects and disguises its operations."[7] The science fiction writer Ursula K. Le Guin makes a similar point in an article entitled "Myth and Archetype in Science Fiction," where she takes a look at some of the stock characters of pop culture—the barbarian heroes of sword and sorcery, mad scientists, private eyes, evil aliens, and bug-eyed monsters—and concludes that "their roots are the roots of myth, are in our unconscious—that vast dim region of the psyche and perhaps beyond the psyche which Jung called 'collective' because it is similar in all of us, just as our bodies are basically similar."[8] And in *The Virgin Land,* his classic study of "The American West as Symbol and Myth," the Americanist Henry Nash Smith defines popular art as "an objectified mass dream." According to Smith, the popular artist works by abandoning his own personality and identifying himself "with the reveries of his readers." Popular art, therefore, expresses "the dream life of the vast, inarticulate public."[9] This function of popular art—its ability to embody, in a very unselfconscious way, mass fantasies and cultural myths—largely accounts for its enormous appeal. It also explains the importance of the popular arts to the cultural critic or social historian. By studying such material, we can get, perhaps better than from anywhere else, important insight into what is going on in the deep imagination of a whole society.

Finally, there is one more element of Jung's theory I must introduce before talking specifically about the sixties. I've said that the compensatory symbol appears, in the case of the individual, in dreams and in the case of the whole society, in its cultural myths as embodied primarily in its popular arts. But these symbols can be seen not only in dream and myth but in human behavior, not only in art but in action. Jung's point is that by raising the appropriate symbol to consciousness, the unconscious tries to correct the one-sidedness of the conscious attitude. But what happens if the conscious mind, as it so often does, ignores the message from the unconscious? How many of us, after all, really pay attention to what our dreams are trying to tell us? As Jung remarks, symbols are "living psychic forces that demand to be taken seriously, and they have a strange way of making sure of their effect."[10] When an archetypal symbol emerges from the depths of the unconscious, it always brings with it what Jung calls a "compelling effect." It exerts a powerful influence on us. It actually has the power to shape our lives to its ends, so that people in the grip of a symbol are impelled not only to portray it in art but to live it out in some way. They become *possessed* by the symbol. Such possession is the way the unconscious has of forcing us to recognize the symbol and to change our lives in accordance with the meaning it represents.

A good example of symbolic possession can be seen in the movie *Close Encounters of the Third Kind,* which portrays precisely this phenomenon: a group of people in the grip of a symbol. What happens to these people? First, they are moved by some inner necessity to embody or portray the symbol in some way: one character sculpts it, another paints it compulsively. But in larger terms, the symbol forces them into an awareness of, or confrontation with, something meaningful that has been completely missing from their lives: a sense of mystery, of the marvelous, the sublime. (The source of the symbol is shown to be outside the people, but this is just a case of what psychologists call "projection.") It seems to me that the decision of the writer-director, Steven Spielberg, to set his movie in an absolutely flat, empty, Midwestern locale and to have the experience happen to utterly ordinary people leading utterly drab and mundane lives was perfect. He's either read Jung or intuited the same truth about compensatory symbols. Because the symbol which grips the imagination of his characters—and dramatically alters their lives—is compensatory to an existence which is completely devoid of any sense of the marvelous, of anything more sublime than a Budweiser beer commercial. The symbol which possesses them is the precise opposite of the mundane; it's otherworldly, celestial—a great, vaulting, magic mountain crowned with a halo of heavenly lights. Essentially it is a religious symbol which these characters are compelled to integrate into their heretofore spirit-less lives, or else run the risk of suffering a total psychic collapse.

So, to sum up, we see that, at certain periods, in societies which have been moving in a dangerously one-sided direction; in which certain values and attitudes are emphasized to the unhealthy exclusion of other important ones; a mythic symbol will arise which will possess the imagination of large numbers of people—dominate their dreams, even shape their destinies. And this symbol will be compensatory to the outlook of the culture at large, to its dominant values and beliefs and practices. It will represent an attempt to correct or redirect the energies of the culture.

II

In our own culture, such a symbol emerged, I believe, during the 1960's. This essay began by saying that the sixties were a mythic age—an era in which a whole generation of Americans was possessed by, or living out, a particular myth (without being aware of it at the time). What was the myth of the sixties? I believe that symbol which dominated the decade is the one which Jungians call the archetype of the *puer aeternus,* the Eternal Child (known also as the Eternal Youth or Immortal Child).

Exactly what is the *puer aeternus?* The standard work on the subject, Marie-Louise von Franz's book *The Problem of the Puer Aeternus,* contains the following definition:

> *Puer aeternus* is the name of a god of antiquity. The words themselves come from Ovid's *Metamorphoses* and are there applied to the child-god in the Eleusinian mysteries. Ovid speaks of the child-god Iacchus, addressing him as: *puer aeternus....* In later times, the child-god was identified with Dionysus and the god Eros. He is the divine youth who is born in the night.... He is a god of vegetation and resurrection, the god of divine youth, corresponding to such oriental gods as Tammuz, Attis, and Adonis. The title *puer aeternus* therefore means eternal youth.... [11]

The term *puer aeternus*, then, applies first of all to certain mythological figures, primarily young male deities who die in their youths and are usually reborn. Frequently, they are vegetation gods, like Attis, Tammuz, or Adonis, who die or are slain and then are resurrected in the spring—so that they become, in effect, undying, immortal, eternally youthful. Sometimes, like Hyacinth and Narcissus, they are reborn or resurrected as flowers—i.e., they are flower-people, flower-children. Mythic figures who fall into the category of *puer aeternus* (besides the ones I've already mentioned) include Dionysus, Hippolytus, Bellerophon, Icarus, Hermes, and Pan.[12]

As I suggested earlier, all myths, all archetypal images, are metaphors or symbols of certain psychological traits (so that when we talk about being possessed by an archetype, we mean that, in such situations, our psychological lives become "mimetic to myths," imitate or recreate myths. Our behavioral patterns match or follow mythic patterns).[13] The primary psychological trait associated with the Eternal Child is, obviously, a refusal to grow up—a desire to remain a child forever. This characteristic is closely connected to several others. First, there is the trait which might best be labelled *timelessness*: the urge to drop out of time and history and inhabit a paradise or Never Never Land free of the responsibilities and obligations of adulthood, to remain in a state of what Norman O. Brown calls "privileged irresponsibility."[14] Second, there is what von Franz describes as a terrible fear pinned down in the "real world," of being caught in a situation from which it may be impossible to slip out again. And this fear is inseparable from another typical *puer* trait described by von Franz: a difficulty with making a definite commitment to another person or to a personal relationship.

Another feature of *puer* psychology discussed by both von Franz and the Jungian analyst James Hillman is "ascensionism": a fascination with ascending, with heights and flying. Von Franz describes ascensionism as "a desire to get as high as possible, the symbolism being to get away from reality, from the earth, from ordinary life."[15] As I indicated earlier, the *puer* types from classical mythology include Icarus, who flew too near the sun on his wings of wax and feathers, and Bellerophon, who tried to ride to the top of Mount Olympus on the back of the winged horse Pegasus.

There is an intense feeling or sympathy for Nature associated with the *puer aeternus*. Many *puer* figures are vegetation gods and are closely connected, in their myths, to Earth Mother goddesses: Attis and Cybele, Osiris and Isis, Tammuz and Ishtar.

Puer aeternus psychology is also distinguished by a tendency to divinize or demonize adults. Just as a child will perceive grown-ups, and especially his parents, as larger-than-life supernatural beings—gods or demons—so there is a corresponding tendency among *puer* types to see adults in this exaggerated fashion.

The Eternal Child is further characterized by androgyny—an ambiguous sexuality or bisexuality which displays both masculine and feminine characteristics.

Finally, two last traits associated with the Eternal Child: Holy Innocence and Tricksterism. By Holy Innocence I mean an attitude of childlike innocence and simplicity in one's dealings with the world. The Holy Innocent is a person who goes against the conventional wisdom of the world. He (or she) does not operate by the usual standards of profit and practicality. Rather, he lives by other, higher laws. He doesn't care about "getting ahead" or "making it," which of course renders him totally unsuited to the "serious" business of the world. Instead of following the dictates of a society that puts a premium on material advancement and financial success, he spends his time in such "idle" pursuits as contemplation or communion with nature. As a result, he's regarded as a fool by those members of society who prize common sense and tough-mindedness (the "when-the-going-gets-tough the-tough-get-going" boys, the hard-chargers). So the Holy Innocent is also sometimes known as the Holy Fool.

By Tricksterism I mean the impulse to play pranks, make mischief, stir up trouble, create chaos, anarchy, revolution, disorder. Especially in American folklore and popular culture, children are associated with Tricksterism. Peck's Bad Boy, the Katzenjammer Kids, Dennis the Menace are all well known examples of the Child-Trickster. The Trickster represents a powerfully anarchic, anti-authoritarian impulse, a drive to revolt, to disrupt or overturn the existing order.

Turning now to American society in the sixties: when we look at the counterculture during those years, we discover that it is characterized by precisely those traits which define the *puer aeternus* archetype. First we find a group of people who identify themselves as children, and not just children but flower-children. As we have seen, the original flower-children were the *pueri* of classical mythology, like Hyacinth and Narcissus. And this fact in itself suggests that what was taking place in the sixties was the revival of an ancient mythic idea—the recurrence of what Jung calls a "primordial image."

That a mythic revival of this sort occurred during the sixties becomes even more clear when we consider a phenomenon like the Paul McCartney Death Rumor. Nearly two thousand years after Ovid composed *The Metamorphoses* (which recounts the story of the beautiful youth Hyacinth, a very literal flower-child, who was slain and subsequently resurrected in the form of the blossom which bears his name), a whole generation of flower-children—members of the counterculture and other rock music fans—were suddenly gripped by the strange conviction that one of *their* heroes, the androgynously pretty Paul McCartney, had been killed in a car accident and then miraculously reborn (in the form of an exact duplicate who looked and sang exactly like, or even better than, the original). This rumor is clearly incredible, and the fact that it was believed by so many people cannot be understood in logical terms, though it can be understood in *mytho*logical ones, as the recurrence of an archetypal idea.

The popularity of the Beatles is in itself a striking sign of the emergence of the myth of the Child because the Beatles were the supreme embodiments of the archetype, and their phenomenal popularity demonstrates the dominance of that symbol during most of the sixties. John, Paul, George, and Ringo, the four mop-tops, were Eternal Children turned into flesh and into art. They were the minstrels of the *puer* state of mind. In his book *Gates of Eden,* Morris Dickstein discusses "the irrepressibly childlike qualities of the Beatles." He describes their "exuberance and effervescence," their "incurable addiction to the pleasure principle," and the "childlike magic" which was so "central to their appeal."[16] The very titles of their songs reveal the group's childlike sensibility: "Yellow Submarine," "Octopus's Garden," "Mother Nature's Son" (which might be the theme song of Attis or Tammuz), etc. As Dickstein notes, "Lennon's lyrics are sometimes so simple they look like children's nonsense verse, which he also writes very well."[17] And Paul McCartney, after leaving the group and forming Wings, even records a version of "Mary Had a Little Lamb."

The retreat into the world of the Child is evident everywhere in the counterculture. There are, for example, the costumes adopted by the "love children." In *Loose Change,* a vivid evocation of the sixties, Sara Davidson describes the guests at a party she attended in Berkeley in 1967: "They were wearing Edwardian velvet gowns, spaceman suits, African robes, cowboy regalia, Donald Duck hats and Indian war paint."[18] Like kids preparing for Halloween or playing with a trunkful of outlandish clothes they have discovered in their grandparents' attic, the hippies loved to dress up.

They also loved bright colors. To recall the sixties is to conjure up a world of posters, light shows, psychedelic art, and supergraphics—an explosion of radiant primary colors.

Toys were another standard feature of the sixties counterculture. The frisbee fad started back in the sixties. "Head shops" did a big business in kaleidoscopes, prisms, reflecting disks of various sorts and—something which has since disappeared from the market, but which enjoyed a good deal of popularity during those psychedelic days—an item called "Ocean in a Bottle" which consisted of a clear plastic cylinder filled with a viscous blue fluid. When the cylinder was tilted back and forth, the fluid recreated the motion of ocean waves.

Like most of the optical toys popular during the sixties, "Ocean in a Bottle" was intended primarily for the enjoyment of people who were stoned (since there is a limited amount of pleasure a sober person can derive from watching some blue liquid slosh back and forth in a container). Drugs—obviously a central feature of the sixties counterculture—were another manifestation of the myth which that generation was caught up in, an expression of what Hillman and von Franz describe as ascensionism: the desire "to get as high as possible." According to von Franz, people characterized by the *puer* psychology are very attracted to such activities as mountaineering and aviation. But, as Harry Chapin points out in his popular song "Taxi" (in which a young man, who had dreamt of becoming a pilot but ended up driving a cab, "flies" instead by getting stoned), there is more than one way to get high.

The desire to drop out—the refusal to enter time, history, or society—is very evident in the sixties, an era in which people were urged to "Turn on, tune in, drop out." Another popular slogan of the time, "Never trust anyone over thirty," captures the corollary of the desire to remain a child—namely the fear of aging and distrust of adults. The same sentiment is powerfully expressed in the Who's anthem, "My Generation," containing the lyric "Hope I die before I get old"—which is of course simply another way of saying "I'll Never Grow Up."

The latter song, "I'll Never Grow Up," comes from the 1950's television production of *Peter Pan,* which I mention here because the title character is a perfect pop representation of the *puer aeternus* archetype. He refuses to grow up, lives with his tribe of lost boys in Never Never Land (an earlier version of Strawberry Fields), has the ability to fly, and so on. Also, interestingly, in both TV versions of the play, his role is played by women—Mary Martin in the 1950's and Mia Farrow in the more recent production. There is something distinctly androgynous about Peter Pan. Androgyny, as I indicated earlier, is a trait of the *puer aeternus*—and again, we see this in the sixties in the move towards what was called "Unisex."[19]

A related phenomenon is the change in sexual behavior which took place in the sixties, specifically a shift to a kind of infantile or "polymorphous perverse" sexuality, which Norman O. Brown defines as "the pursuit of pleasure obtained through the activity of any and all organs of the human body."[20] We find, for example, a marked fascination with—even fixation on—oral lovemaking; an emphasis on "getting in touch with your body," which produces phenomena like the Esalen Institute in California and various "see me, feel me, touch me, hear me" therapies, the "group grope" (as the Fugs used to say).

The fear of being pinned down which von Franz describes—and the wanderlust and restlessness which go along with it—can be seen clearly in the prevalence of what might be called "the highway fantasy": dozens of films and songs about "movin" along the highway" (in the words of Carole King). It is a fantasy perhaps best exemplified by the movie *Easy Rider* and some of the early lyrics of Bob Dylan, whose second album is called *The Freewheelin' Bob Dylan* (a later release is titled *Highway 61 Revisited*). This fantasy, which the comedian Steve Martin parodies with his "I'm a ramblin' guy" pose, is closely related to another typical *puer* trait—the fear of being trapped in a relationship. Once again, Bob Dylan's music provides the prime expression of this feeling, particularly the song "Don't Think Twice It's All Right," in which the singer tells his lover, "When the rooster crows at the break of dawn/Look out your window and I'll be gone."

As for the Holy Innocent (or Holy Fool): this part of the *puer* sensibility is also prevalent in the sixties. The Beatles' "Fool on the Hill" is probably the purest expression of it in rock, though it is also strikingly present in the lyrics of Paul Simon (see, for example, "Save the Life of My Child," "Punky's Dilemma," "Papa Hobo," "Duncan," and "Loves Me Like a Rock") and in the persona of Arlo Guthrie in "Alice's Restaurant." In literature, it informs the fiction of Kurt Vonnegut (particularly *Slaughterhouse-Five, or, The Children's Crusade*), Richard Brautigan, and Joseph Heller's *Catch-22*. Benjamin Braddock, the hero of the movie of *The Graduate* (an important film of the period) is a perfect example of the

Holy Innocent who is regarded as a fool because he doesn't share the materialistic values of his elders; he isn't interested in spending his life in plastics.[21]

The Trickster element of the counterculture has been discussed recently in an article by E. Allen Tiller, who sees the Trickster as the dominant myth of the sixties.[22] While Tilley, in my opinion, puts too much emphasis on the Trickster—which I see as just one aspect of the larger myth of time—he does an excellent job of describing its appearance in such phenomena as the Yippies and Ken Kesey's Merry Pranksters. The Rolling Stones—the Peck's Bad Boys of rock—also embody this aspect of the *puer aeternus* myth.

The feeling for or closeness to Nature that is part of the *puer* myth is obvious in the sixties counterculture. The sixties are the time when the back-to-Nature movement begins to blossom in this country; when the nation's ecology-consciousness begins to be raised; when masses of Americans start dreaming about returning to the land—and many make the attempt; when plant stores and health food shops start popping up in every neighborhood and every item on the market (or so it seems) is suddenly advertised as "all natural."

Related to this new prominence of Mother Nature is the phenomenon Hillman describes: the tendency to divinize or demonize the parents. If one examines fairy tales or children's literature in general, one sees very clearly the child's habit of mythologizing adults, of perceiving them as monumental beings. Mothers may be wicked witches or helpful fairy godmothers; fathers may be cannibalistic ogres or giants (as in "Jack and the Beanstalk") or beneficent Wise Old Man. Once again, when we look at the sixties, we find the same fantasy figures dominating the imagination of the counterculture. We find Mother Nature making a comeback, reverenced in various forms of behavior, from vegetarianism to the ecology movement, and celebrated in poetry, music, and elsewhere.[23] A perfect statement of this feeling for Nature is the song "Mother Earth," written by Eric Kaz and recorded by Tom Rush on his album *Merrimack County:*

> While Mother Earth looks after me
> I will follow faithfully.
> ....
> I am blessed with her devotion
> Mother Earth provides for me.

These lyrics also express a theme which Jungians call "the provisional life"—the childlike fantasy that all our needs will be provided for us by a great, benevolent power, so that we need not worry about working to support ourselves. The Beatles are also, predictably, celebrants of the Good Mother, in songs like "Lucy in the Sky with Diamonds," "Mother Nature's Son," and especially "Let it Be": "When I find myself in times of trouble/Mother Mary comes to me...."

As for the Terrible Mother—her image appears everywhere in the sixties. I don't have the space to list all the manifestations of this mythic figure here, but I will mention a few of the most important.[24] Ken Kesey, an important figure during this decade, portrays a very powerful Terrible Mother figure in his novel *One Flew Over the Cuckoo's Nest:* the monstrous "Big Nurse" Ratched. The Terrible Mother also appears in *The Graduate,* in the character Mrs. Robinson. The so-called New Comix or Head Comix—one of the two characteristic pop art forms of the counterculture—are truly obsessed with the Cannibal Mother. A classic example is Richard Corben's "Gastric Fortitude," from *Death Rattle* #1, in which a young man takes shelter from a storm in a Gothic castle inhabited by a voluptuous woman. When the hero removes his wet clothing, she tells him that he "looks good enough to eat"—and then proceeds quite literally to devour him.

By the late sixties, rock music—the premier art form of the young—also begins to be filled with images of the Terrible Mother. Grace Slick of the Jefferson Airplane, for instance, sings a song called "Silver Spoon," in which she assures her listeners that "You could learn to dine on your friends." It is also around this time that the Rolling Stones, at the very peak of their popularity, adopt as their trademark a pair of thick red lips with a fat tongue thrust out from between them—a caricature of Jagger's own famous liver-lips, but also the symbol (as the Stones themselves were well aware) of the Indian Cannibal Goddess Kali. Immediately the Kali symbol began popping up everywhere—on watches, key rings, pins, pendants, posters. This move by the Stones was not very surprising. If the Beatles celebrated the Good Mother and sang "Let it Be," the Stones could be counted on to celebrate the Terrible Mother and sing "Let it Bleed."

Similarly, as soon as the Beatles released an album *(Sgt. Pepper's Lonely Hearts Club Band)* dedicated in spirit to their Good Father figure, the Maharishi, the Stones rushed out an album dedicated to the Terrible Father: to "His Satanic Majesty." The tendency of the counterculture to create Good Father figures, Wise Old Men, can be seen not only in the sudden celebrity of the Maharishi but in the prominence of all the gurus of the day— Timothy Leary, Baba Ram Dass and so on. Indeed, it is in the sixties that the word "guru" becomes a part of our everyday speech. As for the flip side of that myth, the Negative Father who destroys his

children: he too appears repeatedly in the sixties, in the fantasy of
the hard-hat killer (the best example of which is the popular movie
Joe, in which the title character ends up shooting his own hippie
daughter) and in the fantasy/reality of Nixon, who plays out his
mythic role in this mythic age (because everyone gets up in the spirit
of the time) as the Terrible Father-Destroyer of children.

Destroying children, in fact, has a great deal to do with why the
puer aeternus arose in the first place, as I will explain later.

III

But first, let me summarize: I have tried to show that the
dominant myth of the sixties was that of the Eternal Child—that the
psychological traits associated with this myth were precisely the
ones lived out by the counterculture. The question then becomes:
what caused this particular myth to emerge when it did? It seems to
me that if we look at American society between World War II and the
Vietnam War, when the flower-child generation was being born,
growing up, and coming of age, we see a society which is militaristic,
increasingly mechanized and technologized, which prizes
competitiveness and masculine aggression, defines sex roles very
rigidly, and so forth. Following Jung's theory of archetypal
compensation, which I summed up at the start of this essay, we can
say, I believe, that the counterculture was given shape and direction
by unconscious forces operating on a collective scale and with a
particular purpose because the unconscious, according to Jung, *is*
purposive; it does have a definite aim which is self-regulation, the
maintenance of psychic health and balance. During the sixties, as
in other eras, the unconscious strove to achieve this purpose by
raising the symbol of the neglected values into the cultural
consciousness of mainstream American society, by forcing the
culture at large into an awareness of those values which it had been
denying to its detriment.

Symbolically speaking, the opposite of war, aggression,
competition, death-machinery, is the Eternal Child. Hence, many
anti-war posters used the baby or child as as an image of peace
during the sixties, and a popular slogan of the time went, "War isn't
healthy for children and other living things." The same antithesis
of childhood and war can be seen clearly in the hit movie *M*A*S*H*,
in which the reaction to war is a retreat into the Child-Trickster
behavior of its heroes, Hawkeye and Trapper John, and in which the
best people are Holy Innocents like Radar O'Reilly. The denial of
child values by American society—and the actual destruction of
children (an image bombarding us daily through the mass media)—
led, I believe, to a compensatory reaction among the young, an

exaltation of those values which American society seemed intent on destroying.

To be sure, it's clear—in fact glaringly obvious—that the values and behavior of the counterculture were counter to those of the mainstream culture. But it is my contention that the shape and destiny of the counterculture were determined by deeply unconscious forces—that it was a mass movement created and motivated first and foremost by unconscious compulsions. Only later was the role of the child adopted as a conscious stance and strategy. It is possible of course to look at the sixties counterculture and see its retreat into childhood as merely regressive and infantile behavior—a large scale neurosis. But, while there is an element of truth to this, I think that it's a mistake to see the counterculture as nothing more than a symptom. Jung teaches us to look at neuroses, not symptomatically but symbolically. The counterculture *was* a symptom of a cultural sickness, but it was also the living symbol of the cure, a push towards a new synthesis—an attempt ironically enough to set American society straight.

NOTES

[1]This is made explicit in *The Front,* the recent movie about the McCarthy era, which ends with Frank Sinatra's voice singing over the closing credits, "Fairy tales can come true/It can happen to you..." ("Young at Heart")

[2]Morris Dickstein, *Gates of Eden: American Culture in the Sixties* (New York: Basic Books, 1977), p.ix.

[3]Joseph Campbell, *Hero With a Thousand Faces* (New York and Cleveland: World Publishing/Meridian Books, 1956), p.19.

[4]Joseph Campbell, Introduction to *The Portable Jung* (New York: The /Viking Press, 1971), p.xxii.

[5]Ibid.

[6]C.G. Jung, "Psychology and Literature," in *Modern Man in Search of a Soul,* W.S. Dell and Cary F. Baynes, translators (New York: Harcourt, Brace & World, inc./Harvest Books, 1955), p.166.

[7]Mircea Eliade, *Myths, Dreams and Mysteries: The Encounter between Contemporary Faith and Archaic Realities,* trans. Philip Mairet (New York: Harper & Row/Harper Colophon Books, 1975), pp.27 ff.

[8]Ursula K. Le Guin "Myth and Archetype in Science Fiction," *Parabola,* I, no. 4 (Fall 1976), p.45.

[9]Henry Nash Smith, *The Virgin Land: The American West as Symbol and Myth,* (New York: Vintage Books, 1950), p.101.

[10]C.G. Jung, "The Psychology of the Child Archetype," in *The Archetypes and the Collective Unconscious,* Collected Works, IX, part I, trans, R.F.C. Hull (Princeton: Princeton University Press, 1959, Bollingen Series XX), p. 156.

[11]Marie-Louise von Franz, *The Problem of the Puer Aeternus* (Zurich: Spring Publications, 1970), Section I, p.1.

[12]James Hillman also points out that "students of literature would find the *puer* perhaps in St. Exupery, in Shelley, Rimbaud, in Rousseau; Shakespeare's Hotspur is an example; Herman Melville has at least five such beautiful sailor-wanderers." See "Pothos: The Nostalgia of the *Puer Aeternus,*" in *Loose Ends: Primary Papers in Archetypal Psychology* (Zurick: Spring Publications, 1975), 49-62.

[13]Ibid., p.50.

[14]Norman O. Brown, *Life Against Death: The Psychoanalytic Meaning of History* (Middletown, Connecticut: Wesleyan University Press, 1959), p.24.

[15]*The Problem of the Puer Aeternus,* Section I, p.2.

[16]*Gates of Eden,* pp.202 and 209.

[17]Ibid., p.204

[18]Sara Davidson, *Loose Change: Three Women of the Sixties* (New York: Pocket Books, 1978), p.139.

[19]For a valuable discussion of this phenomenon, see June Singer, *Androgyny: Toward a New Theory of Sexuality* (New York: Anchor Press/Doubleday, 1976).

[20]*Life Against Death,* p.30.

[21]The figure of the Holy Innocent can be clearly seen in the book which is the inspiration for *The Graduate* and indeed which forecasts this whole side of the sixties: J.D. Salinger's *The Catcher in the Rye.* Holden Caulfield considers himself a moron and is regarded as a failure; but his worldly failure is really the correlative to his spiritual superiority. His extreme goodness (as well as his connection to the world of Nature) is demonstrated by his concern over the fate of the ducks in Central Park. This theme has an interesting parallel in the Grimm Brothers' fairy tale "The Queen Bee," which also contains a hero who is solicitous of some ducks. This hero's name is Simpleton: like Holden and Benjamin Braddock, he is a Holy Fool.

[22]"The Counterculture Trickster," *Psychocultural Review,* 2 (Winter 1978), 53-61.

[23]For a fuller discussion of this phenomenon, see my article, "The Return of Demeter: The Poetry of Daniela Gioseffi," *Psychocultural Review,* I (Fall 1977), 452-458.

[24]I discuss others in "Kali on Main Street: The Rise of the Terrible Mother in America," *Journal of Popular Culture,* VII (Fall 1973), 251-263.

Discussing "The Myth of the Eternal Child in Sixties America."

1) The 1920's was also a "decade of youth." What parallels, using Schechter's hypothesis, can be drawn between youthfulness during the Jazz Age and various youth movements during the 1960's?

2) Read *The American Adam* by R.W.B. Lewis (University of Chicago Press, 1955). How does the nineteenth century concept of the American Adam compare with Schechter's description of the Eternal Child archetype?

3) Talk with someone who was a "Hippie" during the 1960's but who is now a "normal" member of society. Find out what attracted them to the Hippie life and what caused them to return to the American mainstream.

4) Schechter argues that the Eternal Child myth gained popularity during the 1960's because it was a corrective for other directions in American society during that time. Was anything really corrected? What are the lasting effects the counterculture had on American life?

Star Trek as Myth
and Television as Mythmaker

By Wm. Blake Tyrrell

The phenomenon of *Star Trek* is unique in television. More popular now than its first run in the late 60's, it has spawned books of adapted scripts and of fandom as well as countless fanzines. *Star Trek* regalia extend to complete blueprints of the *Enterprise* and code of conduct for its personnel. Fan clubs have led to conventions where attendance must be limited. All this is the result of something beyond the dramatic spectacle. *Star Trek* is consistent but often childish science fiction, engaging but often belabored drama. I wish to propose a reason for the phenomenon of *Star Trek* as a contribution to our understanding of the power of television.

Star Trek never had high ratings; it did have in science fiction an intriguing format. By inventing a believable world, *Star Trek* provided the viewer with material for his own imagination. He could elaborate upon the sets and equipment, bandy arcane knowledge, even write his own scripts. That the format had the potential to involve the viewer beyond one hour each week is the initial basis for the phenomenon. *Star Trek's* format created a world alive, turning viewers into fans.

Gene Roddenberry, creator of the series, referred to it, if only in jest, as " 'Wagon Train' to the stars,"[1] and the similarity between groups journeying toward the unknown is evident. Movement is a prominent motif of both Western and *Star Trek* where it is made visual in the flyby of the gliding starship. But the similarity goes deeper. The Western story is the only indigenous mythic narrative of the white American. "The isolation of a vast unexplored continent, the slow growth of social forms, the impact of an unremitting New England Puritanism obsessed with the cosmic struggle of good and

From the *Journal of Popular Culture*, 1977, 10(4), pp.711-719. Reprinted by permission of the editor and the author.

evil, of the elect and the damned, the clash of allegiances to Mother Country and New World, these factors," as Jim Kitses says in *Focus on the Western,* "are the crucible in which the American consciousness was formed."[2] Since the publication in 1893 of Frederick J. Turner's essay "The Significance of the Frontier in American History," the dominant symbol of the Western myth has been the frontier.[3] *Star Trek* views space as "the final frontier."[4] Despite its format *Star Trek* is not speculative fiction in the way of written science fiction or even of *Space 1999* in its first season. It is American myths clothed in the garb of science fiction. "Space — the final frontier" is conceptualized through the same motifs and themes as the Western frontier. A brief example.

The heart of the Western myth is the encounter with the Indian. The myth-making imagination has contained the Indian's alienness in two types: Chingachgook, the noble warrior ever outside White Man's world, and Magua, sly, perfidious, fallen and by that fall, bound to the white world. Both types are found in *Star Trek*. The Romulans, whose name recalls the heroic founder of Rome, are aggressive, militaristic aliens. Nonetheless they are "hard to hate," *The Making of Star Trek* explains, "as they often display enormous courage." The Klingons, a name as low as Cooper's Magua, are ruled by the principle "that rules are made to be broken by shrewdness, deceit, or power."[5] There is nothing admirable about them and with them in time, one episode predicts,[6] the White Man of the *Enterprise* is destined to unite. Though apparently distinct figures in the series (and perhaps in their creator's imagination), their dark, satanic visages reveal Romulans and Klingons as aspects of a whole, the Indian reborn.

Yet *Star Trek* is more than the transposing of visuals and motifs, more than the shifting from one metaphor to another. Myths are narratives with the power to move our psychic energies toward integration of self and of self with the cosmos. Myths define an image of the world within and without and relate us to it emotionally. Myths put in narrative form the unconscious assumptions that constitute the spirit of a culture. They can inspire and direct those energies to monumental achievements of good or ill. During the 60's American myths and the values they supported, after a brief sojourn in Camelot, began coming apart, not to be replaced by those of the counter culture. *Star Trek* revitalizes American myths by displacing[7] them into a futuristic, quasi-scientific setting. In effect, *Star Trek* takes our roots and disguises them as branches for some of us to cling to. Moreover, *Star Trek* put them on television.

Television is the medium of immediate, personal communication. No willed suspension of disbelief occurs; television speaks not to intelligence or to its pilot, the will. It works through the emotions on a non-reasoning level and is thus the medium best suited to the emotional word, *mythos*.[8] *Star Trek* exploits television's intimate communication. Things on *Star Trek* look right. The family of the *Enterprise* is closely knit, appealing and calmly efficient. The men are men, and the women are endowed. (Though set in the 23rd century, sexual roles are those of the 50's.) Kirk, broadly played by William Shatner, projects emotion, strength and unthreatening paternalism. Leonard Nimoy's Spock surpasses him by striving not to emote at all. The result was that *Star Trek's* message of revitalized mythic narrative, brought directly to the emotional needs of the viewer, engendered the feeling that the shows were more than escapist entertainment. They had meaning. That feeling transformed the 48 minute episodes into rituals, and rituals, being group-creating, led to clubs and to the convention. This feeling and the power to generate it are, I believe, what is unique about *Star Trek* and the reason for the phenomenon.

Star Trek is a product of the dreams and nightmares of the 60's. It came to those who needed the confidence and triumph of the American past, while fearing a present that foreboded the disappearance of the American way. The need has become stronger in the diffident 70's. *Star Trek's* vision, as Roddenberry and the authors of *Star Trek Lives!* maintain, is "of a brighter future of man, of a world characterized by hope, achievement and understanding."[9] But *Star Trek's* impact transcends simple optimism for a tomorrow we may never see. *Star Trek* creates a future world where the glories of the past are pristine and the failures and doubts of the present have been overcome. It gives us our past as our future, while making our present the past which, like any historical event for the future-oriented American, is safely over and forgotten. One way that myths function, particularly those of creation, is to anchor the present to the past and place the worshipper in the time of first beginnings.[10] Something similar is the source of *Star Trek's* power. Myths no longer link us to the past, since we know the past is gone and is of historical, not immediate, relevance to the present. Bicentennialism recalls the past. On the other hand, any science fiction can link us to the future. But the future, even that imagined in books, is uncertain. *Star Trek*, by disguising our past as our future, puts us in it — not the historical past but the mythic past of our first beginnings. There ensues a feeling of permanence, stability and renewed confidence. This is what's different about *Star Trek*.

I wish now to illustrate this view by looking at one mythic theme of *Star Trek* — that of paradise, whose role in mythicizing America began before the Puritans touched its shores.[11]

Paradise is a fundamental theme of the series, the subject of at least 13 of 79 episodes.[12] It is imagined as the lost Eden of *Genesis* or as the garden of the New World that lies just beyond the Western frontier. Paradise is destroyed, the victim of *Star Trek's* unquestioned identification of tranquility with stagnation. In *The Apple,* for instance, the crew of the *Enterprise* have happened upon a planet controlled in weather, food supply, everything by a computer named Vaal.[13] The inhabitants are humanoids living in a state of nature. Their single task is to feed Vaal with rocks. Watching the fueling process, McCoy, Spock and Kirk are speaking together:

McCoy:	What's going on, Jim?
Kirk:	Mess call.
Spock:	In my view a splendid example of reciprocity.
McCoy:	It would take a computerized Vulcan mind such as yours to make that kind of a statement.
Spock:	Doctor, you insist on applying human standards to non-human cultures. I remind you that humans are only a tiny minority in this galaxy.
McCoy:	There are certain absolutes, Mr. Spock, and one of them is the right of humanoids to a free and unchained environment. The right to have conditions which permit growth.
Spock:	Another is their right to choose a system which seems to work for them.
McCoy:	Jim you're not just going to stand by and be blinded to what's going on here. These are humanoids. Intelligent. They need to advance and grow. Don't you understand what my readings indicate? There's been no change or progress here in at least ten thousand years. This isn't life. It's stagnation.
Spock:	Doctor, these people are healthy, and they are happy. Whatever you choose to call it, this system works despite your emotional reaction to it.
McCoy:	It might for you, Mr. Spock, but it doesn't work for me. Humanoids living so they can service a hunk of tin.
Kirk:	Gentlemen, I think this philosophical argument can wait until our ship's out of danger.

For the men of *Star Trek* as for the pioneers paradise is to be exploited. Open land beckons the plow, way to the new beginning that brings rebirth. It is the dream our ancestors followed westward;

it launches our descendants into space. Inseparable with rebirth is death: natives of paradise too contented to appreciate the virtues of progress and advancement are reeducated. Kirk violently inflicts Federation enterprise upon them by destroying Vaal. Despite the nagging of its conscience Spock, the series subscribes to McCoy's benevolent imperialism. At the time of *The Apple's* first airing the belief in America as World Peacemaker and Liberator, a belief which is surely an aspect of the myth of the frontier, was coming apart in Vietnam and in Washington, D.C.[14] *Star Trek* assures us of its validity by showing it as the unquestioned truth of the 23rd century. Near propagandizing, to be sure, but *Star Trek* gives out the message to those who want to believe in a way that they can believe.

In one episode the theme of paradise is treated quite differently. The tensions inherent in the myth are relieved, not by the dogmatic destruction of one pole, but by the device of the mediator. Although not typical of the paradise-theme, *This Side of Paradise*[15] is a microcosm for the way the series generates its impact. The plot is as follows.

The *Enterprise* arrives on Omicron Ceti III expecting to find the members of an agricultural colony dead. The planet is bombarded by Berthold radiation that disintegrates human tissue. Yet they are greeted by the colonists. They have survived because of their symbiosis with spores that absorb the radiation. These spores are a group organism; they cause their hosts to lose the sense of self and of self-advancement. No progress has been made toward the goals of the colony. The crew succumbs to the spores and abandons the *Enterprise*. Included are McCoy and Spock, the latter experiencing the only painful conversion. While under the spores Spock falls in love with an old admirer who happens to be on the planet. Capt. Kirk is ovecome by the spores while on the ship, but becomes so angered at the thought of leaving it, that he is released from their influence. He later discovers that violent emotions dissolve the spores. He provokes Spock to a fight in the Transporter Room,[16] and the ensuing violence dissolves his spores. Together they bring the crew to its senses and the *Enterprise* to order.

A mediator is a third between two opposites that shares something of the nature of each. Being anomalous, it may function to overcome the opposition. In *Genesis* the Serpent mediates between Man and God as well as between Man and Woman.[17] In the myth of the frontier the trapper, hunter or scout is the anomaly between White and Red. Fundamental to the psychology informing the myth is the tension between the longing for paradise and the knowledge of its passing. But both paradise myths, *Genesis* and the Frontier, link this tension with others — social, sexual and moral. Such is the way paradise is treated in *This Side of Paradise.*

Paradise as an idea, desirable but manifestly impossible, is mediated by the alien Spock. Paradise as a place lost yet sought after is mediated by the *Enterprise*. These tensions are connected with those over drugs and the differences between generations which had become polarized because of drugs. The structure of the story may be diagrammed:

PARADISE	MEDIATION	PARADISE LOST
Paradise as an Idea		
a. McCoy	Spock	Kirk
b. Spores	Spores then violent emotions	Violent emotions
c. Painless acceptance	Painful acceptance	
d. Abdication of duty	Return to duty	Unquestioned duty
e. Loss of self	Sacrifice of self	Self as all
f. Stagnation	Friendship	Ambition
Paradise as a Place		
a. Omicron Ceti III	*Enterprise* with crew	*Enterprise* empty except for Kirk
b. down	Transporter Room	up

Reading down the columns...McCoy accepts the spores painlessly. Forgetting his duty, he loses his self in the group induced by the spores. He gains peace and contentment, marked by the return of his Southern accent and evoking in the viewer's mind the opening scenes of *Gone With The Wind*, that is, the plantation as paradise. [18] Kirk, his opposite, is briefly affected. Because of his anger, he rejects the spores painlessly and without regret. Though he says he realizes their meaning, his sense of duty is too strong for them. Kirk is left by himself — literally, alone with his self. Spock, the middle ground between them, accepts the spores but painfully. For him as for Kirk they are unnatural; like McCoy, he experiences their effect, wants it and regrets its passing. Spock breaks continuity with the group by asserting his individuality; he fights back when Kirk insults his parentage and logical outlook. When he returns to duty, he does so knowing his loss. He sacrifices the happiness of the spores to his responsibility to others. The cost of the sacrifice is made real through the love affair with Leila. The spores suppress Spock's Vulcan side. Fully human, he can love. Once returned to normal, he can not even speak of his regard for her. Given the characterization of Spock as a constant struggle against emotions and the sexual feelings that he has aroused in viewers, the affair expresses poignantly the pain of paradise lost.[19]

Star Trek is committed to technological progress as the answer to our problems. Roddenberry reiterated in a *Penthouse* interview (March, 1976) his reasons for the series' popularity, one of which is:

> First of all, we live in a time in which everyone, and particularly young minds, are aware that we face huge troubles ahead. There are many people saying, "I doubt if we'll make it through the next twenty or thirty years." And indeed, if you read the newspapers it seems so. "Star Trek" was a rare show that said, "Hey, it's not all over. It hasn't all been invented. If we're wise, why the human adventure is just beginning." And this is a powerful statement to young-minded people, to think that the explorations and discoveries and challenges ahead of us are greater than anything in the past.

For such an attitude as Roddenberry's paradise, a state of wholeness, of unity, can only be stagnation, for paradise denies the need for the quest. Sandoval, head of the colony, says after his release from the spores:

> We've done nothing here. No accomplishments. No progress. Three years wasted. We wanted to make this planet a garden.

Kirk pronounces the moral of the episode:

> Maybe we weren't meant for paradise. Maybe we were meant to fight our way through. Struggle. Claw our way up. Scratch for every inch of the way. Maybe we can't stroll to the music of the lute. We must march to the sound of the drums.

Edifying but unpleasant. There is a third way, one suggested by the structure of the story: responsibility to others. Spock tells Leila:

> I have a responsibility. To this ship. To that man on the bridge. I am what I am, Leila. If there are self-made purgatories, then we all have to live in them. Mine can be no worse than someone else's.

Paradise is knowingly and willingly sacrificed for love of others and for duty.

Omicron Ceti III is depicted as rural America, and the *Enterprise* without its crew as a helpless hulk. The one place expresses the simplicity of the past. Kirk alone on the ship, whose vast technological capabilites are a repeated theme of the series, expresses the loneliness of those who have left the past for the uncertainty of the future. Between them is the *Enterprise* with crew. The struggle between Kirk and Spock that determines Spock's role as a mediator occurs in the Transporter Room, the intersecting point of the 'down' of the planet and the 'up' of the ship. Here the conflict over the idea of paradise is resolved, for here on the ship the sacrifice is ever made.

The authors intend for us to see the story in the context of the drug culture of the 60's. Their intended message is found in the pontifications of Kirk. But the meaning coming from the story's structure is very different: friendship and the self-sacrifice and responsibility it demands offer a middle way between the dropping out of the Flower Children and the rat race of their parents. The episode ends — the last thing we see — with the three friends reunited in the common mission of the *Enterprise*. The mission, stated after the teaser of every show, is never questioned (or questioned in order to be reaffirmed) in this or any episode. The bitter conflict over lifestyles of the 60's, as worked out through the mediator Spock, is relieved by a third: being with friends on a mission whose undoubted worth confers upon existence ready-made meaning and purpose.

In a similar fashion the series itself mediates the tension between the past and the present by establishing a third time, that of first beginnings. It is a time with the anticipation and wonder of the future without the anxieties of the present, with the glory and security of the past without its remoteness. By transcending in an ultimately inexplicable way the sum of message and medium *Star Trek* puts the fan-become-believer in that time. As an indication of what I am saying I quote the following poem from a *Star Trek* fanzine:[21]

> Gliding swiftly through the dark,
> Sailing now in starry space,
> Silently and free you fly,
> Traveling midst time and place
>
> Like a quiet thing, alive,
> Though your engines hum and roar,
> Faster than the speed of light,
> High above the sky you soar.
>
> Oh! To be aboard you now
> As between the stars you roam,
> To be once more upon your decks,
> The Enterprise — my home.

For the believer "Star Trek Lives" is more than the slogan of a TV show that would not die. It is the ritual cry to a world where he belongs, where he has it all together. *Star Trek* offers the comfort of religion.

NOTES

[1]Stephen E. Whitfield and Gene Roddenberry, *The Making of Star Trek* (New York, 1968) 22. The context of Roddenberry's remark is one of throwing sand into the network's eyes in order to get the show on the air. But see Robert L. Shayon's comment in *Saturday Review* (June 17, 1967) 46:

"*Star Trek* is a space version of *Wagon Train*. There's the crew, there's the encountered. The problems arise now from the in-group, now from the out. The future is not without its counterpart of violence in the past and present."

[2]Jim Kitses, "The Western: Ideology and Archetype," in *Focus on the Western,* ed. Jack Nachbar (Englewood Cliffs, 1974) 66.

[3]Frederick J. Turner, "The Significance of the Frontier in American History," *Annual Report of the American Historical Association for the Year 1893* (Washington D.C.), 1894) 199-27. For a more convenient source see Ray A. Billington, *Frontier and Section: Selected Essays of Frederick Jackson Turner,* Englewood Cliffs, 1961.

[4]Stated after the teaser of every episode is the series' continuing theme:

Space — the final frontier. These are the voyages of the Star
Ship *Enterprise.* Its five year mission: to explore strange new
worlds, to seek out new civilizations, to boldly go where no man
has gone before.

[6]Gene L. Coon, *Errand of Mercy,* first shown on March 23, 1967. An adaption of the script has been published by James Blish, *Star Trek, 2* (New York, 1968) 41-54. Although many writers contributed to *Star Trek*, Coon along with D. C. Fontana (see below, note 15) and Roddenberry maintained consistency and provided the series with its best, most characteristic episodes.

[7]This term is Northrup Frye's (*Anatomy of Criticism,* Princeton, 1957) 136-37:

Myth, then, is one extreme of literary design; naturalism is the other,
and in between lies the whole area of romance, using that term to
mean...the tendency...to displace myth in a human direction and yet,
in contrast to "realism," to conventionalize content in an idealized
direction. The central principle of displacement is that what can be
metaphorically identified in a myth can only be linked in romance by
some form of simile: analogy; significant association, incidental
accompanying imagery, and the like.

[8]For the intimate communication of television see Mawry Green, "The Mythology of Television," *Television Quarterly* 9 (1970) 5-13; Robert C. O'Hara, *Media for the Millions* (New York, 1961) 286-306; Horace Newcomb, *TV: The Most Popular Art* (Garden City, 1974) 154-60; 243-64. Ernst Cassirer (*Essay on Man* (Cambridge, 1944); reprint: New Myth and primitive religion are by no means entirely incoherent, they are not bereft of sense or reason. But their coherence depends much more upon unity of feeling than upon logical rules."

[9]Jacqueline Lichtenberg, Sondra Marshak and Joan Winston, *Star Trek Lives!* (New York, 1975) 107-8. More revealing of *Star Trek's* appeal, I believe, is the authors' comment (8) on what the reader may gain from their book:

Most of all, perhaps, we hope you will find that *you are not alone!*
(Author's italics)

[10]Mircea Eliade, *The Sacred and the Profane,* translated by Willard Trask (New

York, 1961) 80-113.

[11]Arthur K. Moore, *The Frontier Mind, A Cultural Analysis of the Kentucky Frontiersman* (Lexington, 1957) 25-37. See also Henry Smith, *Virgin Land, (Cambridge, 1950)*.

[12]The theme of paradise appears in order of airing in: *The Menagerie* (two-part episode), *Shore Leave, This Side of Paradise, Who Mourns for Adonais? The Apple, Metamorphosis, Paradise Syndrome, For the World is Hollow and I Have Touched the Sky, Mark of Gideon,* and *The Way to Eden.*

[13]Max Ehrlick, *The Apple.* All quotations from the episodes are taken from the televised version of the script. There is an adaption of *The Apple* by James Blish in *Star Trek 6* (New York, 1972) 49-68. Blish takes too many liberties with the scripts for his adaptations to be useful for the study of *Star Trek.*

[14]*The Apple* was first shown on October 13, 1967. On October 21 and 22 demonstrations took place in Washington, and in particular at the Pentagon, protesting the number of those killed in Vietnam.

[15]Nathan Butler and D. C. Fontana, *This Side of Paradise*, first shown on March 2, 1967 and adapted by James Blish in *Star Trek 5* (New York, 1972) 58-72.

[16]The transporter is a "device for converting matter temporarily into energy, beaming that energy to a predetermined point, and reconverting it back to its original pattern and structure" (Whitfield (above, note 1) 192). It is the usual means of access to and from the ship.

[17]Edmund R. Leach, "Genesis as Myth," *Myth and Cosmos,* edited by John Middleton (Garden City, 1967) 1-13.

[18]Smith (above, note 11) 145-54.

[19]See Lichtenberg *et al.* (above, note 9) 71-105 for a discussion of Spock from the fan's point of view.

[20]See above, note 4.

[21]J. Clinkenbeard, "Love Poem to a Ship," *Warped Space,* fanzine of the Star Trek Club of Michigan State University, October 31, 1974.

Discussing "*Star Trek* as Myth and Television as Mythmaker"

1) Read John G. Cawelti's "Savagery, Civilization and the Western Hero." In what ways does the Western myth as described by Tyrrell differ from the Western myth as described by Cawelti? In what major ways are they the same?

2) Read Bruce Lohof's "The Higher Meaning of Marlboro Cigarettes." Can an argument be made that if we believe both Lohof and Tyrell, the person lighting up a Marlboro and the person watching *Star Trek* are really experiencing the same myth? Why?

3) The smash hit 1977 movie *Star Wars* was often described as an outer space Western. Is *Star Wars* the 1970's mythic counterpart of *Star Trek?*

4) What other beliefs do you think are attached to the myth of paradise? What examples of these beliefs can you find in American popular culture?

PART TWO
POPULAR ICONS

Introduction

Popular icons are images and objects that suggest emotional and/or intellectual meanings beyond their physical appearance or use. These are the "things" of our culture, including both two-dimensional pictures, such as advertising, and three-dimensional objects, such as buildings and automobiles. The archeologist digging for the remains of a past civilization is looking for material culture, which consists of the artifacts or objects, pottery for example, produced by the past society. The student of popular culture is engaged in above-ground archeology, looking at the things around him/her and trying to understand their meanings.

Not all of the images and objects of our culture, however, are icons. Icons are the things which are symbolic–they communicate beliefs and values, they *mean* something. The word "icon" originally referred to religious pictures and objects, particularly pictures of saints which were meant to be worshipped and cherished. The crucifix, in fact, is an icon, perhaps the most powerful of all. But in our modern and more secular age, we find that many other cultural images and objects besides the purely religious are charged with significance.

Popular icons are all around, as every part of the environment which has been shaped or built by human forces is therefore a reflection of human values. Streets, buildings, signs, and all the other human-made objects are representative of our ideals, fears, and aspirations. The natural world too has to a great extent been altered to meet individual and social needs–the millions of acres of cultivated farmland, the creation of new lakes and rivers, the building of new hills and valleys by giant earth-moving equipment. The world we see around us was made by our society and is our society.

There are in this environment certain images and objects that are especially significant, icons on which a high degree of meaning is focused. Obvious among these are the icons of American nationalism–the United States flag, the White House, the figure of Uncle Sam–all of which carry a heavy load of emotional baggage. Consider another of these patriotic icons, the American eagle, symbol of political strength and military authority. In the founding days of the American republic, Benjamin Franklin seriously proposed the wild turkey as the national emblem. The turkey is indigenous to America while species of the eagle are found throughout the world. Despite Franklin's pleas for the turkey, the eagle was chosen as the national emblem because the founding fathers knew that the eagle had a long tradition from the days of ancient Greece and Rome as a symbol of mastery, strength, vigilance, and fierceness. The borrowing of classical icons extended throughout American life, with public buildings of all kinds constructed to look like Greek temples.

But what of our contemporary built environment, the icons that are being created now? Perhaps the most remarkable American architectural phenomenon of our age is the enclosed shopping mall. Springing up all over the country in the last twenty years, the mall is an oasis of consumerism, a vast structure dedicated to the arts of merchandising. The mall is also now a center of community life, displacing downtown areas as a meeting place for the citizenry. As it recreates the aura and function of the ancient market-place, the mall is a total self-contained environment which is a world of fantasy and fleeting luxury, with spouting fountains, colored lights, and modern sculpture. Every suburb can now have its own miniature version of Disney World.

The history of American icons is the story of a struggle between the old and the new. This tension, according to John Kouwenhoven, is between the cultivated style inherited from Europe and the vernacular (meaning "native") style which arose in America to meet the demands of creating a New World. The cultivated style is decorative, esthetic, ornate, and formal, with overtones of the old aristocratic societies. The new style, the American vernacular, is based on technology and democracy; it is functional, realistic, practical, energetic, and plain. Almost any American artifact will have elements of both styles, but the vernacular will likely have the upper hand. This means of describing artifacts is a useful tool in icon analysis, as it gives us a way of categorizing and of understanding what is typically American.

Icons may also be studied by relating them to age groups. Icons come and go in our lives, as objects lose and gain meaning according to our life situations. These are often personal icons, the things which are significant to the individual: the toddler's teddy bear, the high-schooler's class ring, the young adult's stereo system, the middle-ager's house in the suburbs. Iconic meanings do vary from one person to another, and your most cherished object may mean nothing to your neighbor.

The essential functions of popular icons are part of the function of popular culture in general: to create order out of chaos, to help us define what is important, to serve as tangible reminder of our origin and destiny, to ease our sense of isolation or aloneness, to evoke and resolve human problems, to give significance to the world around us. There are some icons which are the most commonly found symbols of order. The first of these is the image of the common life of the family, the city, and the nation. Despite the rising divorce rate, the family is still seen as a basic symbol of American order, and this is repeatedly reflected in the icons or images of advertising. Advertising, which is a fountainhead of contemporary popular icons, also sets up technology as a symbol of order and progress. American faith in the wonders of science and technology is still alive, and the love of machinery is a key to understanding icons. At the same time, the advertisers tap the American love of nature by presenting all sorts of products, from foods to cigarettes to clothing, as "natural."

The following essays will give you only a sampling of this vast territory of popular icons, hopefully suggesting some approaches to the subject. All of the articles make it clear that icons are closely related to cultural myths and beliefs. Pinball machines are viewed as a climactic example of the American love/hate affair with their gadgets. Songs about cars reveal the changing values of our century, particularly the attitudes of youth. Marlboro cigarettes show us a calculated advertising campaign which has plugged into the powerful American mythology of the frontier. Finally, the ever-present McDonald's restaurant is seen as another means of commercial communion, togetherness and peace through the hamburger.

Whether we choose to examine popular architecture, advertising images, commercial packaging, machine products, clothing, or any other kind of popular icon, we should be aware that all of these things are expressive of our culture. To "read" the icon, ask questions like these: What myths and beliefs are suggested by the icon? Does the icon have magical powers? What is its history?

What ritual behavior is associated with the icon? What does the icon mean to you?

Selected Further Reading

Brown, Curtis F. *Star-Spangled Kitsch*. New York: Universe Books, 1975. A negative view of the subject, but the book gives many good examples of icons with illustrations.

Browne, Ray B. and Marshall Fishwick, eds. *Icons of America*. Bowling Green, Ohio: Popular Press, 1978. Insightful essays on a variety of icons.

Fishwick, Marshall, and Ray B. Browne, eds. *Icons of Popular Culture*. Bowling Green, Ohio: Popular Press, 1970.

Gowans, Alan. *Images of American Living*. Philadelphia: J.B. Lippincott, 1964.

Gowans, Alan. *The Unchanging Arts*. Philadelphia: J.B. Lippincott, 1971.

Kouwenhoven, John A. *Made in America*. New York: Doubleday, 1948. Reprinted as *The Arts in Modern American Civilization*. New York: Norton, 1967. A basic reference on the subject of American artifacts.

National Trust for Historic Preservation, Tony P. Wrenn and Elizabeth D. Mulloy. *America's Forgotten Architecture*. New York: Pantheon, 1976.

Pinball Machine:Marble Icon

By Cynthia Packard and Ray B. Browne

With religious offerings clutched tightly in sweaty fists, the contestant is lured to the flashing lights of the electronic opponent. Plunk...plunk...kerchunck—plunck-kerchunk. Five balls. Four can play—two can play—one can play. Player up. The pinball game is on.

A strange place, perhaps, and an unusual icon, for a religious experience. But so it is. Standing at the foot and looking up at the head the player strokes and manipulates the icon in a strangely medieval sense—like the mythic wrestling match between Gawain and Lancelot, or that earlier match between eyeless Samson and the Temple in Gaza—and is joined in a personal contest with superhuman, perhaps satanic, forces.

This scene of the innocent but hopeful electronic antagonist-worshipper is common in numerous beer joints, arcades, bus stations, lunch counters and laundromats across the U.S. The eager patron directs the flippers, bumps the machine and awaits the outcome of his efforts, secretly praying that this time he—man—can triumph over technology and thereby be reunited with his personal god. The drive is addictive; one game never satisfies. The competitive urge, as in any athletic event, between contending players or between a single player and his score, is obvious. Yet the strongest urge transcends mere human competiton. Player and machine, literally and symbolically, grapple in a bigger-than-life contest between human being and perhaps unknown supernatural force.[1]

In earliest times, great public games, like those in Greek, Mexican, and Egyptian cultures—and present day Olympics—took

From *Icons of America,* Ray B. Browne and Marshall Fishwick, (Bowling Green, Ohio: Bowling Green University Popular Press, 1977). Reprinted with the permission of the editors and the publisher.

place in connection with religious celebrations or ceremonies. Elaborate athletic events, races, contests, and dances became essential facets of religious ritual; man could verify his worthiness to his gods, striving to appease or equal them in some manner.[2]

One game in particular was popular in ancient Mexico, and was closely associated with the priesthood. Tlachtli, as it was known, involved players hitting a rubber ball with their hips and/or knees, attempting to drive the ball through one of several sculptured stone rings placed at the ends of a 150-foot walled-in court.

Tlachtli, according to folklorist Lewis Spence, may have "symbolized a struggle betwixt the powers of light and darkness."[3] More specifically, it may have represented the motions of some heavenly body, the sun or the moon, since the tlachtli ball was often half light and half dark in color. This ritualistic game might represent the myth, found in many ancient cultures, that contending powers toss the fortunes of the universe from light into shadow, in an eternal mythic ball game.[4]

It would be absurd to assume that pinball is a direct descendant of ancient religious games, tlachtli in particular. However, characteristics of each game point to some correlation, as far as ball movement and scoring are concerned. Each is played on a walled-in court, with balls being manuevered toward a goal. The tlachtli goal, a stone ring, could be compared to the various "extra ball" or "extra points" holes found on nearly every pinball table. Propelling the ball through the ring won the tlachtli player honor and fortune (the lighted universe); by tilting the pinball machine, the modern player loses fortune and fame, and plummets into universal darkness—the blinking lights cease to function, darkening the surface of the table. Ultimately, the god of light and darkness has been transformed into technology: the god of "on and off."

A second significant religious "game" which had similarities with pinball playing was the labyrinth ritual of Egypt and, most notably, Crete. This maze was, according to Spence, "associated with the worship of a diety whose image was concealed in the holy of holies at the centre of its complex passages."[5]

The Cretan myth of the labyrinth at Knossos tells how King Minos of Crete blackmailed the Athenians into sacrificing twelve youths and maidens to the half-bull, half-man monster-Minotaur, which lived in the maze. Through various schemes, the Athenian hero Theseus was able to find and slay the Minotaur. This "slaying" became a ritualistic dance, depicting the wanderings and gropings of Theseus in the winding passages of the maze. The ritual is most often associated with the cult of the sacred bull in several cultures, symbolizing man's strength over the powerful and most virile animal, thus reinforcing man's virility.[6]

While pinball is not specifically a "male" game, the fact remains that more males than females play it regularly and definite sex roles are reinforced in the playing.[7] It might follow, then, that threading the silver ball through the labyrinth of lights, buzzers, and traps, in competition for power over a machine is a virility reinforcement for male pinball players. In the wake of automation, computerized jobs, and feminism, playing pinball may be symbolically one of the few physical acts of power and/or virility left for the modern male: a sexual or physical prowess, god-like in nature, exemplified by the scoring of points against an electronic adversary.

Whether these connections are real or not is the province of the interpreter. What remains, is the basic idea that pinball is a game, no matter how uneven the odds of human victory, and any athletic event can be traced to religious ritual of some sort. The energies expended during such events, whether in playing tlachtli, chasing down the Minotaur, or competing with a pinball machine, are symbolically the outpourings of human vigor with the intention of further physical growth for the participant and for the culture, and ultimately for spiritual ecstasy.

If modern man is left powerless by machines, then he is able to grow spiritually by defeating such devices, as in playing pinball. As Marshall McLuhan put it in *Understanding Media,*

> The games of a people reveal a great deal about them. Games are a sort of artificial paradise like Disneyland, or some Utopian vision by which we interpret and complete the meaning of our daily lives. In games we devise means of nonspecialized participation in the larger drama of our time...A game is a machine that can get into action only if the players consent to become puppets for a time.[8]

McLuhan might have gone further and pointed out the general iconic nature of games. Pinball, as we know it today, did not flower until after World War II. But the seeds for these marvelous contraptions were planted long before any other technological device of reverence (i.e. automobiles, telephones, airplanes, electric toothbrushes) in our culture.

Historically, pinball's nearest traceable ancestor is the parlor game bagatelle popular in the nineteenth century. As mentioned in Dickens' *Pickwick Papers,* members of the Pickwick Club visited the Peacock Tavern and "beguiled their time chiefly with such amusements as the Peacock afforded, which were limited to a bagatelle board on the first floor."[9]

In this game, the player used a billiard cue to shoot balls into holes located in the middle of the playing field. In the late 1800's, a game closer to modern pinball, called "Log Cabin," was introduced. This version of bagatelle was a table top game which featured a large high-value "skill hole" located near the top, as well as numerous pegs, and several smaller holes lower down, which counted for lesser point values.[10] One political cartoon from 1862, shows the Union Army defeated at Bull Run, while President Lincoln played pinball (probably bagatelle). In the cartoon are rats and slovenly dressed players, typifying the sleaziness long associated with pinball.[11]

It was not until 1930, however, that pinball was developed and made widely popular. Although Leo Berman introduced in 1930 an adaption of bagatelle which he called "Bingo," it was David Gottlieb who became financially successful at manufacturing the games. Gottlieb, founder of D. Gottlieb and Company, a major manufacturer of pinball machines, introduced his first machine also in 1930, which he called "Baffle Ball." This simple and inexpensive game was a counter-top version of pinball, and had a playing surface that featured four major scoring areas. For one penny, the player could send seven balls onto the board with a wooden plunger. In less than a year, Gottleib sold 50,000 of these machines at an average price of $17.50.[12] Depression-heavy Americans were all too happy to purchase the ephemeral escape of seven clanking steel ball bearings for one cent.[13] In 1931, a second successful game was designed by a young Chicago businessman named Raymond Maloney. His version, "Bally-Hoo," was originally manufactured by Gottlieb, but as sales approached the 70,000 mark, Maloney began making the machines on his own. His firm, now the Bally Manufacturing Corporation, equals Gottlieb's in the pinball field today.[14]

Howard Poe of Rochester, New York, introduced in 1932 what was to become the biggest selling counter game of all time, "Whirlwind." His success prompted many other producers of coin-operated machines to go into the pinball business. From all of these endeavors, features such as curved loops, spring activated kickbacks, and other gimmicks were developed which added much to the action and appeal of the game. Many of these innovations from the early 1930's are standard components on modern pinball machines.[15]

One of the most important innovations in pinball history came in 1933, when Harry Williams, of the Pacific Amusement Co. of California, designed a game called "Contract," which introduced electric circuitry into the pinball industry. "Contract" employed battery-operated gates and kick-out holes, devices which transformed this expanding industry. Williams, later to found another major pinball manufacturing firm, Williams Electronics, used four dry-cell batteries on his machine, which powered lights and rang an occasional bell; 24 volts is still the standard pinball current.[16]

The first solenoid was used on the playfield of "Fleet" in 1935, adding an essential element of action to the advancing game. Other innovations such as electronic tilt devices, automatic scoring, free games, thumper-bumpers, and roll-overs were to evolve later.

By 1940, pinball machines were found in bars, cafes, soda fountains, and arcades all over the country. As with any popular entertainment that seemed to be growing into an obsession, pinball suffered the traditional lashings and criticism from decency leagues, PTAs, church groups, and crime commissions, as a corruptor of youth, addicting and expensive vice, and lastly a gambling device controlled by the "syndicate."

Much of the bally-hoo about pinball being a gambling device stemmed from the fact that Gottlieb and Bally both manufactured slot machines, which were gambling devices. In addition, early pinball machines returned money as rewards for high scoring games; prizes were given for attaining a certain score. Also, in 1940, the pinball player could control the outcome of the game, to a certain extent, only through bumping or jostling the machine with his body. This body English, or "gunching," was the only real human factor in playing pinball.[17]

So strong was the move to "stamp out" these youth-corrupting machines in the early 1940's that New York City's Mayor LaGuardia declared war against pinball machines, slot machines, weighing machines, etc.

Prior to the massive raids on establishments harboring the machines in 1942, the *New York Times* reported that, "One out of every three persons in the pinball business...has been arrested at least once...machines have replaced slot machines as a major industry and...the 11,080 machines now operated in New York bring in a gross 'take' of 20-25 million dollars per year...the average weekly gross 'take' per machine is between 35-40 dollars, of which 40-50% is paid out in prizes."[18]

When you consider that the machines were operated on nickles in 1941, the daily average income per machine reflects an obsessive interest by the general public in playing pinball.

LaGuardia condemned the pinball machines as " 'an evil and a menace' to young persons because they develop the gambling urge in children"[19]. This statement was the springboard for nearly a year of raiding establishments, of arresting operators, and of axing up machines (ala Carrie Nation) in five burroughs of New York City. On January 22, 1942, war was declared against the so-called gambling machines, and in the first nightly raid, 1,802 machines were seized throughout the city.[20] By February 1, 1942, 3,261 machines had been taken and 1,593 summonses issued for possession of the gambling devices.

After World War II, the tables were turned, so to speak, with a historic development, the flipper. Designed by Harry Mabs in 1947, the flipper was not only to save the pinball machine from oblivion, but to remain as an essential device on all machines manufactured since that time. Gottlieb and Co. manufactured the first commercial machine to use flippers, "Humpty Dumpty" in 1947. The flipper, a rubber bat joined to a solenoid, could be controlled by the player by means of pushing a button on the side of the machine.[21] This small, but influential, device moved the pinball machine a little further away from a mere gambling device. In addition, manufacturers began altering their machines to award extra balls or free games instead of cash for a winning score.[22]

Now, skill—required only slightly on the older machines—became a significant part of the game, as one learned to manipulate the flippers.

Today, the pinball industry is flourishing, supplying machines to all parts of the world. Complicated machines with asymetrical playfields, drum scoring counters, messenger balls, captive balls, and electric comic book art are active once again throughout the smoke-filled bars and noisy arcades of America. The manufacturers of these "dream machines" produce six to twelve models per year, with each machine having a specific run of from one to four months. During that period, the company will be producing only one model; so in effect, each pinball machine is a limited edition.[23] Of the 50,000 or so games produced each year, 40% are sold in the U.S.[24]

In recent years, the brightly colored flashing machines have become popular as collector's items. Like Mickey Mouse watches, old comic books, and decoder rings, the older and more rare machines like "Contact," "Bingo," or "Bally-Hoo" are expensive and difficult to obtain. Most who buy machines for home entertainment purchase used ones from a distributor and pay from $500 to $900 for a four-player machine. They then treat the instruments as something far more important and "sacred" than mere machines.

Video games, such as "Pong," electronic tennis, "Gotcha," as well as air hockey, football, and various other electronic games have become popular bar and arcade machines, as well as home entertainment devices. More often than not those machines involve more skill and player to player competition as in a sporting event, than pinball does.

"Your community may be helping perpetuate one of the most vicious of all rackets—one that spreads gambling and corruption to practically every street corner, and has as its potential target every child."[25] No, it's not the slot machine, or even the local numbers racket, but merely the pinball machine. Articles like the one this statement was taken from were quite common prior to the inclusion of manual flippers on the various models of pinball machines manufactured in this country. Still, even after the human factor was admissible in court as evidence that the pinball machine was not wholly a gambling device (providing that it did not pay off in valuables for a good score), public opinion was most always unfavorable toward the amusement device. Quite possibly this public opinion against the pinball machine could be linked to the general attitude toward leisure activities in America, especially prior to the late 1950's. Wasting time was in direct opposition to the Protestant Work Ethic, where working hard was the sum and total within itself.

During the 1950's especially, the pinball machine was under heavy fire from nearly every small town decency organization and family magazine in the country. For instance, this statement from *Better Homes and Gardens,* typifies the middle class opinion of pinballing during this period, especially from the standpoint of community leaders and law enforcement officials:

> Be ready for the argument that pinball is a harmless little game. Here's what one of the country's leading crime fighters, James W. Connor, director of St. Louis Crime Commission says: "Pinball feeds on vast sums siphoned from the worn pockets of those least able to afford the sucker's game of rigged odds. If allowed to get out of hand, it can wreck the civic enterprise and economic well-being of any village, town, or city."[26]

At the same time that article appeared in *Better Homes and Gardens, Harper's Magazine* ran a story written by Julius Segal, entitled "The Lure of Pinball." Here, the middle-class paranoia was mentioned, but the predominant tone was pro-pinball. This article is one of the first in major magazines to point out the differences between pinball of modern times and the slot machines of the 1930's and 1940's. As noted in the article, one pinball player's opinion of the game is much the same as present day views and demonstrates the gnawing sexual-religious overtones of the game and the machine:

> "If I could win on every try," he said "there'd be no fun to this game; losing every time would make me quit, too. It's like chasing a woman. There's always that chance you'll catch her. But if you knew for certain, the chase would hardly be worth it.[27]

With computerization becoming more and more prevalent in business and industry, the assumption here might be that Americans were feeling the pressures of a mechanized society, especially where machines and/or computers were taking over human jobs. The idea of "beating the machine" was raised to an Iconic level in the *Harper's* article:

> In the pinball parlor, the player fancies, there is a machine he can do something about, a contraption he can meet on equal terms, an industrial challenge he can manipulate and master. To prove it, he must deify the machine. Only then does the practice of his crafty (but irrelevent) techniques become appropriate and satisfying.[28]

J. Anthony Lukas, Pulitzer Prize winning free lance writer, set forth part of what might be termed a "pinball philosophy"—again touching on the religious aspect—in a recent article in *New Yorker Magazine:*

> ...the game does give you a sense of controlling things in a way that in life you can't do. And there is risk in it, too. The ball flies into the ellipse, into the playfield—full of opportunities. But there's always the death channel—the run-out slot. There are rewards, prizes coming off the thumper-bumper. The ball crazily bounces from danger to opportunity and back to danger. You need reassurance in life that in taking risks you will triumph, and pinball gives you that reaffirmation. Life is a risky game, but you can beat it.[29]

In recent years the pinball machine has become the "in thing" to analyze in clinical psychology classes, to have in one's rumpus room, and to parallel to sociological patterns. As one psychologist, Ronald F. Balas, noted in a recent *Cleveland Plain Dealer* feature:

> ...Some are attracted by the pitfalls: the tile, the lost ball, the narrowly missed target. He is a loser who is "reinforcing his self-destructive anxiety"...the pinball player is much like the rapist, striving for power over the woman, forcing her into submission. The actual submission is not important, it's the process leading up to it.[30]

For the average player, perhaps, pinball does not control his life. With some, however, the truly iconic characteristics are obvious when, in biblical terms, the flesh and spirit meet in ecstasy approaching religious experience, as explained by one player in *Playboy:*

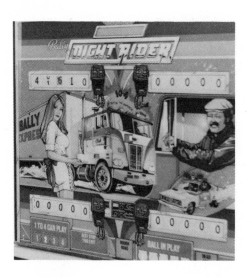

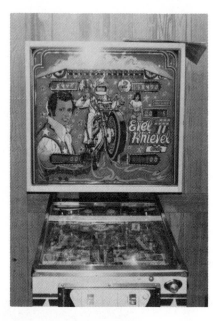

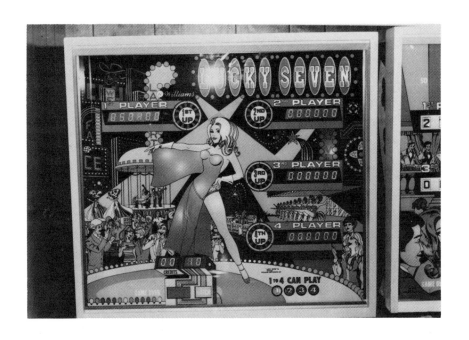

Now I got a steady job, fixing pin machines. I'm 25 you know? Time I was settling down. I got my own apartment—just one room, but I got three machines in it. Also a bed. . . About a month ago, my girl was playing one of my channies and I was balling her from behind, you know? We sometimes like it that way, while she plays the 80,000 points on the first ball. Well, on the second ball she went over 100,000, and then, just as she hit the volcano—that's the big apple on Four Million B.C.—she came. She lost all three balls. They just drained right down: she never even flipped. I think she finished up at 120,000 or so. Not a bad score, but nothing great, either.[31]

Such contemporary thought on pinball drives one to conclude that many players indeed become "one with the machine." In seeking this togetherness some players seek the assistance of body- and mind-altering substances like liquor and marijuana; many, however, feel that liquor or drugs adversely affect playing skills. But of the people who like to take liquor or drugs while playing, a large majority favor marijuana; liquor, they feel, dulls one's senses, while smoking marijuana heightens them and allows the player to lose himself in the game, apparently the goal of nearly half the people who play it. Such attitudes substantiate the assumption that players deify the game and indeed treat the machine as an icon.

As with most religious experiences, the pinball player does not remember occurrences from the middle of the experience. Here, in other words, the player can recall after the game is finished how the game started, and what caused the game to end, but has no actual memory of the experience in between shooting the ball out of the gate, and losing the ball down the run-out passage. The experience of actually playing the game is nebulous; glimpses of points scored, gates opened, and targets knocked down might come to mind, but the experience as a whole is a blur.

Further total concentration is given to the act of playing pinball. Talking, smoking a cigarette, drinking beer or any other liquid refreshment and eating are next to impossible while playing the game. There seems to be a need for isolating oneself from the immediate environment of noisy crowds and interruptions, thus creating a different environment of flashing lights and ringing bells closely related to a hypnotic state, where the participant has no recollection of the intermediate experience.

The belief of many avid pinball players that becoming "one" with the machine enables them to play more effectively could be tied into the idea of the pinball machine communicating with the participant on a religious basis.

If the player's awareness is outside and "above" him, then the entire process of playing pinball, especially the intermediate aspect, is a religious experience. The only personal awareness the player has or ends up with is the realization that he has scored points, and here triumphed over the machine.

Becoming one with the machine implies a loss of self, or a loss of personal awareness for a period of time. Still some type of awareness exists. This communication with the machine, for the player, is in a sense religious awareness, with personal awareness only occurring when the quarter is dropped in the slot and the player shoots the ball onto the playing field. At that point, where the ball is no longer totally in the player's immediate control, the religious awareness begins. At the point where the machine stops communicating to the player, when the ball drops from sight, into the "death channel," the personal awareness of the participant returns. He has scored, and has a basis for judging his endeavor. The act of playing the electronic maze is anomalous, and therefore a sacred or religious experience for the participant.

Evaluating a cultural artifact, like the pinball, under these terms and means is not always an easy task. Documenting assumptions is difficult and sometimes impossible, yet it must be concluded that pinball playing is not merely a game, nor is the instrument merely a machine. It involves altering one's environment to the point of blocking out immediate awareness, psychological readiness and including a pinball "state of mind" where one's hands become extensions of the flippers and one's eyes become analogous to the flashing lights. In such a state one is in a potential religious ecstasy far more intense than that associated with the usual lay icons. Indeed the feeling approaches that of the individual who lays his lands on the Bible or the altar or some other religious holy article.

The people who through the years have railed against the pinball obviously knew that they were combatting a powerful force, one strong enough to shape icons and religious ecstasy—and in more ways just as far-reaching.

NOTES

[1]Spence, Lewis, *Myth and Ritual in Dance, Game and Rhyme*, p.4-5.
[2]Spence, p. 18.
[3]Spence, p.19
[4]Spence, p.20-1.
[5]Spence, p.55.
[6]Spence, p.55-6.
[7]McMillen/McMillen, "Electronic Amusement Devices: Some Considerations of Sex Role Differentiation."
[8]McLuhan, Marshall, *Understanding Media*, p.210-11.

[9]Laurence, Michael, "Great Moments in Pinball History," *Playboy Magazine,* Dec., 1972, pp.162,260.

[10]Sharpe, Roger C., "Boing! Buzz! Tilt!" *New York Times,* December 28, 1975, p.29.

[11]Laurence, p.163.

[12]Sharpe, p.29.

[13]Laurence, p.260.

[14]Laurence, p.260.

[15]Sharpe, p.29.

[16]Laurence, p.260.

[17]Sharpe, p.29.

[18]*New York Times,* December 28, 1941, 25:3.

[19]*Ibid.*

[20]*New York Times,* January 22, 1942, 19:5.

[21]*New York Times,* February 22, 1942, 30:2.

[22]*New York Times,* October 17, 1942, 17:2

[23]*New York Times,* March 7, 1943, 34:1.

[24]Laurence, p.260.

[25]Sharpe, p.29.

[26]*Better Homes and Gardens,* October, 1957, p.142.

[27]Segal, Julius. "The Lure of Pinball." *Harper's Magazine,* October, 1957, p.142.

[28]*Ibid.*

[29]*New Yorker,* June 30, 1975, p.81.

[30]*Cleveland Plain Dealer,* Sunday Magazine, January 11, 1976, p.6.

[31]Laurence, p.260.

Discussing "Pinball Machine: Marble Icon"

1) Study the art on the playing fields and backboards of pinball machines. What values and stereotypes are reinforced? Compare the art work on old and new machines. How does the art reflect other facets of popular culture, e.g. fads?

2) In some states, winning free games and extra balls is illegal. How does this affect the ritual of playing pinball?

3) Are the old-style pinball machines being replaced by the variety of new computerized games, including home TV models? How are these games different?

Croonin' About Cruisin'

By John L. Wright

Popular songs, like other forms of popular art, are expressive of the attitudes and values of their times. The composers of popular music, in order to be successful, must constantly be searching for new grist for their musical mills. Many times the new material will be simply a reworking of age-old themes of popular art—love, laughter, and conflict. Sometimes, though, a combination of social forces produces a more novel form of cultural expression.[1]

The coming of the automobile in the early years of the twentieth century coincided with a golden age in American popular music. At the same time the auto was becoming the universal means of personal transportation, there happened to be an enormous market for sheet music, as these were the days when every well-furnished home included a piano in the parlor. In addition, the growing popularity of the phonograph created an ever-greater demand for musical material.

Naturally, then, the songsters of Tin Pan Alley looked to the automobile as a new vehicle of musical inspiration as well as physical transportation. From those days to now over one thousand different pieces of music have been directly related to the automobile. America is an automotive culture, and the history of auto songs reflects our long love/hate relationship with this super-icon—the car. The automobile is a super-icon in that it is one of the rather small category of things which have so captured the American imagination that they are virtually symbols of American life. While some may look on the car as nothing more than a necessary evil, the majority of Americans, both now and in the past, have seen it as representative of the American dreams of success, mobility, freedom, power, sex, and the good life through the triumph of technology.

It was clear from the beginning that the motorcar was a disruptive force in American society, a force that would forever change the patterns of social life. Although cars had already been around for several years, an opinion pool in 1903 showed only five percent of the American people favoring the introduction of automobiles. This hostility toward the auto was shown in the early years in songs such as: "Keep Away From the Fellow Who Owns An Automobile," "I Think I Oughtn't Auto Anymore," and "Get a Horse!" One big hit, popularized by Al Jolson, was "He'd Have to Get Under, Get Out and Get Under, To Fix Up His Automobile," which related the common and often embarrassing experience of the mechanical breakdown.

The resistance to the automobile was especially strong in rural areas, where social and technological change is traditionally slow and where the motorcar was seen as a noisy intrusion which frightened horses and generally destroyed rustic tranquility. Until 1909, the vast majority of car owners were "city slickers" who to the rural dwellers represented the sinful life of the town. In some rural areas the farm folk actually banded together to block the roads against autos, and there were a number of incidents in which car drivers were shot at by annoyed farmers.

It was the introduction of the Model T by Henry Ford in 1908 that rapidly changed this situation. The Model T was designed as the car for the masses, called by Ford himself "The Universal Automobile." By 1920 half of all the cars in the world were Model Ts; between 1908 and 1927 over fifteen million T-Model Fords were produced. The Model T was by far the most popular auto subject of the tunesmiths too, who dedicated over sixty songs to this one model of car. Thus we may say that until 1930 the story of the automobile in song is largely the story of the Model T, and these songs express a wide range of cultural values.

Because of its low price and durability, the Model T was quickly accepted by farmers as well as city folk. Affectionately dubbed the Tin Lizzie, the car was probably the single greatest influence in breaking down rural isolation. In 1925 only 12% of farm families had running water, but 60% had automobiles. When asked by a pollster why her family owned a car but not a bathtub, one farm wife replied, "Why, you can't go to town in a bathtub."[2]

While the affordable Model T allowed farm families to escape from rural tedium, it also raised fears that young people would be permanently lured away by the excitement of the fast life; how can you keep them down on the farm after they've seen the city? A 1916 song shows this mixed attitude:

Hiram Brown went to town, bought himself a Ford the other day.
Now the charm of the farm loses out whenever he is on his merry
way.

Many of the auto songs similarly symbolized the car as a vehicle
of escape—escape from the drudgeries of work and the cares of daily
life. The automobile provided the actual means for fleeing from the
country to the city or vice versa. Led by Teddy Roosevelt, Americans
had gained new interest in the wonders of nature, and the auto was
now the mode of personal transportation for going wherever the
heart desired.

The automobile, even the lowly Model T, also became a status
symbol. Buyers were willing to put themselves under long-term
mortgages in order to obtain a car. The 1915 song "You Can't Afford
to Marry If You Can't Afford a Ford" describes the saga of two
lovers, Percy and Mary, in which Mary says, "No wedding bells will
chime for you and I, Until you try, a Ford to buy..." In desperation
Percy pawns his watch for a down payment, buys the Model T, and
off they drive to see the parson. Mary's final joyous cry is:

There's no use waiting for the love days in June,
With mellowy moon so we can spoon.
Right in our Ford we'll spend our sweet honeymoon,
As we sing our little tune.

As might be expected, the vast majority of the compositions
adapted the automobile to the eternal subject matter of popular
song—love. But as America moved from the Victorian age to the age
of the flapper, the songs became more suggestive in their portrayal
of love:

For a boy in love, if you haven't anyplace to spoon,
Take a ride, with a gal by your side,
Up and down the Eight-Mile Pike.
There's Fords to the left, and Fords to the right,
But Fords never tell what they see every night,
Up and down the Eight-Mile Pike.

Though moralists inveighed against the evil influence of the auto
upon youth, the car rapidly displaced the parlor in the scheme of
courtship. As one critic noted, "A bulwark of American morality had
always been the difficulty of finding a suitable place for
misconduct."[3] Now that difficulty was overcome, and songs such as
"On The Old Back Seat of The Henry Ford" celebrated the victory.

The Model T was the great equalizer in transportation, as it
made mobility available to almost everyone. Predictably, many of

the popular songs reflected this leveling of class distinctions. Tin Lizzie owners were often depicted as social upstarts, and a recurrent theme is that of the poor but adventurous Model T driver who wins away the girl from the owner of a larger auto. The most popular of all the Model T songs was "The Little Ford Rambled Right Along":

Now Henry Jones and his pretty little queen,
Took a ride one day in a big limousine.
The car kicked up and the engine wouldn't crank;
There wasn't any gas in the gasoline tank.

About that time along came Nord,
And he rambled along in his little old Ford;
He stole that queen as his engine sang a song,
And his little old Ford rambled right along.

One of the ideas in these lyrics, the reliability and economy of the Model T, was the basis for many of the hundreds of jokes about the Model T which were current in its era. The songwriters, too, were quick to capitalize on the affectionate jibes at the car with such lines as, "When she blows out a tire, just wrap it up with wire..." and, "When the power gets sick, just hit it with a brick..." The legendary economy of the Model T perhaps reached a peak in the 1915 composition "My Henry [sic] Ford": "It's the only car made yet, That you can safely bet, That if you run out of gasoline, 'Twill run upon its 'rep.' " These sentiments were echoed in a very different context by an anonymous World War One doughboy who penned a parody of the Kipling poem "Gunga Din," ending with the lines:

Yes it's Tin, Tin, Tin, You exasperating puzzle, Hunk o' tin. I've abused you and I've played you, But by Henry Ford who made you, you are better than a Packard, Hunk o' tin.

As the 1920s roared along, the Model T retained its popularity but became increasingly anachronistic as the public desired greater comfort in their automobiles. The passing of the Model T and the advent of the Model A in 1928 occasioned several new tunes, including "Henry's Made a Lady out of Lizzie":

No more bruises, no more aches,
Now she's got those four wheel brakes...

They used to keep her with the cow,
But gee, you ought to see her now;
Henry's made a lady out of Lizzie.

In the depths of the depression years of the 1930s, the number of car songs by mass-market composers declined drastically. Few persons could afford to buy a car anyway, and it looked for a time as if the American dream was, if not dead, at least in critical condition. The few songs that did appear were usually about expensive automobiles such as Cadillacs and Lincolns, no doubt expressing a longing for unobtainable luxuries.

World War Two brought a rash of songs about the Jeep, which became a special kind of cultural icon of the rugged military life. Totally functional vehicles, Jeeps seemed typically American in a sturdy, no-nonsense way. Most of the Jeep ditties were comic: "Six Jerks in a Jeep," "Little Bo Peep Has Lost Her Jeep," and "Why Don't They Put a Saddle on This Doggone Jeep?"

Throughout the 1930s and 1940s, however, car songs continued to thrive in another area of music, the Negro blues. Catering almost exclusively to a black audience, the bluesmen recorded many original songs which are classics of folk expression. Perhaps the greatest of the country blues singers, Robert Johnson, recorded in 1936 a song titled "Terraplane Blues" which has served as a model for many later auto blues. Explicitly sexual, the song compares his woman to a car and asserts:

> Who's been driving my Terraplane since I've been gone?
> I'm gonna get deep down in this connection,
> Keep tangling with your wires,
> And when I mash down on your little starter,
> Then your spark plug will give me fire.

The car-sex metaphor is found in most of the blues about automobiles, whether sung by men or women. In 1941, Memphis Minnie sang:

> Going to let my chauffeur, going to let my chauffeur,
> Drive me around the, drive me around the world,
> Then he can be my lil boy, yes, and I can be his girl.

Other country blues of this type include "Car Trouble Blues," "T-Model Blues," "Auto Mechanic Blues," and "My Starter Won't Start This Morning."

During these years, the blues were moving from the country to the city, as the black singers and their audiences migrated to the urban centers of the North, particularly to Chicago. The Chicago blues which evolved reflected a very different lifestyle than did the country blues. Where the country blues were usually relaxed solo performances, the city blues used electrified instruments, a fast and

Courtesy of the Ford Motor Company archives

loud beat, but with the same gritty lyrics; this new musical form was well-suited to songs about the automobile. Also, to the urban black dweller, the car was more than ever a symbol of success and sexuality. The Chicago singer Muddy Waters typified this in the song "Tiger in Your Tank":

> I can raise your hood. I can clean your coils.
> Check the transmission, And give you the oils.
> I don't care what the people think,
> I want to put a Tiger, you know, in your tank.

The rough old-time blues were rapidly becoming rhythm and blues, another new music which was still for blacks but in the early 1950s would be adopted by young white singers and a white audience. One of the key figures in the further transition from rhythm and blues to rock and roll was Chuck Berry, whose songs combined the funkiness of the black music with lyrics which appealed to the interests of a newly-rebellious white teenage public. Less explicit than the pure blues, Chuck Berry's great 1954 hit "Maybellene" nevertheless conveyed a feeling of excitement by setting a love affair in the context of a car chase:

> As I was motivatin' over the hill,
> I saw Maybellene in a Coupe De Ville...

> *

> The Cadillac looking like it's sitting still,
> And I caught Maybellene at the top of the hill!

To the American teenager, now relatively affluent, a car represented independence and social status. The concern of the new car songs was with speed and chrome and a garish array of customized accessories. In the best tradition of the icon, the car was an object not just to be used but to be *seen* and admired. Chuck Berry was again there to celebrate this love of gadgetry with the fantasy song "No Money Down":

> Mister, I want a yellow convertible, 4-door De Ville,
> With a Continental spare and wire chrome wheels.

> *

> Yes, I'm gonna get me a car, I'll move on down the road,
> Well, I won't have to worry about that broken-down ragged Ford.

The early 1960s saw the height of the hot-rod era, the age of the "muscle car." Although a nationwide phenomenon, this teenage love affair with the hot rod reached its full flower on the dragstrips, beaches, and freeways of Southern California. Here was (and still is) a culture built entirely around the automobile, a society in which it is almost impossible to survive without a car. Suburbs, restaurants, shopping centers, and every other major part of the social pattern are predicated on car ownership.

The leaders and champions of the hot rod song were The Beach Boys who, besides their surfing music, recorded a multitude of automobile lyrics. Their 1963 album *Little Deuce Coupe,* in addition to the hit title track, contained this roster of car songs, the title of which convey the main topics: "Ballad of Ole Betsey," "Car Crazy Cutie," "Cherry, Cherry Coupe," "409," "Shut Down," "Spirit of America," "Our Car Club," "No-Go Showboat," and "Custom Machine." A related song in the album, "A Young Man is Gone," is a eulogy to James Dean, the film star who died in a horrible auto accident.

Second to The Beach Boys in the hot rod rock scene were Jan and Dean, who scored hits in 1963 with "Drag City" and "Dead Man's Curve," the latter another mythic treatment of the theme of the car crash. In the next year, Jan and Dean followed with "My Mighty GTO" and "The Little Old Lady From Pasadena," and The Beach Boys continued their success with "Fun, Fun, Fun Till Daddy Takes the T-Bird Away," a timeless story of generational conflict.

There were a host of imitators after these successes, as other groups rushed to record hot rod music. The car songs of the 1960s were typified by lyrics which dwelt in detail on the power and beauty of the machine, often in the setting of the street race. "GTO" is a standard product of the genre:

> Little GTO, you're really looking fine,
> Three deuces and a four-speed and a 389.
> Listen to her taching up now, listen to her whine,
> Come on and turn it on, wind it up, blow it out, GTO!

In another area of popular song, country music, there has been a somewhat different attitude toward the automobile. Many of the country car tunes have been mournful songs which tell of tragic accidents, such as "Long Black Limousine," which ironically is describing a hearse:

> When you left you told me some day you'd be returning
> In a fancy car for all the world to see
> Now everyone is watching; you finally got your dream,

You're riding in a long black limousine.

Other country car songs include "Detroit City," "Carroll County Accident," "Automobile of Life," "Welfare Cadillac," this last a harsh satire on "poor" folks who spend their welfare money on Cadillacs. One of the most popular of the country car songs was "Hot Rod Lincoln," by Charley Ryan; this piece has been re-recorded with success by many other artists. And Johnny Cash had a big hit with "One Piece at a Time," the story of a Detroit worker who smuggles out parts from the plant to build his own Cadillac.

The 1970s are nearing a close, with a growing energy crisis and increased concern over environmental pollution. These factors, combined with the general quieting of the youth culture and the maturing of rock music, have contributed to a decline in the number of automobile songs. Many of the cultish aspects of the hot rod music have been transferred to the now-popular van—the love of gadgetry, the customizing craze, the idea of the vehicle as an extension of the owner's personality. Whatever the future holds for the automobile, it seems that for Americans the car is here to stay, in large part because it is a powerful iconic focus for the national ideals of individualism, freedom, and personal power. And the songs that celebrate this great American icon will continue to strike a responsive chord in the American psyche.

NOTES

[1] I am indebted throughout this essay to these articles: Roy C. Ames, "Cars in Song," *Special Interest Autos* (Jan.-Feb. 1977), pp.40-45; Glen Jeansonne, "The Automobile and American Morality," *Journal of Popular Culture* (Summer 1974), pp.125-131. Grateful acknowledgement is also given to The Edison Institute, Dearborn, Michigan, for permission to use material previously prepared for the publication *The Herald*.
[2] Cited in Jeansonne, p.129.
[3] Cited in Jeansonne, p.128.

Discussing "Croonin' About Cruisin' "

1) Examine the iconic image of motorcycles as reflected in popular songs and other media. What does the motorcycle represent? Do the same for vans. What is the image of the semi-truck and the truck driver?
2) How is the car used as an icon in films and on television? Discuss different makes and models of cars.
3) A related phenomenon is the CB craze. Is the CB aerial an icon? What cultural needs are being fulfilled by CB radio?

The Higher Meaning of Marlboro Cigarettes

By Bruce A. Lohof

In 1960, S. I. Hayakawa—then a respected semanticist not yet foundered on the shoals of academic administration—delivered a lecture in which he related a personal and homely anecdote surrounding the birth of the Hayakawa's first child. "I was kind of thrilled and excited," he admitted:

> and so I wrote a poem about it. After it was written my wife pointed out to me:
> "It's a very nice poem, but you can't sell it."
> "Why not?" I asked.
> "Well, Pet Milk and Gerber's Food have taken over those emotions for commercial purposes."

Another reading of the poem told Hayakawa that it was straight copy for a baby lotion advertisement. "All the baby food suppliers, the diaper services, and so on," he discovered, were "exploiting the hell out of mother love for purposes of sale of products."[1]

This technique of exploitation—which Hayakawa calls the "poeticizing of consumer goods"—is, of course, not peculiar to the mother-love industries. Elemental in much effective advertising is the transubstantiation of soup or beer or laxatives into symbols of some higher and more holy good. Thus Brylcreme ceases to be merely a hairdressing and becomes a symbol of teenage sexuality. Volkswagons are turtlesque, nose-thumbing packets of the status which accrues to those who cannot afford, but delight in snubbing, the symbols of automotive hauteur—Cadillac, Lincoln, and Imperial. Pepsi Cola, once a humdrum soft drink, becomes symbolic

From the *Journal of Popular Culture*, 1969, 3(3), 441-450. Reprinted by permission of the editor.

of a whole generation of youth and vigorous funseekers. The Pepsi Generation is:

> ...comin' at ya', goin' strong;
> Put yourself behind a Pepsi,
> If you're livin', you belong.

Teenage sexuality is worthy of our envy, and Brylcreme, therefore, is worth buying. Those who cannot afford the status of a limousine can, nevertheless, take comfort in that certain eccentric nonchalance which cloaks the owner of every "bug." And Pepsi Cola is surely the found potation of those who have searched after the Fountain of Youth. But there is a breed of advertising that transcends the Consumer's itch for sex, status, and eternal youth. The more perceptive of Madison Avenue's moguls sell products by identifying them with what Leo Marx has called a "cultural symbol," i.e., "an image that conveys a special meaning (thought and feeling) to ...[the] large number of people who share the culture" with the advertiser and his product.[2] This transcendent form of advertising confronts the consumer with an image that will evoke a cluster of ideas and emotions which he holds in common with other Americans. It is not simply soap or soft drinks that are being sold. It is not even sex or security. It is, rather, the *merchandising of a metaphor* which will speak to and be understood by the collective imagination of the culture.

Doubtless the finest exemplar of the merchandised metaphor is the Marlboro Man who for the past half decade and more has served as the emblem of Marlboro Cigarettes. Rugged, vigorous, and robust, he strides through the pages of a magazine. He crouches before a daybreak fire to turn the crinkling bacon or pour coffee from a blackened pot. He rides his horse knee-deep in snow, his sheepskin coat warding off the howling winter winds. He gazes serenely over the sturdy neck of his stabled pony. In every case he is "lighting up," and suggesting that you follow his lead. He is the archetypal cowboy, to be sure. But he is much more.

There was a time when he was not even that. For thirty years the "man " in the Marlboro commercial had as often as not been a lady—and always in plush, upholstered surroundings. Marlboro Cigarettes in the days before the Marlboro Man had been "America's luxury cigarette," a genteel smoke available with either an ivory tip or a red "beauty tip." The affluent, textured salons in which Marlboros were smoked connoted a deep-pile luxury and velvet sophistication that bordered on the effeminate. Indeed, Marlboros were widely regarded as a lady's smoke forty years before Virginia Slims Cigarettes congratulated the American woman on having come:

...a long way, baby,
To get where you've got to today;
You've got your own cigaret, now, baby;
You've come a long, long way.

Then the 1950's brought the first cancer scare and, subsequently, a bromide in the form of cigarette filters. A spate of filtered brands entered the market. Among them was the Philip Morris company's early bid. "New from Philip Morris," the slogan said. Marlboros, an old brand in new clothing, now had a "filter, flavor, [and a] fliptop box." Moreover, lest the effeminacy of old be augmented by the sissiness that surrounded the earliest filtered cigarettes, Marlboro was given a new, masculine image—the tattooed man.

By chance, the first tattooed man was a cowboy. No Marlboro Man, he was simply the result of an advertiser's desire to identify his product with "regular guys." As an agency executive later admitted, "We asked ourselves what was the most generally accepted symbol of masculinity in America, and this led quite naturally to a cowboy." No apparent effort was made to magnify this initial cowboy into the cultural symbol which would later emerge. Indeed, the tattooed man soon forsook the range in pursuit of other manly vocations. "Obviously," advertisers erroneously reasoned, "we couldn't keep on showing cowboys forever, although they could be repeated from time to time." In his place came a succession of he-men—explorers, sailors, athletes, and an occasional tuxedoed but no less rugged gentleman. In each case the common denominators were an elemental masculinity and, of course, the tattoo—emblem of those who look "successful and sophisticated but rugged...as though [they] might have had interesting experiences."[3]

But the tattooed man, like the imagination of the culture that smoked his cigarettes, kept returning to the open spaces of his birth. His Madison Avenue parents had meant for him to don cowboy regalia on occasion, but the costume became his natural clothing. In the early '60s the cowboy was promoted to supremacy over other tattooed men. By 1963 the tattoo had disappeared and the Marlboro Man had emerged as the exclusive inhabitant of Marlboro commercials. A cultural symbol had evolved; a metaphor was ready for merchandising.

The Marlboro image, though woven into whole cloth, consists of two elements, each illuminated in the neon of sloganeering. One, naturally, is the Marlboro Man himself. The other is expressed in the ubiquitous phrase : "Come to Marlboro Country."

Marlboro Country, in a sense, is Montana–the Montana which more than twenty-five years ago astounded that eastern erudite

Jew, Leslie Fiedler. "The inhumanly virginal landscape: the atrocious magnificence of the mountains, the illimitable brute fact of the prairies"—this is Marlboro Country. It is, as the license plates say, the "Big Sky Country." Had it not been for Rousseau's romantic myth of noble savagery, Fiedler would have been psychologically impotent in the face of its virginal enormity. He would have had no way of comprehending it. There would have been nothing for him "to do with it...no way of assimilating the land to [his] imagination."[4]

But the Rousseauan legacy, held in trust by Natty Bumppo, Daniel Boone and more recently Ben Cartwright, has made Marlboro Country not only mentally manageable but psychologically fascinating.thus, what might have boggled the national imagination by its sheer immensity in fact evokes within the cultural consciousness a nostalgic and reverent image of its own mythical heritage. Marlboro Country is an environmental memoir, reminding Americans of where they have been and inviting them to vicariously return.

The rustic garden, of course, is a potent symbol in the American mind. Leo Marx has shown the intrusion of "technology" into the "pastoral ideal" or *The Machine in the Garden* to be a "metaphoric design which recurs everywhere in our literature" from James Fenimore Cooper and Washington Irving to Ernest Hemingway and Robert Frost [5] Indeed, so envious are harried twentieth-century Americans of the pastoral ideal that it spills out of their serious art and across their commercial advertising. Once the consumer realizes that "You can take Salem out of the country, but you can't take the 'Country' out of Salem" he and some modern Amaryllis are only a pack of cigarettes away from a gambol through a field of waving grass toward a shadowy glade. Here Rip Van Winkle escaped from the village to a cozy repose in the midst of benign nature. Here menthol-puffing couples meander barefoot across an oaken bridge with never a thought of splinters. Here picnics are antless, summers are sweatless, and autumns are endless (which is to say winterless). Here one can find pleasant refuge from the responsibilities and encumbrances of civilization.

But the trill of shepherds' pipes and the wooded serenity of a Hollywood back lot are, upon closer inspection, strangers in Marlboro Country. They belong instead to the pastoral verdure of Salem Country, that Arcadian middle landscape that edges upon civilization. On the nether edge of Arcadia, however, is the wilderness—violent, primitive, occasionally malevolent. This is the incredible landscape of Fiedler's Montana. This is the monstrous, illimitable home of the noble savage.This is Marlboro Country.

The cursory distinctions between the garden and the wilderness are esthetic: the bucolic greenery of "take a puff, it's springtime," versus the rough-hewn realism of a Frederick Remington painting; the capricious gaiety of flutes versus the strident, robust brass of "The Magnificent Seven," the motion picture whose virile theme accompanies all Marlboro commercials.[6] Beneath the surface, though, lie more important differences. The pastoral ideal connotes a benign nature where conflict, danger, and tension are non-existent. The primitive ideal, on the other hand, speaks of a wilderness which jeopardizes and makes demands upon its residents. Accordingly, the Vergilian shepherd lies in repose, unharassed by either the complicated tensions of the town or the forbidding dangers of the marsh.[7] Meanwhile, his wilderness counterpart stands erect and vigilant. He is a man in conflict with his environment. He is of necessity a man of action and purpose. He is a Marlboro Man.

The Marlboro Man epitomizes the awesome, primitive environment in which he lives. His clothing, his habits, and even his face reflect the competitive spirit which the wilderness exacts from its inhabitants. His garb is not the fringed and bespangled costume of dimestore Texans and backlot cowboys. Nor is it the casual drape of the classic shepherd. He wears instead a rough-spun shirt, sheepskin vest or coat, dungarees, and chaps—nothing for show, nothing for comfort, everything for facing down the elements.

His habits, like his clothing, are dictated by practical considerations. He is, as the jingle says:

Up before the sun,
Travel[ing] all day long.

Each commercial presents another vignette. He rescues a stranded herd from the snowbound uplands; he mends fence; he rounds up stray calves; he thwarts an incipient stampede. Even his leisure moments—gathering water for the morning coffee or competing in a local rodeo—are reflections of his real purpose. His habits are work-oriented, his work a way of life.

But the essence of the Marlboro Man finds its truest expression in his face. His visage does not reflect the placid serenity of the shepherd. Not does it mirror either the cosmetic polish of civilization's winners or the sullen weariness worn by its victims. Like his clothing and his habits, the face of the Marlboro Man comes with the territory—sculptured, cragged, lined not by age but by the elements. He gazes out upon Marlboro Country through what Fiedler called the "'Montana Face' ...a face developed not for sociability or feeling, but for facing into the weather"[8] A rude sagaciousness of eye, a leathery tautness of skin, a wind-cured

ruddiness of complexion—altogether a rugged handsomeness—
signal his sturdy lifestyle.

The higher meaning of this Marlboro Man and the wilderness
he faces down cannot be written in terms of tobacco. Not cigarettes
but metaphors—or in this case a metaphor—are being
merchandised. The Marlboro image is a cultural symbol which
speaks to the collective imagination of the American people. It
speaks of the virgin frontier, and of the brutal efficacy and constant
vigilance which the frontier exacts from its residents. It speaks, as
Frederick Jackson Turner three-quarters of a century ago, of that

> coarseness and strength combined with acuteness and
> inquisitiveness; that practical, inventive turn of mind, quick to
> find expedients; that masterful grasp of material things, lacking
> in the artistic but powerful to effect great ends; that restless,
> nervous energy; that dominant individualism, working for good
> and for evil, and withal that buoyancy and exuberance which
> comes with freedom....[9]

In fine, the image speaks of *innocence* and *individual efficacy*:
innocence in spite of the Marlboro Man's rude sagacity, efficacy
because the territory demands it as the price of survival. It was the
innocence of the Marlboro Man which prompted Fiedler to write
that, in Montana, "there was something heartening in dealing with
people who had never seen, for instance, a Negro or a Jew or a
Servant, and were immune to all their bitter meanings."[10] In
Marlboro Country one finds a breed of humanity untarnished by—
indeed, ignorant of—the acrid fumes of modern civilization. The
naivete of the Marlboro Man is as fresh as the unpolluted air that
sustains him and as pure as the mountain stream which quenches
his thirst. Unsullied is he by the guilt and terror that mingle in the
civilized eye whenever it sees a race riot or a ghetto or a mushroom
cloud. He stands beyond the city's fouled social relations,
compromised political affairs, and clogged streets. He represents a
reprieve from the malaise that hangs darkly over all who have been
accessories to the crimes of civilization.

The Marlboro image, however, is not evocative of simple escape.
To be sure, the Marlboro Man stands apart from civilization. But he
stands apart also from Arcadia, from the simple, purposeless,
unencumbered dawdling of Salem Country. Like civilization,
Marlboro Country makes demands upon its inhabitants. But
responsibilities there are simple. The tasks require vigilance, rigor
and diligence, but there is resolution and accomplishment in the
reward. Possessed of those virtues memorialized by Turner—"that
practical, inventive turn of mind...that masterful grasp of material

things"—the Marlboro Man is "powerful to effect great ends."

The Marlboro image represents escape, not from the responsibilities of civilization, but, from its frustrations. Modern man wallows through encumbrances so tangled and sinuous, so entwined in the machinery of bureaucracies and institutions, that his usual reward is impotent desperation. He is ultimately responsible for nothing, unfulfilled in everything. Meanwhile, he jealously watches the Marlboro Man facing down challenging but intelligible tasks. He sees this denizen of the wilderness living as Thoreau would have: "deliberately...front[ing] only the essential facts of life."[11]

Innocence and individual efficacy are the touchstones of the metaphor employed on behalf of Marlboro Cigarettes. Despoiled by technology, Marlboro Country and the virtues which flourished therein are no more. But technology has a way of reconstituting the commercial purposes that which it has taken away. So it is with the Marlboro Man, his habits and appearance, his virtues, and his territory. A way of life which became a folk myth in the minds of a people is conjured back into "reality" and sent into the marketplace.

A decade ago the editor of a trade journal questioned the "intrusion" of cowboys "into...advertising—as authorities on cigarettes, bourbon and automobiles." Noting the cowboy's alleged penchant "for personal ornamentation, preening, drinking and brawling," his tendency toward "regarding females largely in the herd," and the aroma "of horses, dung and sweaty saddle leather" that follows wherever he goes, the editor thought it paradoxical that "civilized advertising men can parade him before us as someone whose habits are worthy of copying."[12] The resolution to this paradox, of course, is that the Marlboro Man is not simply a cowboy. He is a symbol of irretrievable innocence, and of that illimitable wilderness wherein, as Emerson said, one might have been "plain old Adam, the simple genuine self against the whole world."[13]

NOTES

[1]S.I. Hayakawa, "The Impact of Mass Media on Contemporary American Culture," a lecture delivered at Sacramento State College, Sacramento, California, 1960. Portions of the lecture, though not the anecdote, appear as "Poetry and Advertising" in *Language in Thought and Action*, 2nd ed. (New York, 1964), pp.262-77.

[2]Leo Marx, *The Machine in the Garden* (New York,1964), p.4.

[3]Leo Burnett, "The Marlboro Story: How One of America's Most Popular Filter Cigarettes Got That Way," *New Yorker*, 34 (November 15, 1958), 41-43. See also "Marlboro Won Success by Big Newspaper Ads," *Editor and Publisher*,91 (December 6, 1958), 26; and "PR Man Fones, Adman Burnett Bare 'Secrets' of Modest Marlboro He-man," *Advertising Age*, 29 (November 17, 1958), 3,99.

[4]Leslie A. Fiedler, "Montana, or the End of Jean-Jacques Rousseau," reprinted in

An End to Innocence (Boston, 1955), p. 131.

[5]Marx, p. 16.

[6]It is worth noting that advertisers have recognized that Remington's paintings "would be perfect for a series of outdoor Marlboro posters," and have erected his art work—blown to 300 times its original size—along California's highways. See "Giant Size Remington Reproductions become Marlboro Outdoor Boards," *Advertising Age,* 40 (January 20, 1969), p. 32.

[7]Marx delineates the borders of Arcadia. "One separates it from Rome, the other from the encroaching marshland." Within these borders the pastoral shepherd is "free of the repressions entailed by a complex civilization," but still "not prey to the violent uncertainties of nature." Marx, p.22.

[8]Fiedler, p.134-35.

[9]Frederick Jackson Turner, "The Significance of the Frontier in American History," reprinted in *The Frontier in American History* (New York, 1920), p.37.

[10]Fiedler is quick to notice the darker side of noble savagery, pointing out that these same people "had never seen an art museum or a ballet or even a movie in any language but their own." Fiedler, p.135.

[11]Henry David Thoreau, *Walden* (New York, 1961), p.105.

[12]"Saddlesoap, Please," *Advertising Age* , 31 (March 18, 1960), p.90.

[13]*The Journals and Miscellaneous Notebooks of Ralph Waldo Emerson,* ed. William H. Gilman , et al (Cambridge, 1960), IV, p.141.

Discussing "The Higher Meaning of Marlboro Cigarettes."

1) Examine how advertisements for beer, liquor candy, perfume and other "luxury" goods attract the consumer. Study the ads for a particular product or compare similar products. What are the myths and beliefs which are being exploited?

2) Discuss the recent advertising developments for cigarettes and the proliferation of "low-tar" brands. Compare these with the Marlboro ads.

3) Find other advertisements which use the images of the wilderness and the innocence and ruggedness of the frontiersman.

4) Despite the decline of westerns in movies and on TV during the 1970's, the image of the cowboy continued to be used to sell not only Marlboro's but also several other products such as Big Red chewing gum and Schlitz Light beer. As a student of popular culture, how do you explain this?

The Psychology of Fast Food Happiness

By Gregory Hall

McDonald's Eateries are as common as chewing gum under cafe counters, and more genuinely American. A few facts are in order. As of 1973, McDonald's hatched on the average one fledgling fast food diner each day. In the restaurant business this amounts to a population explosion. It's still happening. Even more staggering is the number of cows that have been ground up for the billion McDonald's burgers sold roughly every four months. Resurrected, these herbivores would ring around an area larger than Greater London. But even this number is far exceeded by the number of American school children who adore Ronald McDonald second only to Santa Claus. Clearly McDonald's is more than just another hamburger joint. It is a hamburger joint that wins the hearts of men. It is itself the product of peculiarly American preoccupations. Its product is fast food happiness.

In 1968, Guy Roderick, successful establishment lawyer, was charmed by McDonald's. He quit a Chicago law practice and joined the growing number of doctors, executives and lawyers who each year take up residence under the golder arches. As of 1973 Roderick owned four of hamburgerdom's mightiest and worked seven days a week behind the counter. Trading 20 years of legal science for fast food vending might seem like a step down, but Roderick insists the change brought him "a million dollars in happiness." What rare fascination does McDonald's hold for establishment professionals? Perhaps those disillusioned with the stress and responsibility of professional life opt for the less demanding, less creative and almost certainly profitable escape McDonald's offers. In return for an initial lavout, the licensee gets to attend Hamburger University and

From the *Journal of American Culture*, 1978, 1(2), 398-402. Reprinted by permission of the editors and the author.

use the McDonald's real estate, name and formula, which earn the operator handsome profits. For many this is a prescription for happiness.

Why do so many hungry Americans prefer McDonald's meals? Because McDonald's is a form of therapy. Like many modern technologies tailored to the consumer market, McDonald's wants to entertain. But the entertainment is subtle, almost imperceptible. "When you are in this business," says Ray Krok, "you are in show business. Everyday is a new show. It's like a Broadway musical—if people come out humming the tune, then the show was a success." Krok, one time barroom piano player and war cohort of Walt Disney, knows how to entertain. His fast food circus stars a clown and a bevy of energetic uniformed kids who welcome the hungry into a carefully designed atmosphere. "We offer people more than just fast food. It's an experience," says John Giles, national director for public relations. "It's an experience of fun, folks and food. We've sold 21 billion hamburgers, but we sell them one at a time." The McDonald's indoctrination begins with elaborate television commercials that illustrate the joyous restaurant atmosphere. Under the arches, we may feel the commercial-related *esprit de corps*. We may be entertained and fascinated by a group of unskilled adolescents who have been miraculously mobilized into an efficient, cheerful, coordinated unit. We may feel the invisible but ubiquitous Ronald McDonald poke and make us vulnerable to happiness.

In form the circus strategy was designed to capture families by first capturing the kids. But it aims equally at luring the passive child consumer from its shallow haunt in the adult ego. In the language of transactional analysis, our child ego state becomes dominant. It is the child who is able to feel the elemental joys of circus and food.

A certain psychological fulfillment is basic to McDonald's success. That is the real feat engineered by Ray Krok and subordinates—the transformation of an American institution, greasy-spoon hamburger joint, into a respectable, superclean, standardized, computerized food production machine that also makes people happy. The capture of America's tummies goes hand-in-hand with giving America a mealtime lift. It is technology used to create the aura of happiness—as contrasted to the growing experience of constraints and frustrations imposed upon daily life by the engine of technical change in a world of discontinuity. In the words of a Fort Lauderdale, Florida 13-year old: "It's a fun place. It's like a circus. I feel happy here."

Escape from stresses of modern life is a national preoccupation aided, in large measure, by the automobile. It is interesting that the auto also plays a big role in precipitating many of the stresses from

which it is used to provide escape, such as increased tempo, traffic, injury or death, financial responsibility, noise and pollution. The uterine confines of the car allow us to make instantaneous decisions to get away, to express and experience "freedom." As ideal transmitters of impulse, autos have become second skins, extensions of the human personality. In the same way McDonald's is a projection, a response to a collective human desire for a certain kind of experience. The McDonald's ethic is closely allied to the values encouraged by the auto. This should be no surprise since the drive-in hamburger joint evolved as a symbiotic adjunct to the car. But McDonald's goes beyond reinforcing the speed-escape ethic. It is an experience qualitatively different and more varied than the auto.

Still, our fascination for McDonald's is like our fascination for the auto. Both are the lure of the slick efficient machine, as well as anticipation of the fantastic built on images of escape. In philosophical terms these cross currents are congruent with Nietzscheian categories, the Dionysian and Apollonian visions. The American experience has at one level been an interplay of these forces, an exploration of stresses set up between the exercise of individual freedom and compromises to a culture of control, between the perfectly ordered, crystalline dream and the ecstasy of spontaneous, uncontrolled, creatively sensuous experience. McDonald's builds these unconscious elements integrally into the machine itself, into the technology of the system. Hence we can see the perfectly ordered, mechanized process in seeming union with the casual, playful, tensionless child-world of the clown.

The drive-in window may serve as a case in point. The window is a common piece of fast food design in many McDonald's as well as most other fast food vendors. It allows for a maximum casual encounter, speed, minimum of customer effort, in a machine-limited interaction. We can remain in our metal bubble while accepting nourishment through the portal. The window becomes our mouth, the first opening of the digestive tract. As gas stations are for cars, so McDonald's are fuel stations, or pit stops, for people whose automobile has become an exoskeleton. The situation becomes a McLuhanesque world of projection and counter-projection: humans are like machines and machines are like humans. It is a world where man is pacified and precariously at home in a technological womb. It is a seeming contradiction that, while allowing the height of informality and relaxed encounter, the drive-in window really perpetuates the American speed syndrome responsible for the hectic pace of life. This is a compromise between *l'homme machine* and his biological/psychological limits. Speed means we can get something or somewhere as quickly as possible. It means escape from the necessity of waiting, of being patient. In our fast moving society, where waiting can demand determination and perseverance, escape from "wasted" time is deliverance, relief, or happiness. Speed may be preferred because it promises a future in which more things can be done in less time. The value of experience becomes a measure of its quantity and intensity. The measure of McDonald's success is in the quantity, the billions of hamburgers sold, and the intensity of happiness ("...fun, folks and food.") it can offer. Ultimately this is the therapy we buy, the carefully designed commercial relief from cooking and waiting.

The mortuary industry has taken a cue from other popular American business and is offering a "drive-in funeral home." Mourners in New Roads, Louisiana may now view the remains of their relatives through a five-by-seven foot window at the Point Coupee Funeral Home. Owner Alven Verette says the new feature allows mourners to pay their respects without getting out of their cars. Explains Verette: "We wanted something for people who didn't have time to dress."

Admittedly, the fast food encounter is qualitatively different from the mortuary experience. The example serves only to illustrate the pervasiveness of the American preoccupation with speed and informality and to make clearer its effect. With the foot on the brake, there is hardly time to view the remains through an antiseptic pane of glass before the machine demands we be carried away. The drive-in window gives us a picture of the distant corpse bathed in a metallic blue neon light. The machine-limited encounter separates us from the experience. In much the same way, the mechanized, ritualized McDonald's process minimizes the possibility of relating to anything but categories or species of situations.

This limitation is an essential ingredient of an efficiently run operation like McDonald's. But it would be enervating if the undifferentiated series of exchanges between members was nothing more than mechanical. If the customer feels he is nothing more than matter in its place, he will not know the thrill of the McDonald's experience. Hence, the machinery must be imbued with a mysterious life. This is accomplished by advertising campaigns which give significance to the ritual around which the McDonald's experience turns.

Dr. Kottak, a University of Michigan professor of anthropology, addressed the 1976 annual meeting of the American Anthropological Association and claimed that McDonald's has become a virtual religious experience for millions of Americans. Kottak believes that McDonald's eateries, much like churches or temples, offer uniformity in an otherwise chaotic world. He says: "From the rolling hills of Georgia, to the snowy plains of Minnesota, with only minor variations, the menu is located in the same place, contains the same items and has the same prices." Accordingly,

"We know what we're going to see, what we are going to say, what will be said to us and what we will eat." From that first request for a Big Mac to the final "Have a nice day!" every move is ritualized much like a religious service.

But the religious experience of McDonald's goes deeper than ritual. McDonald's is the Messiah carrying the new theology into a world of chaos; the Messiah whose Golden Arches are symbols heralding the new age of Yankee fast food technology. Eateries which are the same everywhere destroy the artificial boundaries of local custom and become a unifying force, bringing together all believers in a common brotherhood of those who have been cured of a Big Mac attack. This applies to the people of Europe and the Orient as well as to Americans, because everyone must have a chance to believe. It is understandable why Steve Barnes, head of McDonald's International Operations says of the European campaign, "It's corny, but I feel like a missionary over here."

The McDonald's canon is one of basically Puritan values: law and order, cleanliness, purity, hard work, self-discipline and service. The jingle "We do it all for you," is meant to characterize the selfless aspect of the religious McDonald's. Cleanliness is a personal fetish of Ray Krok's. It is well known among franchise owners that Krok is a self-assigned, plain-clothed policeman who patrols his empire on periodic inspection tours in order to catch deviants. He once walked in a Canadian McDonald's and roared cantankerously. "There was gum on the cement patio, cigarette butts between the wheel stops for the cars," he relates. "There was rust on the wrought iron railing, and the redwood fence needed to be restained. I went in there and said to the manager: 'You get somebody to mop this goddamned floor right now! And if you don't I'll do it myself!' "

McDonald's accepts the beleaguered and hungered modern into its fold and nourishes him. Many find the cheerily bland atmosphere reassuring. It is designed to neutralize anxiety. At this level McDonald's is able to ally the mystery of the computer circuit with the mystery of religious peace. The Golden Arches become symbol as well as sign. Obviously the arches form a letter M for McDonald's. But they also resemble cathedral arches which have been the architectural equivalents of man's ethereal aspirations.

Inspiring values of power, dominance and mastery which produce kingdom, McDonald's is the perfect embodiment of American military prowess. Accordingly, McDonald's has captured the suburbs and, in the language of *Time* magazine, conquered the country. Advertising *campaigns* are waged to win the populace and deliver lethal blows to the competition (Jack-In-The-Box, Whataburger, etc.). Armed with a variety of "secret" sauces and jingles, the fast food brigadiers engage in pitched battle for a bigger

cut of the market. The artillery is in the form of jingles, musical ammunition which lodges in the psyche of the consumer and prods him continually. As Bill McClellan writes:"It is Orpheus in alliance with Pavlov working on the Whimpy in all of us." The roots of this mobilization and expansion are at the heart of the American movement itself, the exploration and colonization of the remaining frontiers. It is Commander Krok who leads the fast food army into fertile territory, current exploitable American preoccupations, winning the natives with Ronald McDonald straws and napkins.

McDonald's has not swept Europe as it has America. Suburban Europe is not as mobile as suburban America. When they moved to the city they found extremely high rent cut their profits substantially, a problem that Kentucky Fried Chicken and Whimpy were able to minimize because of their decreased overheads. Speed does not seem to be as important in Europe as in the United States. Britain's Whimpy and Switzerland's Movenpick do better with slower service. The Germans and Swiss are more likely to remain at home in the evening rather than go out again. So McDonald's has had to depend on weekend shopping crowds for most of its profits.

The McDonald's phenomenon is not necessarily a sign of declining culture. It is more a reflection of basic American values and as such may be a sympton of stresses. Centuries from now, when historians and anthropologists sift through twentieth century artifacts, they will try to make sense of a hamburger joint that inspires religious fervor. If we could hold it up to ourselves like a mirror, we might experience a moment's astonishment. But almost as quickly we might see the signs of hamburger addiction; the gaunt, harried look that precedes a Big Mac attack. Like Faust before the Mater Gloriosa, an irresistable power draws us on and we find ourselves in the sanctum of a McDonald's kitchen. Although we may not genuflect after receiving the great beef cure, we may feel the urge to glance skyward, giving thanks that we do not need to leave a tip.

Discussing "The Psychology of Fast Food Happiness."

1) Compare the advertising slogans of other fast food restaurants with those of McDonald's, What things are promised in each?
2) Read *Little America* by Rob Swigart (Houghton Mifflin, 1977) for a satirical look at the fast food industry.
3) How has the architectural style of McDonald's changed in recent years? Discuss the possible reasons for this change.
4) Review Madonna Marsden's essay on the myth of success. In what ways do Ray Kroc and McDonald's embody this myth?

PART THREE
STEREOTYPES

Introduction

The American civil rights movements of the 1950's and 60's dramatically demonstrated to the world that non-white American ethnic groups, in being considered inferior human beings by a large proportion of the white majority, had also suffered through centuries of horrible social and economic victimization. Conversely, the narrow view of whites as a group of racist exploiters, termed "honkies" by some non-whites during the last quarter century, had led to a hardening of racial resentments by both groups. It is clearer now than it once was that the oversimplification of characteristics in any race of people into a narrow, negative stereotype can have tragic consequences. Black Americans were enslaved through two-thirds of a century during which the United States constitution guaranteed basic human rights. Orientals, characterized in popular books and movies of the 1920's and 30's as vicious, rat-like sneaks, part of a world wide "yellow peril," may have unconsciously been one reason why more than 100,000 Japanese Americans were incarcerated in American concentration camps during the Second World War. Germans, believing Jews to be pollutants of the Ayran master race, stood by doing little or nothing while the Nazis systematically butchered six million men, women and children. It is no wonder that many people feel that the very word "stereotype" is tainted and that stereotyping in any form is evil.

Despite the destructive consequences that stereotyping often initiates, it is incorrect to think of stereotyping as always a bad thing. Stereotyping itself is neither good nor bad, but rather a necessary function of human thought. Because there is so much information about the world which the brain must absorb, the brain makes the continual bombardment of information manageable by placing individual items into general categories. In other words, the unique characteristics of specific people or things are dropped and only general characteristics applicable to an entire group are mentally retained. A stereotype is exactly the same type of generalized idea about a group of individual items that the brain creates every minute. The one significant difference is that stereotypes are shared classifications; the narrow set of characteristics are discussed in common among groups of people. What therefore makes an individual stereotype good or bad is: a) whether or not there is any accuracy in the stereotype; b) the positive or negative emotions aroused by the stereotype; c) the positive or negative actions caused by the stereotype.

There are many areas besides race where stereotyping is common. It is sometimes sexual (Women who work are poor mothers. Men only want one thing from a woman.). It is sometimes vocational (Doctors on TV tend to be wise, compassionate and always right. Nurses in the movies tend to be sexual athletes.). It is sometimes religious (Hindus love cows more than people. Catholics love the pope more than their country. There are no atheists in foxholes.). Sometimes things are stereotyped. Cities, for example, since the late 1960's have usually been pictured as sinkholes of depravity full of sexual perversion (*Midnight Cowboy*), narcotic addiction (*Panic in Needle Park*), homicidal muggers (*Death Wish*), and pathological violence (*Taxi-Driver*). On a smaller scale of things, a television set is often stereotyped by intellectuals as a "boob tube" or "a vast wasteland."

Stereotyping is such a natural human function and is so common that it can actually serve useful functions. For one thing, it is sometimes valuable to create classifications of individuals. The term "freshman" on college campuses brings to mind a popular image of a rather naive newcomer who is in the dark about both the social and intellectual life of a campus. Of course many freshmen don't fit this narrow picture. Nevertheless, the stereotype of the freshman serves the purpose of encouraging professors to construct introductory courses for those with no experience in the subject matter and it also encourages campus social organizations like fraternities and sororities to sponsor group activities planned especially for campus newcomers.

Another useful function of stereotypes is they can act as a corrective for harmful stereotyping. Movies of the 1960's and early 1970's such as *Guess Who's Coming to Dinner, Shaft,* and *Buck and the Preacher,* the pop music of James Brown and television shows like *I Spy* and *Brian's Song* all featured dynamic, ambitious, and talented black males. Such a positive stereotype corrected earlier media stereotypes of black males which had pictured them as lazy and cowardly, always ready to sleep on the job, steal a chicken or run wide-eyed from ghosts.

A third legitimate use for stereotypes is as conventional characters in popular stories. This will be discussed further in the section on popular formulas. It should suffice at this point to say that stereotyped characters allow the storyteller the luxury of not having to slow down to explain the motivations of every minor character in the story. This permits the storyteller to get on with the plot itself and to concentrate on suspense and action. In a Western we don't need to know the inner psychology of the bad guy. It's enough to know he's a murderous rustler. What we really want to see or read about is the gunfight in the dusty streets at sundown.

Christopher Geist, as a popular culture historian, uses a chronological overview to examine the evolution of stereotyped images of blacks in American popular culture. Going back to sixteenth century Europe, he traces black stereotypes into the plantation slave experience and into the nineteenth century minstrel show. His purpose is to discover the origins of well known and long-lived stereotypes and to suggest how and why these images have been incorporated into some more recent popular art forms.

Another, more specific historical approach is taken by J.Frederick MacDonald. Concentrating on just one period, 1900-1945, and just one type of popular fiction, the juvenile series, MacDonald demonstrates that almost all ethnic groups were negatively stereotyped in America. MacDonald's conclusions show that stereotypes tell us more about who believes them than whoever is being stereotyped. The fact that we have denigrated nearly everyone not exactly like "average" Americans indicates a problem, MacDonald argues, with the American people who until recently formed their ethnic prejudices from the ignorance of a centuries-long tradition of isolated xenophobia.

Deborah Weiser, instead of examining the historical past, concentrates on the speculative future. Science fiction, because it is free from the necessities of historical fidelity or realism, may explore any number of alternatives to traditional stereotypes. Weiser is therefore disappointed when she finds that science fiction mainly relies on the same narrowly defined women characters that are found in other types of popular literature.

Since stereotypes show us how groups of people think and feel about other people and things, they are direct expressions of common beliefs. Stereotypes are also good barometers of changing patterns of belief. The successful 1930's novel *Gone with the Wind* describes a simplified picture of the pre-Civil War South as an idyllic paradise. *Mandingo,* a bestseller during the 1950's and much imitated ever since, was also a novel about pre-Civil War plantation life. The world described in *Mandingo,* however, is not idyllic at all. Instead, the slave-maintained plantations are infested with lust, sadistic cruelty and every variation of human depravity. *Mandingo,* of course, is as stereotyped and oversimplified a picture of the old South as is *Gone with the Wind.* The real point though is that the great differences in how the two novels stereotype the South offers some clues to changing American attitudes towards slavery in America. This in turn offers suggestions as to why 1930's America made little headway in civil rights whereas by the end of the 1950's millions of people were emotionally sympathetic to the efforts of that period to end segregation.

Popular stereotypes are too often an ugly and cruel set of popular beliefs we could all do without. But the best way to rid ourselves of them and to use those that serve a worthwhile function, is to understand what stereotypes are, what they can do, and what they reveal.

Selected Further Reading

Barshay, Robert. "Ethnic Stereotypes in *Flash Gordon,*" *Journal of Popular Film,* 1974, 3(1), 15-30.

Bogle, Donald. *Toms, Coons, Mulattoes, Mammies, and Bucks: An Interpretive History of Blacks in American Films.* New York: Viking, 1973.

Chung, Sue Fawn. "From Fu Manchu, Evil Genius, to James Lee Wong, Popular Hero: A Study of the Chinese-American in Popular Periodical Fiction from 1920-1940," *Journal of Popular Culture, 1976, 10(3), 535-547.*

Haskell, Molly. From Reverence to Rape: The Treatment of Women in the Movies. New York: Holt, Rinehart and Winston, 1974.

Tuchman, Gaye, Arlene Kaplan Daniels and James Benet. *Hearth and Home: Images of Women in the Mass Media.* New York: Oxford, 1978.

Sambo, Zip Coon, and Mammy: Origins of Black Stereotypes

By Christopher Geist

Webster's New World Dictionary (1966 edition) defines the word "stereotype" as follows:

> ...an unvarying form or pattern; fixed or conventional expression, notation, character, mental pattern, etc., having no individuality, as though cast from a mold: as, *the Negro is too often portrayed as a stereotype.*[1]

Webster's use of the black race in the definition should come as no surprise. With the possible exceptions of Native Americans and women, no other group in the United States has been so consistently linked with stereotyped presentation in the popular and folk arts. "Sambo," "Mammy," "Zip Coon" (the urban dandy version of Sambo), "Uncle Tom," and others have been used in crude racial jokes, in popular literature (both children's and adults'), in song lyrics, in films, in advertising campaigns, on radio, in folktales, as trademarks, and on television. Since the days before the Civil War whites have developed their perceptions of the black race and its culture through reference to the stereotypes which have permeated American culture.

As is the case with most stereotypes, black stereotypes were developed by individuals and groups who focused on superficial characteristics and exaggerated them. Often the creators (white writers, illustrators, actors, etc.) had little or no personal contact with blacks. Seen from a distance, it was obvious that blacks were different. First, and perhaps most obviously, blacks have been set apart by their color. A white ethnic has the opportunity, at least through his/her chldren, to escape any derisive ethnic stereotype associated with his/her background. An Italian might escape the image of "Greasy Wop" by Anglicizing his name (or changing it through marriage, if female), learning English, obtaining an American education, and abandoning Italian traditions. In the course of a few generations, perhaps even one, a German immigrant family might alter its name (say from Braun to Brown) and blend inconspicuously into the mythical melting pot. That same family could, of course, decide to maintain its heritage and discover a sense of pride in its ethnic origins. Either way, there is a choice which is not available to blacks. Though blacks, too, might fall back on their African heritage, whites still tend to feel threatened and puzzled by such displays. Somehow, in the 1960s when the "Black Pride" movement gained momentum it also gained a revolutionary aura. A Saint Patrick's Day parade is a festive occasion–long live the Irish! Even non-Irish can look on and enjoy the spectacle. A "Black Pride" parade would probably be characterized as a "demonstration."

Stereotypes are great levelers. Simply speaking, a stereotype develops, exaggerates, and exploits one or two seemingly unusual attributes of a given group or class of people and applies those attributes to *all* members of that group or class without discrimination. In what sense may those attributes be termed "unusual?" They are unusual in that they are outside the experience of the observer. For example, all whites know that *all* blacks have stiff, kinky hair. This stereotypical trait has provided the punch line for innumerable jokes. Yet, as numerous authorities have pointed out, all blacks do not have "wool" for hair. In fact, the range of black hair types includes dozens of variations–straight, wavy, tightly curled, thin, thick, soft, etc. Why are these variations so conspicuously absent from popular representations of blacks (at least until the last few decades)? Stereotypes pare down and simplify reality; too many variations would complicate and confuse. Stereotypes tend to remain direct and undiluted. Their purpose is to set a group apart from the mainstream. To endow that group with too much variety in appearance or actions might well make them too real, too human.

Fear of the unknown contributes to the creation of stereotypes. When European whites were first establishing contacts with blacks (in the 1500s) they really knew very little about the black race and the continent of Africa. Early explorers and traders returned from the Dark Continent with fantastic stories of strange beasts. Among those newly discovered marvels of nature was the black man-ape with "large Breasts, thick Lips and broad Nostrils."[2] Direct contact with blacks was not a part of the experience of most Europeans. Thus, from the earliest periods, white men and women relied on a relatively small number of observers who wrote travel accounts which tended to focus on the facets of African life and culture which seemed most unusual from their European perspective. They felt free to invent details, to fabricate amusing anecdotes, and to rely on hearsay. Bizarre tales (most of them incapable of being substantiated) soon began to circulate which linked blacks with magic, bestiality, and cannibalism.

Perceiving their own whiteness as "normal," whites attempted to account for the "abnormal" color of the Africans. Some blamed the Africans' black skin on the effects of the intense, equatorial sun. Those who adhered to this theory believed that blacks who were transported to the more temperate areas of the world would soon be "cured" and would return to "normal" color. Another theory linked the skin color of Africans with a Biblical and Talmudic curse. Ham had committed the sin of looking on his drunken, naked father, Noah, and was told that this indiscretion would cause his descendants to be "ugly and dark skinned." Furthermore, in the Biblical version of the tale, Ham and his progeny would forever be "servant of servants."[3] This final phrase would have obvious utility later in the defense of slavery in the United States.

Curiously enough, the true source of any white fear of Africans may be rooted even more deeply than in black facial features and the mysteries of the African continent. Winthrop D. Jordan, in his monumental study of white racism, *White Over Black,* has pointed to the long history of English aversion to blackness. The *Oxford English Dictionary*, notes Jordan, provides the following definition of "black" *prior to the sixteenth century:*

> Deeply stained with dirt; soiled, dirty, foul.... Having dark or
> deadly purposes, malignant; pertaining to or involving death,
> deadly; baneful, disatrous, sinister...Foul, iniquitous,
> atrocious, horrible, wicked....Indicating disgrace, censure,
> liability to punishment, etc.[4]

Jordan goes on to say that the color had already become "the handmaid and symbol of baseness and evil, a sign of danger and repulsion" before Africans and Englishmen came into contact.[5] Shakespeare and other Elizabethan artists used black to symbolize evil and danger, and black is also associated with evil and uncleanliness in the folklore of many European countries. Even today we resort to black to symbolize mourning, but the "purity" of white is associated with such symbolic rites of new birth as the wedding. Perhaps long-held, unconscious cultural meanings associated with their color has helped insure that blacks are stereotyped as base and inferior.

In the early history of slavery in the United States, many of the most enduring black stereotypes were developed. Though the formation of these caricatures undoubtedly drew upon the earlier experiences of the Europeans, there is ample evidence to suggest that various stereotypes grew out of the slave experience itself. Some slaves, for example, may have "shuffled," acted ignorantly, and moved slowly as a ruse to fool their masters. "Indolent, faithful, humorous, loyal, dishonest, superstitious, improvident, and musical, Sambo was inevitably a clown and congenitally docile."[6] Sambo put on the mask of ignorance and incompetence, and if the master was convinced that Sambo's act was real then he could not expect too much from this docile, dumb slave around the plantation.

Sambo became one of the most enduring and popular of the black stereotypes. It is fairly easy to see why. Sambo's mindless frolicking, his intense loyalty to his master, and his childlike need for protection and guidance were just the proper traits the planters needed to justify their version of slavery. Sambo was basically a happy child (Fig.1). Given freedom of choice he would not work a single minute of his life. He would dance, fiddle, and spend his hours in wanton idleness. Sambo needed his master as much as his master needed him. To enslave another race some justification is needed. The Sambo stereotype, coupled with the "Curse of Ham" and other Biblical passages, helped to provide that justification. Besides, all whites, whether slaveholders or not, could and did look upon all blacks as inferior. Thus, no matter how poor, no matter how ignorant, whites could always see in Sambo someone below themselves.[7]

Another stereotype which developed on the plantations of the Old South was almost the reverse of Sambo. "Nat," the dangerous, rebellious black, terrorized whites. He was probably a necessary creation to remind white slaveholders that, in spite of gentle old Sambo, some slaves could be dangerous. Though historians have shown that there were relatively few major slave rebellions in the United States, none of them successful,[8] a few bloody uprisings (such as Gabriel Prosser's in 1800 and Nat Turner's in 1831) struck fear in the hearts of whites. Nat Turner and his band had slain over fifty whites before their rebellion was contained. These random incidents helped to convince the slaveholders and their nonslaveholding neighbors that lurking behind Sambo's broad grin and "Yassa Massa" personality was a potentially dangerous revolutionary.

The successful slave rebellion in Haiti in the 1790s also helped to persuade whites that slaves could be devious and dangerous. Never turn your back on a slave–remember old Nat. Then, too, mysterious acts of covert defiance around the plantation

Figure 1 Sambo

strengthened the stereotype of the black as rebel. Tools and heavy equipment seemed to break down at crucial times. Food disappeared from the master's larder. Clumsy slaves "accidentally" ruined a portion of the crops or seriously injured a valuable animal. Sure, they grinned back in Sambo-like puzzlement at such bad luck, but wasn't Nat really behind all those shining teeth? Old Nat would do almost anything to defy and harm his Ol'Massa. Perhaps some of the mistrust and fear of blacks we see among whites in the twentieth century had origins in the Nat stereotype.

Every plantation had its fat, jolly, motherly cook—or so we have been taught through the popular arts. Remember Hattie McDaniel as the mammy in *Gone With The Wind?* (Fig.2). Remember Aunt Jemima? These happy-go-lucky mammies took care of the children, prepared the sumptuous plantation banquets, despised "poor white trash," and loved Ol'Massa and his family more than anything in the world. Mammy was so loyal that she would reject a chance of freedom just to remain with her white family. She was probably so fat because she sampled too much and too frequently from the kitchen she oversaw. She was a good slave because she lived in the Big House and was able to realize just how fine and good Ol'Massa really was through her close association with him. She was a credit to her race.

Figure 2 Mammy and Scarlett from *Gone With the Wind.*

More than likely Mammy lived with Uncle Tom, an older slave who had served the master competently and faithfully for many years. Now old Uncle Tom just lazed around the plantation, worked a bit at light tasks, and generally entertained Ol'Massa and others with tall tales and fiddling. He was now enjoying a life of ease which the master provided as reward for past service--a slave's retirement. He had virtually no worries, for the kindly master provided for his every need. Contented Old Uncle Tom was a stereotype which helped reinforce the planters' assertion that slavery was a necessary institution which benefitted the blacks. What would an old man such as Uncle Tom do for a living if it was not for the goodly Ol'Massa?

Always, of course, Uncle Tom and Mammy were careful to teach young slaves how fine their master was and how contented a slave's life could be if he/she followed a few simple rules. Neither Uncle Tom nor Mammy would dream of any other life. They might not be bright, but at least they knew their place. Slavery was a good thing for blacks; freedom would make them miserable. Work for the master and he would feed you, clothe you, provide you with a Christian religion, and care for you in your old age. Who took care of old free blacks? Yes, Uncle Tom and Mammy were perfect slaves. There are two important questions which relate to these stereotypes. First, did the slaveholders create Mammy and Uncle Tom to represent idealized versions of the perfect slave? This would allow them to be used to educate young blacks. Second, did the slaveholders create these stereotypes to convince themselves that they were good masters and that slavery was a moral and righteous task which helped care for an inferior race? The answer in both cases is, at least partially, in the affirmative.

The diffusion of these and other black stereotypes through the popular culture has a long and interesting history. Perhaps the single most important influence was the nineteenth century minstrel show. Minstrelsy had its origins in the years following the War of 1812 when traveling "African delineators" began to perform songs and dances which they supposedly drew from authentic black sources. These performers were whites who blacked in their faces and applied white make-up around their eyes and mouth to give themselves a wide-eyed, grinning Sambo look. During the 1840s and 1850s the "African delineators" evolved into the minstrel show, one of the earliest and most important forms of popular entertainment. The heart and soul of the minstrel show was the portrayal of blacks by whites. It was on the minstrel stage that many Americans of the nineteenth century received their only impressions of blacks and their culture. It was from the minstrel stage that black stereotypes were widely diffused. Eventually these same stereotypes would enter into film, radio, and television, sometimes with very little change.

Sambo came in two varieties in the minstrel show. In a rural plantation setting he was an ignorant, fun-loving buffoon. He was also portrayed as the urbanized, free black dandy in flashy clothing. This second stereotype became known as "Zip Coon." Zip Coon was overly pretentious, was a womanizer, and was just as lazy as his rural cousin, Sambo. The difference was that Zip Coon was a Northern black stereotype. He was totally unequipped to deal with the life of a free man. He could not hold a job, he did not understand the urban north, and he could never succeed on his own. He was foolish, tended toward exaggerated speech inflections and malapropisms, and walked with a ridiculous strut. Zip Coon helped to demonstrate the basic inferiority of blacks and helped to convince Northern whites that blacks were better off down on the plantations of the South.

Another typical presentation of the minstrels was that of Mammy. One song characterized her as follows:

> She'd joke wid de old folks and play wid de child
> She'd cry wid de sorrowing, laugh wid de gay;
> Tend on de sick bed, and join in de play
> De fust at de funeral, wedding, or birth
> De killer ob trouble and maker ob mirth
> She spoke her mind freely, was plain as de day
> But never hurt any by what she might say
> If she once made a promise, it neber was broke.[9]

Mammy was truly a lovable, jolly old slave who demonstrated by her life and actions that even slaves could be happy and content. Old Uncle Toms also cavorted about the minstrel stage. They, too, were dedicated and contented blacks who knew their proper role in society.

Always and in every conceivable manner the white minstrel performers portrayed the blacks in gross stereotypes. So strongly were these portrayals accepted that when blacks began to enter minstrelsy after the Civil War they were forced, to a certain extent, to adopt the conventions. Some blacks even appeared in burnt cork make up![10] Robert C. Toll, whose *Blacking Up* is the finest book on minstrelsy, has described the manner in which white minstrels depicted blacks:

> Minstrel blacks did not have hair, they had "wool"; they were "bleating black sheep," and their children were "darky cubs." They had bulging eyeballs, flat, wide noses, gaping mouths with long, dangling lower lips, and gigantic feet with elongated, even

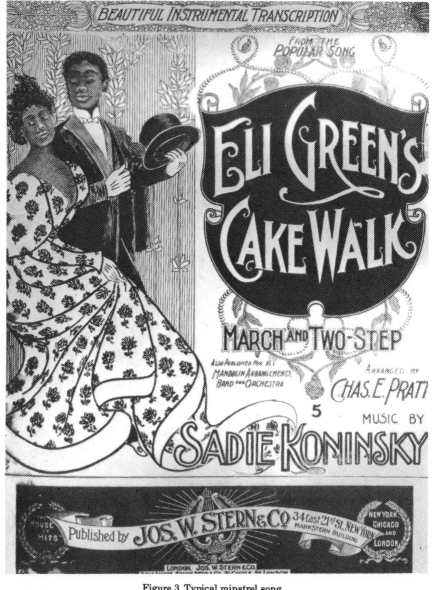

Figure 3 Typical minstrel song

flapping heels. At times, minstrels even claimed that Negroes had to have their hair filed, not cut. . ."

The minstrels also lampooned black diet, dress, and beliefs. They portrayed blacks as lovers of music and dance. In short, the minstrel show helped to popularize all the major conventions which have made up the various black stereotypes in the other popular arts. It is important to note that these stereotypes were created by whites for a predominantly white audience.

As the years rolled on, the stereotypes popularized in the minstrel shows were adapted to other art forms. Early film images of blacks were quite similar to the minstrel version. In fact, many "blacks" in early American films were actually whites in blackface make up.[12] Black actor Stepin Fetchit eventually came to epitomize the Sambo stereotype in American films. There was a great deal of the minstrel tradition in radio's "Amos 'n Andy" (both characters were portrayed by whites). Aunt Jemima could not have sold so many pancakes without the effective use of the Mammy stereotype. *Uncle Ben's Rice* utilized a modernized version of Uncle Tom to promote sales. The "J.J." character in television's "Good Times" may be viewed as a modern version of Zip Coon. There are hundreds of other examples which might be cited, but the important point is that black stereotypes still exist. Even though they may be toned down, stereotypes still provide all too many white Americans with their only perceptions of the black race and its culture. Total racial equality and understanding may never be possible until the last remnants of those stereotypes have disappeared.

NOTES

[1]Emphasis added.

[2]Winthrop D. Jordan, *White Over Black: American Attitudes Toward the Negro, 1550-1812* (New York: W.W. Norton & Company, Inc., 1977), p.8. The quoted passage dates from 1738 but is similar to statements found much earlier.

[3]*Ibid.,* pp.17-18. See also *Genesis,* Chapters 9 and 10.

[4]*Ibid.,* p.7.

[5]*Ibid.,*

[6]John W. Blassingame, *The Slave Community: Plantation Life in the Ante-Bellum South* (New York: Oxford University Press, 1972), p.134. This work is an excellent study of the origin of the plantation stereotypes.

[7]Edmund S. Morgan has even argued that slaveholders actively promoted racial animosity, partially through stereotypes, in order to insure that slaves and poor whites would not combine to oppose the privileged planter class. See his *American Slavery, American Freedom: The Ordeal of Colonial Virginia* (New York: W.W. Norton & Company, Inc., 1975). See also William H. Cohn, "Popular Culture and Social History," *Journal of Popular Culture,* XI (Summer, 1977), 167-179.

[8]A standard work on slave revolts is Herbert Aptheker, *American Negro Slave Revolts.*

[9]Robert C. Toll, *Blacking Up: The Minstrel Show in Nineteenth-Century America* (New York: Oxford University Press, 1974), p.79.

[10]*Ibid.*, pp.200-201.

[11]Ibid., p.67.

[12]Some of the finest studies of black stereotypes in recent years have dealt with American films. The best of these is Thomas Cripps, *Slow Fade to Black* (New York: Oxford University Press, 1977).

Discussing "Sambo, Zip Coon, and Mammy: Origins of Black Stereotypes."

1) Compare issues of two popular magazines meant primarily for black readers that are at least ten years apart. What are the major similarities and differences between the images of blacks in these four magazines? How do these images differ from images of blacks that appeared in general circulation popular magazines of the same period?

2) Read Thomas Cripps' article, "The Noble Black Savage: A Problem in the Politics of Television" in *Journal of Popular Culture,* VIII:4, pp.687-695. What are the major developments in the changing black stereotypes as seen on television? Compare these with the images discussed by Geist.

3) Suppose Africa was discovered in the present time. Given the quick dissemination of information possible via the mass media and current attitudes towards cultures we know little about, what stereotypes about blacks and black cultures do you think would emerge?

The "Foreigner"
In Juvenile Series Fiction, 1900-1945

By J. Frederick MacDonald

*I'm not a native or even a foreigner. I'm an American citizen.*___[1]

As with much in the history of American popular culture, little serious study has been directed toward the juvenile literature that flourished in the first half of the present century. Some writers have attempted to assess the more popular series—Tom Swift, Nancy Drew, Hardy Boys, Bobbsey Twins—but there exists no systematic and inclusive investigation of the hundreds of fictional series that entertained American youth for generations.

Several factors help to explain this academic hiatus. Traditionally, books of this type have been avoided by university libraries. Therefore, the scholar in search of collections of juvenile series finds his task almost impossible. There also exists no accurate information regarding the expanse of series titles. Literally scores of publishing houses churned out hundreds of these series and each series contained a proliferation of titles. In seeking data regarding authorship, moreover, the researcher discovers that authors often resorted to pseudonyms and mass-production techniques, both of which help to blur the line between the literary and commercial.

Nevertheless, despite inherent problems in dealing with juvenile series fiction, where sizable collections of these books have been assembled, the researcher is able to gather useful insights and poignant conclusions about the values and attitudes propounded to American youth. In particular, with reference to the manner in which young American minds were shaped to consider the non-

From the *Journal of Popular Culture*, 1974, 8(3), 534-548. Reprinted by permission of the editor and the author.

American—the foreigner, and therefore the rest of the world—this literature reveals a dramatic picture of race-consciousness, xenophobia, and imperialism. Whether the foreigner is encountered at home or abroad, juvenile series fiction usually paints him in negative colors, and always causes him to run second-best to the healthy, intelligent, rational, and White American heroes. Compared to the Anglo-Saxon surnamed heroes of this fiction (Brewster, Swift, Drew, Hardy, Porter, Fielding, Tyler, Gordon, Scott, Kent, Darrin, Ford, Merriwell, etc.), the foreigner is portrayed in general as an ignorant, unwashed, thieving and sinister character who is alien to American values.

One way in which the negative attributes of the foreigner is poignantly described is in repeated references to appearances. By referring to physiognomy, series authors make the point that evil looks and evil character are synonymous. Thus, young readers encounter such conclusions as the fact the German "looks stupid" but his leaders are worse;[2] that "villainous-looking" Chileans all resemble the "bloated-faced," fat, greasy-looking, and "probably lazy" stereotypes encountered by handsome American heroes;[3] that all residents of the Middle East look alike, regardless of ethnic affinities;[4] that dark skin gives "a hideous appearance" to natives of the East Indies;[5] and that Japanese are all "buck-toothed" and evil "brown rats," or as one hero phrased it, "the little Jap... showed his buck teeth in a broad smile that started forward... like a little brown terrier on the end of a leash."[6]

Character assessments drawn from such observation usually contain strong racist overtones. Here dark skin color and/or race-mixing are usually portrayed as vile and debilitating, and definitely in contrast to the characteristics of the American hero. Typical of such an attitude is the remark by one of the Battleship Boys in regard to two Hawaiian crewmen who deserted the ship: "Those black-faced fellows from the other side of the world sailed into me as if they wanted to eat me up," and he concludes that with these Hawaiians "black goes all the way through; I'll bet they're black clear to the bone."[7] This condemnation is amplified when, after mistakenly referring to the Hawaiians as "niggers," one character concludes that "all Blacks look the same to me."[8]

The debasing effect of race-mixing is also a theme of this juvenile literature. One book assails the Yaqui Indians of Mexico for such activities. According to this book, after mingling "with negroes, degenerate Spaniards and Mexicans until it is almost an insult to apply the name 'Indian' to them," the Yaquis "live like beasts," have "lost the ideals of their race," and are "a dragged-out remnant, steeped in crime."[9] The ultimately uncivilized nature of inter-racial mating seems to be the theme of one description of an unsavory restaurant in the Phillipines for:

> The only thing French about the Cafe de Paris was the fact that
> one of the proprietors was a low-caste Spaniard, and the other a
> Filipino mestizo, or half-breed.[10]

As further testimony to the debauched results of miscegenation, a
White American hero encounters in Singapore a veritable
Dantesque underworld where his Sumatran contact is "a hideous
looking creature" with "all the bloods of the Far East in his veins,"
and where he observes in dingy bars "men who once had claimed
kinship with the white races but had sunk so low they were no longer
any part of a white man."[11]

Thus, being a White man is in series fiction an almost-sacred
virtue. It is an attribute which the dark-skinned people of the world
can never achieve. Yet more importantly, it is a virtue lost forever to
the half-breed. Nowhere is this more strongly evidenced than in the
case of Bomba, the Jungle Boy, who is a White American youth
living *aux primitifs* in the South American jungle. Here his
triumphs among his dark peers are often attributed to the inherent
superiority that comes with being White. Hence, when Bomba wins
a struggle, "it is the White blood in Bomba that helped him to fight
so bravely," and when he reasons and speaks, he betrays the racial
superiority of the White man.[12]

If looks and racial constitution impart to the readers of juvenile
series the picture of the relatively regressive character of the
foreigner, so too does the authors' use of dialect. It is not easy for a
child to read and comprehend the stumbling butchery of the English
language which is the literary use of dialect. It is intended to bring
humor and authenticity to a character, but in children's literature it
adds confusion, derision and inferiority. All social and ethnic
groups are submitted to the humiliating rendering of dialect.
Usually such accents are reserved for antagonists where it is an
accompaniment to sinister and alien qualities, or for comic
characters where it is used to emphasize ignorance and buffoonery.
Thus the likes of enemy agents in the United States, or cunning men
encountered abroad, generally handle English in a halting, yet self-
assured dialect; while malapropisms and stupidity are conveyed in
the dialects of comic types such as Tom Swift's butler Eradicate
Sampson, who is an Afro-American, and Lt. Stan Wilson's pal, Lt.
O'Malley, who is Irish.[13]

It is interesting to note that most accents are those of European
natives dealing with the English language. In particular, Italians,
French, Irish, Dutch, German, Spanish, and Russian speakers
frequently betray strong dialects in their speech. Other familiar

accents are those of Chinese, Japanese, Mexicans, and American Indians. In several cases, however, authors have had problems with less familiar dialects. Thus, in one book a Norwegian is presented speaking perfect English, while all Latin American dialects are the same as the Mexican accent, and stereotypic American Indian dialect is used to convey the speech of South American Indians, Eskimos, and Hawaiians.

A prevalent bias is encountered by the reader of juvenile series in the continual comparison of American habits and attitudes with those of foreigners. Here the reader is led invariably to the conclusion that people from other countries and other ethnic groups are inferior to White middle-class America, the social source of most series heroes. Whether the hero is sampling unfamiliar food, observing habits of personal hygiene, visiting foreign cities, or even making jokes, he betrays xenophobic prejudices. Thus, when a series hero tastes an exotic cuisine, it is usually described as unfit to eat, or certain to lead to sickness, or at least tasteless. Perhaps the closest remark to a compliment is one author's note that Peruvian food is "almost as good as in Texas."[14]

Many of the foreigners are described as living in messy and dirty homes, a situation reflective of the shabby and unkempt personal appearance of the foreigners themselves. This theme of cleanliness is carried one step further in the Polly Brewster books where, while visiting foreign countries, the heroine and her friends assail the stench of the marketplace in Kingston, the "insufferably hot" and inferior hotels of Colombia, and the generally uncivilized nature of life in Haiti.[15] In a second book, these youthful American tourists berate the odor of Paris; the poor, dirty, and debilitated condition of Ireland; and the over-abundance of pigeons living in Venice.[16]

Even in the jokes and humorous expressions that series heroes sometimes use, a definite prejudice against foreigners is noticeable. In some cases this racial humor is ironic as, for instance, when the pink-cheeked Peggy Lee, newly arrived at an American girls' school from her father's Nicaraguan coffee plantation, is tauntingly asked by fellow students if she is an immigrant or an American. Her mocking reply is that "I'm a Chinaman—I've lost my pigtail."[17] Much more racist is the observation of Dave Dawson when he meets a "squat, chunky Jap" that reminds him of a "fire hydrant with a face."[18] Even when heroes search for cliches typifying the extremes of stupidity, they resort to phrases such as "if I don't get to the bottom of this, you can call me a Chinaman,"[19] and "if that wasn't Bill Bender, I'm a Dutchman."[20] And humorous puns can also be concocted from foreign names, as in the case of the Russian Ivan Barsky, which causes Tom Swift's chum, Ned Newton, to muse: "I hope his bite isn't as bad as his bark-sky."[21]

Historically, American juvenile series fiction began to flourish at the beginning of the twentieth century after having emerged from the lengthy, but limited success of writers of the previous century like Oliver Optic (William Taylor Adams) and Harry Castlemon (Charles A. Fosdick). Emerging as it did at the time of the American adventure into imperial expansion and world politics, series fiction displays prominently the blend of manifest destiny and *noblesse oblige* which is associated with American imperialism. One manner in which such an attitude is expressed is through the use of chauvinistic statements and incidents. In this regard, the youth series are full of flags, patriotic music, valiant deeds, righteous indignations, duly impressed foreigners, and properly humble American heroes.

The message of America as "Great White Father" is also propagated in more subtle ways in this literature. One method is to portray the foreigner as diminutive and child-like and, therefore, in need of the paternal guidance of the more advanced and taller Americans. This is especially true of the natives of those countries either annexed or dominated by the United States after its war with Spain. Citizens of Puerto Rico, Cuba, and the Phillippines are usually depicted as "little people" who desire and require the benefits of Yankee civilization. An interesting example of this mentality occurs when Sunny Boy, a five-year old series hero, is found wandering in the market place of San Juan by a Puerto Rican adult. When the man returns Sunny Boy to the correct hotel, the child, despite the difference in age and maturity, is still able to inform his parents that "That man brought me. See? The little one in the white suit going up the street."[22]

The stigma of smallness is reserved almost exclusively for dark-skinned foreigners. Thus, European types are seldom short while Latin Americans and Orientals invariably are depicted as such. One book links the short stature of Nicaraguan soldiers with the lack of muscularity and relative inefficiency.[23] Mexicans are generally portrayed as short people, as in the case of the "ragged, stupid-looking, undersized man, evidently of the peon class" encountered by the Boy Scouts,[24] and the "queer but plucky little chap" who happens to be the father of ten children in the Ted Scott series.[25] Japanese, Chinese, and Eskimos are also "little people" in juvenile fiction. In one story, however, the author has an apparently difficult time in keeping straight the skin color of his "little people," as he refers to the Japanese as "these industrious little yellow people," then as the "little brown people," but finally he refers to them as "olive-colored."[26]

Because American heroes bring with them the products of a

technological society, they make more than small impressions on the less mechanical foreigners they encounter. Airplanes, firearms, radio equipment, ascension balloons—all so glorified in series fiction—provide youthful readers with many instances of foreigners fully impressed with American prowess. This is graphically illustrated in one Don Sturdy book when a South American aboriginal chief expresses his amazement with American technology by falling to the ground and rubbing his face in the dirt at the feet of the young American.[27] When a Mexican aviator meets the youthful American air ace, Ted Scott, the foreigner is described as showing "awe and an almost dog-like devotion in his eyes."[28] The awe with which a group of Colombians observe an American monoplane in one of the Exploration Series titles is called "almost childish in its sincerity."[29] And typical of the theme of White-Man-Become-God-Among-the-Dark-Natives is the story of the Boy Explorers in Borneo. Here it is rifles that cause the indigenous Dyaks to elevate one of the White explorers to the ranks of deity.[30]

If the themes of race-consciousness, xenophobia, and imperialism are consistent themes throughout the history of modern juvenile series fiction, nowhere is there a more successful blending of these themes than in times of international warfare. In all the major and minor struggles of the United States in the twentieth century, youthful fictional heroes find themselves embroiled. And whether they are combating Spaniards, Filipinos, Mexicans, Nicaraguans, Germans, Bolsheviks, Italians, or Japanese, somehow the young heroes manage to extricate themselves and the honor of the flag and homeland. As might be expected, however, in the process of victory the full descriptive arsenal of anti-foreigner prejudice is unleashed upon the enemies of America.

During World War I the Germans were especially assailed in juvenile literature. Thus the "Huns," "Boche," "Heines," "Teutons," "Prussians," or "Fritzies," were also called "Hun-baby-killers," "Huns, fit descendants of Attila,"[31] "like a lot of savage dogs,"[32] "German madmen,"[33] and "barbarians" who "wasted land, ruined homes, orphaned and mutilated little children [and] butchered old people."[34] The Germans were also credited with certain distasteful national characteristics. Included among these inhospitable traits were the necessity to "rule or else lick the boots of those over them"[35] of possessing a " 'yellow streak' all through the nation,"[36] of feeling that the "dirtier the deed the greater the pride,"[37] of being a "race lacking in all sense of gratitude,"[38] and of taking "a savage delight in bombing hospitals."[39] Interestingly, antipathy toward the Germans did not die easily. As late as 1922 juvenile fiction was still condemning Germans for having "never understood the fundamentals of Christianity," and suggesting that the "Germans might have saved us a lot of trouble if they had used the sulphur for self-extinction purposes."[40]

Although there are ethnic slurs in the criticism of Germans in World War I, series fiction writers could not escape the fact that the enemy in that war was also Caucasian. Thus, the writers were compelled to curb racial biases and content themselves with calling the Germans uncivilized and inhuman. If one looks for stronger forms of racial disparagement, one must look to the wars and adventures involving the United States with dark-skinned enemies. In particular, during World War II the Japanese provided an especially obvious target for racist prejudice. While the Nazis were being painted as treacherous and ruthless, and while the Italians were portrayed as uninspired and even apologetic, the Oriental enemy was castigated in racial as well as political terminology. Not untypical of this style was the War Adventure Series of R. Sidney Bowen in which the young aviator hero, Dave Dawson, helped to win the war. Here the Japanese were described as "those dirty brown devils,"[41] "slant eyes,"[42] "monkey men of the Far East,"[43] and "buck-toothed, throat-slitting sons of Nippon."[44] In one particularly inspired passage, Bowen referred to the Japanese as "the hordes and hordes of little brown rats [who] were going to spring savagely at white men's throats."

The threat of Communism is also a theme of juvenile series fiction. As such, it also reveals the general antipathy of the literature to anything, even ideas, that is not home-grown. Even before the Bolshevik Revolution of 1917 the problem of Russian radicalism was handled in the Tom Swift Series. Here both extremes, the corrupt Czarist establishment and the nihilist and anarchist alternative, were denigrated. Instead, the hero appears more disposed toward the moderate reformist position maintained by the emigre he helps.[46] Fourteen years later, despite the creation of a Communist regime in Russia, Tom Swift had not become a raving anti-Bolshevik. Instead, he dismissed Communism as alien to America and a "part of their religion." Although he confessed that he did not expect Bolshevism to take root in the United States, he did agree, nonetheless, to "keep my eye" on a suspected foreign employee.[47] Much more typical of traditional intolerance, however, was the comment of the youthful aviators of the Pilots of the Air Mail Series. In flying westward across the entire Eurasian land mass, these heroes denounced "these excitable Chinks doing their little revolutionary act, or the Bolsheviks of Russia and Siberia whose minds are turned upside down regarding the rest of the world."[48]

As well as approaching the problem of the foreigner from a

thematic point of view, it is also informative to assess the phenomenon from a geographical vantage. By drawing composite pictures of the foreign types most frequently appearing in series fiction, the researcher is led once again to the conclusion that in this juvenile literature little understanding of foreign societies is evidenced, and almost no respect for such groups is generated. This will be made clear in the following paragraphs dealing with the three most prevalent foreign elements in this literature: Latin Americans, Europeans, and Orientals.

LATIN AMERICANS

The Mexican appears more frequently than any other Spanish-speaking foreigners in series fiction. The "Greasers," as Mexicans are often called, are not pleasant people. They live in a "murder-ridden country;"[49] they are the evil-looking types one "wouldn't want to meet...in an alley;"[50] and they are usually linked with filth, thievery, laziness, and general disorder. Although several later books do treat Mexicans with dignity and fairness,[51] the picture of the Mexican is usually that "for a United States half dollar a lazy half breed Mexican" would do anything.[52] One of the most thorough discussions of Mexican character and history occurs in *Boy Scouts in Mexico* where the author berates the Mexicans for being "selfish and cruel" and for never having "been favored as the people of our country have...they've got years of national childhood to go through yet before they become a great people." Although he does trace Mexican "weakness" back to the instinctive murderousness of the Aztecs, he blames the present debilitation of the Mexicans on alcoholism and ignorance:

> What they need here is less strong drink and more school-houses...more real freedom and less mere show of republican government.[53]

It is interesting that for the most part the stereotype of the Mexican—from his character to his dialect—is the brush with which all Latin Americans are painted. Instead of demonstrating national and linguistic differentiation, series fiction pictures Latin America as an ethnic monolith. Thus, South American women in general are called ugly;[54] Honduran architecture is "beautiful in its barbaric style;"[55] Nicaraguan laborers are called "none of the brightest of mankind;"[56] Nicaraguan workers do not mind having to sleep on filthy cots;[57] natives of Tierra del Fuego are called "half-naked savages" and "naked imps of darkness;"[58] gauchos of Argentina are remonstrated for being "a wild set" with "Indian blood in their veins;"[59] and Bolivian villages are "miserable" and filled with "villainous-looking natives."[60] In a significant convergence of racial prejudices, one author urges the Chileans to beware of the Chinese "who are creeping into South America, just as they crept into California and other places on the western coast of the United States." This author maintains that authorities in Chile would have to be careful lest "they will be overrun by the yellow race."[61]

In the Polly Brewster Series the Latin American stereotype is applied to much of the West Indies. In a particularly effusive manner Spanish-, English-, and French-speaking islanders are painted in pejorative terms. In meeting Cubans in Havana, they are described as shysters and cheats who are lazy, immoral, and continually seeking American money. In Jamaica, the young heroine encounters everything from a malodorous, fly-ridden marketplace, to a farcical trial of a Black defendant in the Kingston Court House. The most stinging rebuke, however, is reserved for Haitians since in the words of one character:

> Morally, the Haitians are not to be trusted. All the old superstitions of barbaric Africa prevail to such an extent that no right-minded person wishes to visit there.[62]

EUROPEANS

In the portrayal of Europeans, juvenile series fiction makes a significant distinction. The Catholic and Latin countries are usually presented in a negative manner, the stress being placed here upon social and economic backwardness rather than inherent racial weakness. Protestant countries, however, are generally depicted in a positive light, and a relationship is often made between these nations and the United States. The one glaring inconsistency, however, is the case of Germany.

Whether encountered as immigrants in the United States, or as citizens within their own countries, Catholic Europeans are described as misfits. Poles and Irishmen are generally shown as stupid, inept clowns, and in many books they appear as comic relief in relation to the hero. Italians, on the other hand, are for the most part villainous types who, with their propensity to steal, are also ill-mannered, dirty, but romantic. During World War II this latter trait was often emphasized as many series books maintained that the Italians were poor soldiers who were in the war only because they were forced by Hitler and his dupe, Mussolini.

In dealing with the French, series authors fluctuate. In the war years, they were presented as valiant heroes defending civilization against Germanic barbarism. But in times of peace, the French are usually rude and inhospitable. In stories set in Canada, moreover, the French-Canadian often provides the sinister characteristics needed for the villain.

In the northern, Protestant countries, the heroes of juvenile series meet a more positive stereotype. The Dutch, for instance, are generally portrayed as clean and efficient people whose sense of democracy and freedom is related to American values. Compared to the "filth and shiftlessness of the peasants in Ireland," Polly Brewster finds in the Netherlands only "spotless homes," "prim and pure" white-washed cottages, and in general a "vast difference in living" between the Dutch and the other Europeans.[63] Miss Pat, another series heroine, finds only friendly people and delightful streets in Dutch cities. She is moved, moreover, to comment: "See how placid and happy everything looks in the sunset. Everything is so permanent and so—conscientious."[64] In seeking causes for the radical differences between European societies, youthful readers are cautioned in one book that "it is not poverty alone that does this...one must go way back and seek deep for the causation of such conditions." One ancient difference, it is quickly learned, is the fact that the Pilgrims had actually lived in Holland before sailing for the New World.[65]

The British are the most favorably depicted foreigners in the juvenile series. Dating back to the nineteenth century when British writers like G. A. Henty and Bracebridge Hemyng strongly influenced series fiction, the kinship of England and the United States was forged in this literature. On occasion titles dramatically linked the two nationalities, as for instance in *With Lawton and Roberts, or a Boy's Adventures in the Philippines and the Transvaal.* The author of this volume prefaced the story with his hope that the book might help create "that closer union of Anglo-Saxon folk the world over—American, English, Canadian, Australian, or wherever the language of Shakespeare and that of Washington make all such nations kin."[66] Even when series fiction turned to the Revolutionary War in search of wartime settings, the writers tended to picture the British as honorable and decent types for, as one author phrased it, "Besides, were they not of the same blood?"[67]

Edward Stratemeyer, who was responsible for the bulk of series fiction in the twentieth century, was an Anglophile from the beginning of his career. In his early titles Englishmen were often heroes, or at least the rescuers of young American heroes overseas. In one book an English character defends civil rights, refuses to buckle before a Norwegian bully, and paternalistically admonishes an American hero, "Never let them walk over you. Old England every time, I say." This character confesses later that, "Well, next to being English, I'd prefer to be an American."[68]

As well as descriptions of beautiful countryside, elegant hotels, and general hospitality, the political and ethnic bond with America is emphasized when dealing with the English. In wartime series, young Americans fought alongside the British long before the United States government abandoned its neutrality. Thus fictional heroes like the Boy Allies in the First World War, and Red Randall, Lucky Terrell, and Dave Dawson in the Second World War, found themselves involved with the British cause even when the official American posture was non-involvement. Demonstrative of this spiritual and political commonness, series heroes give three cheers for the British navy,[69] join the Canadian Air Force in order to help defend England from the Nazis,[70] or even confide that, "I don't blame you for being proud that you're English, pal. . . so would I, if I wasn't Yank."[71]

In dealing with the Germans, series fiction faces an interesting quandary. Half-Catholic and half-Protestant, technologically advanced, efficient, and ultimately Anglo-Saxon, the Germans, nevertheless, were the enemy in the two world wars. This latter situation tends to diminish the value of whatever positive attributes the Germans demonstrate. In the First World War the Germans were usually pictured as brutally inhuman; in the Second World War they were portrayed as cunningly inhuman. Not much was done with the Germans in the years before 1914, but after World War I, Germans could not escape the stigma of being callow and mechanical people, barely qualifying as civilized. As mentioned above, even into the 1920's series books discussed Germans in light of the war. The Polly Brewster books in particular castigated the Germans for being self-centered and "bringing forth only the *material* emblems of brain and earthly power."[72] Five years after the war had ended this series was still integrating anti-German war stories into its otherwise formula books.[73]

ORIENTALS

The Orient does not present the strong differentiation that one encounters in the portrayal of European nationalities. For the most part, series literature has depicted the Oriental—whether Chinese, Japanese, or any other—in pejorative terms. Perhaps a general epitomization of attitudes toward Orientals is the remark elicited from one series heroine after an involvement with an Indian murderer:

> How I hate those hideous Eastern creatures! They go about spoiling the world for other people. They aren't fit to breathe the same air with decent people.... Oh, I loathe and abominate and abhor the East. Nasty, creeping, underhand, greedy *tigers*— that's what they are.[74]

Although stories have been set in the East Indies and Central Asia, most series attention and characterization is aimed at the Chinese and Japanese. Of the two, however, the Chinese have been more consistently and quantitatively the target of the prejudices. Although the Chinese do appear as a positive force in some of the anti-Japanese books from World War II, they have been generally distorted by series authors. As early as 1911 Edward Stratemeyer warned of the danger of being innundated by the "yellow race."[75] Since then, the Chinaman, Chink, "yellow-faced man" or whatever he was derisively called, has been more than a little abused. Typical of the traits ascribed to Chinese civilization are the "pigtails and powder" anticipated by Polly Brewster when she learns she is to visit China.[76] Chinese characters often are given awkward and ridiculous dialects, and then portrayed as stupid because American heroes cannot understand their speech.[77] They have been sketched as beasts of burden for, as one hero phrased it, "These coolies are just like horses; it's hard to realize that they are really human beings."[78] When crowds of Chinese surround visiting young Americans, the natives are called "ominous and evil looking" and impart to the heroes "only distrust for the yellow races."[79] Chinese homes are castigated for having a "vile odor"—more specifically, the scent of "opium smoke...mixed with smells of cooking."[80] And even when a Chinese is encountered within the United States, series fiction first calls attention to him as "a copper-colored man with slanting eyes," and notes, "Queer fellows, these Chinese. Always suspicious."[81]

Juvenile series fiction does recognize one positive feature in the stereotypic Chinese. Even when he is castigated and mocked, series writers credit him with being a good businessman. Thus, in many cases in steamy Oriental settings it is the Chinese who maintain the shops into which go the touring young American heroes. In an ironic manner the character in one book compliments the business acumen of the Chinese when he remarks:

You Chinese beat the world for doing business straight, taking
all risks and holding your tongues like so many clams. Pay a
Chinaman enough and he'll risk hanging or any other
unpleasant fate.[82]

The Japanese, interestingly, have not been consistently
denigrated in series books. Perhaps because of the late emergence of
Japan from its self-imposed isolation, or perhaps because of the
political and economic success of the Japanese until World War II,
juvenile fiction only mildly mocked the Japanese before the 1940's.
Certainly skin color and diminutive stature have been derisive
themes, but lacking is the vicious intent more associated with the
Chinese. One book credits the Japanese with great courteousness,
for "so courteous are the Japanese that they will sacrifice their own
convenience and pleasure to please strangers."[83] Another author
credits the Japanese with being excellent gardeners and for being
industrious and technologically-minded. But the same author
concludes that although Tokyo is a pleasant city, there are "many
queer things" about Japan. Nevertheless, this writer does pay to the
Japanese one of the highest forms of compliment in series fiction
when he calls them "the 'Yankees of the East.' "[84]

For half a century fictional American boys and girls ventured
into the world and encountered the rest of humanity. At home and
abroad these representatives of White middle-class American
civilization met foreigners and found them generally less educated,
speaking other languages, and going about their less-technological
business. Therefore, in most cases these American heroes found the
foreigner an inferior entity.

These young travellers were the epitome of patriotism and
honesty and strength. Like the young aviator Ted Scott, they were
"the young idol of the American people."[85] They were also like
Frank Sheldon of the Army Boys who was

A stalwart young American who had been born and reared in
Camport, a prosperous city of about twenty-five thousand
inhabitants. He was a bright, likeable fellow, a leader in athletic
sports and a general favorite. Above all, he was a hundred per
cent American...[86]

Wherever they went, the series heroes went like Uncle Sam's
Boys, as "representative here of American power, law and
dignity."[87] Thus, they could conclude with Dave Darrin that, "We do
not belong to ourselves but to the United States."[88] Above all, by
encountering relatively retarded forms of civilization, series heroes
help to reenforce the myths of American life. Epitomizing this

164

aspect of series prejudices, one book relates the routine life of Chinese living on junks, to that of globe-travelling wealthy Americans:

> "Don't use all your films for the shipping," advised Mr. Dalken. "You'll want to get a number of scenes along the streams we shall see, where the thousands of junks lie along shore; junks that are the only homes the owners know of; where they are born, live, and die, never dreaming of an outside world, and ways of living." "How awful that must be," remarked Mrs. Toller. "Think of the drab monotomy of such a life," sighed Polly. "Quite a contrast to the way we live, eh?" suggested Dodo.[89]

Historians, sociologists and political scientists have criticized Americans for maintaining for the rest of the world a disdain and distaste. Whether it is recognized in the political isolationism of the period 1919-1941, or whether one traces it back to the original motives in the foundation of the nation in the seventeenth century, the fact remains that the United States and the mainstream of its citizenry have had little experience outside the geographic confines of the nation. Although realities following World War II have tended to alter this situation, during most of the present century the heritage of isolation has been only augmented.

This study of juvenile series fiction in the period 1900-1945 confirms the picture of a detached and self-assured America. In terms of race consciousness, xenophobia, and general imperialistic attitudes, this literature propagated to generations of American youth the legacy of centuries. Today such literature is no longer produced. The few series that have survived are being reedited so as to remove prejudiced and denigrating terminology, and new titles avoid the old stereotypes altogether. Seemingly this development reflects a general shifting of values within the society, and hopefully children's series fiction in the future will impart to young readers ideas that are healthier and more idealistic.

NOTES

[1]Philip Jasper, *Uncle Sam's Navy Boys with the Marines; or Standing like a Rock at Chateau Thierry* (Chicago, 1919), p.7.

[2]H.Irving Hancock, *Dave Darrin and the German Submarines* (New York, 1919), p.181.

[3]Edward Stratemeyer, *Chased Across the Pampas, or American Boys in Argentine and Homeward Bound* (Boston, 1930), pp.1-2, 153.

[4]Edward L. Beach, *Ensign Ralph Osborn, The Story of His Trials and Triumphs in a Battleship's Engine Room* (Boston, 1911), p.266.

[5]Fenworth Moore, *Wrecked on Cannibal Island, or Jerry Ford's Adventures Among Savages* (New York, 1931), pp.104-105.

[6]R.Sidney Bowen, *Dave Dawson at Singapore* (New York, 1942), pp.196, 202.

[7]Frank Gee Patchin, *The Battleship Boys' First Step Upward, or Winning their Grades as Petty Officers* (New York, 1911), pp.101-102.

[8]*Ibid.,* p.162.

[9]Willard F. Baker, *The Boy Ranchers Among the Indians* (New York, 1934), p.102.

[10]H.Irving Hancock, *Uncle Sam's Boys on Their Mettle, or a Chance to Win Officers' Commissions* (Philadelphia, 1916), p.40.

[11]Bowen, pp.69, 89.

[12]Roy Rockwood, *Bomba the Jungle Boy Among the Slaves, or Daring Adventures in the Valley of Skulls* (New York, 1929), p.127.

[13]An interesting comparison of those using accents is provided by the German accent of Professor Dundlass who is an educated inventor in Clarence Young, *The Motor Boys in the Clouds, or A Trip for Fame and Fortune* (New York, ca. 1910), p.61; and the accent of the Chicago criminal underworld found in Roy J. Snell, *Triple Spies* (Chicago, 1920), pp.187-88.

[14]E.J. Craine, *Airplane Boys at Platinum River* (Cleveland, 1931), p.11.

[15]Lillian Elizabeth Roy, *Polly's Southern Cruise* (New York, 1923) pp.175, 266, 105.

[16]Roy, *Polly and Her Friends Abroad* (New York, 1922), pp.146, 106, 210.

[17]Anna Andrews, *Peggy and Michael of the Coffee Plantation* (New York, 1931), p.154.

[18]Bowen, p.202.

[19]Homer Randall, *Army Boys on German Soil, or our Doughboys Quelling the Mobs* (Cleveland, 1920), p.11.

[20]Howard Payson, *The Boy Scouts of the Eagle Patrol* (New York, 1911), p.89.

[21]Victor Appleton, *Tom Swift and His Chest of Secrets, or Tracing the Stolen Inventions* (New York, 1925), p.52.

[22]Ramy Allison White, *Sunny Boy on the Ocean* (New York, 1925), p.187.

[23]Wilbur Lawton, *The Boy Aviators in Nicaragua, or At War With the Insurgents* (New York, 1910), pp.68, 272, 277.

[24]Frank Stuart, *The Boy Scouts of the Air in the Lone Star Patrol* (New York, 1914), p.170.

[25]Franklin W. Dixon, *South of the Rio Grande* (New York, 1928), p.101; and *Across the Pacific* (New York, 1928), p.59.

[26]John Prentice Langley, *Masters of the Air-Lanes, or Round the World in Fourteen Days* (New York, 1928), p.59.

[27]Victor Appleton, *Don Sturdy in the Land of Giants, or Captives of the Savage Patagonians* (New York, 1930), pp.161-162.

[28]Dixon, *South of the Rio Grande,* p.110.

[29]James Foster, *Secret of the Andes* (New York, 1933), p.78.

[30]Warren H. Miller, *The Boy Explorers in Borneo* (New York, 1922), p.107.

[31]Jasper, pp.20, 192.

[32]John Blaine, *The Boy Scouts on a Submarine* (Chicago, 1918), p.196.

[33]Hancock, *Dave Darrin and the German Submarines,* p.223.

[34]George Durston, *The Boy Scouts to the Rescue* (Chicago, 1921), p.171.

[35]Jasper, p.144.

[36]Randall, p.85.

[37]Homer Randall, *Army Boys Marching into Germany, or Over the Rhine with the Stars and Stripes* (Cleveland, 1920), p.188.

[38]Clair W. Hayes, *The Boy Allies in Great Peril, or With the Italian Army in the Alps* (New York, 1916), p.124.

[39]Charles Amory Beach, *Air Service Boys Flying for Victory, or Bombing the Last German Stronghold* (Cleveland, 1920), p.97.

[40]Roy, *Polly and Her Friends Abroad*, p.182.

[41]R. Sidney Bowen, *Dave Dawson with the Pacific Fleet* (New York, 1942), p.237.

[42]Bowen, *Dave Dawson on Guadalcanal* (New York, 1943), p.40.

[43]Bowen, *Dave Dawson with the Flying Tigers* (New York, 1943), p.39.

[44]Bowen, *Dave Dawson at Singapore*, p.232.

[45]*Ibid.*, p.216.

[46]Victor Appleton, *Tom Swift and His Air Glider, or Seeking the Platinum Treasure* (New York, 1912), pp.19-20. The theme of an American hero being mistaken for a European anarchist is found also in Edward Stratemeyer, *Dave Porter in the Far North, or The Pluck of an American Schoolboy* (Boston, 1908).

[47]Appleton, *Tom Swift and His Chest of Secrets*, p.49.

[48]Langley, p.162.

[49]H.Irving Hancock, *Dave Darrin at Vera Cruz, or Fighting with the U.S. Navy in Mexico* (New York, 1914), p.61.

[50]Dixon, *South of the Rio Grande*, p.2.

[51]See Craine, *Airplane Boys at Platinum River*; Laura Lee Hope, *The Bobbsey Twins in Mexico* (New York, 1947); and Elizabeth Borton, *Pollyanna's Castle in Mexico* (New York, 1934).

[52]Stuart, pp.105, 53-55.

[53]G. Harvey Ralphson, *Boy Scouts in Mexico, or On Guard with Uncle Sam* (Chicago, 1911), pp.136-42.

[54]Noel Sainsbury, Jr., *Billy Smith—Mystery Ace, or Airplane Discoveries in South America* (New York, 1932), p.51.

[55]Victor Appleton, *Tom Swift in the Land of Wonders, or The Underground Search for the Idol of Gold* (New York, 1917), p.208.

[56]Lawton, p.75

[57]Andrews, pp.132-22.

[58]Roy Rockwood, *Under the Ocean to the South Pole, or The Strange Cruise of the Submarine Wonder* (New York, 1907), pp.139, 143.

[59]Stratemeyer, *Chased Across the Pampas*, p.240.

[60]*Ibid.*, pp.1-2.

[61]*Ibid.*, pp.80. An interesting variation of the theme of the Yellow Peril occurs when the Japanese are linked to plots with Mexicans to wage war on the United States; See Ralphson, pp.123-24, and Howard Payson, *The Boy Scouts and the Airship* (New York, ca. 1911), pp.70-71.

[62]Roy, *Polly's Southern Cruise*, p.105.

[63]Roy, *Polly and Her Friends Abroad*, pp.177, 106-07.

[64]Pemberton Ginther, *Miss Pat in the Old World* (Philadelphia, 1915), p.211.

[65]Roy, *Polly and Her Friends Abroad*, p.177.

[66]Elbridge S. Brooks, *With Lawton and Roberts, or A Boy's Adventures in the Philippines and the Transvaal* (Boston, 1900), p.vi.

[67]Frank Ralph, *The King's Messenger, or The Fall of Ticonderoga* (Philadelphia, 1904), p.211. For an example of British officers actually voting on the future of a captured Colonial spy, see Stephen Angus Cox, *The Dare Boys in Trenton* (New York, 1910), pp.85-89. An interesting contrast is the portrayal of British atrocities against Colonial soldiers as described in a book based largely upon historical reality: William P. Chipman, *The Boy Spies at Fort Griswold. The Story of the Part They Took in Its Brave Defense* (New York, 1900), pp.183-90.

[68]Stratemeyer, *Dave Porter in the Far North*, pp.177-78.

[69]E. L. Beach, *Ensign Ralph Osborn*, p.152.

[70]Canfield Cook, *Spitfire Pilot* (New York, 1942), pp.17-18.

[71]Bowen, *Dave Dawson at Guadalcanal*, p.53.

[72]Roy, *Polly and Her Friends Abroad*, pp.182-82 [my italics.]

[73]Roy, *Polly's Southern Cruise*, p.226ff.

[74]Ginther, p.149.
[75]See footnote No.59.
[76]Roy, *Polly in the Orient* (New York, 1927), p.201.
[77]Hancock, *Uncle Sam's Boys on Their Mettle,* pp.27-30.
[78]E.L. Beach, *Ensign Ralph Osborn,* p.152.
[79]Langley, pp.70, 183.
[80]Snell, p.12.
[81]Moore, pp.24, 26.
[82]Hancock, *Uncle Sam's Boys on Their Mettle,* p.33.
[83]Roy, Polly in the Orient, p.177.
[84]Langley, pp.42-44.
[85]Dixon, *South of the Rio Grande,* p.181.
[86]Randall, *Army Boys Marching into Germany,* p.17.
[87]Hancock, *Uncle Sam's Boys on Their Mettle.* p.13.
[88]Hancock, *Dave Darrin and the German Submarines,* p.252.
[89]Roy, *Polly in the Orient,* p.206.

Discussing " 'The Foreigner' in Juvenile Series Fiction, 1900-1945."

1) Investigate the stereotyped villains of superhero comic books, which are today's equivalent of juvenile series fiction. What similarities and differences are there between the comic book stereotypes and the stereotypes described by MacDonald?

2) At one time America was known as the "melting pot" where immigrants could lose their foreign heritage and become Americanized. Today, many ethnic groups in this country are proud of their heritage and struggle to preserve it. What factors account for this change in attitude?

3) Review some popular jokes you have heard lately that insult specific ethnic groups. Do these jokes reveal attitudes similar to those shown in earlier juvenile series fiction or are there other factors that cause the jokes to be told and enjoyed?

The Female Image in Speculative Fiction

By Deborah Weiser

I

Science fiction is often defined as that genre of literature that deals with what could be or fiction that speculates on the future. It is a relatively young genre, one that only now is becoming widely popular. The reason for its recent popularity is probably its growing tendency to cover a wider array of scientific fields. Much early-twentieth century sf dealt with the advent of technology and its influence on society. In the seventies, sf encompasses the "soft" science of psychology, cultural anthropology, communication.

Earlier in this century, sf was a man's domain. Written almost entirely by males, stories revolved around men and their battles with aliens/machines/technological destruction. The popular short stories were published in pulp magazines whose audiences were mostly male. Women writing sf often used male pseudonyms so that their stories would be accepted by readers and by editors. Even with some women writing in the field, strong female characters were rarely developed.

As early as 1957, critics noted this lack of women. One psychologist, Ednita Bernabeu, commented that sexuality is scarcely mentioned and women are conspicuously absent."[1] She believed that women were unnecessary in formulaic sf since reproduction could be carried on without them. Robots and androids were manufactured asexually, thereby proving that it was possible to maintain the population without women. Bernabeu felt that the male readers had "severely repressed their sexual desires"[2] and were reading sf for symbolic expression of these desires. Bernabeu saw spaceship lift-offs as a sort of birth that liberated men from dependence on women. The wish to leave the mother planet actually denoted the desire to escape from women into a world inhabited only by men. Both of these 'escapes' are futile since outer space (read 'vagina') is unattainable. Believing that sf is the "new mythology," Bernabeu was concerned about its readers' "regressive defenses."[3]

Beverly Friend divides sf into three categories centered around themes: gadgets, adventure, and social consequences. Friend believes that women in gadget and adventure sf are often androids and hostages, respectively. It is in the literature of social consequences that women characters are most often found. Examples will be taken from a random selection of sf.

First, there is woman as a gadget. The classic example of this is Lester del Rey's "Helen O'Loy." The only woman here is a robot who becomes influenced by the serials (soap operas) on the television. She takes on the stereotyped housewife role replete with worries, nagging, and hysteria. Finally, one of her designers finds he loves Helen and they marry. She is a perfect wife and, aided by cosmetics, "grows old" with her husband. This theme is still present in modern sf. In Ira Levin's *The Stepford Wives,* women are not only robots, but their human counterparts are murdered in order to keep society safe for men. The 'new' wives are physically perfect; their lives center around serving their husbands' every desire. The difference between del Rey's and Levin's stories demonstrate growth in sf. Helen O'Loy reflects society where a docile housewife was every man's dream. Levin's tale expresses the nightmare that could result when a stereotype is imposed without regard for human individuality.

Lest it be said that only male authors wish women were docile machines, look at Anne McCaffrey's "The Ship Who Sang." Here, the brain of a deformed woman is trained, then implanted in a spaceship. "She" then may choose the mobile half of her partnership, "a man or a woman, whichever she chose."[4] Helva's only choices are men, known colloquially as 'brawns.' She falls in love with her brawn and together they enjoy several space missions. At last, Helva's brawn dies in a catastrophe. She is heartbroken, can think of no other men, considers "going rogue." But going rogue means being alone and "it's exactly the thing we're conditioned against," Helva is told.

On occasion, to be quite fair, men are the gadgets. Joanna Russ writes of this in "An Old-Fashioned Girl." Her Davy is an end-product of cybernetics—"the Playboy Bunny with testicles."[5] Russ admits in her afterword that this idea is not original, but mere role reversal.

Women as gadgets, then, is the logical (?) theme in a world where women are looked upon as passive objects around which the important action of life occurs.

The female characters in adventure sf are also objects,

reflecting the traditional idea that men are the only people able to function in the outside world. An example of this would be any of Harry Harrison's Stainless Steel Rat stories.

An example of adventure sf with a female protagonist is Naomi Mitchison's *Memoirs of a Spacewoman*. The narrator's forte is the science of communication because it is "so essentially womanly. It fits one's basic sex patterns."[6] Women are taught to adapt to another way of thinking, the socially accepted male viewpoint. This makes communication an obligation of the woman: understand men because they rule the world. Mitchison's narrator's communication science is legitimized telepathy. Often, women characters in sf have capabilities that are traditionally associated with women, such as intuition or telepathy, which require no formal training or physical strength.

The narrator of *Memoirs* is preoccupied with romantic interests. Mingling with aliens, roaming the planets, she views every male as a possible father of her children. The males are quite willing to fulfill her desires, but are not interested in being stay-at-home fathers. More important tasks await them on other planets. The women must allay their adventurousness to the "natural" role of mother.

An sf suspense story using the double standard is Tom Godwin's "The Cold Equations." Here a stowaway is discovered to be a young girl who must be ejected into space since the ship carries a minimum of fuel. Over and over, the narrator bemoans the situation. Had the stowaway been a man, of course, he would have been ousted with relish. But a girl...

Falling back on stereotyped sex roles is not a failing found only in sf. Setting up a plot wherein the characters act as expected (by socialized human beings) makes it easier to work on other elements in the story. This leaves us, however, with one-dimensional, cardboard characters which may be the mark of a less imaginative writer. On the other hand, a writer may be trying to appeal to a wide audience. Then the stereotyped characters make a fantastic plot more recognizable, easier to grasp. Joe Haldeman's *The Forever War* is an example of this. A colonization/defense team composed equally of men and women battle their way across the universe. Even though both sexes fight together, individuals still are typed by sex. The women are the emotional ones, displaying jealousy, frivolity, flightiness. The men are sex-crazed bed-hoppers, making risque wisecracks to pass the time.

Staying clear of sexual stereotypes is a difficult task for many authors. Pamela Sargent blames this on cultural spillage. A writer is influenced by his or her own cultural environment. This influence shows up in the attitudes, moral codes and typed behavior of his/her fiction. The more inventive the writer, the less culturally bound will his/her works be.

The "New Wave" science fiction authors are credited with breaking away from these cultural bonds, exploring characters in futuristic situations that are more imaginative. These New Wave writers deal in "speculative fabulation," a more open genre than early technology-oriented science fiction. Some critics claim that the New Wave is no longer concerned with true sf. Isaac Asimov hopes that "when the New Wave has deposited its froth and receded, the vast and solid shore of *science fiction* will appear once more."[7] This would be unfortunate for sf. It would remain a narrow literature, confined to formulaic elements. The growth and extrapolation of the New Wave opens the genre to more imaginative stories and, consequently, to a wider audience.

Kate Wilhelm's *Where Late The Sweet Birds Sang* is a fine example of visionary sf. This post-holocaust novel describes the last bastion of human civilization. All the men have become sterile, and perpetuation of mankind depends on parthenogenesis. The clones are re-cloned again and again. Parties of explorers are sent to unearth useful remains from the demolished cities. These explorers, attached mentally to their clone groups, are unable to function when separated from home base. They have become emotionally sterile. By chance, one child is sexually reproduced.

His mother is an outcast because she has a distinct personality that disturbs her clone sisters. The child, Mark, leaves the sheltered complex because he cannot cope with the sterility of the clones. He, along with several fertile women, begin repopulating the earth which has recovered from its sterility caused by the ecological disaster.

Wilhelm starts with conventional elements of sf: the end of the world, parthenogenesis and hoarded technology as the last hope of a dying earth. However, her imagination leads her beyond formula. Her characters are real people with wide ranges of emotions and reactions. The clones are carbon copies of their "parents" and their creativity declines with each successive generation. The individuals, the saviors of civilization, are not limited characters. The novel warns against an over-reliance on technology. Scientific knowledge alone will not save the world. Mankind must retain its independence and spirit so that humanity, not just people, will be preserved.

This is the direction sf should take: true speculation on the future of both technology *and* humanity.

II

Stories and novels are not the only forms of sf. The genre

functions in other media. One medium that may never outgrow its sexual stereotypes is the superhero comic book. Here supermen and not-so-superwomen battle the forces of evil. Many times the women seem to be merely plot devices. Superwomen are hostages, a bargaining lever to be used by the villains.[9]

Women superheroes are invariably defined in terms of their men. Medusa and Crystal, sister superheroes, are good examples. When first introduced to the comic's audience, Medusa's biography tells us that her heart belongs to "the brooding Black Bolt."[10] Crystal can influence fire, water, and air "just as she has already influenced the heart of Johnny Storm,"[11] the Human Torch of the Fantastic Four. Male superheroes rarely have time for their women, however.

Even when women are involved in crime-fighting with the men, they are given tasks fit for a woman. When the men of the Justice League of America bring an old-time villain out of suspended animation, black Canary, the only woman, redesigns his costume. The men handle the real work of rewiring circuits and activating the electronic brain.[12]

While most male superheroes are physically strong, women superheroes have more typically feminine powers. Saturn Woman is a mind reader—glorified intuition. Crystal has powers over fire, water, and air, like Mother Nature.

It seems the readers of superhero comics like the femininity of superwoman. This audience is generally younger than the readers of short stories and novels, however. It should be possible, then, to present women in less stereotyped roles since the readers should have fewer preconceived ideas. Black Orchid was an atypical superwoman. She vanquished men relentlessly, particularly savoring the deflation of egotistical chauvinists. After three issues, Black Orchid was phased out of the DC Adventure line. Too much independence isn't good for a superwoman.

Superhero comic books are much like old wave sf. Women are beautiful, but mostly kept in their place. Readers must look to very recent sf for an upgrading of women's images. This is a reflection of the increasing attention given to the women's movement by society in general.

Once again, I would emphasize that sf is not the only genre guilty of sexual stereotyping. However, it is the best hope for the liberation of ideas. Nearly every other form of fiction is set in the past or the present. Sf is forward-looking, by definition a literature that extrapolates about the future. As it becomes more popular, sf will influence a larger audience. So that society can break from narrow cultural biases, the popular audience must have new visions on which to model their tomorrows. Sf, speculative fabulation beyond science fiction, will provide these new visions.

NOTES

[1]"Science Fiction" in *Psychoanalytic Quarterly*, Oct. 1957, pp.527-535.

[2]Ibid.

[3]Ibid.

[4]McCaffrey in "The Ship Who Sang" in *Women of Wonder*, Pamela Sargent, ed.

[5]Russ in her afterword to "An Old-Fashioned Girl" in *Final Stage*, Ferman and Malzberg, eds.

[6]Mitchison in *Memoirs of a Spacewoman*, p.16.

[7]Quoted in a review of Judith Merril's works by Theodore Sturgeon, in *National Review*, 18 Nov. 1969, p.1174.

[8]See *Justice League of America*, June 1969 (DC Comics), or *Legion of Superheroes*, #3, 1976 (DC Comics), or *Collector's Item*, #3, 1966 (Marvel Comics).

[9]*Collector's Item*, #3, 1966 (Marvel Comics).

[10]Ibid.

[11]*Justice League of America*, #112, 1974 (DC Comics).

Discussing "The Female Image in Speculative Fiction"

1) Review the women characters in recent science fiction films and TV shows. Are Weiser's conclusions about women in science fiction literature also true about women in these other media?

2) Read Joanna Russ' "Someone's Trying to Kill Me..." How different are the women characters in gothic romances from the women in science fiction? Why?

3) What other stereotypes are common in science fiction? What do these suggest about the status of these stereotyped figures in American culture?

PART FOUR
POPULAR HEROES

Introduction

Popular heroes, whether real or imaginary, are people who represent for the members of a culture the ideals of that culture. They are human icons representing as individuals the best person a culture is capable of producing. Odysseus, with his combination of great physical strength and cunning wits thus represents the ideal human qualities revered by the ancient Greeks. The first legendary American hero was Daniel Boone, who came to represent virtues of which Americans were particularly fond: skills in the wild, bravery, and a strong commitment to assist in the civilizing of a new land. Such heroes as Odysseus and Boone provide a valuable function for the other, less talented members of a culture. First, they provide us with concrete images of what we all can strive to become. They stand and beckon to us from the pinnacles of the mountain we all try to climb. Second, heroes represent a perfected member of a culture that is a source of pride to that culture because it is the culture itself that has produced such perfection.

There are great differences in the qualities that grace heroes from different cultures but three main conditions must be present for a person to gain true heroic status. The first condition is that the person must be exceptionally gifted in some way. Professional athletes, for example, have become heroes in the twentieth century because we can read about and witness their extraordinary physical skills. T.V. sets all over the country were tuned to Henry Aaron as he belted the homer that beat Ruth's record and within a few minutes Aaron had become a national hero. O.J. Simpson became an athlete-hero not only because he was the first pro football player to rush for over 2000 yards but also because we could watch his amazing feats over and over again in video-taped slow motion replays. Other heroes display non-athletic gifts. Charles Lindburgh was a skilled pilot. Robert E. Lee was a great military strategist. Thomas Edison was a great inventor.

American heroes George Washington and Abraham Lincoln illustrate the second necessary condition for heroic status—the hero must possess qualities the culture highly values. Historically, George Washington seems to have been a man with gifts as a military and political strategist. What we remember most affectionately about Washington, however, are two other qualities, both of them immortalized through legends. The famous telling of the truth after little George chopped down his father's cherry tree never happened. But it illustrates a prized American quality, telling the truth. Since Americans prize individualism as a virtue, it has always been our belief that a person should have nothing to hide. Therefore, George's telling the truth testifies to his dignity as an individual. The other legendary event, the terrible winter at Valley Forge, exemplifies the American virtue of perseverance, of sticking to something no matter how hard until the job is done. (This of course links Washington to a major American myth already discussed—the myth of success.) Lincoln, as his nickname "Honest Abe" clearly shows, is also admired as a teller of the truth. Another Lincoln nickname, "The Great Heart" illustrates another admired American quality Lincoln is said to have in great measure—compassion for the unfortunate. Just as we applaud a Horatio Alger boy who gives his last nickel to a starving chum, Lincoln is still praised for his plans to gently welcome back the South into the Union.

The third necessity for the true popular hero is his duty to the culture itself. Heroes must be defenders of their culture; they must put their gifts and qualities to work so the culture is preserved and made prosperous. It is the third necessity that has made the soldier such a popular hero type throughout history. England has its St. George, France its Joan of Arc and South America its Simon Bolivar. In the United States, men like Washington, Andrew Jackson, Teddy Roosevelt, and Dwight Eisenhower have attained heroic status through military feats and have used this status as springboards to the presidency. It is of some interest to note that the last two American wars in Korea and Viet Nam have produced no heroes. In earlier wars Americans felt their way of life was directly threatened or their quest for territory justifiable. Military heroes naturally resulted because it was clear that soldiers were either protecting or spreading the American way of life. Asia, on the other hand, is so far away and the ideological basis for fighting in Korea and Viet Nam was so ambiguous that the military connection with preservation of prosperity was ambiguous. The resultant mixed feelings about these wars created a national mood unreceptive to soldier heroes.

F.R. Lloyd in "The Home Run King" discusses the gifts and qualities that made Babe Ruth a hero for millions, especially during the 1920's. Just as important is Lloyd's description of how Ruth's growth to heroism fits Orrin Klapp's very well known pattern of how heroes come to be. According to Klapp there is a five part process:

1. Spontaneous popular homage
2. Formal recognition and honor
3. Gradual formulation of a legend
4. Formal commemoration of the hero
5. An established cult to preserve the legend and fame of the hero

Our description of the popular hero so far has focused on what can be termed the "traditional" hero. A number of cultural analysts, as Pam Ecker points out in her essay on Farrah Fawcett-Majors, have been concluding lately that in fact there aren't very many traditional heroes anymore. One reason for this has been a trend in recent historical studies to critically re-examine traditional historical interpretations. The result has been the discovery that many of our past heroes had all-too-human faults. Another reason is the emergence of psychology as a major influence on modern thought. Freudian psychology, for instance, hints that some heroic action may actually be symptomatic of certain neuroses. Behaviorial psychologists might argue that all action, heroic or otherwise, is no more than learned responses to specific stimuli. At any rate, as we seem to grow more and more disillusioned with traditional heroes, two other types of heroes are becoming more and more common.

The first type of alternative hero, the rebel hero, is shown by Al-Tony Gilmore in his article on the life of heavyweight boxing champion Jack Johnson. According to an article by Anthony Hopkins, "Contemporary Heroism — Vitality in Defeat," rebel heroes are not heroic because they defend the dominant culture but because they oppose it. Because they are against the mainstream culture, the very act of rebellion becomes a quality admired by certain cultural sub-groups who are also in rebellion against the majority. Also, rebel heroes may or may not possess remarkable talents, but they are most notable for possessing a great zest for living. Outlaws since at least the time of Robin Hood have been popular rebel heroes. In America Jesse James, Billy the Kid, John

Dillinger, and Bonnie and Clyde all are popular outlaw heroes. Gilmore's discussion of Jack Johnson reveals a man of vital appetites rebelling against a racist white society but loved within the black sub-culture. Rebel heroes are especially interesting to cultural analysts because knowing about them provides clues about conflicts within a culture. Rebels usually represent certain resentments against mainstream culture which because of fears of reprisal, sub-cultures might be reluctant to otherwise articulate.

Farrah Fawcett-Majors, as pictured in Pam Ecker's irreverent personal essay, is the very essence of a second type of alternative hero, the celebrity. Celebrities, as Ecker shows, neither represent nor rebel. All they do to be "heroic" is become and remain famous. Jackie Kennedy Onassis, Patty Hearst, and Johnny Carson are other notable examples. The fact that pure celebrities seem to be getting more and more attention is indicative of the immense impact the mass media has on life in the twentieth century and hints at the cynicism that most people currently seem to feel about the possibilities of real heroism.

If real heroes exist at all these days they tend to exist in fictional forms rather than in real life. Perhaps people can more easily appreciate and identify with heroes if they know ahead of time that the heroes are merely fantasies. Spider-Man is the most popular comic book super-hero to emerge during the 1960's.

Salvatore Mondello in "Spider-Man: Superhero in the Liberal Tradition" demonstrates how Spidey was such a perfect heroic representation of the 60's era. In addition it might be noted that Spider-Man, along with the other costumed crusaders of the comics such as Superman, Captain Marvel, and Wonder Woman all have plain-folks alternate identities. Reading these comics calls forth the belief in perfectability discussed in the general introduction. Just beneath the drab clothes of the ordinary looking citizen is a wonderful costume and a hero whose powers are perfect beyond the possibilities of normal human hope. The chart below provides a quick comparison between the three types of heroes. In doing your own analysis of the significance of a specific hero the chart may act as a guide for asking yourself helpful questions about the hero. What are his-her gifts? Why is he-she famous? What sub-groups admire this rebel hero? The questions will change with each hero. But, as usual, the answers will offer hints as to what is on the collective minds of us all.

Traditional Heroes	The Rebel Hero	The Celebrity
1. Exceptionally Gifted in some way	1. Often gifted but mainly characterized by a great VITALITY for life.	1. Nothing beyond very minor gifts. (Fame results only from being well known)
2. Epitomizes cultural values	2. Epitomizes the values at best of only a cultural sub-group. Mostly he/she epitomizes the idea of individualism against conformity.	2. Represents certain immediate cultural interests
3. A defender of the culture	3. A rebel *against* the dominant culture	3. Neither a notable defender/nor rebel usually. Mostly the celebrity is just there

DEVELOPMENT	DEVELOPMENT	DEVELOPMENT
1. Spontaneous popular homage	1. Spontaneous homage (not necessarily on a large scale)	1. Formal recognition (Person is known ONLY thru the media)
2. Formal recognition and honor	2. Formal recognition (In the media it's often of an uncomplimentary nature)	2. The establishment of a cult (Which usually lasts only as long as the personality is receiving media exposure)
3. The building up of a "legend"	3. The building of a legend	
4. Commemoration of the hero	4. An established cult (Especially important for rebel heroes)!!!	
5. An established cult (especially for dead heroes . . . and most especially for dead YOUNG heroes)		

Selected Further Reading

1) Boorstin, Daniel J. *The Image: A Guide to Pseudo-Events in America*. New York: Harper and Row, 1964.

2.) Browne, Ray B., Marshall Fishwick and Michael T. Marsden, eds. *Heroes of Popular Culture*. Bowling Green, Ohio: Popular Press, 1972. An anthology of essays on popular heroes from music, athletics, television, literature, etc.

3) Campbell, Joseph. *The Hero With a Thousand Faces*. Meridian Books: New York, 1949. An analysis of the elements shared in common by popular heroes in all cultures.

4) Fishwick, Marshall. *The Hero: American Style*. Van Rees Press: New York. 1969.

5) Klapp, Orrin E. "Hero Worship in America." *American Sociological Review,* XIV February, 1949., p.53-62.

6) Monaco, James. *Celebrity: The Media as Image Makers*. New York: Dell Publishing Co., 1978.

7) Wecter, Dixon. *The Hero in America*. New York, Charles Scribner's Sons: 1941.

The Home Run King

By F. R. Lloyd

On a warm midsummer afternoon in 1926 a billikin-faced baseball player approached home plate in Yankee Stadium with a curiously mincing stride. He stepped into the batter's box, selected a pitch, and hit the ball out of the park. His blow reverberated halfway across the continent, breathing life into a group of fans clustered about a newspaper scoreboard in Omaha. "'Twas an attentive but undemonstrative mob," the *Literary Digest* reported,

> sufficiently interested, as by ingrained habit, but on the whole silent, expectant, waiting to be shown. Suddenly a shout—a swelling, spreading, roaring tidal wave of delight. The mob had awakened. The released life force flashes in its eyes, thunders in its composite voice. What has come to pass a thousand miles away, to work such a miracle in Omaha, and doubtless in many another place from ocean to ocean? Behold the answer on the scoreboard—Babe Ruth has hit another home run. Wow! The sun shines brighter, "God's in his heaven: all's right with the world."[1]

To this Omaha crowd and to many others, Ruth's home runs were dramatic events which made him the object of the kind of public hero-worship Orrin Klapp described ("Hero-Worship in America," *American Sociological Review,* XIV (February 1949), 53-62). Ruth was a celebrity; he was the object of spontaneous adulation; he was accorded more formal honors; legends grew about his life and

From the *Journal of Popular Culture,* 1975, 9(4), 983-995. Reprinted by permission of the editor.

career, and he was commemorated as a hero after death. This public behavior indicates the esteem in which many people held Ruth and the record numbers of home runs he hit. During the period of his greatest popularity, however, Ruth was esteemed as more than a home run hitter. Ruth's home runs, to judge from expressions in the popular press, could have been evaluated as sources of wealth and celebrity, for their cathartic regenerative effects on the game of baseball and its fans, and for their apparent affirmation of qualities like strength, self-sufficiency, gallantry and even destructiveness. These diverse associations are unified, however, by a largely amoral uniqueness and superiority. These qualities, moreover, extended from Ruth's home runs to his person. Thus, during the period 1919-1935, Babe Ruth was esteemed as the Home Run King, the unique superior individual, as well as the hitter of home runs.

Prior to his sale to the Yankees in 1920, Ruth was well-known among baseball fans, "the unquestioned star of the best team in baseball."[2] Ruth then performed deeds which raised him suddenly to national prominence. He hit home runs in record numbers. In 1919, with Boston, he hit twenty-nine home runs to break the record of twenty-seven set in 1884. Robert Creamer shows that these home runs "made him a national sensation."[3] The next year, with the Yankees, Ruth hit fifty-four, and in 1921 he hit fifty-nine to set a record for the third consecutive year. He broke these records in 1927 when he hit sixty homers. F.C. Lane, often critical of Ruth for making Ty Cobb's aggressive intellectual style of play obsolete, admitted that Ruth's 1920 achievement was unprecedented: "Babe stalked the baseball horizon literally as a superman. He had smashed all precedents, upset all accepted standards, and stood forth as the prodigy of the diamond."[4] Ruth's home run totals were not only enormous in contrast with previous records, they were monumental relative to his contemporaries. On August 28, 1927, for instance, when Ruth had forty-one homers and Lou Gehrig had forty, the next best American League slugger had but sixteen, and the top National Leaguer had twenty-three. Even Gehrig, from 1925, his first full year in the league, was but a lesser Ruth. The Babe hit nineteen home runs in September 1927; Gehrig managed but seven. Gehrig also lacked Ruth's dramatic timing. He followed Ruth's "called-shot" blow with a home run of his own, and he hit four home runs in one game the same day John McGraw retired as manager of the Giants.

Ruth's home runs were regarded as dramatic events. A "highbrow critic" admitted that although it is hard for an individual to appear glamorous on a baseball field, Ruth is

personally, and quite irresistibly compelling and dramatic.

> Ruth came to bat. There was a man or two on base and the score
> was close. At first there was a throaty cheer from the multitude,
> but after a moment, as he stood there motionless at the plate, his
> bat poised at his shoulder, a dead hush fell. The air seemed to
> tighten, as if under some pressure which threatened to release
> itself in a moment with a terrific explosion. The outfielders
> drifted casually back against the fences. The pitcher glanced
> around to see that all was well. Even the peanut vendors paused
> in their shouting and turned to watch.[5]

This quality of tense anticipation even made Ruth's strike outs
dramatic. As Bozeman Bulger wrote, "There is something of drama
in the way he strikes out. It only adds to the thrill of the next home
run... For Ruth, the stage seems always set, and he, consciously
or unconsciously, enacts the star part."[6]

People flocked in record numbers to witness these dramatic
events. Before Ruth came to the Yankees, "Olympian heights" of
attendance were considered one million spectators. In 1927, the
Yankees played to 2,220,200 fans—1,200,000 at home.[7] Yankee
attendance in 1920 was 1,289,422, double the 1919 figure (619,164).[8]
Gate receipts were so high that Ruth commanded princely salaries,
and he spectacularly indulged his legendary tastes in food, clothes,
cars, and women. In 1921, Ruth made $20,000 per year. In 1922 his
salary was raised to $52,000. His pay jumped again in 1927 to
$70,000 and finally to $80,000 in 1930.

Ruth was also the object of the kind of hero-worship Klapp
describes. He was famous, a celebrity. Details about his personal life
were painstakingly reported in the public press. Public concern for
Ruth's physique, for example, was a vernal rite. The New York
Times weighed and measured Ruth and published his special diet.[9]
The paper indulged in hyperbolic rejoicing when it was apparent
that one of Ruth's "startling" rejuvenations was complete:

> Bounding youthfully two steps at a time, the Babe ascended the
> stairway to the Yankee office...and rushed into the presence of
> Edward Grant Barrow...[who] desired to see for himself if it
> were true that George Herman had shoulders like Atlas, biceps
> like Thor, a chest like Hercules and a waist of which Archilles
> would not have been ashamed....Contrast this picture with the
> vivid memory of that day last April when Ruth, a few minutes
> after he had fainted and brought his head into smart contact
> with the floor of a Pullman car, was lifted on a stretcher through
> the car window and bundled off to the hospital. Contrast this
> picture also with that of the portly but feeble individual who
> could barely carry his own weight at the Yankee Stadium in
> June and July.[10]

Babe Ruth

Ruth's celebrity made it possible for him to endorse products, like a candy bar, and other people, like Al Smith, for whom Ruth campaigned in 1928. " 'Governor Smith,' " Ruth claimed, " 'is the type of man who appeals not only to the baseball fan, but to all red-blooded lovers of American sport.' " Babe did not " 'know anything about tariffs and those kinds of things,' " but voting was a pocketbook issue, and Smith's " 'friendship for baseball' " made big crowds and large salaries possible. Ruth also praised Smith for rising from humble beginnings to the top of his chosen profession, just as the Babe had risen from the Baltimore waterfront.[11] Even though he endorsed Smith, Ruth did not vote for the first time until 1944.[12]

People not only gained access to Ruth through reportage and trusted his judgment, they flocked to his magic presence off the diamond to offer him spontaneous homage, often involving feelings of familiarity and possessiveness. Babe Ruth's stalled car, for example, once attracted 1500 people. The ensuing traffic jam was unsnarled only when Ruth distributed bats and balls left in his car from a visit to an orphanage.[13] In 1929 one hundred fifty uninvited people gathered at six-thirty on a rainy April morning to glimpse Ruth at his wedding ceremony. Most "crowded around to touch the national hero, and to cry 'Good Luck!' " Ten or twelve boys crowded at the altar rail, and the altar boys were presented with autographed baseballs.[14] Ruth often tried to dodge such attention, but he was known to "secretly" revel when fame found him. The New York Times reported that he would quit cards, arguments, his saxophone or anything to make an impromptu public appearance, but his brief remarks usually consisted of something like, " 'Why don't you folks go to bed? Don't you ever sleep around here?' "[15]

In addition to this kind of renown and spontaneous homage, Ruth was accorded more formal recognition, and he was commemorated. He was made an Elk and selected for such honors as touring the Boston jail and greeting the Queen of Rumania. He was enshrined in Baseball's Hall of Fame, and a monument to him stands in center field in Yankee Stadium. This monument is being preserved in the plans for remodeling the stadium.

Legends also formed about Ruth's life, especially its little-known aspects. Returning from spring training in 1925, Ruth mysteriously was taken ill in Asheville, North Carolina. As noted in the Times above, he had fainted in a Pullman car, and he was weak and ineffectual for most of the season. Legend has it that he suffered a monumental stomach ache from eating twelve hot dogs, a quart of orange soda, and an apple before an exhibition game. After his recovery, he could not regain proper condition in midseason.[16] Ruth's teammate and companion, Joe Dugan, confided to Roger

Kahn, however, that his "bellyache heard round the world" " 'was something a little bit lower.' "[17]

The "called-shot" home run Ruth hit in the 1932 World Series is one of the most famous instances of this kind of legend formation. Mark Koenig, a former Yankee star ending his career with the Cubs, had been denied a World Series share by the Chicago club. This led to ill-feeling between the two teams and precipitated much verbal abuse. During one game, Ruth was being ridden especially hard by the Cub bench and most of all by Guy Bush, the next day's pitcher. At one time at bat Ruth raised a finger on his right hand for each strike and a finger on his left for each ball. When the count reached one ball and two strikes, Ruth pointed out towards the field and hit the next pitch out of the ball park. He circled the bases laughing and gesticulating. Legend has it that he "called the shot" in order to quiet the boisterous opposition and their fans and that he circled the bases flapping his arms in imitation of the ball. Charlie Root, the pitcher, and Charlie Grimm, Cub first baseman, deny that Ruth called his shot. Grimm believes Ruth was pointing to the mound where Bush would be the next day. Root and Grimm further contend the pitch Ruth hit was a change-up, and that Root would never have offered Ruth such a fat pitch had he in fact called the shot. Nevertheless, the umpire, the next Yankee batter (Lou Gehrig), and four houndred sportswriters seem to have regarded the home run as called. Ruth himself apparently never clarified the point.[18] When Ford Frick asked Ruth if he really pointed to the stands, Ruth cryptically relplied, " 'Why don't you read the papers? It's all right there in the papers.' "[19]

This behavior characteristic of hero-worship—spontaneous homage, formal recognition, commemoration, and legend formation—indicates that Ruth and his home runs were valued. Many may have admired the wealth and celebrity home runs brought Ruth. Perhaps surprisingly, though, many seemed less certain as to the value of these material rewards. "If you crave a monument to his deeds," the New York *Evening World* admonished, perhaps sarcastically,

> go up to the Harlem River, stand on its banks, and gaze at that mammoth structure known as the Yankee Stadium. In the golden hush of sunset, when the tumult and the shouting have died, it has the austere dignity of a national bank, and for the same reason. Money speaks there in the low modulated voice that is more eloquent than the shouts of a mob storming the Bastille.
>
> Home runs built it. This is no mere record about to be marked up in perishable chalk. It is the middle of an epoch.[20]

Ruth and his home runs also were identified widely as the authors of a profound change in the offensive philosophy of the game of baseball, and this change was evaluated positively as a kind of regenerative force. The popularization of this change brought baseball back to "public favor" after the Black Sox scandal broke in 1920.[21] Ruth's home runs were credited with lifting baseball from this nadir because they were thrilling. Albert Britt, for example, wrote that Ruth "has brought a vivid personality and a thrill into a sport that sometimes threatens to become a dull and drab commercial affair. To see him set his monumental legs at the plate and wing into a fast one with a resultant white streak going over the fence brings a sensation worth going many miles to feel."[22] This sensation was the kind of *"katharsis"* described by a writer for *The Weekly Review:*

> let no one suppose that baseball is a game. It is a symbol; and the home run is its perfect expression, its pearl, whole, unique, finished. No such *katharsis* anywhere as your home run; it clears the passions as it clears the bases. Purged and refreshed, life is for the moment radiantly conscious of itself. In a world of tentatives, of frustrations, of mis-directions, it is the one thing complete and satisfying, transmuting the raw materials of life into the perfect product and leaving nothing at loose ends.[23]

The effect of this *"katharsis"* was liberating, exalting, and moral as baseball could transform 55,000 people "from money-grubbing human animals, with bills to meet and bosses to please, into a holiday throng, with laughter in their voices and contentment in their eyes,"[24] or, in the words of the New York *Times*, "its influence is beneficent. It makes sound and vigorous men."[25] Ruth's feats, then, were believed to have tonic effects for baseball because they had tonic effects for the fans.

This restorative quality was extended to Ruth's off-field presence. Ruth was given to youth as a moral counsellor. He gave speeches warning of the dangers of smoking and of straining one's eyes in artificial light. He exhorted boys to work and study hard in order to get to the top.[26] He was also a source of regenerative power. The stories of sick children healed by Ruth are legion: a paralyzed boy sat up to cheer Ruth in Tampa;[27] Ruth roused a country boy from delirium by travelling twelve miles from Vicksburg one rainy night;[28] a scalded three-year old cried feebly, "Where's Babe?" as the slugger passed on a visit to a ward of children injured in a panic at Yankee Stadium.[29] The most famous of these cases is that of Johnny Sylvester, homer-hitting juvenile third baseman. Johnny was seriously ill, perhaps near death, some say with a sinus infection, others with blood poisoning. The boy's father, a New York banking executive, contacted Ruth in St. Louis during the 1926 World Series and arranged for Babe to send Johnny autographed baseballs. Ruth also promised to hit a home run for Johnny, and he hit three—a record. Ruth later paid Johnny a dramatic visit to which the boy's recovery was credited. An account of the confrontation was syndicated by Universal News Service:

> Just as natural and casual as if he were mortal, Babe Ruth popped into the little second story room where 11 year old Johnny Sylvester was getting the edge in a fight with death today and seemingly turned death's retreat into a rout...[Johnny's] hand was tingling from a grip that beneficent Providence designed to fit just at the small end of a ball bat, and his ears heard a voice from Olympus.[30]

Truly Ruth could assure people, "God's in his heaven: all's right with the world."

Not everyone regarded Ruth's alteration of the game so positively. Some, like F.C. Lane, believed the "revolutionary change in the game"[31] wrought by Ruth's home runs to be a deplorable corruption rather than a thrilling tonic.[32] In 1922, for example, a writer for *The Sporting News* described Ruth as

> a third-rate outfielder. As a baserunner he is in a class by himself. I'm not complimenting him, either.
>
> As a batter, Ruth is an accident. He never plays inside baseball at the plate. He goes up trying to take a swing on every strike, a style that would cause any other player to be benched. He either knocks home runs or strikes out. Any man who strikes out as many times as Ruth did last year can never be classed as a great hitter.[33]

After Ruth had been held to a .118 batting average by the New York Giants' pitching staff in the 1922 World Series, Joe Vila, a New York baseball writer since before the turn of the century, wrote, " 'The exploded phenomenon didn't surprise the smart fans who long ago realized he couldn't hit brainy pitching. Ruth, therefore, is no longer a wonder. The baseball public is onto his worth as a batsman and in the future, let us hope, he will attract just ordinary attention.' "[34] As Vila indicates, this view is that of a kind of cognoscente, a group of insiders who know baseball far better than the casual fan or member of the general public. It seems to be, therefore, a minority view. Vila himself changed his opinion of Ruth by 1935. At that time Vila wrote, " 'Ruth became the greatest ball player the game has ever known, a player beside whom the other great players—and this goes for Cobb and Speaker and all the rest—were as little boys playing with a man.' "[35]

Ruth and his home runs could have been evaluated at least as restorative forces or as corrupting agents. The latter seems to have been a minority view. The interpretation of Ruth and his home runs as regenerative forces could have been valued positively for several reasons. Roderick Nash believes people became aware of the "transforming effects of population growth, urbanization, and economic change"[36] during the height of Ruth's career. These transformations were believed to threaten time-tested valued concepts associated with the frontier: "courage, strength, and honor and...the efficacy of the self-reliant, rugged individual."[37] Ruth's deeds, to Nash, could restore faith in these ideas, for in sports arenas, as on the frontier, men confronted and overcame tangible obstacles "with talent and determination."[38] Leverett Smith argues that Ruth's regenerative power could have been evaluated in terms of concepts other than those associated with the frontier. Smith notes that baseball changed its public image between 1919 and 1922 to preserve its economic structure. As a result of the Black Sox scandal, baseball's understanding of its relation to society became that of a moral example; its political community became authoritarian and hierarchical, and, thanks to Ruth, the style of play changed to slugging. Consequently, Smith contends, baseball came to be associated with authoritarian concepts. Ruth, the hero of this transformation, was the ideal citizen of the structured authoritarian community. He was a hard worker but not a shrewd opportunist. He was instinctual and child-like, and he was motivated by love of the game.[39]

The imagery associated with Ruth in the press suggests, however, that Ruth and his deeds were most likely valued as affirming a concept more appropriate for a frontiersman than for a citizen of an authoritarian community: the unique superior individual. Ruth was sometimes linked with these concepts by frontier imagery. When pitchers faced Ruth "they felt like the coon did when he saw Davy Crockett point his rifle,"[40] because he possessed the strength to wield "that big wagon tongue bat."[41] Ruth was necessarily self-sufficient because he was unique, the pioneer in the vanguard. He "long ago blazed a trail into an unexplored territory of herculean feats...Babe Ruth, the pioneer, the worker of miracles, has left all competitors far behind."[42] He was also dependable "Old 'Wagon Wheels'—Still Rollin' Home."[43] Frontier imagery also attributed destructive strength to Ruth. In spite of the strength, self-sufficiency, and dependability the frontier connected with Ruth, he was "George Herman Ruth...on the warpath...about ready to rush down the dusty trail, swinging his trusty tomahawk at every head..."[44] This destructiveness accompanied other positively valued concepts suggested by additional important images associated with Ruth.

Ruth was also linked to the concept of the unique superior individual by images appropriate to technological progress. The New York *Evening World,* again perhaps sarcastically, asserted Babe Ruth's five hundredth home run should

> be bracketed with our skyscrapers, our universities, our millions of automobiles, as a symbol of American greatness. Bells should have rung when this thing came to pass, and firecrackers set off, and traffic halted for one minute throughout the length and breadth of the land; in addition, Mr. Ruth should have had his picture taken with Thomas Edison, Harvey Firestone, Charles A. Lindbergh, and Henry Ford. Is he not as eminent as they?[45]

Ruth persevered at his specialty until, as the Des Moines *Register* explained, "he succeeded...with a completeness that delighted a people to whom specialization has become a religion. He was an orphan boy who made good, a tradition that is taught in all our schools."[46] He was dependable and efficient, a "great machine,"[47] whose skills were reduced to mechanical components: "a heavy bat that can still be swung quickly, hitting the ball at approximately 45° off the bat, a fair horizontal angle, strong arms, quick eyes and reflexes."[48] If these elements seemed obvious to even a non-scientific observer,[49] Professor A.L. Hodges concluded that the "king of home run makers is then working at the rate of forty-four horsepower every time he cracks out one of his long hits, but he maintains this rate for such a brief length of time that not very much actual work is involved."[50] Yet, like his frontier strength and self-sufficiency, Ruth's technological power, efficiency, and specialization were not necessarily benevolent. The illustration accompanying Professor Hodges' scientific explanation of Ruth's home runs shows an enormous bat smashing a skyscraper.

One of the most common images associated with Ruth was a military one in which he appeared gallant and brave. His bat was often characterized as a "war club,"[51] and Grantland Rice modernized this image for Ruth and Gehrig: "every homer they struck off left the old ash gun with a tail of fire attached. On each occasion the ball left the bat as a six-inch shell leaves the muzzle of a howitzer, with a screech and a roar, to soar far above the roof of the outfield stands and disappear from sight."[52] As a military hero, Ruth's bravery and gallantry were responsible for the rejuvenation of his teammates. The day he hit three home runs in a World Series game, for example, the New York *Times* described the "bulky, swaggering figure" behind whom the Yankees "marched to an overwhelming victory....When they were going down for the third and almost last time, Ruth tossed them the rope of three homers. He took personal charge of the world's series and made the game his greatest single triumph. He led the charge of a faltering battalion and turned the tide of battle..."[53] As a result,

> there have been few more gallant figures than Ruth leading the charge of the Yanks today....There have been few figures as gallant as Ruth as he strode from the bench to receive the thrice repeated homage of an enemy crowd—his portly frame swaggering ever so slightly, his face alight with the fire of determination.
> If the Babe was going down, he would go down fighting.[54]

Ruth could be chivalric with foes as well as gallant with teammates. When a girl pitching for the Chattanooga team faced Ruth in an exhibition, he struck out. The Cincinnati *Times-Star,* reporting the event, explained,

> so men have been doing ever since the days of Atlanta. Sometimes they make a mistake, as Achilles did when he slew Penthesilea, the Amazon queen before the walls of Troy, and it grieves them. In general their attitude is that of Bob Fitzsimmons, champion heavyweight, when he exhibited a black eye, and with a proud grin explained: 'The little woman thinks she can lick me.'
> 'The bravest are the tenderest.'[55]

Yet Ruth's force that inspired these military associations, although gallant when serving teammates, often was amoral and destructive. His war club often became a "bludgeon."[56] He was known as "Batterin' Babe" and, with Gehrig, as the "Busting Twins." According to Walter Johnson, Ruth "might be expected to inspire terror in the heart of every pitcher...like dynamite, Ruth is always dangerous."[57] Grantland Rice memorably characterized this destructiveness when describing the 1926 World Series in which Ruth gallantly slugged his three home runs in one game;

> Babe and Lou stalked through this series like the 'Four Horsemen of the Sock Eclipse'—Dynamite, Demolition, Destruction and Death....In addition they were a pounding pestilence, a mauling misery, a clouting contagion, a black plague of mighty wallops that continued to clear the right field wall and threaten the lives and homes of those benighted denizens who lived in gun-fire range...they left a thundering echo of destruction that will haunt St. Louis as long as long-

rusted cannon still haunt Verdun and the Marne.[58]

This warlike, destructive force had little to do with right, wrong, or virtue. It transcended partisanship, for, as *The Literary Digest* reported, "Even the rabid rooters of the Mound City realized that when a hero like Ruth put on such a magnificent feat, party lines were minor matters and that there were bigger things in sport than the insignia on the uniform."[59] Grantland Rice added that the dominance of Ruth and Gehrig proved that "might can crush right or wrong, that the slam is mightier than the brain; that mind is only superior to matter when there is nothing the matter, as Don Marquis once said."[60]

This destructiveness may be simply the hyperbole characteristic of sportswriters who, by the 1930's were imitating Grantland Rice's excessive style.[61] Rice's description of Ruth and Gehrig in the 1926 World Series, for example, echoes his own earlier description of the 1925 Notre Dame backfield: " 'outlined against a blue-gray sky, the Four Horsemen rode again. In dramatic lore they are known as Famine, Pestilence, Destruction, and Death. These are only aliases. Their real names are Stuhldreher, Miller, Crowley, and Layden.' "[62] Yet if this destructiveness is characteristic hyperbole, the application to Ruth merely is extended to a type of athletic hero. The association with awesome destructive power, moreover, certainly existed no matter how hyperbolically it was expressed by the imagery. It is impossible to tell how many people took this awesomeness seriously, but Rice's own respect for Ruth is apparent in his poem, "Game Called."[63]

This array of conflicting imagery associated with Ruth emphasizes the concept of the unique superior individual. He was the pioneer in the vanguard, the machine-like specialist, the leader of the charge, yet in each of these roles he displayed awesome destructive power. In view of Ruth's uniqueness and superiority, it is not surprising that the imagery most commonly associated with him was regal. He was the home run king, the home run rajah, the sultan of swat, the potentate of the pill, the mighty maharajah of maul, the crown prince of home run hitters, and the wizard of wallop. These images reaffirm Ruth's omnipotence at his specialty rather than a set of specific virtues. *The Literary Digest* cited the transformation Ruth wrought in the game of baseball as the source of this superiority:

> now and again a superman arises in the domain of politics of finance or science that plays havoc with kingdoms or fortunes or established theories. Such a superman in a narrow but none-the-less obvious field is Babe Ruth...the true Home Run King in a

larger sense than is commonly understood. For he has taken the place hit from its pedestal as the batter's universal model and has set up in its place the home run.[64]

But it was the kind of cathartic effect noted by Britt, which also was responsible for this transformation of the game, that made Ruth unique as well as superior. His record-breaking home runs were thus treated with regal pageantry befitting the Home Run King. When Ruth hit the first home run to left center field in Boston's Fenway Park, for example, the New York *Times* reported a "sixteen year old record fell before the mighty wand of King Ruth and once again the Boston populace rose to cary [sic] 'Long live the King!' "[65] The *Times* also reported Ruth's sixtieth home run in 1927 as a royal triumph:

> while the crowd cheered and the Yankee players roared their greeting the Babe made his triumphant, almost regal tour of the paths. He jogged around slowly, touched each bag firmly and carefully and when he embedded his spikes in the rubber disk to record officially Homer 60 hats were tossed into the air, papers were torn up and tossed liberally and the spirit of celebration permeated the place.
>   The Babe's stroll out to his position was the signal for a handkerchief salute which all the bleacherites, to the last man, participated. Jovial Babe entered into the carnival spirit and punctuated his kingly strides with a succession of snappy military salutes.[66]

Ruth's thus-celebrated prowess, like his regenerative influence, could have been extended to his off-field activities. It is already clear that Ruth could gain money and fame by hitting home runs, but he could also do so by performing acts sure to retain the public eye. These acts were nearly always excessive—speeding, eating too many hot dogs—but these apparent violations of norms were nearly always excused, even, as we have seen, to the point of touting Ruth as a moral counsellor. By excusing this behavior, people behaved as if they valued it and the concepts by which they excused it. A writer in *The Literary Digest,* for example, indicates that while Ruth's faults are common enough, his material success vindicates them: Ruth "has all our faults, and in spite of them all the material success we should like to have."[67]

Ruth was excused also because he was boyish: a "lovable, big-hearted, simple, careless, reckless, easily led, seldom thinking or caring for consequences, . . . big, overgrown, naughty boy."[68] He was excused because he was penitent. At a baseball writers' dinner in 1922, then-State Senator Jimmy Walker recounted a ragged urchin's demand for a dime of the Senator so the boy could " 'get me a cap

with Babe Ruth on it...like the rest of the gang.' " Upon realizing
the esteem in which he was held by the city's " 'dirty faced little
boys,' " Ruth burst into tears, did public penance for his excesses
and promised to reform.[69]

Ruth also was excused these excesses because, like his
prodigious home runs, they proved him unique and superior. His
teammate, Joe Dugan marveled at Ruth's superhuman ability to
perform successfully while pursuing a dissipated lifestyle:

> He wasn't human. He was an animal. No human could have
> done the things he did and lived the way he did and been a
> ballplayer. Cobb? Could he pitch? Speaker? The rest? I saw
> them. I was there. There was never anybody close. When you
> figure the things he did and the way he lived and the way he
> played, you got to figure he was more than animal even. There
> never was anyone like him. He was a god.[70]

Red Smith indicated that these excesses which proved Ruth superior
also proved him unique:

> As John Kieran sang many years ago:

> 'My voice may be loud above the crowd
> And my words just a bit uncouth,
> But I'll stand and shout till the last man's out,
> There was never a guy like Ruth!'

> The fact is, there never was and almost certainly never will be.
> Ruth was more than a ball player. He was youth and health and
> success and fun. He was at least a demigod. He was the superb
> extrovert, the greatest eater, the heaviest drinker, the longest
> hitter, the lustiest competitor, and most profligate spendthrift:
> the warmest personality in the world was his.[71]

Babe Ruth and the record numbers of home runs which called
national attention to him were widely valued between 1919 and
1935. People regarded Ruth as a celebrity, and he was accorded both
spontaneous and formal adulation. Legends grew about his life and
character, and he was commemorated. This behavior lavished
wealth as well as acclaim on Ruth, and some members of the public
evaluated Ruth's deeds on the basis of this material success. Ruth's
home runs seem to have been evaluated most widely, however, as
restorative forces. Some evaluated this rejuvenation negatively as a
corruption of the game of baseball, and some evaluated it positively
as affirming concepts like strength, self-sufficiency, dependability,
efficiency, gallantry, and awesome destructive power. All these

concepts by which Ruth and his home runs seem to have been evaluated, however, emphasized the uniqueness and superiority proved by his tonic effects on and off the diamond. These qualities unite in Ruth's popular image as the Home Run King.

NOTES

[1]"The Babe's Big Effort to Come Back," *Literary Digest,* XC (July 31, 1926), p.46.

[2]Robert W. Creamer, "And Along Came Ruth," *Sports Illustrated,* XL (March 18, 1974), p.76.

[3]Creamer, p.87.

[4]F.C. Lane, "Babe Ruth and Frenzied Finance" in Sidney Offit, ed., *The Best of Baseball* (New York, 1956), pp.83-84.

[5]"Professor Ruth and Dr. Cobb Tickle a Highbrow Critic," *Literary Digest,* LXXXIX (June 12, 1926), p.77.

[6]Boseman Bulger, "And Along Came Ruth," *Saturday Evening Post,* CCIV (November 28, 1931), p.6.

[7]"What is Babe Ruth Worth to the Yankees?" *Literary Digest,* CIV (March 29, 1930), pp.41-42.

[8]Lee Allen, *The American League Story* (New York, 1962), p.108.

[9]New York *Times,* January 15, 1926, p.24.

[10]New York *Times* January 18, 1926, p.19.

[11]New York *Times* October 20, 1928, p.5.

[12]Roger Kahn, "A Look Behind a Legend," in *How the Weather Was* (New York, 1973), p.24.

[13]New York *Times,* June 10, 1928, p.28.

[14]"Wedding Bells—and a Home Run to Left Field," *Literary Digest,* CI (May 4, 1929), pp.66-68.

[15]New York *Times,* June 10, 1928, p.V9.

[16]Murray Olderman, *Nelson's 20th Century Encyclopedia of Baseball* (New York, 1963), p.62.

[17]Kahn, p.22.

[18]The "called-shot" home run is discussed in Allen, pp.131ff.; John Durant, *Highlights of the World Series* (New York, 1971), p.75; Joseph J. Kreuger, *Baseball's Greatest Drama* (Milwaukee, 1943), pp.297-298.

[19]Robert W. Creamer, "Colossus of the Game," *Sports Illustrated,* XL (April 1, 1974), p.48.

[20]"Babe Ruth's Five Hundredth," *Literary Digest,* CII (September 7, 1929), p.62.

[21]Des Moines *Register,* January 11, 1930, p.4.

[22]Albert Britt, "Another Popular Idol Upset by the Public Who Made Him," *Outing,* LXXX (August, 1922), p.209.

[23]"Batter Up!" *The Weekly Review,* II (June 16, 1920), p.124.

[24]"Highbrow Critic," pp.77-78.

[25]New York *Times,* October 8, 1926.

[26]Three such speeches are reported in Bulger, *SEP* (December 19, 1931), p.36; New York *Times,* April 14, 1932, p.28; and New York *Times,* May 21, 1926, p.3.

[27]Bulger, *SEP* (December 5, 1931), p.50.

[28]Bulger, *SEP* (December 19, 1931), p.36.

[29]New York *Times,* May 21-22, 1929, pp.33,3.

[30]New York *Times,* October 8, 1926, p.17; October 12, 1926, p.1; Des Moines *Register,* October 12, 1926, p.11; New York *Times,* April 12-13, 1927, pp.1,27.

[31]Bulger, *SEP* (December 5, 1931), p.50.

[32]"Baseball Shudders at the Home Run Menace," *Literary Digest,* LXXX (January 5, 1924), pp.57-61; "Enter Baseball, But Where Are the Pitchers?" *Literary Digest,* LXXX (March 29, 1924), pp.50-54.

[33]Quoted in Leverett Smith, "Ty Cobb and Babe Ruth and the Changing Image of the Athletic Hero," in Ray B. Browne, Marshall Fishwick, Michael T. Marsden, eds., *Heroes of Popular Culture* (Bowling Green, 1972), pp.78-79.

[34]Quoted in Lee Allen, *The World Series: The Story of Baseball's Annual Championship* (New York, 1969), p.106.

[35]Quoted in Allison Danzig and Joe Reichler, *The History of Baseball* (Englewood Cliffs, New Jersey, 1959), p.167.

[36]Roderick Nash, *The Nervous Generation: American Thought, 1917-1930* (Chicago, 1970), p.126.

[37]Nash, p.127.

[38]Nash, p.127.

[39]Smith, pp.73-74, 81-84.

[40]Sidney Reid, "Meet the American Idol," *The Independent,* CIII (August 14, 1920), p.193.

[41]"How the World's Batting King is Regarded By the King of Pitchers," *Literary Digest,* LXVI (September 18, 1920), p.83.

[42]"Dope for Babe Ruth Notebooks," *Literary Digest,* CXI (November 28, 1931), p.31.

[43]"Babe Ruth—A 'Bat Buster's' Last Stand," *Literary Digest,* CXVIII (July 21, 1934), p. 32.

[44]New York *Times,* March 7, 1928, p.20.

[45]"Babe Ruth's Five Hundredth," p.62.

[46]Des Moines *Register,* January 11, 1930, p.4.

[47]"Babe Pitches His Way to New Glory," *Literary Digest,* CVIII (October 11, 1930), p.51.

[48]"Babe Ruth's Forty-Four Horsepower Swats as Analyzed by Science," *Literary Digest,* LXVI (August 21, 1920), pp.91-93; A.L. Hodges, "Science Explains 'Babe' Ruth's Home Runs," Des Moines *Register,* July 25, 1920, magazine section.

[49]See Walter Johnson's analysis of Ruth's skill in "How the World's Batting King is Regarded by the King of Pitchers," pp.82-84.

[50]"Babe Ruth's Forty-Four Horsepower Swats," pp.91-93.

[51]See, for instance, "Dope for Babe Ruth Notebooks," p.32.

[52]"Babe Ruth's Record-Breaking World Series," *Literary Digest,* XCIX (October 27, 1928), p. 56.

[53]New York *Times,* October 7, 1926, p.1.

[54]New York *Times,* October 7, 1926, p.20.

[55]"The Girl Who Fanned Babe Ruth," *Literary Digest,* CIX (April 18, 1931), p.42-43.

[56]See, for instance, "The Babe Shows How," *American Magazine,* (September, 1930), p.108.

[57]"How the World's Batting King is Regarded by the King of Pitchers," p.82.

[58]"Babe Ruth's Record-Breaking World Series," p.52.

[59]"Babe Ruth's Record-Breaking World Series," p.52.

[60]"Babe Ruth's Record-Breaking World Series," p.58.

[61]Kahn, pp.6-10.

[62]Kahn, p.7.

[63]In R.R. Knudson and P.K. Ebert, eds., *Sports Poems* (New York, 1971) p.24.

[64]"The Babe Ruth Epidemic in Baseball," *Literary Digest,* LXIX (June 25, 1921), pp.51-54.

[65]New York *Times,* July 24, 1928, p.15.

[66]New York *Times,* October 1, 1927, p.12.

[67]"The Threat to Babe Ruth's Home Run Record," *Literary Digest,* CXIV (August 12, 1933), p.23.

[68]"The Babe's Big Effort to Come Back," p.46.

[69]Bulger, *SEP* (November 28, 1931), pp.7,36.

[70]Kahn, p.26.

[71]Red Smith, "If the 'Mantle' Shines—?" in Offit, pp.245-246.

Discussing "The Home Run King"

1) Sports heroes like Babe Ruth obviously have great skills and often possess qualities admired by the culture, but how can it be said they have the third element of heroism, being defenders of the culture?

2) Compare the apotheosis of Babe Ruth with that of Jack Johnson. How do these illustrate the principle differences between traditional and rebel heroes?

3) Examine the role of the contemporary mass media in shaping our perceptions of recent sports stars. Is the relationship between star and media now so important that sports heroes are no longer heroes at all but rather celebrities?

Jack Johnson, the Man and His Times

By Al-Tony Gilmore

From 1908 to 1915, Jack Johnson, boxing's heavyweight champion, was public news number one in the United States. He attracted more attention on a national level than any black man in this century's history to that time. One writer even goes as far as to say that his "impact on popular feeling was sharper than [President] William H. Taft's."[1] At one time or another during his reign as champion, almost every newspaper, governor, mayor and political aspirant in America voiced strong opinions on Johnson's life style, or on what he meant symbolically as the conqueror of white hopes. Much of the controversy and discussion surrounding the champion stemmed from the fact that he was unlike any publicized black man America has ever known.

Jack Johnson was his own man when it was not economically or physically advisable for blacks to be "men." He refused to allow anyone, white or black, or anything, including laws and customs, to dictate his place in society or the manner in which he should live. Born black in Galveston, Texas, in 1878—fifteen years after the Emancipation Proclamation and one year after the official ending of Reconstruction—he came to be the first of his race to fight for and to win boxing's heavy-weight championship. However, in order to appreciate the impact on and the significance of this achievement to Americans, it is necessary to understand the man and the times in which he lived.

In America, during Johnson's reign as world champion, there was a color bar, referred to as Jim Crow, that almost amounted to apartheid. The color bar received legal approval in the *Plessy vs. Ferguson* decision of 1896, when the Supreme Court upheld

From the *Journal of Popular Culture*, 1973, 6(3), 496-506. Reprinted by permission of the editor and the author.

segregation in public transportation. In the following years the
segregation principles were applied to nearly every facet of
American life. There were unbelievably few places where blacks
would be allowed in a hotel, theatre, church, educational institution,
train or even a restroom occupied by white Americans without being
restricted to the "Colored Section."[2] Even conservative black
spokesman Booker T. Washington, who accepted segregation, was

surprised when he drew the scorn of whites, in 1901, for dining at the
same table with President Theodore Roosevelt in the White House.[3]
By 1903, the racial situation was so despairing that militant black
leader W.E.B. DuBois was moved to say that, "the problem of the
twentieth century is the problem of the color-line."[4]

Indeed the Jim Crow policies of the nation proved to be a formidable obstacle for blacks. What tended to complicate and make the situation more firmly rooted, however, was that this dehumanizing segregation was rationalized on the widespread assumption that blacks were inherently physiologically and mentally inferior to whites. Blacks were not believed to be "full-fledged" human beings. A vicious cycle operated here as the beliefs of the general white population were confirmed as "racial truths" by many white scientists. The basic purport of most of their pseudo-scientific studies was that the mental endowments of blacks were considerably less than whites, and that human intelligence increases in direct proportion to the amount of Caucasion blood. Such "findings" reinforced the beliefs of whites, and the cycle continued.[5]

Consequently, when Johnson won the title, alarm developed among many whites who felt that serious doubt was now cast over their highly revered notions of white supremacy. Seemingly, it should not have been a difficult task to explain away Jack Johnson. One need simply to accept the proposition that all races could produce men of superior physical endowments. But, as long as Americans found themselves under the spell of a racist ideology which declared that it was the Anglo-Saxon "manifest destiny" to rule over the darker, weaker peoples of the world, such an admission was difficult. Racist ideology, although stressing physiological and mental characteristics, did not ignore physical attributes. The Social Darwinian theory of evolution, with its physical implications, greatly influenced white social thought in the late nineteenth and early twentieth centuries.[6] The nature of society, nation, or race was presumed to be a product of natural evolutionary forces. "The evolutionary process was characterized by a struggle and conflict in which the stronger, more advanced...would naturally triumph over the inferior weaker...peoples." Thomas Gossett explains in his study, *Race: The History of an Idea:*

> The idea of natural selection was translated to a struggle between individual members of a society; between members of classes of society, between different races. This conflict, far from being an evil thing, was nature's indispensable method of producing superior men, superior nations, and superior races.[8]

Hence, many whites used the "natural laws" of Social Darwinism to justify policies and practices of white supremacy. What Johnson as champion implied was that non-whites could triumph in the "struggle between individual members of society." He was a notable contradiction to one of the fundamental tenets of white supremacy. Thus, few stones were left unturned in search of ways to restore the heavyweight crown to the white race. Yet, it would be grossly inaccurate to assert that this was the only reason why whites overwhelmingly opposed Johnson. Equally important was the nature of the champion's character, personality, and life style.

One scholar of Afro-American folklore has compared Johnson to sociologist Samuel Strong's definition of a "bad nigger". This personality type was one who adamantly refuses to accept the place given to blacks.[9] This idea and image of the bad nigger is the most important model to help us understand Johnson the man, and his impact on both whites and blacks.

One characteristic of the life style of the "bad nigger" is an utter disregard of death and danger.[10] In this sense, Jack Johnson was truly a "bad nigger." Never once was his head bowed in mental acknowledgement of the superiority of white man, for he feared no one. During his reign as champion, when the Ku Klux Klan and other anti-black organizations and individuals ranged the swamps, bayous, and mountaintops of "Dixie" as well as other places; when, at least 354 blacks were lynched, eighty-nine of whom were accused of insulting, assaulting, or raping white women; and when, in most states, it was illegal for black men to marry white women and strongly forbidden by social custom in others, Johnson married two white women and made no secret that he had had intimate relations with an entourage of others.[11] In fact, he conspicuously paraded all of his white women as if to flout the laws and customs of the nation.

Johnson undoubtedly took pleasure in aggravating whites. For example, upon entering his integrated night club, in Chicago—his city of residence—the Cafe de Champion, one was first met by a larger than life-size portrait of the champion embracing his white wife. And if that was not enough for openers, the champion would grace the bandstand with his bass violin and sing his favorite son, "I Love My Wife."[12] Such actions of Johnson are to be disassociated from the black males of the period who were less well known and who sometimes crossed the color line for marital happiness, because Johnson was the most publicized figure of his race with the heavyweight crown perched atop his black, cleanshaven head.

To intimidate Johnson was practically impossible, regardless of how trying the circumstances may have been. Shortly after his first white wife committed suicide in 1912, he was arrested on the charges of abducting a nineteen-year-old white woman. He was jailed until proper bond could be posted, and disorder among the white prisoners erupted when they learned that Johnson had been locked up in the white, instead of the "Negro section," of cells. One white prisoner shouted, "Lynch him," and Johnson, in return, shouted back loudly, "I'll give just fifty dollars to slug that one."[13] After being transferred to the "Negro section," he displayed no signs of being frightened or concerned about the seriousness of the charges against him when he shouted to the guards, "I want a dozen candles so I can have more light, a box of cigars and a case of champagne."[14] Johnson's aides posted bond the following morning and the champion was released. By this time news had spread of the charges, and angered whites made numerous threats and attempts at his life. One rumor was spread to the effect that Johnson had been shot and killed. The rumor reached Johnson's friends, and they rushed excitedly to his home to find out if it was true. They found the champion unharmed and told him of the rumor, to which he replied, "Me shot? No such luck."[15] When the arraignment on the abduction charges was held, Johnson was, again, a "bad nigger" to the core as he showed no evidence of fear to the charges. The Chicago *Daily News* reported that "Johnson appeared at the Criminal Court in a high powered automobile and with a bodyguard of two other negroes [sic] and three white men...the Negro strolled into the courtroom half an hour late, carrying a long black cigar in his mouth, and smiling every step."[16]

Perhaps nothing demonstrated Johnson's fearlessness clearer than his actions in the ring. Given the violence against blacks during the period, many feared that the angry white spectators would storm the ring; yet this strong possibility never seemed to worry Johnson. In fact, he took pride in exhibiting his bravery in the ring. According to one sports writer, he was so cocky in the ring "that during an average bout, he carried on more conversation with his opponent, ringsiders, handlers, and officials than a committee of neighborhood gossips."[17] And almost always his white wife or woman, depending on his marital status of the moment, was seated at ringside beautifully attired and wearing many diamonds.

Other aspects of Johnson's personality indicate that he was more than a "bad nigger." One historian has pointed out that in the North during slavery, next to the "bad nigger," the most despised black was the "uppity nigger." This personality type had achieved a degree of economic security and was relatively independent of whites.[18] It is doubtful that northern white views of blacks changed by the time Johnson became champion. Writing of Southern attitudes toward blacks, a sociologist says that even without economic security, "The Negro male who dresses well consistently (i.e., without overalls or work clothes on weekdays), or who in bearing or manner, does not suggest a certain deference or humility...is in danger of being labelled a 'smart nigger'."[19] Hence, Johnson, by his very life style was not only a "bad nigger" as well. His financial holdings and his ostentatious manner of dress will attest to this fact.

With his ring earnings and the money that he made from theatrical tours throughout the black "belts" of the nation, Jack Johnson lived a life of luxury.[20] At a time when most blacks were barely carving out a living with their meager earnings, Johnson was busy purchasing expensive automobiles and clothing. Not one to be modest about his income, he told one black newspaper, while on vacation in New York, that he was "in town to pick up some diamonds and other souvenirs."[21] The Boston *Globe* was quite accurate in its description of him when it wrote:

> Good clothes and plenty of them; enough diamonds to illuminate his shirtfront and hands to make him a conspicuous figure when he promenades the streets. . . . Seldom does a day pass but what he will appear on the streets three or four times in changed attire from head to foot.[22]

The champion was well aware of the privilege that his money could afford. He knew that enough money would grant him and his family certain immunities from many of the racial policies of the period. For instance, when it was announced that Johnson's mother and sister wanted to leave Chicago for a vacation in Galveston, railroads sent their representatives to his home. The Rock Island Railroad made the best offer by giving the Johnson's a written guarantee that it would "not only put them there but would give them first class passage all the way and that they may go to dinner at any call they choose and use the library or do anything that any of the other passengers are allowed."[23]

Another facet of Johnson the "bad nigger" was his insatiable love of having a good time.[24] Oldtimers still living in Chicago and New York remember the "good old days" when Johnson would frequent the night spots, "fingering an inevitable roll of gold-clipped thousand dollar bills." They recall that whenever he entered a club, it was a signal for champagne for everyone; and that he almost always had a "darling pink lady dangling on his bulging biceps."[25]

Money was never an object of consideration to the champion if enjoyment was to be had. After collecting more than $60,000 from one of his fights, he told reporters that he had reaped enough "spending money" to last a week.[26] On another occasion, while vacationing and hunting in Maine, he missed his regularly scheduled train, and to the astonishment of all, rented an entire train to transport his wife, manager, and himself to the big game country.[27]

Nothing in the way of circumstance or even personal tragedy stood much chance of deterring the champion from having a good time. On the day after the funeral of his first wife, it was reported that "men and women of both races" were in the Cafe de Champion "Having the time of their lives" and that Johnson "joined the band with his bass fiddle and played several lively and catchy selections."[28] One of the most obvious displays of Johnson's desire of having a good time came when he married his second wife. Circumstances surrounding his personal life were tense. Not only had he recently been released of charges accusing him of having abducted a young white woman, but he was also out on bond awaiting trial for charges of having violated the Mann Act with another white woman—the transportation of women across state lines for immoral purposes. Consequently, the wedding was expected to be a calm, solemn, non-boisterous affair. Johnson, however, was not to be denied the opportunity of having a good time. As soon as the nuptial vows were taken, he exhibited his showmanship by performing for the guests all of the latest dances including the "Grizzly Bear" and the "Bunny Hug." After dancing Johnson went to one of his favorite pastimes—drinking champagne. He had bought twenty-four cases for the wedding, and boasted to reporters that he and his "henchmen" would drink it all before morning.[29]

Still another way in which Jack Johnson liked to have a good time was by racing at high speeds in his high powered automobiles. During his ring career, he was arrested and given scores of traffic citations for speeding.[30] He raced his automobiles so often the New York *Age* was moved to joke that his gasoline bill alone was "materially helping to increase the net earnings of the Standard Oil Company."[31]

While the "nigger" concept explains to a great extent why many whites deplored Johnson, it also aids significantly in an understanding of what he meant to many blacks. As Samuel Strong has pointed out, inarticulate and illiterate blacks admire the "bad nigger" even though they are "afraid to follow him."[32] Strong's contentions were well supported by one of Johnson's avid backers, the Richmond *Planet,* when it warned blacks that "a colored man who imagines himself Jack Johnson, will get an awful beating."[33] The Johnson image as a hero among many blacks also sounds very much like Roger D. Abraham's definition of the "hard hero" as being that hero who "is openly rebelling against the emasculating factors in his life."[34] Given the background of the repression of blacks, Johnson's personality elevated him to hero status, particularly among the more deprived of his race, because his exploits and publicized manner of living gave them the vicarious experience of leaving their inferior position.

Whenever Johnson visited black communities across the nation the excitement was stupendous. It was not uncommon for police officials to put extra officers on duty when the champion travelled to their cities.[35] So popular was he, that the black baseball leagues often requested Johnson to umpire their games, hoping that attendance would be increased.[36] One black writer described his return to Chicago after a victory:

> Jack Johnson came to his own with the "blare of trumpets." The citizens clung to the wheels of his chariot; drew from there the horses and bore him on broad shoulders high above the shouting multitude. Not since the gladiator days of Rome has there been a scene enacted as that which greeted Johnson's return from Reno. His pathway was strewn with flowers; rich and poor alike lost distinction in the crushing throng to seize his hand.[37]

In that same crowd, it was observed that "gray-haired grandfathers" were carrying their grandsons, hoisting them high above the shoulders "that the little fellows might gaze upon Johnson." "Now watch close, dere, honey," one grandfather is supposed to have said, "'cause you'se goin' to see the greatest cullard man dat ever lived."[38]

Although it is difficult to discern exactly how inarticulate and illiterate blacks reacted to Johnson at a specific moment or in a specific incident, black folklore helps to understand how they perceived him generally.[39] That perception was positive. Apparently what they liked best about Johnson was his ability to outwit whites. Much of the folklore on Johnson deals with this aspect of the man. One humorous story on his cleverness in the ring goes:

> Man, Jack was too smart for them white fighters. He'd get them in a corner and pin their arms at the elbow joint between his thumb and index finger. Then he would smile sweetly and kiss them on the cheek. Man, this would make these fighters so mad they would forget about boxing and come out swinging wild. that was all old Jack wanted. He'd step inside their leads and counter punch them to death.[40]

Another, dealing with the champion's ability to always "get the best" of whites, is about Johnson as a refused passenger of the ill-fated *Titanic*:

> Look where and what has been done—1912, 12th day of May, when the *Titanic* sink in the sea. When they was getting on board [there] was no colored folks on. There was not no Negroes died on that ship. But Jack Johnson went to get on board. "We

are not hauling no coal" [they said]. So Jack Johnson didn't like what the Big Boss said. He went and tried to do something about it, but it was so much Jim Crow he could have no go. And a few hours later Jack Johnson read the papers when the *Titanic* went down. Then the peoples began to holler about the mighty shock. You might have seen Jack Johnson doing the Eagle Rock so glad that he was not on that ship.[41]

As should be expected, there is also folklore which involves Johnson in direct confrontation with Jim Crow restrictions. One story with a surprising and amusing ending follows:

> Jack Johnson went to a Jim Crow Hotel and asked the desk clerk for a room. When the clerk raised and saw that the man was black he angrily responded, "We don't serve your kind here." Johnson again asked for a room and the clerk replied the same. The champion then laughed, pulled out a roll of money, and politely told the clerk, "Oh, you misunderstand me, I don't want it for myself, I want it for my wife—she's your kind!"[42]

In addition to that folklore which dealt with the champion's ability to "put one over" on whites there are also items of folklore which glorify his fast life style. One story is concerned with Johnson and his automobile:

> It was on a hot day in Georgia when Jack Johnson drove into town. He was really flying: Zoooom! Behind his fine car was a cloud of red Georgia dust as far as the eye could see. The sheriff flagged him down and said, "Where do you think you're going boy, speeding like that? That'll cost you $50,000." Jack Johnson never looked up; he just reached in his pocket and handed the sheriff a $100,000 bill and started to gun the motor: ruuummmmm, ruuummm. Just before Jack pulled off the sheriff shouted, "Don't you want your change?" And Jack replied, "Keep it, 'cause I'm coming back the same way I'm going!" Zoooooom.[43]

Other blacks, however, were not so fond of Johnson's antics or his life style. They, swayed by fear of white reprisals, condemned the man whose conduct in public tended to embarrass them. More often than not, these were articulate men, newspaper editors, preachers, teachers and race spokesmen.[44] Many black men of their category, however, were ardent supporters and followers of the champion. Thus, there was clearly no monolithic black view of Johnson. How one might judge Johnson at a given moment was highly dependent on the circumstances in which he was involved at the time.

This was Jack Johnson and the time in which he lived. Sports writer Dick Schaap, aptly summarized Jack Johnson when he wrote, "think of the forces that shaped him, of the time in which he lived, and accept one conclusion: He must have been some man."[45]

NOTES

[1]John Lardner, *White Hopes and Other Tigers* (Philadelphia: J. B. Lippincott, 1951), p.13.

[2]One of the better accounts of segregation policies of the early twentieth century is C. Vann Woodward's, *The Strange Career of Jim Crow* (New York: Oxford University Press, 1966).

[3]Albon L. Holsey (ed.), *Booker T. Washington's Own Story of his Life and Work* (Naperville, Illinois, and Toronto: J.L. Nichols and Company, 1915), pp.282-285.

[4]W.E.B. DuBois, *Souls of Black Folk* (New York: New American Library, 1969), p.54.

[5]Phett Jones, "Proving Blacks Inferior, 1870-1930," *Black World* (February, 1971), pp.4-19.

[6]Louis L. Knowles and Kenneth Prewitt (eds.), *Institutional Racism in America* (Englewood Cliffs, N . J.: Prentice Hall, 1969), p.9.

[7]*Ibid.*

[8]Thomas Gossett, *Race: The History of an Idea* (Dallas: SMU Press, 1963), p.18.

[9]William H. Wiggins, Jr., "Jack Johnson as Bad Nigger: The Folklore of His Life," *Black Scholar* (January, 1971), pp.4-19.

[10]Samuel M. Strong, "Negro-White Relationships as Reflected in Social Types," *American Journal of Sociology,* LXII (1946), p.24.

[11]Lynching figures cover the period from December 26, 1908 to April 5, 1915—the dates that Johnson won and lost the title respectively. Excluded are black women. National Assocation for the Advancement of Colored People, *Thirty Years of Lynching in the United States, 1889-1918* (New York: Arno Press and the New York Times, 1969).

[12]Chicago *Broadax,* September 26, 1912, p.2; Chicago *Defender,* July 13, p.1.

[13]Minneapolis *Tribune,* November 10, 1912, p.2.

[14]Indianapolis *Freeman,* November 23, 1912, p. 7.

[15]Chicago *Daily News,* October 19, 1912, p.1.

[16]*Ibid.*

[17]S. Young, "Was Jack Johnson Boxing's Greatest Champion?" *Ebony* (January, 1963), p.67.

[18]Leon Litwack, *North of Slavery: The Negro in the Free State, 1790-1860.* (Chicago: University of Chicago Press, 1961), p.179.

[19]Hylan Lewis, *Blackways of Kent* (Chapel Hill: University of North Carolina Press, 1955), p.54.

[20]New York *Age,* July 7, 1910, p.6.

[21]Boston *Guardian,* January 6, 1912, p.7.

[22]*Globe,* December 27, 1908, p.10.

[23]*Defender,* February 18, 1911, p.1.

[24]Wiggins, "Bad Nigger," p.36.

[25]Pittsburgh *Courier,* March 5, 1960, p.M.2-3.

[26]St. Louis *Post-Dispatch,* July 8, 1910, p.12.

[27]Baltimore *Afro-American Ledger,* November 26, 1910, p.2.

[28]*Broadax,* September 27, 1912, p.2.

[29]*Freeman,* December 14, 1912, p.7; New York *Herald,* December 4, 1912, p.6.

[30]*Defender,* April 8, 1911, p.1; on June 10, 1946 Johnson was killed in an automobile accident.

[31]*Age,* January 10, 1910, p.6.

[32]Strong, "Negro-White Relationships," p.24.

[33]*Planet,* July 16, 1910, p.1.

[34]Roger D. Abrahams, "Some Varieties of Heroes in America," *Journal of the Folklore Institute,* III (1966), p.35.

[35]*Defender,* March 23, 1912, p.5; Galveston *Daily News,* July 10, 1910, p.11.

[36]Robert Peterson, *Only the Ball Was White* (Englewood Cliffs, N.J.: Prentice-Hall, 1970), p.61.

[37]*Freeman,* July 16, 1910, p.7.

[38]*Daily News,* July 7, 1910, p.1.

[39]In 1910, 30.4 percent of all blacks over age ten were defined as illiterate. Literacy was determined by the ability to write. U.S. Bureau of Census, *Negro Population in the United States, 1790-1915.* (Washington: Government Printing Office, 1918).

[40]Wiggins, "Bad Nigger," p.43.

[41]Letter from Huddie Ledbetter to Moses Asch in Asch and Alan Lomax (eds.), *The Leadbelly Songbook* (New York: Oak Publications, 1962), p.26.

[42]Folklore told to writer by humorist, folklorist, Rudy Ray Moore, Toledo, Ohio, April, 1972.

[43]Wiggins, "Bad Nigger," p.46.

[44]Because folklore does not deal with the negative images of its subjects, it is possible that, at a given time, many inarticulate blacks also condemned Johnson.

[45]Schaap Introduction in Jack Johnson, *Jack Johnson Is a Dandy: An Autobiography* (New York: New American Library, 1969), p.16.

Discussing "Jack Johnson, the Man and his Times"

1) Compare Jack Johnson's career with that of Muhammed Ali. (see *Rolling Stone,* #265, May 18, 1978 for details on Ali.) Can they both be classified as rebel heroes? Does Ali's public emphasis on his religion make him a stronger or weaker hero than Jack Johnson?

2) Name five other rebel heroes of the last ten years. Do their careers parallel Johnson's or do modern rebel heroes obtain their heroic status in substantially different ways?

3) Most rebel heroes either see their lives destroyed, like Johnson, or are killed, like Jesse James and Butch Cassidy and the Sundance Kid. Why are these kind of tragic endings so appropriate for rebel heroes?

My Affair With Farrah

By Pamela S. Ecker

It began innocuously enough. I saw her picture on a magazine cover. It might have been *TV Guide*. Probably September 25, 1976. That was the week it really began. The magazine arrived in the mid-week mail. The label covered her face. I could see Kate and Jaclyn clearly. And I could see her hair. No eyes, no smile, no face at all. No body either. Just her hair.

I'd see that hair again and again. It would come to haunt me. I'd see it on magazine covers. Hundreds of magazine covers. I'd see it on book covers. *Farrah: An Unauthorized Biography*. Or *Welcome to Farrah's World*. Or *Lee and Farrah*. I'd see it on more magazine covers. I'd see it on television. Vic Tanney. Mercury Cougar. Wella Balsam. An occasional nostalgic Noxema. And "Charlie's Angels," of course. I'd see it on still more magazine covers. I'd see it on wigs. On dolls. On posters. On people.

Her name and her face were everywhere. Spring and summer of 1977 belonged to her. I learned about her childhood, her marriage, her career, her dreams, her diet and exercise tips. I devoured each new article and studied each new photo layout. I became expert at bringing her name into any conversation. I wondered if I should do something to my hair.

By May 21, 1977, *TV Guide* had proclaimed her a "phenomenon." She'd already been a *People* Magazine "Most Intriguing Person of 1976." She'd already made the cover of *Time*.

College professors and learned journalists discussed and analyzed her popularity. Newspaper columns and magazine pages were filled with her exploits. Rumors spread. *New York* Magazine said she had scars on her legs. The *New York Post* said she had been arrested for shoplifting. Someone on campus said someone on a radio station said she said she was gay. Or that she was leaving her husband. Or that she was leaving "Charlie's Angels."

Late in May, 1977, she left "Charlie's Angels."

The production company sued her. Cheryl Ladd replaced her. Farrah went to New York to make a movie. She appeared on fewer magazine covers. Her name was mentioned less frequently. She changed her hair.

In November, 1976, *Us* Magazine had put her on the cover of their premiere issue. They wanted a cover that would stimulate sales. In May, 1978, *Us* put Shaun Cassidy on their cover. Inside, they proclaimed Farrah a has-been. They said, "She was overblown, overexposed and overdone."

I wondered if it was true. Did Farrah really fly so high, and sink so low? And what about me? What was I to do with my mountains of magazines, my pile of pictures, my cases of clippings? And what about my hair?

I delved into history for guidance. Surely there had been others before Farrah. Certainly there had been others like me.

Once upon a time, I learned, there had been heroes. They were usually Generals, Presidents, and Religious Leaders. People admired their great deeds and their charismatic personalities. Heroes were treated with respect and adulation. Statues were erected in their honor. Libraries and museums were named after them. Their heroism was celebrated in song and legend, with parades and ceremonies. Heroes were very special people. One nineteenth-century writer said that heroes could "... hallow a whole people and lift up all who live in their time."

Technology changed heroism. As methods of communications and means of information dissemination became more rapid and efficient, heroes became harder to maintain. Great Events were superceded by current events. Newspapers and newsreels had to find subjects and objects to cover. Radio and television had to find topics and types who could fill up air time. Each development of each new communications medium gave the public more chances to know more things about more people. Photography and film let the public see those who previously could only be described and imagined. Heroes were good people for the new mass media to deal with, but there weren't enough heroes to go around. Heroes gave way to celebrities.

According to Daniel Boorstin, a celebrity is "a person who is well known for his well-knowness." According to James Monaco, celebrities are "passive objects of the media." In either case, celebrities are different from heroes. Heroes do things. Celebrities simply are. Celebrities are highly visible. They are media created and media maintained and media distributed. Some celebrities have records of accomplishment, as actors, musicians, athletes, politicians, writers. Some celebrities are "personalities" alone. They present themselves to the public regularly, as sidekicks or guest hosts or contestants or panelists. Or as gossip column items.

Charles Lindbergh was a hero who became a celebrity. In 1927, Lindbergh flew a small airplane alone, nonstop, from New York to Paris. His act was courageous, and inspired others. His deed made him a hero. The deed was celebrated, by the people and by the media. Lindbergh's name became known.

When the deed was long past, Lindbergh was still known. The media still celebrated his name—the name of one who was well-known. Lindbergh did no more great deeds. He remained well-known. He was a celebrity.

Lindbergh's celebrity increased in 1932, when his son was kidnapped. Sixty newspaper reporters came to Lindbergh's home the day the kidnapping was announced. Their only story was Lindbergh's tragedy, and his well-knownness. The child's body was found. A trial was held. Lindbergh did no more great deeds. Eventually, his name left the news. In 1977, the fiftieth anniversary of his flight was celebrated. Media were filled with stories about the deed, and the well-known man. But by 1977, Lindbergh was dead.

The Dionne Quintuplets were never heroes, but they were celebrities. They achieved celebrity status on May 28, 1934, by being born. They were the five identical daughters of a shy Canadian couple who disliked publicity.

The doctor who delivered the quints, Allan Roy Dafoe, was different. He liked to talk to reporters, to give speeches, to eat at New York City restaurants, to see his picture in newspapers dressed as Santa Claus with five identical little girls dressed as elves surrounding him. Newspapers and newsreels liked to write about and photograph Dr. Dafoe. Testimonial dinners were held for him, speaking tours were arranged, contracts were signed.

The Dionne name and the five Dionne faces were sought out by advertisers. The Dionne Quintuplet name and photo was attached to Lysol disinfectant, Colgate dental cream, Quaker Oats cereal, Carnation milk, Palmolive soap, General Motors autos, Remington Rand typewriters, and calendars and toys and sheet music and other commodities. Tourists flocked to Canada to see "Quintland" and to buy souvenirs at the Dionne home and at the brand new Dafoe Hospital. By 1940, the six-year-old Dionnes had been superceded by other celebrities. In 1943, Dr. Dafoe Died. The estate of the once-penniless doctor was worth over $182,000.

Charles Lindbergh and the Dionne Quintuplets were the first among many. In twentieth-century America, celebrities multiplied at ever-increasing rates. Movie stars were celebrities.Radio stars were celebrities. Television stars were celebrities. Rock stars were celebrities. Sports stars became celebrities. Models became celebrities. Lawyers became celebrities. People who climbed the sides of buildings or rode motorcycles over canyons or fell off high wires were also celebrities. People who were kidnapped or killed sometimes became celebrities. People like Patty Hearst and Jimmy Hoffa became celebrities when they disappeared. People like Stephen Weed and Rosemary Woods and Althea Flynt became celebrities, because they associated with people who were celebrities.

Present-day celebrities get lots of help getting lots of hype. Since 1974, three magazines, *People, Celebrity* and *Us,* have been created for the purpose of spotlighting celebrities. The magazine pages stay filled with stories of celebrities of all types. The magazines stem from respectable sources—*People* is a creation of Time-Life; *Us* belongs to the New York Times publishing group. Both magazines are prosperous. They supplement traditional "fan magazines," some of which have existed for nearly fifty years, and many of which are specialized to deal with celebrities of film or music or daytime television or nighttime television.

Six television shows provide places for celebrities to gather and talk. (Johnny, Merv, Dinah, Dick, Phil and Tom host these gatherings.) Countless numbers of local tv talkers and radio interviewers fill the same function. News programs are stuffed with "personality profiles." Sports events are supplemented with similar segments. Newspapers and newsmagazines are replete with gossip and celebrity sections. Each day, more people fill more media time and space with more data about more people. As Boorstin points out, the famous folk who once engaged private secretaries to protect them from the public now hire press secretaries, to make sure they stay close to the public.

Which brings me back to Farrah. Farrah has excellent press secretaries.

In 1966, Farrah came to Hollywood from the University of Texas, because publicist David Mirisch had encouraged her. Mirisch had chosen Farrah "Most Beautiful Freshman" at U. of T., after studying photos of Farrah and nine other beautiful Texas coeds.

Publicist Mirisch introduced Farrah to Agent Dick Clayton. Clayton found Farrah modeling jobs, commercials, occasional television roles, and parts in the movies "Logan's Run" and "Myra Breckinridge."

Personal Agent Clayton introduced Farrah to Commercial Agent Marge Schicktanz. Schicktanz arranged Farrah's contracts with Wella Balsam shampoo and Mercury Cougar cars. Under Schicktanz' management, Farrah became able to earn $30,000 a week as a commercial model.

Through Clayton, Farrah also met Talent Coach Renee Valente. Valente's New Talent Program taught rising media stars necessary performing skills. Traditional acting techniques were supplemented with "now" talents, like karate.

Farrah's hairstyle resulted from a meeting with Hairdresser Hugh York. In 1970, York urged Farrah "not to look like a dumb blond." Farrah's hyphenated name was created in 1973, when she married Actor Lee Majors.

When Farrah and Lee were just dating, they sometimes had double-dated with Television Producer Aaron Spelling. When Spelling and his partner, Leonard Goldberg, were looking for a blond actress to group with the two brunettes they had already selected for their new ABC-TV series, "Charlie's Angels," Spelling suggested Farrah. Goldberg approved. So did network programmer Fred Silverman, who remembered Farrah from three ABC made-for-TV movies.

As Farrah's popularity rose, Marge Schicktanz' arrangements increased. Schicktanz negotiated contracts for posters, dolls, commercials, clothes, public appearances, books, autograph sessions, TV guest shots, T-shirts, and magazine covers. And magazine interviews. And special magazines.

When Farrah left "Charlie's Angels," after one phenomenal attention-getting season, she left with commercial contracts, movie contracts, modeling contracts, and hundreds of thousands of dollars worth of appearance and product contracts. Farrah left her television series with agents, publicists, and managers. She left with lots of publicity, lots of security, and incredible wealth.

I understood Farrah's celebrity. I knew how it was managed and packaged and sold. But why, I sometimes wondered, was she the one? What made her so infinitely salable? Was it her hair? Her smile? Her braless look? Was it some intangible essense of the personhood, perhaps?

Then I looked again at my mountains of magazines and piles of pictures and cases of clippings, and I understood. Farrah was significant because she was omnipresent. She was a celebrity because I saw her everywhere, and I saw her everywhere because she was a celebrity. Her face (her hair? her nipples?) sold magazines and newspapers and posters and products. Those things sold because they included her. I was obsessed with Farrah because I knew her. I knew her because she was everywhere. She was the most well-known of all the well-known people I knew. For a while.

In spring of 1978, Farrah went on trial in Los Angeles, charged with breach of contract. On April 13, 1978, Farrah and Spelling-Goldberg Productions reached an out-of-court settlement. Farrah agreed to return to "Charlie's Angels." She would be contracted, I read and heard, to appear in six episodes of the television series, over two years.

And I began to wonder again about my hair.

Discussing "My Affair with Farrah."

1) In what ways does television provide continuing opportunities for celebrities to remain well known, sometimes even after they are dead? Consider such programming as game shows, awards ceremonies, salutes to deceased stars, and, most obviously, talk shows.

2) Examine one type of celebrity magazine: rock stars, movie stars, soap opera stars, or general celebrity magazines such as *Us* or *People*. In general what are the methods these magazines use to keep the personalities they feature attractive to read about? What is it about the people within the magazines that makes them admirable and worth imitating?

3) Ecker writes of her own "relationship" with a famous celebrity. Consider your own relationship with a celebrity and ask two of your friends to do the same. Are your experiences similar to Ecker's? Can you determine any kind of pattern of events in the way a fan developes an interest in a celebrity?

Spider-Man:
Superhero in the Liberal Tradition

By Salvatore Mondello

The cover of *The Mighty Marvel Bicentennial Calendar* shows Spider-Man, the Hulk, and Captain America as imposing members of a fife and drum corps. Behind the superheroes are soldiers of the American Revolution. Like his two companions, Spider-Man has become an important fictional hero and is entitled to be represented as an American patriot on such a calendar celebrating American independence. Yet, in the beginning, his days as a superhero—like his country's first years of freedom—seemed numbered.

Even Stan Lee, Spider-Man's creator, saw little hope of success for his new comic book superhero when he introduced him to the public in Marvel's *Amazing Fantasy* #15 for August, 1962. That publication had become a financial liability, couldn't compete for readership with other Marvel titles, and was scheduled for cancellation with the August issue.[1]

Written by Lee and illustrated by Steve Ditko, the original tale stuck closely to time-tested formulas used by comic book writers and artists since the late 1930's. Shy, studious, and introspective Peter Parker, a student first at Midtown High School and later at Empire State University, is ridiculed by his classmates. While attending a science lecture and demonstration, he is bitten by a radioactive spider and acquires its characteristics. Using his knowledge of science and technology, Peter adds to his already considerable powers by inventing a web-shooter for each hand, enabling him to swing easily from one rooftop to another. He creates for himself a costume of red and blue and decides to embark upon a career as a television entertainer, hoping thereby to repay his Aunt May and Uncle Ben for the love, care, and affection they have given their

From the *Journal of Popular Culture*, 1976, 10(1), 232-238. Reprinted by permission of the editor and the author.

orphaned nephew over the years. At the television studio, Spider-Man refuses to assist a security guard pursuing a thief, the very robber who later invades the Parker residence and kills Uncle Ben. Capturing the murderer in an abandoned warehouse, blaming himself for his uncle's death, Spider-Man swears to avenge the crime by waging relentless war against the forces of evil.

Teenage superheroes, such as Airboy, Robin, and Bucky, appeared years before Spider-Man; arachnids, like the Spider, feared by both the police and the underworld, were staple fictional characters in the old pulp magazines and movie serials; revenge following the murder of loved ones was a gambit used by countless comic book heroes, such as Batman and Blackhawk to name two of the most famous; and orphaned kids who became superheroes abounded in the comics, with Superman leading the pack.[2]

Granted all this, Spider-Man *did* become the comic book superstar of the sixties, entitled to his own magazine, *The Amazing Spider-Man,* as early as March, 1963. Why did Spider-Man merit such a large, diverse, and enthusiastic audience, including many college students? From the start, Spider-Man was given unique characteristics for a superhero; human characteristics and problems with which readers could identify. He always finds it hard to make ends meet and even tries to sell his services as a crime fighter to the Fantastic Four only to learn that they are a non-profit organization. He offers to pose for bubble gum cards, but is turned down by the card manufacturer who tells him he is a has-been. So, as Peter Parker, he must work for a pittance as a part-time photographer for *The Daily Bugle.* That newspaper's publisher, J. Jonah Jameson, pays him little for his action-filled photographs of Spider-Man in deadly combat with supervillains. And, to add insult to injury, Jameson detests Spider-Man, considering him a glory-hound and criminal.

The Amazing Spider-Man has found an enthusiastic young audience because it deals fundamentally with titanic battles between a teenage superhero and middle-aged supervillains—an impressive rogues' gallery which includes such memorable knaves and grotesques as the Vulture, Doc Ock, the Sandman, Kraven the Hunter, Electro, the Evil Enforcers, Mysterio, the Green Goblin, the Scorpion, the Rhino, the Shocker, The Kingpin, the Lizard, Hammerhead, and the Jackal, names which shake the very soul of every True Believer. With each battle between Spider-Man and one of his tormentors, we enter the realm of high adventure, knowing full well that the hero's victory will only be temporary, for the villain will return time and again to haunt and pursue him.

Many of the supervillains degenerate into knaves as a result of scientific accidents. Some examples will suffice here. Doc Ock was working at an atomic research center, designing a contraption with four metal tentacles which would enable him to conduct all sorts of nuclear experiments. An accident occurred, causing brain damage to Ock and causing his mechanical device to adhere to his body. Flint Marko, escaping from a maximum security prison, finds himself in an atomic devices testing center; a nuclear test takes place and the molecules of his body fuse with the molecules of sand under his feet—ergo, Sandman, capable of assuming many shapes. (Once, Spidey captured Sandman by sucking him up with a vacuum cleaner.) Dr. Curtis Connors, a brilliant surgeon and devoted family man, lost his right arm in war. He studies lizard life, discovering a serum which restores his arm but changes him into a giant lizard whose only interest is to destroy mankind.

Now Spider-Man himself is the result of a scientific mishap. But what is incontrovertible is that the accident brought out Peter's best attributes, including his willingness to question power and to assume public responsibilities, while the accidents which befell the others brought out their evil side. We must especially ask why the sensitive Dr. Connors becomes a misanthropic grotesque while the less sophisticated Peter Parker becomes a crusader for social justice.

The answer is found in the age of the protagonists. *The Amazing Spider-Man* appeals to the young. As Peter Parker, he must accept abuse from Jameson, must not miss any more classes or his teacher will fail him, must call his cloying Aunt May to assure her he will take his vitamin pills. And what has he gained from all this? An ulcer. But as Spider-Man, he is the superior of any middle-aged person. He can swing freely with his webbing from rooftop to rooftop without giving his aunt a second thought, or he can playfully suspend himself on his webbing outside Jameson's office window and taunt him mercilessly. Through Spider-Man, Stan Lee has brought redemption to America's Peter Parkers.

But Lee tried to do more than that, and *The Amazing Spider-Man* was used skillfully to bridge the generation gap which was tearing the nation apart in the late sixties and early seventies. He introduced Captain George Stacy, a retired policeman who understood teenagers, all this at a time when our more radical youth were calling cops "facist pigs." He introduced Joe Robertson, a black journalist, who also tried to relate to young people and who fought for responsible reporting of the news at a time when many Americans believed our journalists were concerned only with sensational headlines calculated more to sell newspapers than to report events accurately. *The Amazing Spider-Man* was intended to find an irenic solution to the challenges facing America.

While many novelists have bemoaned the growing pervasiveness of urbanization and technology upon American

society, *The Amazing Spider-Man* treats these as controllable forces.[3] Spider-Man does not work in some fictionalized urban center like Metropolis or Gotham City, but lives and goes to school in New York City. He is New York's Tarzan swinging from rooftop to rooftop as the Lord of the Jungle swings from tree to tree. Spider-Man seems less agile when pursuing adversaries in New York's suburbs, for buildings there are too low for him to leap with ease from place to place.

Spider-Man deals with supervillains possessing considerable technological skills. He manages to more than hold his own against their mechanical devices. On occasion, he uses technology to fight technology. Discovering that the Vulture can fly because he has harnessed magnetic power, Spider-Man invents an anti-magnetic inverter. At other times, he relies on Yankee ingenuity or just plain common sense to thwart the nefarious designs of his enemies. He once defeated the mighty Electro by spraying him with a water hose. And when all else fails, Spider-Man, like John Wayne, still knows what to do with his fists. He once floored Doc Ock with a smashing right to the jaw. In this case, human, not super-human powers, triumphed over the mechanical tentacles of his opponent. Morally superior to his adversaries, Spider-Man can always beat them even when they match his scientific genius. Even the Shocker's two vibro-smashers are unequal to Spider-Man's powers, which are not artificial but an integral part of his very being.

Spider-Man has mastered his technology and crippled that of his opponents because he has learned to control his emotions. If this were not the case, Spider-Man would have long been driven to insanity by the diabolical Mysterio, who fights him by creating illusions. In 1965, Mysterio, disguised as Dr. Ludwig Rinehart, visited Jameson and told him that Spider-Man is a human who wants to be a spider. Hence, he should eventually suffer a mental breakdown. Jameson printed Rinehart's views in *The Daily Bugle,* and Peter, after reading the account, began to fear the posssibility of having a nervous collapse. Using his scientific skills, Mysterio creates visions of Doc Ock, Sandman, and the Vulture, but when Spider-Man attempts to fight them, they vanish. Utterly bewildered, Spider-Man goes to see Rinehart, hoping he can save him from the horrors of madness. Entering his office, he finds that the entire room and its furniture, including Rinehart sitting at his desk, are upside down. He finally learns that Mysterio actually constructed the room that way, even nailing the furnishings to the ceiling, in order to drive Spider-Man insane.

Mysterio has never been able to understand how Spider-Man manages to maintain his equilibrium. But the Mindworm knows. Born a freak, the Mindworm drove both of his parents to madness and then to death. In 1974, the Mindworm placed hundreds of people in a trance in Far Rockaway, New York; he is forced to do this, for his mind feeds upon controlling the will of others. He yearns to dominate Spider-Man's mind. This would represent his greatest victory. He tells Spider-Man: "You're not like them. You feel things...you're more involved...your emotions are so deep, they intoxicate me..."[4] With this incisive statement, the Mindworm gives us the key to Spider-Man's greatness—his ability to control his emotions, his ability to dominate himself. Since Spider-Man has mastered himself, he can master the technology around him.

The Amazing Spider-Man is a historical document that reflects three periods from our recent past. From 1962 to 1967, Spider-Man mirrored an era still dominated by Cold War diplomacy and a citizenry still concerned more with personal gratification than public service. In 1963, Spider-Man foiled the Chameleon's attempt to turn over secret documents from an American defense installation to the Communists. In that same year, he fought the Vulture for personal gain—to pay his aunt's mortgage—not to rid society of a public menace. The July 1967 issue of *The Amazing*

Spider-Man, is an important historical document, for it marks a significant turning point in the development of the superhero and perhaps of his nation. Peter decides to abandon his career as a crime fighter. As he throws away his costume in a garbage can, he says to himself: "Can I be sure my only motive was the conquest of crime? Or was it the heady thrill of battle...the precious taste of triumph...the paranoic thirst for power which can never be quenched?" When the Kingpin learns that Spider-Man has become inactive, he unleashes a reign of terror upon New York City. Peter, rescuing a security guard who is being manhandled by two thugs, realizes that he must continue as Spider-Man as long as people need his assistance.

From 1967 to 1973, Spider-Man addressed himself to every important issue confronting American society. He fought drug abuse and drug pushers, organized crime, pollution, and racial bigotry. It was in this period that superheroines made their appearance in the periodical, compelling Spider-Man to deal with the feminist movement. In 1970, he battled the glamorous Black Widow, who at first wanted to imitate his style as a superhero but finally decided against it, noting that she had her own special destiny to fulfill.

In an era demanding relevance, few magazines were more topical or current than Lee's comic book. It was in this period that *The Amazing Spider-Man* became popular on college campuses throughout the United States. Once contemporary issues were discussed, *The Amazing Spider-Man* became a subtle persuader, fashioning and reflecting public and popular attitudes under the rubric of entertainment. During World War II, comic book superheroes, such as Superman, Batman, and Captain America, to name only the most celebrated, had come to the assistance of our government and its armed forces as we engaged the Germans, Japanese, and Italians in combat. At that time, comics were doing more than simply entertaining the young. But our early superheroes were presiding over a united people, all intent upon defeating the Axis powers. Spider-Man's stand on crucial issues during the late sixties and early seventies could bring him not only supporters but critics, for America was divided on every public question. Superman came to us in a period of consensus; Spider-Man had to find consensus in an era of conflict.

In 1971, Stan Lee was quoted as saying that he was neither a hippie nor a conservative.[5] The same may be said for Spider-Man. During the late sixties and early seventies, we learned that the young man behind the mask was a resolute defender of traditional American liberalism, especially the liberalism fashioned by Franklin D. Roosevelt and other New Dealers.

Let us study the record. Peter Parker believes in equal justice for black Americans, but he has never joined a protest movement to defend that principle. Like his fellow liberals, he feels that blacks will attain full social and political parity with whites by working in the system. In 1968, he was asked to participate in a student protest, and the issue for which his classmates were demonstrating was abundantly clear. The petrified clay tablet—with its inscribed hieroglyphics revealing the secret of eternal youth to anyone capable of deciphering the symbols—was being displayed at Exhibition Hall of Empire State University. After the show, the university planned to convert Exhibition Hall into a private dormitory for visiting alumni. Among the protesting students who wanted the place to become a low-rent dormitory for needy students were two black youths, Josh and Robertson's son Randy. When the protesters invited Peter to join in the rally, he refused, telling them he wanted to hear the Dean's position on this matter. Secretly, he sympathized with their demands but felt further consultations between the students and administrators would break the impasse. (It eventually did in favor of the protesters.) When the demonstrators entered Exhibition Hall, one of the security guards nervously reached for his gun but the other guard restrained him, showing that not all policemen were intent upon shooting young college protesters. During the ensuing commotion, the Kingpin entered the building and made off with the tablet, proving that protest rallies benefited only the criminal elements in American society.

In the late sixties and early seventies, Spider-Man confronted the problem of drug abuse as energetically as Captain America battled the Red Skull during World War II. Spidey was so moved upon seeing a black youth, under the influence of drugs, jump off a roof thinking he could walk on air that he remarked: "My life as Spider-Man is probably as dangerous as any . . . but I'd rather face a hundred super-villains than toss it away by getting hooked on hard drugs! . . . cause that's one fight you can't win!"[6] When his rich friend Harry Osborn began taking drugs, Peter recognized that drug addiction had reached epidemic proportions, not restricted solely to ghetto youngsters. He became so enraged that as Peter Parker, he beat to a pulp three drug pushers.

At the very moment America was experiencing the tragedy of Attica, Peter was sent by Jameson to photograph a riot at city prison. He discovered that most of the inmates were only trying to improve living conditions at the jail. Shortly thereafter, Spider-Man made a television appearance and gave a talk on the need to better prison life.[7]

As Peter Parker, he was deeply troubled by the American

involvement in the war in Vietnam. Like most middle-class young men, he never talked about it. But after saying farewell to his friend Flash Thompson, who is leaving for a tour of duty in Vietnam, Peter thinks to himself: "Which is worse...? Staying behind while other guys are doing the fighting...? Or fighting in a war that nobody wants...against an enemy you don't even hate?[8]

By 1970, Spider-Man seemed worried about political extremism, especially from the right. He was suspicious of a law and order spokesman, Sam Bullit, a former policeman running for district attorney. Bullit, who made pronouncements against "left-wing anarchists," employed thugs to threaten or assault his opponents. When Robertson uncovered evidence exposing him as a fraud, Bullit had him kidnapped. While Jameson had initially lent Bullit full support, Peter and Robertson had viewed the law and order candidate as a fake from the very beginning. The danger from the extreme right to America's freedoms was as evident to Spider-Man as it was to Pogo.

Since 1973, Spider-Man has been locked in combat with such villains as the Jackal, Tarantula, the Cyclone, and the ever popular Doc Ock, among others. Occult themes have become popular. But, Spider-Man as an embattled defender of American liberalism, as a hero trying to update and revise that political ideology, ended with the termination of our involvement in the war in Southeast Asia. By the mid-1970's, Americans, Spider-Man included, had grown weary of crusades and crusaders.

Since 1962, *The Amazing Spider-Man* has helped to shape and reflect the American character and deserves special attention from students of American history because it has enjoyed a popularity and thus an influence second to no other comic book. Like the McGuffey readers and the *New-England Primer* of earlier times, *The Amazing Spider-Man* has helped to educate America's young people. During 1960's, many older Americans feared the teenagers in their midst, stereotyping them as flag burners, pot smokers, and police baiters. By the mid-1970's, however, most of our young adults—former members of the so-called lost generation of the sixties—were responsible, moderate men and women, bringing up families, putting in a full day of work at the office, taking their children on patriotic pilgrimages to Philadelphia and Washington, D.C., to celebrate their country's two-hundredth birthday. Such behavior was only natural from a generation that had been educated by superheroes like Spider-Man. During the late sixties and early seventies, Spider-Man helped to keep alive American liberalism among the young, a tradition stressing cooperation among individuals and minorities rather than conflict, moderation in politics rather than extremism, and the right of each American to social recognition and economic opportunity.

After W.atergate and Vietnam, Americans found themselves plagued by serious economic ills. Little wonder that they wanted Spider-Man to take them away from harsh social realities and transport them into the world of fantasy, circuses, and the occult. But a people and a superhero who had confronted the great social problems of the sixties with courage and decisiveness may have been so changed by that experience that they could hardly be expected to dwell in a fantasy world for very long.

NOTES

[1] For an inside view of how Spider-Man was created, see, Stan Lee, *Origin of Marvel Comics* (New York: Simon and Schuster, 1974), pp.131-138.

[2] The superheroes of the "Golden Age" of comics are discussed in James Steranko's *History of Comics,* I (Reading: Supergraphics, 1970).

[3] For an analysis of the relationship between technology and the Fantastic Four, see, Arthur Asa Berger, *The Comic-Stripped American* (Baltimore: Penguin, 1973), pp.197-207.

[4] "Madness Means the Mindworm," *The Amazing Spider-Man,* Marvel, No. 138 (November, 1974), p.30.

[5] Robin Green, "Face Front: Clap Your Hands! You're on the Winning Team," *Rolling Stone* (September 16, 1971), p.34.

[6] "And Now the Goblin," *The Amazing Spider-Man,* Marvel, No. 96 (May, 1971), p.14.

[7] "Panic in the Prison," *ibid.,* No. 99 (August, 1971), pp.18-19.

[8] "The Schemer," *ibid.,* No. 83 (April, 1970), p.10.

Discussing "Spider-Man Superhero in the Liberal Tradition"

1) Compare Spider-Man with other superheroes of the 1960's and 70's. Are Spider-Man's liberal views unique to him or are they typical of the entire Marvel comics line of super heroes? Compare the ideologies of the superheroes in Marvel comics and DC comics.

2) Compare Spider-Man as a fictional hero of the 1960's with some real heroes of the era, especially the Kennedy brothers and Martin Luther King, Jr. Do all of these men possess the same heroic qualities or are there some basic differences?

3) Go back and re-read Harold Schechter's article on the myth of the eternal child in the 1960's? Does Spider-Man fit into the myth as discussed by Schechter? Why?

PART FIVE
POPULAR RITUALS

Introduction

What do family reunions, rock concerts, and beauty pageants have in common? They are all part of a vast array of popular culture that we call rituals. Of all the dimensions of the culture, popular rituals are probably the most taken-for-granted, simply because they are so much a part of our everyday experience. Yet these popular rituals are important because they give meaning and structure to our lives.

Popular rituals may range from the most casual kinds of experiences to the most spectacular historical events. A coffee break with a group of friends is a common occurrence, while a nation's Bicentennial is an event that happens only once in a country's history; both are popular rituals. Rituals may be classified roughly on a scale from the most personal to the most public. One of the things which makes an activity a ritual is that it is repeated on a more or less regular basis, whether publicly or privately.

Just because an action is repeated, however, does not make it a *popular* ritual. Popular rituals are collective experiences—they occur in a social setting. There may be as few as two people involved, as in a card game. More likely, though, there will be a number of people, both participants and spectators, as in a football game.

It is the kind of ritual that involves a larger group of people that is usually of most concern to the student of popular culture. This is because these large-scale rituals are expressive of the beliefs that are shared by the participants. For most people it is not enough just to believe in an idea. We usually have a desire to demonstrate our belief, to show ourselves and the world that the belief is real and that we really believe it. A popular ritual, therefore, is symbolic—it is a statement of an abstract, sometimes vague idea through action. Sometimes the expression is clear, as in the carrying of the American flag in a Fourth of July parade. Sometimes, though, the meaning of the action is buried in the past, as with the throwing of rice at a wedding, an ancient custom symbolizing fertility. By looking closely at the components of a popular ritual, we may be amazed by how much we do without understanding why we do it. Throwing rice, tying old shoes to the car, carrying the bride over the threshold, the wearing of a wedding veil-all of these traditional wedding components have been perpetuated even though their original meanings have been lost or distorted over the years.

The word ritual may suggest a picture of savages dancing madly around a crackling fire, but every society, including our own, depends on rituals for entertainment, enlightenment, instruction, and emotional satisfaction. For the purposes of simplicity all popular rituals (also called rites) may be divided into three major groups; rites of passage, rites of unity, and rites of season. A particular social ritual may have elements of all three of these types, but most rites will be classifiable into a category.

Rites of passage are the rituals which are designed to publicly mark a transition in the social status or lifestyle of a person or group. Rites of passage include the rituals surrounding birth, baptism, the first haircut, the first day at school, graduations, club initiation ceremonies, showers and weddings, and finally funerals.

A rite of passage involves three main stages, the first of which is the preparation for the change that is to come. In this state we look back on the old life that is to be discarded. The period of preparation may be serious, as in many initiations, or it may be joyous, as in the parties preceding a wedding. Many times the old life is celebrated with drinking and dancing. The second stage is the transition period, the time when the participants exist in a sort of limbo between two lives, the old and the new. For example, there is a period in many high school graduations when one has lost the identity of high-schooler but is not yet clearly into any other identity. For some, this loss of identity is traumatic, and it may take many months or years to find a new life role. It is precisely the purpose of the rite of passage to ease the transition from one role to another. Rituals provide a structured way for persons to make changes and for society to acknowledge these changes, to make them official. Thus rites of passage attempt to give stability to the emotions of the participants as well as to reinforce the social order.

There is usually a moment of action in rites of passage that marks the exact time of transition. This moment may be expressed, for instance, by moving the tassel on a graduation cap. The moment often follows a pronouncement by a representative of the social order, such as a school superintendent, conferring the new status on those making the transition.

The last stage in the rite of passage is the period following the moment of transition. This stage is definitely marked by celebration of the event, with eating, drinking, dancing, and other festivities, all of which symbolize the joining of the initiate with the new group.

Rites of unity, our second type, likewise may be associated with merrymaking, as in the parties which often accompany athletic contests. Rites of unity primarily celebrate the togetherness of the social group, as participants revel in the virtue of belonging, of being part of something. One of the functions of unity rites is thus to combat the individual's feeling of alienation or loneliness. There are many degrees of belonging, from the closeness of a family group to the relative looseness of a crowd at a basketball game. Team sports events are in fact primarily rites of unity in which a group, both players and spectators, band together in loyalty to a particular school or city, usually represented by an icon (see Icon section of this book) such as an animal figure.

There may be no other bond among the fans besides their loyalty to the team. As Michael Real shows in his article here on the Super Bowl, there may even be little more than a rather artificial excitement generated by media hype or by the sheer size of the spectacle. At the same time, the Super Bowl is seen as a means of social indoctrination into American values and beliefs. Rituals are in this way an acting-out of dominant cultural myths. In his essay on disco-mania, James Von Schilling similarly points out that phenomena such as dance crazes are related to trends in the broader social and political environment.

Rites of season, on the other hand, are generally more traditional, often having their roots in the depths of prehistory. In his classic study *The Golden Bough*, Sir James G. Frazer showed how many social customs, especially seasonal rites, are common throughout the world and are many times based on "primitive" rituals of tribal societies. Rites of season such as spring festivals often follow the structural pattern of symbolic death and rebirth. In the earliest agricultural societies, for instance, rites of springtime celebrated the death of winter and the rebirth of the earth, the return of fertility to the land. Anthropological studies leave little doubt that many of our Christian seasonal rites are historically related to the earlier pagan ceremonies marking the stages of the year.

But many of the holidays we now celebrate are more modern inventions, such as the Fourth of July, and others such as Father's Day are purely commercial creations. A question the popular culture student should address is the degree of meaning any of the holidays now have in a mass-mediated society. Have we lost the significance of these important days or has the meaning changed to fit the times? In his essay on Halloween, Gregory Stone finds that this old autumn ritual has been changed to a training ground for American consumerism.

Jewett and Lawrence posit another kind of ritual—the norm demolition derby. Their concept of the rite of reversal is a very useful one which may be applied to all three of our previous ritual types; rites of passage, unity, and season each contain some elements which are temporary escapes from the constraints of everyday life. Indeed, all mass social rituals represent a break from the mundane work routine. They are all forms of play, even if the play is sometimes serious.

The popular culture student would do well to begin with those rituals which are closest to home, part of his or her own life. Everyone belongs to a variety of social subgroups, and each of the groups has its own rituals. Look at these as if you were a visitor from another planet—what do they mean? What is their function? How do they shape people's lives? The answers may be surprising.

Selected Further Reading

Arens, W. and Susan P. Montague. *The American Dimension.* Alfred Publishing Co.: Port Washington, N.Y. 1976. Essays on football, rock concerts, coffee breaks, and poker playing.

Cox, Harvey. *The Feast of Fools.* Harvard University Press: Cambridge, Mass. 1969.

Dulles, Foster R. *America Learns to Play.* Appleton: New York, 1940.

Jahn, Raymond. *Concise Dictionary of Holidays.* Philosophical Library: New York, 1958.

Owens, Bill. *Our Kind of People: American Groups and Rituals.* Straight Arrow Books: San Francisco, 1975. A photographic essay.

Seligson, Marcia. *The Eternal Bliss Machine.* William Morrow: New York, 1973. A sarcastic look at American weddings.

The Super Bowl:
Mythic Spectacle

By Michael Real

NBC Television Sports' "proud" presentation of Super Bowl XI to 85 million Americans from the Rose Bowl, January 9, 1977, ushered in a popular spectacle of intriguing cultural significance. Gilbert Seldes notes that the instant fame of Lord Byron upon the publication of "Childe Harold's Pilgrimage" reached some 2,000 people, while, in the era of mass culture, Lassie's first film meant for the dog "adoration on the part of ten million." A quarter entury later in 1969, whe Joe Namath led the New York Jets to victory in Super Bowl III, announcing the coming of age of the American Football Conference and the end of the Green Bay Packer dynasty, four or five times Lassie's original followers saw it all in their living rooms while it happened. And by 1974, when the Miami Dolphin line and Larry Csonka moved through the Minnesota Vikings for a 24 to 7 victory, more Americans watched than had seen the first man walk on the moon and only slightly fewer than the record 95 million who watched the funeral of President Kennedy.

What makes the Super Bowl the most lucrative annual spectacle in American mass culture? To answer that question this case study utilizes the 1974 Super Bowl VIII telecast on videotape as a data bank of cultural indicators...and then interprets that data to explain both the inner structure and the social function of the Super Bowl as a total mass-mediated cultural event. Methodologically it draws on a variety of communications-related disciplines to achieve a balance between Anglo-American emphasis on empirical data

Reprinted from Michael Real, *Mass-Mediated Culture,* Englewood Cliffs: Prentice-Hall, 1977, by permission of the publisher.

and Continental interest in philosophical implications. The thesis that emerges is this: The Super Bowl combines electronic media and spectator sports in a ritualized mass activity; it structurally reveals specific cultural values proper to American institutions and ideology; and it is best explained as a contemporary form of mythic spectacle. A cross-cultural mythic approach to Super Bowl VIII indicates why the annual Super Bowl may not be culture with a capital *C* but is popular with a capital *P* surrounded by dollar signs and American flags....

Sports and Electronic Media: A Marriage Made in Heaven

By successfully blending electronic media and spectator sports, the Super Bowl has become the capstone of an empire. Even oddsmakers agree it is the number-one game in what 1972 public opinion surveys found was the number-one sport in America. The president of the United States concocts plays and telephones them to coaches in the middle of the night; astronauts listen in orbit; cabinet members, top corporate executives, and celebrities vie for tickets to attend the game in person. In its first eight years, the Super Bowl surpassed the one-hundred-year-old Kentucky Derby and the seventy-year-old World Series as the number-one sports spectacle in the United States. Commercial time on the Super Bowl telecast is the most expensive of the television year, surpassing even the Academy Awards presentation. These are the figures on Super Bowl VIII:

> Live attendance: 71,882
> Television audience: 70 to 95 million
> CBS payment to NFL for television rights: $2,750,000
> CBS charge for advertising per minute: $200,000 to $240,000
> Total CBS advertising income from game: over $4 million
> Estimated expenditures in Houston by Super Bowl crowd: $12 million
> Words of copy sent out from newsmen: over 3 million

Curiously, this mass cultural impact revolved around a telecast that was composed of a distribution of elements as illustrated in Figure 1. The excitement seemed to be about a football game, but the total play-action time devoted in the telecast to live football was less than ten minutes. How has the combination of spectator sports and electronic media evolved into such curious and powerful expressions of mass-mediated culture?

Super Bowl VIII was only a recent climax in the sacred union of electronic media and spectator athletics. The courtship began with Edison's film of the Fitzsimmons-Corbett fight in 1897 and was consummated nationally in 1925 when the first radio network broadcast Graham McNamee's description of the World Series, and in 1927 when the first cross-country radio hook-up carried the Rose Bowl...

The marriage, one is tempted to say, was made not in heaven but somewhere between Wall Street and Madison Avenue. The combination of television and sports has created substantial incomes for each, spilling into major corporate coffers. In addition, the viewing experience of the Super Bowl, taken in mythic perspective, has become peculiarly appropriate in life in the Wall Street—Madison Avenue dominated advanced industrial state. Of course, big-time football was not the only offspring of the wedding of electronic media and spectator sports. Over two and a half years in advance of the events, ABC had sold its television commercial time for the 1976 Summer and Winter Olympics for $62 million....

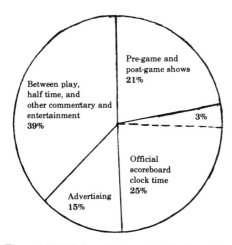

Figure 1 Distribution of elements in the Super Bowl telecast

Inside Super Bowl VIII: A Structural Analysis of Football

Myths reflect and make sacred the dominant tendencies of a culture, thereby sustaining social institutions and life-styles. What are the common structural constituents that underlie both the parent American society and its game-ritual offspring, the Super Bowl?

Cummings takes a step toward a structural, semiotic analysis of American sports when he writes:

> The essential aspects of American sport are basic expression of the American cultural pattern... The very forms of our sports indicate dominant temporal and spatial national features. If the

hunt was the central expression of sport in pre-industrial, state-of-nature America with its expansive landscape and assertion of a primal relationship between man and nature, then baseball, football, basketball and the like are the central expressions of an urban, technological, electronic America reflecting its concern with social structure and interpersonal relationships... Since industrial America severed work from a sense of fulfillment, we have turned more and more to sport as an accessible means of self contemplation. This is the reason for the cheer and sense of release when the batter sends the ball soaring out of the park; the pleasure of the stuff shot, the break-away; the satisfaction of the bomb, the punt return, the long gainer. Our modern sports are attempts to break out of an artificially imposed confinement. [Ronald Cummings, "The Superbowl Society," in Browne, Fishwick, and Marsden, eds., *Heroes of Popular Culure* (Bowling Green, Ohio: Bowling Green University Popular Press, 1972), pp.109-10].

But such surface observations do not touch the deep structure of any single sport. Football is not a mere parable or allegory of American life. It is not a story outside and about a separate referent. Rather, it is a story that is also an activity and a part of the larger society. Moreover, it relates organically to the larger whole. As such, the Super Bowl is a formal analog of the institutional and ideological structure of the American society and culture it is "about." *In the classical manner of mythical beliefs and ritual activities, the Super Bowl is a communal celebration of and indoctrination into specific socially dominant emotions, life styles, and values.*

The nationalism of American sports is made explicit with the National Anthem at the beginning of virtually every competition from Little League baseball to the Super Bowl. Super Bowl VIII offered an ideal popular singer for middle America, Charley Pride, who is both black and country-western-working-class American, Archie Bunker and Fred Sanford, all rolled into one. The CBS announcer had the right country but the wrong song, when he proclaimed that Charley Pride would now sing "America, the Beautiful." (After Pride finished the "Star Spangled Banner", it was correctly identified.) Further appeal to middle America was evident when the six officials were introduced as "a high school teacher in Ohio...a paint company official...a medical supplies salesman..."

What is the relationship of this packaged experience to the concrete lives of viewers and the surrounding political-economic system? The Super Bowl, like the bulk of mass-mediated culture, is at once a celebration of dominant aspects of a society and a diversion from unmediated immersion in that society.

Despite all the Super Bowl's overt and latent cultural

significance, it is popular as a *game*, that is, the formal competition itself has no overt functional utility. It is apart from the viewers' work, from bills, from family anxieties, from conflicts in the community, from national and international politics. Total psychic involvement becomes desirable because the game is enjoyed for its own sake, unlike most activities in the deferred-reward world of laboring for salaries, home, and self-improvement, or eternal salvation. In contrast to wars or family problems, the viewers are aware that they can enjoy or even opt out of the Super Bowl with the same free choice that they entered into it because "it's only a game." In this manner, the Super Bowl is typical of mass-mediated culture in arousing all the emotions of excitement, hope, anxiety, and so on, but as a displacement without any of the consequences of the real-world situations that arouse such feelings.

For the viewer, the Super Bowl, like much of television and mass culture, provides a feeling of a "separate reality." Despite its mass standardization, it has something of the magic and awesome appeal of the "non-ordinary states of consciousness"... The satisfaction that viewers seek in the Super Bowl is born in a hunger not unrelated to the search for ecstasy and comprehension around which mystic and esoteric traditions have been built. In the Super Bowl, however, the yearning is arrested at a low level, subject to what [William F.] Lynch calls the "magnificent imagination" that fixates rather than challenges the human capacity for creative imagery and symbolic formulations.

Historically, the Super Bowl parallels the spectacles of the Coliseum in Rome where the spoils of imperialism were grandiosely celebrated. As a game, the Super Bowl is not a simple, traditional diversion in the way that playing a hand of cards is....

An understanding of contemporary media, the functions of mythic rituals, and the structural values of professional football in a cross-cultural framework takes one sufficiently inside the Super Bowl to explain why 85 million Americans watch it and, at the same time, provides the aesthetic distance to question the Super Bowl's global significance. The Super Bowl recapitulates in miniature and with striking clarity certain dominant strains in the society in which it was born and that takes such delight in it. As a mythic spectacle, the Super Bowl has developed as a perfect vehicle for reinforcing social roles and values in an advanced industrial state.

The structural values of the Super Bowl can be summarized succinctly: *American football is an aggressive, strictly regulated team game fought between males who use both violence and technology to win monopoly control of property for the economic gain of individuals within a nationalistic, entertainment context.* The Super Bowl propagates these values by elevating one football game to the level of a mythic spectacle that diverts consciousness from individual lives to collective feelings, and completes the circle by strengthening the very cultural values that gave birth to football. In other words, the Super Bowl serves as a mythic prototype of American ideology collectively celebrated. Rather than a mere diversionary entertainment, it can be seen to function as a "propaganda" vehicle strengthening and developing the larger social status quo.

While the critics may overstate their case, viewing the Super Bowl can be seen as a highly questionable symbolic ritual and an unflattering revelation of inner characteristics of mass-mediated culture in North America. Nevertheless, to be honest, for many of us it still may be a most enjoyable activity.

Whatever the judgment, the next time a network "proudly presents" a Super Bowl or its mass-spectacle successor, it may well be ushering in a communications event more culturally and symbolically significant than even the traditional American icons of apple pie, motherhood, and the flag.

Discussing "The Super-Bowl: Mythic Spectacle"

1) Contrast the differences between baseball-loving America and the U.S. in the era of the Superbowl. What cultural myths are expressed in baseball? In basketball? In ice hockey? In any other sport?

2) Study the impact of television on sports in America. How have the games themselves been changed? How have the attitudes of the spectators and players been changed?

3) Examine in detail some other television spectacular, such as a beauty pageant or a holiday special. Explain the appeal of the spectacle.

Halloween and the Mass Child

By Gregory P. Stone

I set these notes down with a sense of déjà vu. Certainly it has all been said before, and I may have read it all somewhere, but I cannot locate the sources. I have often thought about these things in the past. Then, too, as a sociologist, I like to think I am providing observations as well as impressions for my audience. I cannot recall any other counts and tabulations of the very few facts and happenings that I counted and tabulated this year in a small "near southern" town on the traditional hallowed evening.

In brief, I found that Riesman's "other-directed man" may have exported his peculiar life style—tolerance and conformity organized by the prime activity of consumption—from his suburban northeastern habitat to areas westward and southward perilously close to the Mason-Dixon line. The town I speak of is a university town. As such, it has undoubtedly recruited "other-directed's" from the universities of the northeast. For example, I have been there. Moreover, the part of town in which I carried on my quantitative survey (properly speaking, a "pilot study") is a kind of suburb—a sub-village, perhaps an "inner-urb"—the housing section maintained by most large universities where younger faculty are segregated from the rest of the community in World War II officers' quarters. "Other-directed's" are younger and better educated than "inner-directed's."

You will recall the main theme of *The Lonely Crowd*: the very *character* of American life has been revolutionized as the fundamental organizing activity of our waking hours has shifted

From *American Quarterly*, 11(3). Fall 1959, 372-379. Reprinted by permission of the author and the *American Quarterly* of the University of Pennsylvania. Copyright 1959 by Trustees of the University of Pennsylvania.(Footnotes have been omitted.)

from production to consumption. We used to work—at least ideally and Protestantly—because work was our life. By our works we were known. Max Weber, among others less careful and profound, has attempted to explain this in his *Protestant Ethic and the Spirit of Capitalism,* showing how a vocabulary of motive was required to consolidate the spread of capitalism in society and arguing that the sheer dialectic of class antagonism was not always sufficient to account for the institution of pervasive economic change. *Every social change requires a convincing rationale.* Protestantism supplied this in part, and its persistence may still be seen in the contrasting attitudes toward gambling (gaming), for example, held by Protestant and Catholic churches. Only in the 1920's did the American Protestant churches relax their bans on such games, and then it was with the stipulation that they be played for amusement only. Risk and gain were cemented in the context of work; never in the context of play. The place of consumption in the "old" society— the industrial society—may be caricatured by referring to Marx's view that the cost of labor was the money and goods required for laborers to exist and reproduce themselves. Abbreviated: we consumed so that we might work. Today, for the most part, we work to live and live to consume. Abbreviated we work to consume.

"Trick or Treat" is the contemporary quasi-ritual play and celebration of Halloween. Characteristically, the "trick-or-treater" is rewarded not for his work, but for his play. The practice is ostensibly a vast bribe exacted by the younger generation upon the older generation (by the "other-directed's" upon the "inner-directed's"). The doorbell rings and is answered. The householder is greeted by a masked and costumed urchin with a bag— significantly, a *shopping bag*—and confronted with dire alternatives: the unknown peril of a devilishly conceived prank that will strike at the very core of his social self—his property; or the "payoff" in candy, cookies or coin for another year's respite from the antisocial incursions of the children. The householder pays.

In his *Psychology of Clothes,* J.C. Flugel has noted that the mask and costume free the individual from social obligation by concealing his identity and cloaking him in the absurd protective anonymity of a mythical or legendary creature—a clown, a ghost, a pirate or a witch. The householder must pay. For, by "dressing out," the urchin is symbolically immunized against those punishments that might ordinarily inhibit the promised violations of property and propriety. Punishment presupposes the identity of the offender.

Nonsense! This conception of "trick or treat" is clearly and grossly in error. In the mass society, the "protection racket" seems as archaic as the concepts of psychoanalysis. To revive either in the analysis of contemporary life betrays the nostalgia of the analyst.

Both are but the dusty wreckage of long dead romances. Moreover, as we shall see, the mask invites the ready disclosure of the wearer's identity. Instead of protecting the urchin, the costume is more akin to the Easter bonnet, designed to provoke the uncritical appreciations of the audience.

Even so, we can apprehend the "trick" as production; the "treat" as a consumption. Just twenty-five years ago, when I was an urchin, Halloween was a time set aside for young tricksters—a time for creative productions. Creativity, I might remind the reader, is inevitably destructive, as it pushes the present into the past. Of course, it is never merely nor exclusively the destruction of established forms. Our destructive productions were immense (I wonder at my adolescence, as Marx wondered at the *bourgeoisie!*). I don't know now how we managed silently to detach the eave troughs from the house of the neighborhood "crab," remove his porch steps, then encourage him to give chase by hurling those eave troughs, with a terrifying clatter, upon his front porch. I do know it was long, hard and careful *work*. The devices of Halloween were also artfully and craftily produced, like the serrated spool used to rattle the windows of more congenial adults in the neighborhood. We had no conception of being treated by our victims, incidentally, to anything except silence which we hoped was studied, irate words, a chase (if we were lucky), or, most exciting of all, an investigation of the scene by the police whom we always managed to elude. Our masks, we believed, did confound our victims' attempts to identify us.

In sharp contrast to these nostalgic memories are the quantitative findings of my "pilot study." Being a sociologist, I must apologize for my sample first of all. An editorial in a local newspaper warned me that between seventy-five and one hundred children would visit my home on Halloween. Only eighteen urchins bedeviled me that evening, a fact that I attribute to two circumstances. First, I unwittingly left my dog at large early in the evening. A kind animal, a cross between a Weimeraner and some unknown, less nervous breed, she was upset by the curious costumes of the children, and, barking in fright, she frightened away some of the early celebrants. Second, I think that our segregated "inner-urb" was neglected in favor of more imposing, perhaps more lucrative, areas of town. My eighteen respondents ranged in age from about four years to about twelve. Half were girls and half were boys. Two of the six groups—one-third—were mixed. Twenty-five years ago the presence of girls in my own Halloween enterprises was unthinkable.

Was the choice proffered by these eighteen urchins, when they whined or muttered, "Trick or treat?" or stood mutely at my threshold, a choice between production and consumption? Was I being offered the opportunity to decide for these youngsters the ultimate direction they should take in later life by casting them in the role of producer or consumer? Was I located at some vortex of fate so that my very act could set the destiny of the future? Was there a choice at all? No. In each case, I asked, "Suppose I said, 'Trick.' What would you do?" Fifteen of the eighteen (83.3%) answered, "I don't know." The art of statistics, taken half-seriously, permits me to estimate with 95% confidence that the interval, .67-1.00, will include the proportion of children who don't know what a random sample is (this is a ruse employed by some sociologists who find out belatedly that the sample they have selected is inadequate). Yet, it seems that at least two-thirds of the children like those who visited my house on Halloween probably have no conception of producing a trick! They aren't bribing anybody. They grace your and my doorsteps as consumers, pure and simple.

What of the three—the 16.7%—who did not respond, "I don't know"? One said nothing at all. I assume he really didn't know, but, being a careful quantitative researcher, I cannot include him with the others. Another did, in fact say, "I don't know," but qualified his reply. Let me transcribe the dialogue.

> Interviewer: Hello there.
> Respondent: (Silence)
> Interviewer: What do you want?
> Respondent: Trick or treat?
> Interviewer: Supposing I said, "Trick"?
> Respondent: (Silence)
> Interviewer: What would you do, if I said, "Trick"?
> Respondent: *I don't know.* (Long pause.) I'd *probably* go home and get some sand or *something* and throw it on your porch. (Emphasis mine.)
> Field Notes: The porches of the old officers' quarters are constructed from one-by-three slats so that about an inch of free space intervenes between each slat. In short, the porch simply would not hold sand, and the "trick" of the urchin could never be carried off!!
> Interviewer: O.K. I'll have to treat, I guess.

The third answered, without prompting, that he'd go home, get a water pistol and squirt my windows (which could have used a little squirting). The "tricks" did not seem so dire, after all! Moreover, the "means of production"—the sand and the water pistol—were left at home, a fact that reminds me of one of Riesman's acute observations to the effect that the home has become a workshop (work is consumed) and the factory, a ranch house (consumption is work).

Did the masks and costumes provide anonymity? To the contrary! I asked each child who he or she was. Happily and trustfully each revealed his or her identity, lifting the mask and disclosing the name. Had they ripped off my eave troughs, I would have had the police on them in short order! "Trick or Treat" is a highly personalized affair so that even its ritual quality is lost (for their persistence, rituals depend upon impersonal enactments), and my earlier use of the term, "quasi-ritual," is explained.

On the possibility that the costume might have been a production or a creation, I noted the incidence of ready-to-wear costumes. Two-thirds had been purchased in their entirety. Four of the others were mixed, consisting of homemade costumes and commercial masks. Two were completely homemade: one a ghost outfit, consisting of an old tattle-tale gray sheet with two eye holes; the other, a genuine creation. It was comprised by a mesh wastebasket inverted over an opening in a large cardboard box with armholes. On the front of the box, printed in a firm adult "hand," were the words: Take Me to Your Leader. Occasionally, adults produced, but only to ratify or validate the child in his masquerade as a consumer.

To ascertain the part played by adults in "Trick or Treat," I must, unfortunately, rely on recollections. In preparing my interview schedule and observational data sheets, I had not anticipated the adult, thinking that the celebrants of Halloween would be children. This impression was confirmed by my local newspaper which published the rules of Halloween, stipulating its age-graded character. "Trick or Treat" was set aside for the preadolescents of the town, while teen-agers were obliged to celebrate the event at parties. The rules were apparently enforced, as this news item on the November 1 front page shows:

> Police yesterday afternoon arrested, then released, a youth they said was dressed in a Halloween costume and asking for tricks [sic] or treats at downtown stores.
> They said the youth was about 17. He started the rounds of the stores early, he said, because he had to work last night.
> Police said they lectured the youth and explained the traditional [sic] trick-or-treat routine is normally reserved for children.

What adults were to do was not clarified by the local press. What many did do was to ease and expedite consumption by clothing their preadolescent children for the role, providing them with shopping bags and, in many instances, accompanying them on the rounds. At least three of the six groups of urchins that called at my house on Halloween were accompanied by adults (the father was always there, one alone!) who lurked uneasily and self-consciously in the darkness where night was mixed with the shadowed shafts cast by my porch light. In one case, a peer group of adults lurked in the shadows and exceeded in number the peer group of children begging on my porch. There they were: agents of socialization, teaching their children how to consume in the tolerant atmosphere of the mass society. The "anticipatory socialization" of the children—accomplished by an enactment of roles not normally played at the time, but roles that would be assumed in the future—was going on before my eyes. I wondered whether the parental preoccupation with the child's adjustment in the larger society could not have been put aside just for Halloween. Perhaps the hiding in the dark allegorically complemented my wish in the tacit expression of shame.

They were teaching a lesson in tolerance, not only a lesson in consumption, encouraging their children to savor the gracious and benign acceptance of their beggary by an obliging adult world. My questions made them nervous. The lone father was silent. He turned his face skywards, studying the stars. One couple spoke rapidly in hushed whispers, punctuating their remarks with nervous laughter. In another couple, the mother said sheepishly, "I wonder what they'll say? They've never been asked that." All the parents were relieved when I tactfully rescued the situation from deterioration by offering to treat the children with (purchased) goodies. Consider a typical protocol.

Field Notes: The bell rings. I go to the door. On the porch are three children between five and nine years old, two boys—one in a clown suit, the other in a pirate suit—and a girl in a Japanese kimono, holding a fan. On the sidewalk are a mother and a father whose faces are hidden darkness.

Interviewer: Hi!
Respondents: (Silence.)
Interviewer: What do you want?
Respondents: (Silence.)
The clown: Candy.
Interviewer: Why?
Field Notes: The married couple giggles. They shift their feet.
Japanese girl and clown: (Silence.)
Pirate: I don't know.
Field Notes: I look questioningly at the girl and the clown. Each is silent.
Interviewer: What are you supposed to say?
Japanese girl: I don't know.
Interviewer: Have you heard of "Trick or Treat"?
Clown: No
Field Notes: The married couple is silent. They lean forward

expectantly, almost placing their faces in the circle of light arching out and around my porch and open front door, almost telling me who they are.

Interviewer: Well, I guess I'll have to treat.

Field Notes: I get a handful of candy corn from the living room and divide it among the three outstretched open shopping bags. All the respondents laugh in an appreciative, relieved manner. My study is passed off as a joke. The world has been tolerant after all.

I am reminded of Ortega's remonstrances against the Mass Man, for whom *privileges had become rights*. Standing there, existing, it was the clown's right to receive the treat, the candy. The treat or gift was at one time an act of deference in recognition of esteemed friendship. Herbert Spencer wrote of it in that way—the gift was a privilege. On Halloween, the gift has become the right of every child in the neighborhood, however he or his family is esteemed. Now, rights are not questioned. That such rights would be questioned was hardly anticipated by those who claimed them. It made them ill-at-ease and nervous, perhaps lest the questions betray an indignation—a state of mind more appropriate to an age when people were busy, or perhaps busier, more productive.

Yet, this is not a plea for a return to the "good old days"— ridiculous on the face of it. Certainly, the farther south the tolerance of the mass society creeps, the happier many of us will be. It seems to be unquestionably true that the younger people of the south are less opposed to segregated schools than the adults. There is nothing morally wrong with consumption, per se, as production was often the setting for ruthless destruction. The conformity of "other-direction" (no trick-or-treater came to my door by himself) need not disturb us. Each society must secure conformity from a substantial majority of its members if that society is to persist. Instead, I have tried to show only two things. First, Riesman's character type of "other-direction" may, indeed, be a *prototype* of American character and not some strange mutation in the northeast. Consumption, tolerance and conformity were recognizable in the Halloween masquerade of a near-southern town. Production, indignation and autonomy were not. Second, national holidays and observances may have been transformed into vast staging areas for the anticipatory socialization of mass men. By facilitating this change in life style, they can give impetus to the change in character conceived by Riesman (and many others). I am being very serious when I say that we need studies of what has happened to all these observances—the Fourth of July, Thanksgiving, Christmas and Easter—in all parts of America. After reading this report, you will agree that we need a study of

Halloween.

It is not only as a sociologist, however, that I ask for these studies. Something does trouble me deeply about my observations—the "I don't know." Here is the source of our misgivings and dis-ease with respect to the mass man. It is not that he consumes, but, to the profit of the "hidden persuaders," that he consumes, not knowing why or just not knowing. It is not that he is tolerant, but that he is *unreasonably* tolerant. It is not that he conforms, but that he conforms for conformity's sake. *The mass society, like the industrial society, needs a vocabulary of motive—a rationale—to dignify the daily life.* That's what troubles me about my findings on Halloween. It was a rehearsal for consumership without a rationale. Beyond the stuffing of their pudgy stomachs, they didn't know why they were filling their shopping bags.

Discussing "Halloween and the Mass Child."

1) How have other traditional holidays been changed to "rehearsals for consumership?"
2) Stone mentions the ritual of "masking" — costuming to conceal one's identity. Discuss masking in other popular rituals, e.g. in parades. What functions do the costumes or uniforms of sports players serve?
3) Stone says, "Today, for the most part, we work to live and live to consume." Discuss.

Norm Demolition Derbies:
Rites of Reversal In Popular Culture

By Robert Jewett and John Lawrence

Rites of reversal are a well-known phenomenon to students of anthropology and primitive religion. As Edward Norbeck puts it, these rituals feature an "... upside-downing during which the social hierarchy is inverted, customary rules of moral behavior are suspended, and other ordinary behavior, is done 'backward.' "[1] Walking and dancing will be done backwards, costumes switched, and sexual roles reversed. In some cultures there are special groups such as the "Contrary Warrior" among the Cheyenne Indians who solemnly said yes for no and reversed many other forms of acceptable behavior.[2] In other cultures there are regular festivals in which "commoners may insult kings; women may deride men; and resentments of all kinds may be expressed with impunity. Obscenity, lewdness, sexual license, theft, and assault or mock assault may be permissible."[3] Despite this flouting of tradition and authority such rituals are not chaotic, for they begin and end with religious regularity and there are accepted limits and forms for the role reversals. Anthropologists tend to see these rites as providing "safety valves"[4] for aggressive impulses: Gluckman sees them as "periodic, cathartic expressions of rebellion against authority which, unlike revolt against authority, is only temporary and serves as a social binder."[5] By letting off steam, such rituals end up reinforcing the very norms which are flaunted and then cheerfully reinstituted at the end of the prescribed festival.

We find it curious that rites of reversal have been seldom

From the *Journal of Popular Culture,* 1976, 9(4), 976-982. Reprinted by permission of the editor and the authors.

identified in American popular culture. With the exception of Victor Turner, who has recently introduced the notion of "secular ritual" and applied it to contemporary behavior,[6] anthropologists have devoted their attention to sacred rituals in exotic, traditional societies. This professional focus seems to inhibit recognition of secular, commercialized counterparts in the familiar American environment. However, excluding Mardi Gras and other similar carnival celebrations which appear to be heavily influenced by European precedents, Puritan and post-Puritan America has provided few officially sanctioned rites of reversal since the elimination of Thomas Morton's May-Pole festivities in the 1620's.[7]

Our thesis is that several unofficial, though widely accepted, artifacts of popular culture fit the role reversal pattern. Both in their ritual form and their apparent function for the participants, these elements from American popular culture seem to fit the patterns discovered in other societies by anthropologists. A critical analysis of these rites may provide some clues to measuring the strength and weaknesses of popular culture as it deals with important human problems.

I

In an article entitled "Clean Fun at Riverhead," Tom Wolfe has described a unique American sport which constitutes, though he does not use this term, a rite of reversal.[8] An auto demolition derby begins with twenty to thirty junky cars, positioned around the circumference of a track, driving at top speed toward the center of the field to see which one can survive the wreckage the longest. Enthusiastic audiences have cheered the demolition of tens of thousands of automobiles since the sport began at the Islip Speedway in 1961. With only a little tongue in cheek, Wolfe terms this "...culturally the most important sport ever originated in the United States, a sport that ranks with the gladiatorial games of Rome as a piece of national symbolism."[9] Given the "quasi-religious dedication"[10] to the automobile on the part of the American public, there is justification in seeing the demolition derby as somehow symbolic of the national consciousness. But Wolfe never comes to terms with the oddest feature of this symbol: why should that which is quasi-sacrosanct be demolished? If one is so hooked on cars, wherein lies the pleasure of destroying them?

Wolfe's theory of the function of demolition derbies for their audience helps lay the basis of our hypothesis of a ritual role reversal. He suggests that with the elimination of direct conflict in modern society, "Americans have turned to the automobile to satisfy their love of direct aggression. The mild-mannered man who turns into a bear behind the wheel of a car—i.e., who finds in the power of the automobile a vehicle for the release of his inhibitions—is part of American folklore." Teenagers similarly use cars to experience a "triumph over family and community restrictions."[11] It is the combination of venting aggressive impulses and transcending communal restrictions which suggests the presence of an unconscious, unacknowledged rite of reversal. Whereas it is not at all clear that the mild-mannered man or teenager would derive pleasure from ruining his favorite high-powered vehicle, there are deep satisfactions to be gained from temporarily thwarting communal norms in an aggressive though socially approved ceremony. The element which confirms the presence of a rite of reversal is norm violation. In the destruction derby the audience participates in the violation of two norms which are crucial in the American education system: the sanctity of property and the voluntary acquiescense in traffic regulations. That one must respect the possessions of others is stressed from the kindergarten socialization process until the high school civics classes; some view it as an essential component of the capitalistic ethos. Since modern society provides no *lex talionis* procedures by which damage to my property can be avenged by my destruction of yours, this property ethic is conducive to frustrations and even at times to rage. One thinks of the widespread public outrage at the Briney case in Iowa, in which a farmer was successfully sued by a thief injured by a booby trap shotgun blast while breaking into a deserted farm building. The pressure of such frustration would be effectively released in a demolition derby in which "getting even" is socially condoned. The audience cheers most at the particularly destructive and disabling crash in which one driver really gives it to another, and drives off triumphant though battered.

The violation of traffic regulations in a demolition derby offers a similar release. The American public has internalized the traffic regulations to an extent amazing to foreign observers: we stop at stop signs even when no one is coming and no one is looking. Apparently there are millions of us who would feel a real sense of guilt if we did not. But this highly developed superego provides the basis for enormous frustration when one is the victim of someone else's traffic aggression. In heavy traffic conditions there are drivers who seethe with rage because of offenses perpetrated by anonymous competitors whose aggression cannot be avenged because of the traffic rules. They may have the urge to ram the rear end of a car which has just slipped in front of them, but if they do, they will be powerless to plead the justice of their cause as the Brineys were with their shotgun-rigged house. That demolition derbies are appealing to lower and middle-class Americans with strongly conformist tendencies is therefore perfectly understandable when one understands the function of a rite of reversal. And it goes without saying that the appeal of such rituals does not depend in the least upon an ability to articulate fully the function of role reversals. A typical response to the question as to why he entered a demolition derby was offered by Tommy Fox, age 19: "You know, it's fun. I like it. You know what I mean?" What was fun about it? "Well," he said, "you know, like when you hit 'em, and all that. It's fun."[12] Although he never heard of reversal rites, it is clear that he finds it pleasurable to destroy the otherwise off-limits property belonging to someone else, in violation with all the normal rules of the road.

II

An even more widely popular rite of reversal in American culture is embodied in the television program "Truth or Consequences." This program, which enjoyed decades of popularity on radio before becoming a regular television program, is virtually a perfect paradigm of the rites of reversal. One might call it, taking a cue from Wolfe's brilliant essay, a norm demolition derby. It features an explicit focusing on normally held values. The consequences of being unable to "tell the truth"—and the audience would be shocked and disappointed if someone were actually able!— are that one is forced to violate some norm of behavior. The entertainment value of the consequences lies in the ritual flaunting of usually accepted behavior. The more outlandish or scandalous the punishment, the more the audience responds—up to a limit. What one would never feel comfortable doing otherwise, one does without compunction because it is part of the game. The rules of the game and the authority of the game-master, Bob Barker* combine to provide a sort of ritual release from the hold of traditional values. But this release is always tightly controlled. One might speak of a threshold beyond which Barker can be trusted not to ask people to go. Within that threshold, violation is safe and even pleasurable. If participants did not trust the keeper of this threshold, one suspects they would not be willing to be such good sports. The consequence is that the value systems of the society are not seriously challenged. Here one finds that distinction noted by the anthropologists, between role reversal rites and actual revolt against authority. Finally the traditional values are reaffirmed at the conclusion of the ritual. The participants go back to their households and businesses, while the master of ceremonies appears on the next program, in the same straight, conforming attire, the very model of propriety.

In an episode we watched recently,[13] the function of "Truth or Consequences" as a norm demolition derby was perfectly clear. The program opened with the icon which must have been used for

*(Eds. note: Essay was written while Barker was host.)

literally thousands of times, but which suddenly gained significance as part of a role reversal rite. There is a halo over the word "Truth" and a pitchfork over "Consequences." Since the questions are unanswerable, the dramatic interest undoubtedly lies in the devilish aspect of the program. Then Bob Barker appears from behind the wall and the curtain, Hell's crater as it were, and takes up the satanic role of manipulating people into violating their usual standards of behavior. In this particular instance, the audience included a church group and an employees' association from a large retailer. A man from each group is asked to tell the "truth" about "How could the man tell that he'd been drinking too much?" Unable to answer with the line, "By the handwriting on the floor," they face the consequences of being placed in a control room monitored by a hidden camera to see if they would closely examine the pin-up photo on the coffee table before them. Barker's comments to the audience during this silly ordeal indicate the expectation of role reversal. "Hopefully," the man from the church group will pick up the picture of the "lovely girl in a rather fetching costume," but since he is here with this particular group, "he may be on his good behavior. Of course, he is the all American type..." The church group cheers when he does not pick it up, "That's our boy!" But when Bob Barker opens the microphone to the control room to "find out what part of the picture you looked at," he finds that the saintly young man has indeed glanced at the photo sufficiently to get the name of the model. The audience cheers this violation of the churchly mores. The worldly contestant gets cheered as he enters the control room with Barker's comment that this one will certainly look hard at the forbidden object; the audience laughs as he looks at the photo, and then applauds when he is able to relate not only the name but the precise vital statistics in small print at the bottom of the photo. Hips, waist, height, age and weight are requested in turn, but Barker refrains from the bust measurement.

The female contestants from the same audience were given the "consequence" of learning to tap dance in one quick lesson. They emerge at the end of the program in scanty follies costumes to carry out their ridiculous dance before a *Dames at Sea* set, a mock destroyer turret with two gigantic guns protruding. Introduced as the "Truth or Consequences Scandals," these proper ladies do their thing in front of the phallic symbols, to the wild cheers of the audience. At the end the contestants all receive their totem objects, consumer goods like clocks and hairdryers, in lieu of the real phallic rewards which would have been enjoyed in some primitive rites of reversal.

The norms violated in this particular program were those associated with petty Puritanism: don't look, don't touch, don't have sexual interests, and don't disclose your bodies lewdly. But within the narrow threshold of temptation guarded by the M.C., the contestants were expected to violate these values. The audience pleasure was directly proportional to the readiness for violation. At the end, values of proper, consumer-oriented behavior were reinstated. No one could doubt that the M.C. and his contestants would revert to the traditional mores after the close of the ritual-game. Barker's admonition at the close of the program, "May all your consequences be happy," implies keeping such temptations within bounds so as to avoid unhappy violations of the norms. This is a sort of ritual closure by which the traditional norms are reinstated after the completion of the rite of reversal.

III

This pattern of temptation and temporary norm demolition within narrowly prescribed threshholds may well characterize other peculiar customs and artifacts in current popular culture. One thinks of the Shriners' conventions and parades in which ordinarily conforming males take up the roles of clowns, court jesters and rowdies. Their escapades during the period of the "rites of reversal" seem to be socially acceptable, their drunkenness and pinching of pretty waitresses evocative of laughter rather than rage. But when others take up such behavior, the police are likely to be called. A bellhop in a metropolitan hotel was complaining this spring about the behavior of the state basketball tournament teams but saw no parallel whatsoever with the recent shrine convention in which middle-aged men acted in precisely the same way. Does this not suggest the presence of an accepted role reversal rite in the one instance and not in the other, so that the violation of norms which evoke rage in one situation can be applauded in another?

The peculiar American Halloween customs may be another case in point. In this instance the norms to be violated are those of Puritan self-reliance. It is generally assumed to be bad taste to receive charity, and even more humiliating to ask for it. "Let him who will not work not eat!" But on Halloween there is a reversal by which children can approach perfect strangers with the demand "Trick or Treats!" If the reversal rites are not reciprocated, the child has the privilege of violating still another norm of respecting other people's property. They may soap windows or teepee trees, just as in the older times, they overturned outhouses and shaved family pets. Victor Turner has noted that the masks employed during Halloween grant anonymity and serve the purpose of punishment-free aggression.[14] Such behavior is sternly condemned outside the night allocated to the ritual role reversal.

The American New Year's Eve ritual also seems to exhibit some role reversal features. Non-convenanted partners may be kissed at the appropriate time, childrens' horns are blown by adults, silly hats are worn by serious oldsters, heavy drinking and carousing is expected of those who are otherwise models of propriety. The peculiar American customs of Sadie Hawkins' days and Corrigan Week, not to speak of Leap Year, feature well developed role reversal patterns in which females take up the aggressive sexual habits of males. The even more peculiarly American invention of beauty contests feature violations of the norms concerning exhibition of the body and sexual modesty, but do so within such narrowly prescribed thresholds that the values of virginity are maintained. Far from being a "brothel in noble dimensions," as Harvey Cox puts it, such ritual reinforces the norms against libertinism by ritual norm demolition within such safe margins.[15]

Whether these customs fit the pattern of reversal rites ought to be investigated in greater depth than we are able to do here. If they do, and indeed if our hypothesis concerning the auto demolition derby and "Truth or Consequences" is substained, a series of issues emerge for further investigation. Do these modern rituals actually provide adaptations to the norms of society? What effect do they have on participants? Mary Douglas has remarked in her study of purification rites in primitive cultures, "Whenever a strict pattern of purity is imposed on our lives it is either highly uncomfortable or it leads into contradiction if closely followed, or it leads to hypocrisy. That which is negated is not thereby removed. The rest of life, which does not tidily fit the accepted categories, is still there and demands attention."[16] Her comment raises the possibility that *Truth or Consequences* may function as a ritual celebration of hypocrisy, a public assurance that we cannot really act out the values which we profess. How healthy are the norms which seem to be virtually violated and then reinstated in the end? And to what extent do these rites already fill the gap which Harvey Cox discovered in the wake of the modern abandonment of the "feast of fools?" During the medieval holiday, "no custom or convention was immune to ridicule and even the highest personages of the realm could expect to be lampooned... Its faint shade persists in the pranks and revelry of Halloween and New Year's Eve... Often it did degenerate into debauchery and lewd buffoonery. Still, its death was a loss. The Feast of Fools had demonstrated that a culture could periodically make sport of its most sacred royal and religious practices."[17] Perhaps American popular culture, in a series of customs and rites, is attempting to devise albeit unconsciously some safer, less degenerate forms of the Feast of Fools.

NOTES

[1]Edward Norbeck, *Religion in Human Life: Anthropological Views* (New York: Holt, Rinehart, Winston, 1974), p.37.

[2]E. Adamson Hoebol, *The Cheyennes: Indians of the Great Plains* (New York: Holt, Rinehart, Winston, 1960), p.17.

[3]Norbeck, pp.37-38.

[4]Gregory Bateson, *Naven* (Stanford: Stanford University Press, 1958), p.495.

[5]Max Gluckman, *Rituals of Rebellion in Southeast Africa* (Manchester: University of Manchester Press, 1954), p.54.

[6]cf. Victor Turner, *The Ritual Process: Structure and Anti-Structure,* (Chicago: Aldine Publishing Co., 1969). The chapter "Humility and Hierarchy: The Liminality of Status Elevation and Reversal" comments upon Halloween, Hell's Angels and other contemporary forms of group behavior.

[7]Morton, Thomas, *Encyclopedia Britannica, Fourteenth Edition,* Vol. XV, pp.832-833.

[8]Tom Wolfe, "Clean Fun at Riverhead" in *Side Saddle on the Golden Calf,* George H. Lewis (ed.), (Pacific Palisades, California: Goodyear Publishing Co., 1972), pp.37ff.

[9]Wolfe, p.38.

[10]Wolfe, p.41.

[11]Wolfe, p.40.

[12]Wolfe, p.41.

[13]"Truth or Consequences," (April 2, 1975).

[14]*Op. cit.,* p.172.

[15]Harvey Cox, "A Brothel in Nobel Dimensions: Today's Sexual Mores," in *Sex, Family and Society in Theological Focus,* J.C. Wynn (ed.) (New York: Association Press, 1966), pp.33-60.

[16]*Purity and Danger: An Analysis of the Concepts of Pollution and Taboo,* (New York: Frederick Praeger, 1966), p.163.

[17]Harvey Cox, *Feast of Fools* (Cambridge: Harvard University Press, 1969), p.3.

Discussing "Norm Demolition Derbies: Rites of Reversal in Popular Culture."

1) Compare Jewett and Lawrence's explanation of Halloween with that of Gregory Stone in his essay.

2) What other rituals or arts in American society might be seen as rites of reversal? Apply this principle to popular literature or film.

3) Study the norms and the treatment of those norms in other TV game shows besides "Truth or Consequences." What values are being flouted or reinforced?

Disco-mmunity, or
I'm OK, You're OK, America's OK,
So Let's Dance!

By James Von Schilling

"Our long national nightmare is over," proclaimed Gerald T. Ford on August 9, 1974, upon taking the oath of office following the resignation of President Richard M. Nixon. In less than a dozen years, the United States had experienced the killing of four of its most significant leaders and the maiming of a fifth, the deaths of close to 50,000 of its males in the most controversial war in its history, the resignation of both a president and a vice-president in mammoth political corruption scandals, a Cold War confrontation that brought the country to the brink of a nuclear war, rioting and destruction in a score of its major cities, disruption and violence on many of its college campuses, a gas-shortage crisis, a serious recession, and soaring crime rates, unemployment statistics, and public welfare rolls. As President Nixon himself expressed in his resignation speech, "By taking this action I hope that I will have hastened the start of the process of healing, which is so desperately needed in America."

With the nation's eyes and ears riveted on events in Washington that summer, few took notice of an unusual development in the popular culture area. That July a record came literally out of nowhere to top both the "Hot 100" and "Soul" charts listed in *Billboard*. The song was "Rock the Boat," recorded by a previously unknown group called the Hues Corporation. It had been out for a year, with few sales, no promotion, and no radio airplay, before being discovered somehow by New York City dance hall audiences. Simply by word of mouth among the dancing set, sales of the record increased steadily. It climbed the *Billboard* lists until reaching a point where radio stations had no choice but to play it, and it soon topped the charts.

Only a gifted prophet could have foreseen back in the Summer of '74 that, indeed, the long national nightmare was over and that the next era would be marked not by the variety and number of social and political crises, but by the absence of any. And only a very gifted prophet could have anticipated that the triumph of "Rock the Boat" against the overwhelming odds of the tightly-controlled, promotion-oriented music industry would signal the beginning of a new era, in which the style of entertainment this song represented would soon take over widespread areas of our popular culture.

"It is unlikely that any major trend (a Presley or Beatles type phenomena) is going to overtake us,"[1] *Billboard* predicted at the close of 1974. Yet, within three years, disco virtually owned *Billboard's* record charts. Twelve of the top twenty-five pop singles and twenty-two of the top soul singles featured disco music during a typical week in February, 1978.[2] The soundtrack album from "Saturday Night Fever," all disco music, was firmly enthroned atop the album charts, selling a phenomenal 800,000 two-album sets per week. One cut from the album, the Bee Gee's "How Deep Is Your Love," had just completed a record-tying eighteen weeks in the Top Ten (more than any other record in rock history); the movie itself had been ranked second in weekly total grosses every week since its premiere the previous December.

By the Winter of '77-78, disco music had also become the dominant background music on TV programs, commercials, and movie soundtracks. Looking beyond the music, though, disco has profoundly affected other American businesses. As reported in *Newsweek*.

> "Disco is the greatest thing that ever happened to restaurants," says Ron Briskman, a Chicago restauranteur-turned-disco entrepreneur. "The Loop is dead at night, but suddenly, with discos happening, we're busy every night. We just take away the tables. It's a new source of income."[3]

The disco boom has reverberated throughout the nightlife business (estimates of new dance halls have totaled 10,000), bringing new life to urban downtowns; it has also exploded the dance-studio business and influenced even the fashion industry.

Why did disco happen and why in the mid-70's? Is there a connection between this popular culture phenomenon and the social and political events (or non-events) of the decade? The first step in analyzing what happened is to understand just what disco—both the music and the industry surrounding it—is all about.

Songs I used to think were boring, like "The Hustle," I like now, because they're good to dance to.[4]

My attitude is that everyone wants to dance. Even if you can't dance, I'm going to try to make you.[5]

These two statements—the first from a *Rolling Stone* correspondent, the second from Bunny Sigler, a top disco artist/producer—illustrate by far the most important point to realize about disco music: it's for dancing. Everyone involved in the process of creating a disco hit, from the producers and composers through the performers and promoters down to the dee-jays and audiences, treats this music as a means to stimulate dancing. This attitude is hardly new in popular music history; it's been prevalent, to varying extents, in connection with soul, rock 'n' roll, rythm-and-blues, mambos and cha-chas, swing, "hot jazz" (Dixieland), ragtime, and even waltz music.

When dance hall audiences in New York and other cities demanded rhythmically-charged, highly-danceable music in the mid '70's, and when the record industry responded to that demand, both groups were following a pattern that extended back not only through our cultural history, but even back across the Atlantic. The bond between music and dancing has always been an undeniably strong feature of African culture, as J.H. Nketia discusses in *The Music of Africa:*

Although purely contemplative music is practiced in African societies in restricted contexts, the cultivation of music that is integrated with dance, or music that stimulates affective motor response, is much more prevalent.[6]

Since the contribution of Afro-American culture is so basic to American popular music—disco itself originated as black music and dance—what Nketia then says about the function of African dance is especially intriguing:

The importance attached to the dance does not lie only in the scope it provides for the release of emotion stimulated by music... Because the dance is an avenue of expression, it may be closely related to the themes and purposes of social occasions, though the guiding principle may be complex.[7]

In an earlier chapter, Nketia outlines two "guiding principles" behind the function of music and dance in Africa: (1) to encourage involvement in the community, and (2) to strengthen its social bonds and values. In other words, music and dance in Africa function as social and cultural rituals, and are crucial in both establishing and maintaining a community, as well as expressing its values. But can this ritualistic approach to dance and music be applied to American popular culture in general, and to disco in particular? Certain dance situations common in the United States can no doubt be judged as contributing to the strength of the community involved: e.g. square dances, firemen's balls, block parties, cotillions, school proms. But can a large-scale popular culture movement, such as disco, be considered a type of national ritual? Does it help bind a people together and express their communal values?

Popular music historian Ian Whitcomb chooses the ritualistic approach to analyze ragtime music and its related dance craze in his history of American popular music, *After the Ball*. Ragtime began as a style of piano playing and composition, accompanying a turn-of-the-century dance called the cakewalk. Once the music caught on, a large number of dances spun off from it, including the turkey trot, bunny hop, and grizzly bear. The result was the Dance Mania of 1911-17; Whitcomb notes, "In 1913, as the song said, 'My Wife Is Dancing Mad!' and no restaurant could hope to survive without a dance floor."[8] The music publishing industry, centered in New York's "Tin Pan Alley," worked ragtime into every conceivable song and, in doing so, sold these songs at an unprecedented rate. The craze brought booming business to cafes, cabarets, night clubs, and dancing schools, and even stimulated interest and sales in a brand-new piece of entertainment technology, Edison's cylinder record player.

Why did pre-World War I America take up dancing with such enthusiasm? Whitcomb attributes the ragtime Dance Mania to post-Victorian social movements toward greater freedom for women, ethnic groups, blacks, and in sexual relationships. He describes how urban blacks, through ragtime music and dancing, brought a strong and sensuous emotionalism to American nightlife. Women became equal partners in ragtime dancing and their movements became more sexual. Nightlife in general, where "immediate satisfaction, by instant contact, was promised,"[9] exploded in popularity and resulted in an ethnically-mixed, sexually-stimulating social atmosphere.

Even the briefest comparison of ragtime and disco shows that the two crazes had strikingly similar effects on the music and entertainment industries of their respective times. Whether or not they both reflect similar social values and movements is a more complex matter, and merely posing the question assumed that a popular dance craze can be treated as a national ritual. But if that assumption is made, then the issue of "Why disco in the mid-70's?" becomes not a matter of musical tastes, but of social forces and cultural values. The question now becomes, as Whitcomb raised in dealing with ragtime, "Why did America in the 70's take up dancing with such enthusiasm?"

> By his leaving, Nixon seemed at last to redeem the 1968 pledge he took from a girl holding up a campaign sign in Ohio: BRING US TOGETHER.[10]

Time's comment about Nixon's resignation may have been wishful thinking at the time it was published, yet no doubt the era of social and political stability following that summer of '74 served to reverse some of the disruptive, divisive results of the previous dozen years. A profound psychological difference exists between a country fighting an unpopular, seemingly-endless war, bursting from inside with dissension and disorder, poisoned with corruption in its highest offices, and a country that appears to have put these matters to rest. That difference can be summarized in just one word essential to the survival of any community: security.

Is a society that feels more secure about itself more likely to make dancing a key element in its popular culture? A quick run-through of American popular dance crazes reveals that each swell of enthusiasm took place during one of the more peaceful periods, socially and politically, of this century: Ragtime—mid-1910's; Jazz (Charleston)—mid-20's; Big Band—late 30's; Mambo and Cha-Cha—mid-50's; Twist—early 60's. And what history demonstrates also makes sense from a cultural viewpoint. Any group of people brought together for whatever purposes must feel relatively secure from direct outside pressures and, perhaps more importantly, secure about each other. What's significant about the group brought together by disco, as compared, for example, to the protest and rock-festival groups of the 60's, are the broad economic, age, and lifestyle bases being drawn from. Disco's popularity is hardly limited to the "swinging singles" set most closely associated with it; as *Newsweek* describes.

> The chance to boogie again is appealing to the Beautiful People, the bourgeoisie and the blue-collar worker alike... There are kiddie discos, senior-citizen discos, roller-skating discos and discos on wheels, which carry their canned music and lights to suburbia. Disco franchizers talk about becoming "the McDonald's of the entertainment business."[11]

Could any craze have attracted such a diverse following during the late 60's and early 70's, when the mention of just one issue, the Vietnam War, might split any community into heated factions? Whether such a craze could or couldn't, the fact remains that none did. Apparently by the mid-70's, however, enough cultural values were shared by enough groups of people, with divisive issues at a low enough level of intensity, for a broad-based community to jell around disco.

If such a community exists, and if disco is a national popular ritual helping to establish and maintain it, then what values does the "disco-mmunity" share and express? Returning again to the Summer of '74, a clue to one key value may be found in this speculatory comment on the Ford presidency, from political scientist Richard E. Neustadt:

> He may be conservative, but he appears to be the kind of guy who knows who he is and is not worried about it. We have had recent experiences with two men who were enormously worried about their own securities. [These wounds] should be healed somewhat by the Ford presidency.[12]

The increase of security on the national level during the mid-70's, along with a sense of more secure leadership in the Ford and Carter Administrations, is likely to have resulted in greater personal security for the individual American. And dancing, after all, is an assertive act of personal self-expression; people "enormously worried about their own securities" are perhaps generally too inhibited to enjoy stepping out on the floor and dancing in front of others, especially large groups of strangers. (It's interesting to note that the only President in recent times to enjoy dancing was Gerald Ford.)

The title of one of the 70's leading bestsellers, I'm OK, You're OK, could just as easily serve as the title of a disco hit. The security and assertiveness it projects is a key force behind learning the steps, buying the clothes, fixing the hair—symbolizing the desire to look and feel good on the dance floor of life. It's perhaps not so much a drive to be the best dancer or even the best-looking dancer, though competition is surely a factor, but to be successful in a community where everyone looks, dances, and feels good. Perhaps the perfect blending of national security, personal assertiveness, and the disco lifestyle is expressed in the following quotation from Barry White, the disco composer/orchestrator/bandleader/singer/superstar:

> My thing, you see, is whatever you dig doing, right on! That's the freedom of America. That's why I say there's no place on earth I'd rather be.[13]

That Barry White, a black American, should be waving the flag with such patriotic fervor is, in itself, a key feature of the 70's disco-mmunity. Numerous aspects of the whole movement demonstrate that many blacks have climbed up the economic ladder onto more secure and assertive rungs. For once, black artists, producers, and record company staffs have not been "co-opted" by the white-controlled popular music industry (as had been the pattern since ragtime); in fact, the top disco company, Philadelphia International, has blacks in all the higher positions and hires whites as recording sidemen. Radio programming, too, has never been as integrated, with black artists topping white playlists and vice versa. As evidence of changing popular attitudes, the lyrics of black disco songs contain little social protest and even less blues-content. Singer/composer Issac Hayes, for example, once wore chains as a sign of black militance, but his new lyrics now reflect rising status: "I took you out of the ghetto," he sings to a female partner, "but I couldn't get the ghetto out of you."

Disco also reflects changes in public attitudes toward sex and women's roles. Although the lyrics to many disco hits simply encourage or describe dancing (the last thing a disco composer wants the audience to do is stop and catch the words), other songs are strikingly erotic, from the titles ("Keep It Comin', Love") to the lyrics ("Don't Leave Me This Way") to the vocal inflection (anything by Donna Summer). In fact, one critic labeled Summer's debut album as "the first frankly erotic album ever to achieve wide currency and airplay."[14] Disco lyrics also frequently present a more assertive role for women, especially in sexual relationships. In songs such as "Best of My Love," "Doctor's Orders," "Don't Leave Me This Way," and again anything by Donna Summer, females are no longer asking for sexual satisfaction, they're demanding it.

Earlier in this essay, ragtime and its Dance Mania were described as creating an "ethnically-mixed, sexually-stimulating atmosphere" for the 1910's nightlife. The achievements of all the post-Victorian social movements were acted out on the ragtime dance floors, just as the results of the "New Morality" and liberation movements of the 60's and 70's are seen every night on the disco floor. Various social critics have described discos as zones of acceptance and interaction between males and females, gays and straights, whites and blacks and Hispanics, urbanites and suburbanites, the old and the young, the rich and the poor and the average:

Superflies, hobbits, dream queens and punks—the crowds are as democratic as they were in anybody's cafetorium.[15]

There is no stigma attached to girls dancing with girls or boys with boys—and no compulsion to find a mate.[16]

In Detroit, discos are one of the few places where blacks and whites truly mingle. "I've been prejudiced all my life and only now am I beginning to relax with blacks... People feel comfortable here."[17]

The movie "Saturday Night Fever," released in December '77, captures perfectly the spirit of the assertive, interactive disco-mmunity. With a racially- and ethnically-integrated cast and musical soundtrack as the backdrop, the hero and heroine (John Travolta and Karen Lynn Gorney) meet, dance, pair off, dance, flirt, dance—all on the urban disco floor. Both characters are noticeably proud, secure, sociable, assertive, competitive, and successful. Gorney, in particular, is an upwardly-mobile career person; Travolta becomes one through her. The disco-mmunity they inhabit is portrayed as sexually stimulating and morally uninhibited, although, perhaps as a nod to women's lib, the movie closes not with the customary hero/heroine kiss, but with a long, firm, lingering handshake.

The characters Travolta and Gorney portray, along with the whole disco-mmunity they represent, might be described in a far less flattering term: narcissistic. In his influential essay on the 70's, "The Me Decade and the Third Great Awakening," Tom Wolfe describes numerous cultural symptoms of what he calls "The luxury enjoyed by so many millions of middling folk, of dwelling upon the self."[18] He and other contemporary social critics see the 70's as a decade of rampant self-interest, with the emphasis on strictly personal gratification reflected in such popular advertising slogans as "Have it your way," "You--you're the one," "We built one for you," "Hey, that's my Dodge," and "Me and my RC."

If the 70's are indeed "The Me Decade," then perhaps the disco experience represents the ultimate narcissistic goal of mass-mediated America: stardom. At a disco, the audience is no longer just the audience; as Barry White describes it,

The record buyer can be the rock star...
People can dress up in the baddest fashions and look like they're in somebody's group. The hippest mother gets a shot at stardom at the disco.[19]

The disco dancer's sense of being "on stage" is heightened by all the spotlights and flashing colors, the costumes, the special effects (e.g. laser beams, fog machines), and the all-encompassing, high-volume music. Everyone gets the chance to play celebrity at a disco, or at least the chance to play John Travolta playing celebrity at the disco in "Saturday Night Fever." In an era when rock stars make millions, lead flashy and well-publicized lives, make the covers of top magazines, achieve international fame, and even live in old Hollywood mansions, the appeal of this aspect of the disco lifestyle is certainly understandable.

Will history look upon disco as the self-indulgent ritual of a decadent society, dancing into the wee hours of civilization, as the world ran through its energy resources, fought over territory and politics and religion, proved incapable of controlling terrorists or population or nuclear materials, and spent almost $1 million per minute arming itself? Or will a positive view prevail, in which the disco ritual comes to symbolize a healthy and secure society, promoting the freedom and assertiveness of its groups and individuals?

At this point, late in the 70's, the jury is still out on disco and the society it represents. But history has provided four precedents this century, all adding up to the same lesson: whether the popular ritual of dancing is viewed positively or negatively, each dance craze since ragtime ended abruptly when national or international problems became too severe to ignore any longer. What will empty the dance floors this time? The answer may already be there, somewhere outside, heading toward us.

NOTES

[1]*Billboard*, January 4, 1975, p.14.

[2]*Billboard*, February 18, 1978.

[3]"Get Up and Boogie!" in *Newsweek*, November 8, 1976, p.95.

[4]Cindy McEhrlich, "Confessions of the Disco Kid," in *Rolling Stone*, August 28, 1975, p.47.

[5]Tom Vickers, "Disco Stars," in *Rolling Stone*, August 28, 1975, p.64.

[6]J.H. Nketia, *The Music of Africa*, p.206.

[7]Nketia, p.207.

[8]Ian Whitcomb, *After the Ball*, p.33.

[9]Whitcomb, p.33.

[10]*Time*, August 10, 1974, p.8.

[11]*Newsweek*, p.94.

[12]*Time*, p.65.

[13]John Lombardi, "Barry White," in *Rolling Stone*, August 28, 1975, p.54.

[14]Albert Goldman, "Disco Fever," in *Esquire*, December, 1977, p.60.

[15]McEhrlich, p.47.

[16]*Newsweek*, p.95.

[17]*Newsweek*, p.95.

[18]Tom Wolfe, "The Me Decade and the Third Great Awakening," in Paul J. Dolan and Edward Quinn, ed., *The Sense of the Seventies*, p.39.

[19]*Newsweek*, p.95.

Discussing "Disco-mmunity, or I'm OK, You're OK, So Let's Dance"

1) Discos attract such a broad-based collection of individuals that the disco experience may represent different things to different people. Discuss how the disco experience can be either a rite of unity, passage, reversal, or possibly season or humanity, depending on the individual. If possible, base part of your discussion on quotes from actual participants.

2) The various ways we experience music in popular culture can all be seen as rituals. Using Nketia's guiding principles for the function of music as a ritual (to establish and maintain a community, and to express its values), discuss these music experiences: 1) listening to the radio, 2) purchasing and listening to records, 3) attending a small club or coffeehouse, 4) attending a large concert, and 5) performing music.

PART SIX
POPULAR FORMULAS

Introduction

The concept of formula in the popular arts gives us another tool for understanding the large and seemingly chaotic realm of popular culture. Note here that the popular arts may be differentiated from some of the other areas which have been covered earlier in this text, such as popular rituals, icons, and heroes. You should be aware, though, that these are by no means rigid categories; rather they are often just different ways of looking at the same thing. Any single phenomenon may be approached from a variety of angles. Take one of the earlier topics, Jack Johnson, who is placed in the Heroes section of the book. Jack Johnson may also be understood in terms of the myths he embodied, in terms of the sports ritual of boxing, as a victim of stereotyping, or even as a human icon. All of these approaches are legitimate, and all will hopefully provide fresh insights into the phenomenon of Jack Johnson. Popular culture study demands, then, a total view of any cultural product, and this should include the placing of the product or phenomenon in both a cultural and an individual context. By cultural context is meant the general social atmosphere and structure in which the product is produced and received. By individual context is meant the actual experience of the individual person or consumer of the product, what it is like for you or someone else to witness or be part of the particular experience.

With this in mind, we may define popular formulas as structures of conventions which are commonly employed in a great number of works of popular art. Each kind of popular art, like a recipe, is made up of special ingredients. The most popular art forms, like the most popular foods, are usually composed of ingredients with which we are familiar. We have tasted them before, know that we like them, and will consume them again. In the popular arts, the familiar ingredients in the formula are the *conventions,* the components which are usually already known to both the creator and audience beforehand. Conventions include the settings, heroes, stereotypes, myths, rituals, artifacts, and other elements which are generally used over and over in a certain kind of popular art. As you see, then, the concept of formula embraces all of the areas of popular culture previously covered in this book, by placing them in the works of the popular arts.

The popular arts include the content of almost all of the media of communication. The medium of print gives us popular fiction, nonfiction, and poetry, conveyed in books, magazines, and newspapers. The medium of live presentation gives us circuses, concerts, and popular theater. With the advent of the electronic media, most entertainment forms are now carried by means of film, radio, and television. Another area of the popular arts, music, is conveyed in a number of ways—by recordings, live performances, or again, by the media of radio and television.

The concept of formula may be applied to any work of popular art in any of the media. In popular music, for example, we may study both the music and song lyrics in terms of formula. In the music itself, formula may consist of rhythms, melodies, certain techniques, and other elements which are generally familiar to the audience. Stylistic trends in popular music, in fact, are often so obvious that we take them for granted. The concept of formula implies artistic imitation, and a musical formula, such as the now-popular disco music, is usually a phenomenon which begins with a small group of culture leaders and then spreads quickly throughout the culture through imitation and repetition. In the present popular culture such formulas may be short-lived because they suffer from overexposure and media saturation. The audience rapidly becomes bored with what only recently seemed so fresh and new. On the other hand, there is considerable continuity to many aspects of formula, as with the lyrics of popular songs. Conventional themes, such as the lament of lost love, may persist for centuries, even though the vehicle, or musical style, is constantly changing.

Conventions are important to the audience of popular art because they do assert a shared continuity of values; they bind a culture together through the artistic expression of commonly known and accepted ways of thinking and doing. The conventions of popular art filter reality for us by selecting out, from among infinite possibilities, a rather narrow range of expressions. Conventions are thus comforting, since they tell us that we live in an orderly world, a world that can be controlled through popular art. Conventions do not threaten us with startling new ideas or patterns of action but give us ideas, characters, and actions which are predictable.

The predictability of popular art does not necessarily imply inferiority, nor does it mean that the popular arts are basically boring. There seem to be certain patterns of art which have such strong appeal to the popular audience that they can be repeated indefinitely, with only minor variations, without becoming stale. The timeless theme of the triumph of good over evil, for instance, takes many conventional forms in popular art. The forces of good usually representing the social order may be detectives, policemen, doctors, cowboys, firefighters, or just plain folks who are called upon by an unusual situation to perform heroic deeds. The forces of evil, whether they are criminals, fires, diseases, natural disasters, or monsters, disrupt the social order and must be destroyed. The acting out of a theme such as this is found in popular art from the time of the classical myth narratives through the troubadors of the Middle Ages to today's movies and television shows.

The formulas of popular art include such conventional themes, but they are more than themes, as they encompass the whole structure of the work, every part of the book or TV show or piece of music or whatever. Many formulas may be found in a variety of media. These formulas are narrative structures such as the detective story, the science fiction story, the domestic comedy, the western, and the soap opera. Within these broad categories may be found many standard variations of the basic formula. The detective story, for example, may be divided into such sub-formulas as the old genteel story of detection, the hardboiled or tough-guy private eye story, and the domestic sentimental mystery.

It is important here to remember that the study of popular art begins with the individual work. You might, then, look at a particular television drama to discover its conventions. Describe the character types, the setting, the events of the story, the artifacts which appear, the ideas which are expressed by the narrative. Having done this, you may compare the individual work to others and fit it into a broader formulaic category. This sort of study requires familiarity with a wide range of popular art, a familiarity most of us have through a lifetime of media exposure.

While the study of formulas mainly concentrates on conventions, popular art also contains *inventions,* elements which are innovative or which make the work unique. These inventions may be such things as different turns of plot or characters who seem individualized rather than typed. Inventions may be little more than minor variations within a basic formula, but they are important psychologically because inventions can introduce new ideas and help us adjust to change. Inventions are also necessary to maintain audience interest, so that each episode of a TV series, for instance, will likely introduce some slightly new character, setting, plot, theme, or other variation at the same time it retains the same basic structure of conventions, its formula.

Because the concept of formula applies to virtually all of the popular arts in all media, the four essays which follow can only serve as sample approaches. John Cawelti's essay on the Western outlines the method of formula analysis by applying it in broad terms to one of the most distinctive and enduring types of American popular narrative. Cawelti has been one of the pioneers of formula study, and his book *Adventure, Mystery, and Romance,* cited in the following brief bibliography, is highly recommended reading for any student of popular formulas. Note that Cawelti focuses on what makes the Western formula unique, the characteristics that distinguish it from other story forms. This may be a useful approach for the student of popular culture—to ask what makes a particular work or kind of work special, to enumerate all the characteristics that make it what it is.

While Cawelti's attitude to his subject is respectful, Joanna Russ's approach is much more critical, even satirical. Yet she is able to define sharply the outstanding elements of the Modern Gothic formula. Her essay is also a useful example because it combines close analysis of the works themselves with an understanding of the reader's responses to the novels. The experience of art is a personal experience, and Russ is aware that the work exists in an interaction between the printed page and the reader.

Walter Evans's essay on the monster movie formula may strike you as an exaggerated interpretation, but he backs up his sexual theory with good examples and reasoning that is difficult to dispute. At its best, analysis of the popular arts can be as lively and provocative as the arts themselves. And since the student of popular culture is often exploring territories which have been neglected by traditional scholars, it may take some imaginative leaps of mind to gain an understanding of the material under study. There are few books in the library to serve as ready references for popular culture analysis, so you must often rely on native knowledge of your culture and on general tools of thought.

The last essay, by David Sonenschein on romance magazines, provides an example of the sociological approach, in that it draws conclusions about broad cultural beliefs regarding love, sex, and marriage. Sonenschein also utilizes the method of content analysis in examining a "scientific" sampling of magazines. This method is useful for dealing with a great number of works because it gives a statistical breakdown of the conventions found in the material. Sonenschein then uses his data as a solid base for a general discussion of the cultural functions of the romance magazines. This combination of detailed data analysis and generalization is effective.

Whatever approach you choose to take toward the study of the popular arts and whatever special art form you choose to examine, the concept of formula will be an essential part of your study. For in almost all of the popular culture, repetition, imitation, and familiarity are key principles of understanding.

Selected Further Reading

Cawelti, John G. *Adventure, Mystery, and Romance.* Chicago: The University of Chicago Press, 1976.

Grant, Barry K., ed. *Film Genre: Theory and Criticism.* Metuchen, NJ: The Scarecrow Press, Inc., 1977.

Greene, Suzanne Ellery. *Books for Pleasure: Popular Fiction 1914-1945.* Bowling Green, Ohio: Popular Press, 1974.

Harper, Ralph. *The World of the Thriller,* Baltimore, Md.: Johns Hopkins. University Press, 1974.

Hart, James D. *The Popular Book: A History of America's Literary Taste.* New York: Oxford University Press, 1950.

Landrum, Larry, Pat Browne, and Ray B. Browne. *Dimensions of Detective Fiction.* Bowling Green, Ohio: Popular Press, 1976.

Marcus, Greil. *Mystery Train: Images of America in Rock n' Roll Music.* New York: E.P. Dutton, 1976.

Newcomb, Horace. *TV: The Most Popular Art.* Garden City, New York: Anchor Press, 1974.

Nye, Russel. *The Unembarrassed Muse: The Popular Arts in America.* New York: Dial Press, 1970.

Savagery, Civilization
and the Western Hero

By John G. Cawelti

The Western formula emerged as American attitudes toward the frontier gradually underwent significant change around the middle of the nineteenth century. It was possible for Americans in the early nineteenth century to treat the frontier as a symbol of fundamental moral antitheses between man and nature, and, consequently, to use a frontier setting in fiction that engaged itself with a profound exploration of the nature and limitations of man and society. However, the redefinition of the frontier as a place where advancing civilization met a declining savagery changed the frontier setting into a locus of conflicts which were always qualified and contained by the knowledge that the advance of civilization would largely eliminate them. Or, to put it another way, the frontier setting now provided a fictional justification for enjoying violent conflicts and the expression of lawless force without feeling that they threatened the values or the fabric of society.

The social and historical aspects of setting are just as important in defining the Western formula as geography. The Western story is set at a certain moment in the development of American civilization, namely at that point when savagery and lawlessness are in decline before the advancing wave of law and order, but are still strong enough to pose a local and momentarily significant challenge. In the actual history of the West, this moment was probably a relatively brief one in any particular area. In any case, the complex clashes of different interest groups over the use of Western resources and the pattern of settlement surely involved more people in a more

Reprinted John Cawelti from, The Six-Gun Mystique, Bowling Green University Popular Press, Bowling Green, Ohio. Reprinted with the permission of the author and publisher.

fundamental way than the struggle with Indians or outlaws. Nonetheless, it is the latter which has become central to the Western formula. The relatively brief stage in the social evolution of the West when outlaws or Indians posed a threat to the community's stability has been erected into a timeless epic past in which heroic individual defenders of law and order without the vast social resources of police and courts stand poised against the threat of lawlessness or savagery. But it is also the nature of this epic moment that the larger forces of civilized society are just waiting in the wings for their cue. However threatening he may appear at the moment, the Indian is vanishing and the outlaw about to be superseded. It is because they too represent this epic moment that we are likely to think of such novels as Cooper's *Last of the Mohicans,* Bird's *Nick of the Woods,* or more recent historical novels like Walter Edmonds' *Drums Along the Mohawk* as Westerns, though they are not set in what we have come to know as the West.

Why then has this epic moment been primarily associated in fiction with a particular West, that of the Great Plains and the mountains and deserts of the "Far West" and with a particular historical moment, that of heyday of the open range cattle industry of the later nineteenth century? Westerns can be set at a later time—some of Zane Grey's stories take place in the twenties and some, like those of Gene Autry, Roy Rogers or "Sky King," in the present—but even at these later dates the costumes and the way of life presented tend to be that of the later nineteenth century. Several factors probably contributed to this particular fixation of the epic moment. Included among these would be the ideological tendency of Americans to see the Far West as the last stronghold of certain traditional values, as well as the peculiar attractiveness of the cowboy hero. But more important than these factors, the Western requires a means of isolating and intensifying the drama of the frontier encounter between social order and lawlessness. For this purpose, the geographic setting of the Great Plains and adjacent areas has proved particularly appropriate, especially since the advent of film and television have placed a primary emphasis on visual articulation. Four characteristics of the Great Plains topography have been especially important: its openness, its aridity and general inhospitability to human life, its great extremes of light and climate, and, paradoxically, its grandeur and beauty. These topographic features create an effective backdrop for the action of the Western because they exemplify in visual images the thematic conflict between civilization and savagery, and its resolution. In particular, the Western has come to center about the image of the isolated town or ranch or fort surrounded by the vast open grandeur of prairie or desert and connected to the rest of the civilized world by

The stagecoach enters the savage grandeur of Monument Valley in *Stagecoach.*

a railroad, a stagecoach, or simply a trail. This tenuous link can still be broken by the forces of lawlessness, but never permanently. We can conceive it as a possibility that the town will be swept back into the desert—the rickety wooden buildings with their tottering false fronts help express the tenuousness of the town's position against the surrounding prairie; nonetheless we do not see the town solely as an isolated fort in hostile country, like an outpost of the French foreign legion in *Beau Geste,* but as the advance guard of an oncoming civilization. Moreover, while the prairie or desert may be inhospitable, it is not hostile. Its openness, freshness and grandeur also play an important role in the Western. Thus, the open prairie around the town serves not only as a haven of lawlessness and savagery, but as a backdrop of epic magnitude and even, at times, as a source of regenerating power.

This characteristic setting reflects and helps dramatize the tripartite division of characters that dominates the Western pattern of action. The townspeople hover defensively in their settlement, threatened by the outlaws or Indians who are associated with the inhospitable and uncontrollable elements of the surrounding landscape.The townspeople are static and largely incapable of movement beyond their little settlement. The outlaws or savages can move freely across the landscape. The hero, though a friend of the townspeople, has the lawless power of movement in that he, like the savages, is a horseman and possesses skills of wilderness existence. The moral character of the hero also appears symbolically in the Western setting. In its rocky aridity and climatic extremes the Great Plains landscape embodies the hostile savagery of Indians and outlaws, while its vast openness, its vistas of snow-covered peaks in the distance, and its great sunrises and sunsets (in the purple prose of Zane Grey, for example) suggest the epic courage and regenerative power of the hero. Thus, in every respect, Western topography helps dramatize more intensely the clash of characters and the thematic conflicts of the story.

The special openness of the topography of the Great Plains and western desert has made it particularly expressive for the portrayal of movement. Against the background of the terrain, a skillful director can create infinite variations of space ranging from long panoramas to close-ups and he can clearly articulate movement across these various spaces. No matter how often one sees it, there is something inescapably effective about that scene, beloved of Western directors, in which a rider appears like an infinitely small dot at the far end of a great empty horizon and then rides toward us across the intervening space, just as there is a different thrill about the vision of a group of horses and men plunging pell-mell from the foreground into the empty distance. Nor is there anything which quite matches the feeling of suspense when the camera picks up a little group of wagons threading their way across the middle distance and then pans across the arid rocks and up the slopes of a canyon until it suddenly comes upon a group of Indians waiting in ambush. Moreover, the western landscape is uniquely adaptable to certain kinds of strong visual effects because of the sharp contrasts of light and shadow characteristic of an arid climate together with the topographical contrasts of plain and mountain, rocky outcrops and flat deserts, steep bare canyons and forested plateaus. The characteristic openness and aridity of the topography also makes the contrast between man and nature and between wilderness and society visually strong.

Perhaps no film exploits the visual resources of the western landscape more brilliantly than John Ford's *Stagecoach 1939*. The film opens on a street in one of those western shanty towns characterized by rickety false fronts. By the rushing motion of horses and wagons along the street and by the long vista down the street and out into the desert we are immediately made aware of the surrounding wilderness and of the central theme of movement across it which will dominate the film. This opening introduction of the visual theme of fragile town contrasted with epic wildernesss will be developed throughout the film in the contrast between the flimsy stagecoach and the magnificent landscape through which it moves. Similarly, the restless motion of the opening scene will be projected into the thrust of the stagecoach across the landscsape. This opening is followed by several brief scenes leading up to the departure of the stagecoach. These scenes are cut at a rather breathless pace so that they do not slow down the sense of motion and flight generated by the opening. Visually, they dwell on two aspects of the town, its dark, narrow and crowded interiors and its ramshackle sidewalks and storefronts, thus establishing in visual terms the restrictive and artificial character of town life. Then the stagecoach departs on its voyage and we are plunged into the vast openness and grandeur of the wilderness with the crowded wooden stagecoach serving as a visual reminder of the narrow town life it has left behind. Ford chose to shoot the major portion of the stagecoach's journey in Monument Valley, a brilliant choice because the visual characteristics of that topography perfectly embody the complex mixture of epic grandeur and savage hostility that the film requires. The valley itself is a large, flat desert between steep hills. Thrusting up out of the valley floor gigantic monoliths of bare rock dwarf the stagecoach as it winds across this vast panorama. This combination of large open desert broken by majestic upthrusts of rock and surrounded by threatening hills creates an enormously effective visual environment for the story, which centers around the way in which the artificial social roles and attitudes of the travellers break down under the impact of the wilderness. Those travellers who are able to transcend their former roles are regenerated by the experience: the drunken doctor delivers a baby, the meek salesman shows courage, the whore becomes the heroine of a romance and the outlaw becomes a lover. By stunning photographic representation of the visual contrasts of desert, hills and moving stagecoach, Ford transforms the journey of the stagecoach into an epic voyage that transcends the film's rather limited romantic plot.

Costume—another feature of the Western setting—has also contributed greatly to the Western's success in film. Like topgraphy, western costume gains effectiveness both from intrinsic interest and from the way writers and filmmakers have learned how to make it reflect character and theme. In simplest form, as in the B Westerns, costumes symbolized moral opposition. The good guy wears clean,well-pressed clothes and a white hat. The villain dressed sloppily in black. The importance of this convention, simple-minded as it was, became apparent when, to create a more sophisticated "adult" Western, directors frequently chose to dress their heroes in black. However, the tradition of western costume also contains more complex meanings. An important distinction marks off both hero and villain from the townspeople. The townspeople usually wear the ordinary street clothing associated with the later nineteenth century, suits for men and long dresses for women. On the whole this clothing is simple as compared to the more elaborate

One of silent films' greatest western heroes, William S. Hart. His costume reveals him as a "man in the middle."

fashions of the period and this simplicity is one way of expressing the Westerness of the costume. However, in the midst of desert, the townspeople's clothing has an air of non-utilitarian artificiality somewhat like the ubiquitous false fronts on the town itself. It is perhaps significant that even in westerns purportedly set at a later date, the women tend to wear the full-length dresses of an earlier period.

The costumes associated with heroes and outlaws or savages are more striking. Paradoxically, they are both more utilitarian and more artificial than those of the townspeople. The cowboy's boots, tight-fitting pants or chaps, his heavy shirt and bandana, his gun, and finally his large ten-gallon hat all symbolize his adaptation to the wilderness. But utility is only one of the principles of the hero-outlaw's dress. The other is dandyism, that highly artificial love of elegance for its own sake. In the Western, dandyism sometimes takes the overt and obvious form of elaborate costumes laid over with fringes, tassels and scrollwork like a rococo drawing room. But it is more powerfully exemplified in the elegance of those beautifully tailored cowboy uniforms which John Wayne so magnificently fills out in the Westerns of John Ford and Howard Hawks.

The enormous attraction of this combination of naturalness and artifice has played a significant role in both popular and avant-garde art since the middle of the nineteenth century. Baudelaire's fascination with the dandyism of the savage which he described as "the supreme incarnation of the idea of Beauty transported into the material world," is just one indication of the nineteenth century's fascination with the mixture of savagery and elegance which has been implicit in the costume of the Western hero from the beginning. Cooper's Leatherstocking even gained his name from his costume, suggesting the extent to which this particular kind of dress excited Cooper's imagination. Like later cowboys, Leatherstocking's costume combined nature and artifice. His dress was largely made of the skins of animals and it was particularly adapted to the needs of wilderness life. Yet at the same time it was subtly ornamented with buckskin fringes and porcupine quills "after the manner of the Indians." Still, it is important to note that Leatherstocking's costume developed along the same lines. In its basic outlines it resembled town dress more than that of the Indian, yet it was more functional for movement across the plains than that of the townspeople. At the same time, the cowboy dress had a dandyish splendor and elegance lacking in the drab fashions of the town and based on Indian or Mexican models. In later Westerns, the hero shared many of these qualities with the villain, just as Leatherstocking had a touch of Indian, despite his repeated assurances that he was "a man without a cross," i.e. actual Indian

The western outlaw as rebel hero. An advertisement for a nineteenth century dramatic romanticization of the life of Jesse James.

kinship. But the hero's costume still differentiated him from the savage, whether Indian or outlaw, both by its basic resemblance to civilized dress and by its greater restraint and decorum. Thus costume, like setting, expressed the transcendent and intermediate quality of the hero. By lying between two ways of life, he transcended the restrictions and limitations of both. Or, to put it another way the Western setting and costume embody the basic escapist principle of having your cake and eating it too.

As already indicated, there are three central roles in the Western: the townspeople or agents of civilization, the savages or outlaws who threaten this first group, and the heroes who are above all "men in the middle," that is, they possess many qualities and skills of the savages, but are fundamentally committed to the townspeople. It is out of the multiple variations possible on the relationships between these groups that the various Western plots are concocted. For example, the simplest version of all has the hero protecting the townspeople from the savages, using his own savage skills against the denizens of the wilderness. A second, more complex variation shows the hero initially indifferent to the plight of the townspeople and more inclined to identify himself with the savages. However, in the course of the story his position changes and he becomes the ally of the townspeople. This variation can generate a number of different plots. There is the revenge Western: a hero seeks revenge against an outlaw or Indian who has wronged him. In order to accomplish his vengeance, he rejects the pacifistic ideals of the townspeople, but in the end he discovers that he is really committed to their way of life (John Ford's *The Searchers*). Another plot based on this variation of the character relations is that of the hero who initially seeks his own selfish material gain, using his savage skills as a means to this end; but as the story progresses, he discovers his moral involvement with the townspeople and becomes their champion (cf. Anthony Mann's film *The Far Country*). It is also possible, while maintaining the system of relationships, to reverse the conclusion of the plot as in those stories where the townspeople come to accept the hero's savage mode of action (cf. John Ford's *Stagecoach* or, to a certain extent, Wister's *The Virginian*). A third variation of the basic theme of relationships has the hero caught in the middle between the townspeople's need for his savage skills and their rejection of his way of life. This third variation, common in recent Westerns, often ends in the destruction of the hero (cf. the films *The Gunfighter* or *Invitation to a Gunfighter*) or in his voluntary exile (*Shane, High Noon, Two Rode Together*). The existence of these and many other variations suggests that the exploration of a certain pattern of relationships is more important to the Western than a particular outcome, though it is also probable that they reflect different components of the mass audience, the simpler variation being more popular with adolescents and the more complex variations successful with adults. In addition changing cultural attitudes have something to do with the emergence of different variations, since variation two is clearly more characteristic of early twentieth century Westerns, while variation three dominates the recent "adult" Western.

Discussing "Savagery, Civilization and The Western Hero"

1) Several popular American formula stories have adopted elements of the Western formula into themselves. What elements of Westerns appear in hard-boiled detective stories? In space opera like *Star Wars?*

2) It is notable that within the Western formula as described by Cawelti there seems to be very little room for themes of love and sex which are at the heart of so many other popular formula stories. Why are love and sex so conspicuously absent from a great many Westerns?

3) Westerns have been called the American myth narrative. Do you agree? How many American myths described throughout this book can be found in the typical Western?

Somebody's Trying to Kill Me and I Think It's My Husband: The Modern Gothic

By Joanna Russ

What fiction do American women read? God knows. When pressed she mumbles about ladies' slicks, fashion magazines, best-sellers, *et al.,* but if you pray earnestly and add that you want to know about fiction read exclusively by women, she finally relents and hands you three genres: confession magazines, nurse novels—and the Modern Gothic.

Anywhere paperback books are sold you will find volumes whose covers seem to have evolved from the same clone: the color scheme is predominantly blue or green, there is a frightened young woman in the foreground, in the background is a mansion, castle or large house with one window lit, there is usually a moon, a storm, or both, and whatever is occurring is occurring at night.

These are the Modern Gothics. If you look inside the covers you will find that the stories bear no resemblance to the literary definition of "Gothic." They are not related to the works of Monk Lewis or Mrs. Radcliff, whose real descendants are known today as Horror Stories. The Modern Gothics resemble, instead, a crossbreed of *Jane Eyre* and Daphne Du Maurier's *Rebecca* and most of them advertise themselves as "in the Du Maurier tradition," "in the Gothic tradition of *Rebecca,*" and so on. According to Terry Carr, an ex-editor of Ace Books, their history in this country:

> began in the early '60s. . . . But books like this have always been written especially in England, where they were called romances. . . from about 1950 on; they were never big things over

From the *Journal of Popular Culture,* 1973, 6(4), 666-691. Reprinted by permission of the editor and the author.

there, just a steady small market. It started at Ace...[which]
bought some novels by Victoria Holt and Phyllis A. Whitney.
They sold like anything....[Ace] continued and expanded the
Gothic list here, including especially buying rights to early
novels by Dorothy Eden and Anne Maybury...both now big-
selling writers.[1]

Modern Gothics unlike nurse novels and the confession
magazines, are read by middle-class women or women with middle-
class aspirations, and for some reason the books written by
Englishwomen have remained the most popular, at least at Ace. In
1970 I asked Terry Carr to provide me with some of their longest-
selling and best-selling books; according to Mr. Carr they are
"representative of the higher ranges of the field" and all seem to be
reprints of earlier works (one as early as 1953).[2]
Also according to Mr. Carr:

> The basic appeal...is to women who marry guys and then
> begin to discover that their husbands are strangers...so there's
> a simultaneous attraction/repulsion, love/fear going on. Most
> of the "pure" Gothics tend to have a handsome, magnetic suitor
> or husband who may or may not be a lunatic and/or
> murderer...it remained for U.S. women to discover they were
> frightened of their husbands.[3]

Here are the elements:
To a large, lonely, usually brooding *House* (always named)
comes a *Heroine* who is young, orphaned, unloved and lonely. She is
shy and inexperienced. She is attractive, sometimes even beautiful,
but she does not know it. Sometimes she has spent ten years nursing
a dying mother; sometimes she has (or has had) a wicked
stepmother, a bad aunt, a demanding and selfish mother (usually
deceased by the time the story opens) or an ineffectual, absent, or
(usually) long-dead father, whom she loves. The House is set in
exotic, vivid and/or isolated *Country*. The Heroine, whose reaction
to people and places tends toward emotional extremes, either loves
or hates the House, usually both.
After a short prologue, this latter-day Jane Eyre forms a
personal or professional connection with an older man; a dark,
magnetic, powerful, brooding, sardonic *Super-Male,* who treats her
brusquely, derogates her, scolds her, and otherwise shows anger or
contempt for her. The Heroine is vehemently attracted to him and
usually just as vehemently repelled or frightened—she is not sure of
her feelings for him, his feelings for her, and whether he (1) loves her,
(2) hates her, (3) is using her, or (4) is trying to kill her.
The Super-Male is not the Heroine's only worry. In the

emotionally tangled and darkly mysterious "family" set up in our House are hints of the presence of *Another Woman* who is at the same time the Heroine's double and her opposite—very often the Other Woman is the Super-Male's present wife or dead first wife; sometimes she is the Heroine's missing cousin, or the woman the Super-Male appears to prefer to the Heroine. The Other Woman is (or was) beautiful, worldly, glamorous, immoral, flirtatious, irresponsible, and openly sexual. She may even have been (especially if she is dead) adulterous, promiscuous, hard-hearted, immoral, criminal or even insane. If the Other Woman is alive, the Heroine knows—in anguish—that the Super-Male cannot possibly prefer her to this fascinating creature; if the Other Woman is dead, the Heroine believes she cannot possibly measure up to the Super-Male's memories. Her only consolation is to be kind, womanly, and good, both to the Super-Male and sometimes to a *Young Girl,* often the daughter of the Super-Male and his first wife. The Young Girl (if she exists) is often being corrupted or neglected by the Other Woman (if alive); in one case there is a Young Man (son of the Super-Male) who is being neglected by his father. One Heroine has a younger sister, or a missing younger cousin (who is combined, in this case, with the Other Woman). The Heroine's task, in all cases, is to win the confidence of this young person, and convince him/her of her/his personal worth. If the person is a girl, this is done by buying her clothes.

In addition to the Heroine's other troubles, she gradually becomes aware that somewhere in the tangle of opppressive family relationships going on in the House exists a *Buried Ominous Secret,* always connected with the Other Woman and the Super-Male (whatever relation they happen to bear one another in the novel). The Super-Male is at the center of the Secret; when she unravels the mystery about him (does he love her or is he a threat to her?) she will simultaneously get to the bottom of the Secret. Then the plot thickens.

Her happpiness with the Super-Male is threatened.

Her life is threatened (sometimes several times).

Minor characters are killed.

Storms take place.

There is much ad-libbing of *Ominous Dialogue.*

And so on.

At some point—either because of other people's detective work or by chance—*the Secret is Revealed.* It turns out to be immoral and usually criminal activity on somebody's part centering around money and/or the Other Woman's ghastly (usually sexual) misbehavior. The six Gothics considered in this paper employ the following Secrets: jewel smuggling, theft, and murder (*Columbella*);

murder, impersonation, drug addiction, and intended blackmail (*I am Gabriella!*); an insane mass-murderer *(The Least of All Evils)*; another insane mass-murderer with a clothing fetish (*The Brooding Lake);* diamond theft and murder *(Nightingale at Noon);* murder and illegitimacy (*The Dark Shore*).

Coincidental with the revelation of the secret is the untangling of the Heroine's emotions—she is enabled to "sort-out" the Super-Male (who is invariably guiltless, although he may have appeared otherwise) from everyone else, especially from a character I call the *Shadow-Male,* a man invariably represented as gentle, protective, responsible, quiet, humorous, tender and calm. The Shadow-Male either wants to marry the Heroine or has—in one case—actually married her. This personage is revealed as a murderer and (twice) as an insane mass-murderer of a whole string of previous wives. There are variations; sometimes two roles may be combined in one character, although in general it is astonishing how constant the elements remain. In one novel the Other Woman is a vanished cousin, in another an old school-friend; her villainy may range from crime to mere irresponsible flirting (which is, however, regarded very seriously by the novel). Sometimes the Other Woman is a minor character (*Nightingale*) but in every case the Other Woman is more worldly than the Heroine, more beautiful, and more openly sexual. The Other Woman is *immoral.* The Heroine is *good.* The Super-Male's competence ranges from Judo *(I am Gabriella!)* through a *sardonic cynicism that always puts the Heroine in the wrong (Brooding Lake)* to the less tangible attributes of being a Canadian and a millionaire (*Dark Shore*). Although scenery ranges from exotic New Zealand to exotic Northern Ontario (the novelist is English in this case), the House, the Heroine, the Super-Male, the Other Woman, the Ominous Dialogue, the Secret and the Untangling are staples of every one of these books.

Certainly the Gothic is worth some study as a genre written for women and by women; even the paperback editors who choose manuscripts are women, although their employers are men. In some ways these stories resemble the tales in the true-confession magazines. In a recent issue of the *Journal of Popular Culture*[4] David Sonenschein has analyzed 73 such tales and drawn the following conclusions:*

> The main "other" was usually a male...older... either the narrator's spouse of a previously unmarried single male (p. 404).
> ...the feeling of uneasiness underlying each story (p.495).
> ...we also get a sense of some of the risks that simply being a woman may entail...(p. 402).
> Relationships are volatile, hostile, and even dangerous; in

*(Eds. Note: Essay included in this volume.)

contrast to male-oriented erotica, *it is trauma, rather than sex, which is "just around the corner"* (p. 405, italics mine).

It is tempting to view the Gothics, with their perpetual Houses (in which, typically, the Heroine has a large emotional investment), their families or quasi-families, their triangles of young girl, older man, and older man's first wife, as a family romance. But the books are not love stories *per se*, nor are they usually concerned (except peripherally) with erotica; the culminations of the books' plots almost always involve attempted murder—the Heroine's being chased along a cliff by someone who wants to kill her (*Shore*), being locked into a room by a madman who earlier almost drowned her *(Lake)*, being pushed over a cliff and later shut in a wall to suffocate *(Evils)*, or being sexually attacked after having been exposed to diamond thieves,believing that literally everyone in her family is trying to kill her and her younger sister, *and* finding out that her adored blind father is a criminal and has pretended blindness for years, *and* believing that the man she loves is a murderer (*Nightingale*). As the Heroine of this one says, with some justification, all is "a swirling vortex of confusion" (p. 136). Other Heroines are trapped alive in caves, almost murdered, and flung against a wall by a "tall figure enveloped in a hooded robe" *(Columbella*, p. 204), and almost run over by a car. The commonest emotion in these novels is fear—but they are horror stories; the plot always involves murder (but they are not stories of detection), and while the Heroine is rewarded with love (without having caused it, deserved it, revealed it, or even asked for it) there is no tracing of the growing bond between the lovers. The Modern Gothic is episodic; the Heroine does nothing except worry; any necessary detective work is done by other persons, often the Super-Male. Whenever the Heroine acts (as in *Lake*) she bungles things badly. There is a period of terror, repeated sinister incidents, ominous dialogue spoken by various characters, and then the sudden revelation of who's who and what's what. In terms of ordinary pulp technique, these novels are formless. Even so, they obey extraordinarily rigid rules. There must be a reason for these rules.

I would propose that the modern Gothics are a direct expression of the traditional feminine situation (at least a middle-class feminine situation) and that they provide precisely the kind of escape reading a middle-class believer in the feminine mystique needs, without involving elements that either go beyond the feminine mystique or would be considered immoral in its terms.

For example, the Heroines are either on vacation, on a honeymoon, or too young to do housework. If they spend ten years caring for an invalid mother, the book begins just after the mother's death; if they have married (and they marry wealthy men) the book begins with the honeymoon; if they are poor, they are too young to cook and clean and the poverty is only temporary, anyway. They always find themselves in exotic locales (the Virgin Islands, the French Wine country, New Zealand, The Camargue, etc.). They are essentially idle women. *Nonetheless,* whenever the occasion arises—and it is always an interpersonal occasion, never a housewife's vocational one—they have a keen eye for food, clothes, interior decor, and middle class hobbies (e.g., collecting sea shells, weaving or collecting china). The novels contain some extraordinarily impersonal descriptions of meals, rooms and dresses, e.g., "crisp native pastry filled with cocoanut" (*Columbella,* p.84), "the cool sharp tang of lime" *(op. cit.,* p. 57) and "coffee that had been perfectly brewed" (*op. cit.,* p. 37). In *Evils* the Heroine is treated to "airy little shells bursting with a delectable and spicy hot mixture" and later "golden wheat cakes and amber syrup, the crisp bacon and plump sausages, the chilled melon with gobbets of fat, whiskery raspberries clinging to it" (pp. 30, 56). In *Nightingale* the heroine's family is too poor to buy good food (tea is "four pieces of bread and butter on a plate and one plain biscuit"—p. 24). When the family can afford steak, strawberries, and whiskey, however, it is not the Heroine who does the cooking. Even *Lake,* in which the Heroine hardly eats from arrival to attempted murder, contains the following housewifely diagnosis: "a plate of thick porridge, some toast which had already absorbed its butter and gone cold, and a cup of weak tea. Dundas had said that his daughter was a good housekeeper... did he really always have this kind of fare?" (pp. 98-99). If the above sound like ladies'-magazine articles, that is because they are; the vacationing protagnists of *Gabriella* subsist on hotel food, which allows the author to produce the following:

> *fricasee de poulet* with puffed out, golden potatoes and apples crystallized whole in sugar (p.23)... jellied eggs with mushroom mayonnaise, *canard a l'Orange*... with a few drops of orange curacao liqueur sprinkled on the slim slices of duck (p. 61)... River trout and then... purple grapes folded into a kind of *crepe suzette* (p. 137)... a long, crusty French loaf, some cheese, half a pound of wild strawberries, some cream, and a bottle of wine (p. 160).

The oddity of such technical expertise in the midst of terror, romance, and murder is not that of the great detective's playing the violin; it is merely off-key. Consider:

> I played with a beautiful *omelette fines herbes* and managed a *souffle.* But all the time I was conscious of the slow

approaching shadow of menace and our unrealized part in it
(*Gabriella,* p. 107).

Even more relentless is the author's eye for female dress. For
example, in *Columbella* no female character ever appears without
careful note being taken of her clothes:

> ...a long-legged, graceful teenager in blue Bermudas and a
> nautical white middy with a blue tie that matched her shorts
> (p.37)...She wore pale green capris that stretched tightly over
> her girlishly flat stomach, rounded hips, and hugged her thighs
> neatly with scarcely a wrinkle. A bit of sleeveless white pique
> tied in a bow between her breasts (p. 40)...I was dressed suitably
> enough for town in a blue denim skirt with deep side pockets that
> I found handy, and a blue cotton overblouse. (p. 130)...The
> princess lines of the linen dress were subtle and set off the
> rounding of her slim young figure. From a circular neckline the
> dress curved gently at the waist and flared to wider gores at the
> hemline (p. 134).

Dark, given more to the mystification possible with a mosaic of
different points of view, still notes the various amenities of dressing,
bathing, and noting what other women look like:

> She wore a plain linen dress, narrow and simple, without
> sleeves. (p. 117)...She didn't dare stop to re-apply her lipstick.
> There was just time to brush her hair lightly into position. (p.
> 73)..."Dinner will be in about half an hour and the water's hot if
> you should want a bath." (p. 71)...Her mouth was slim beneath
> pale lipstick, the lashes of her beautiful eyes too long and dark to
> be entirely natural, her fair hair swept upwards simply in a soft,
> full curve. (p. 42)...there was even more of a rush to have a bath,
> change, and start cooking for a dinner-party...she had just
> finished changing...(p. 16).

Clothes in *Lake* play too much part as clues (a pair of shoes, a
red nightgown, an old wedding dress) to be considered inorganic to
the plot, but here, as in *Columbella*—the Heroine shows her
goodness of heart by helping a young girl uncertain of her looks to
dress up for a party; moreover, an evening memorable mostly for
ghostly voices and a tropical storm includes "the pale blue satin
nightdress...spread on the bed for her." The young lady of the
house then enters in "a turquoise-colored velvet dressing-gown, her
hair brushed down on her shoulders" (pp. 80-81). Later another girl
chooses a green coat, "lingering over it longingly because it was the
one she wanted most, but its price was too high" (pp. 146-147).

Despite the poverty of the family in *Nightingale,* we still have one character's brief scarlet shorts and snow-white sun top (p. 45), and a dress the Heroine borrows for a party, "an inch too short and a couple of inches too wide, but the color, a muted aquamarine, and its straight, deceptively simple cut, had overcome my scruples" (p. 80). She too dresses up the Younger Girl (her half-sister) for the same party (p. 81). If nothing else, she can reflect that she has "put on Lucille's blue dress, brushed my hair, and piled it high" (p. 102). Let a well-dressed stranger appear and the author immediately reverts to type:

> The shoes came first, black sandals with stiletto heels...slender legs, then an oyster[5] skirt, tight about slim thighs...Indigo-black, bouffant hair caressed her cheeks and forehead (p. 84).

In *Gabriella* we have:

> A crocodile handbag, chocolate-brown gloves (p. 5)...an expensive suit of dark green raw silk, with a clip made of crimson stones shaped like an eagle, in her lapel (p. 18)...a pleated cream nylon dress and gold slippers (p. 82)...a jewel case with a soft zip top (p. 112)...a white silk dressing gown I had bought in Paris (p. 154)...a blouse...of hand blocked silk with green stars and moss roses...tan gloves (p. 118)...a tomato silk housecoat (p. 216).

When the Heroines of Gothics are not noticing other people's clothes (or their own) or being thrown off cliffs, or losing the men they love, they often spend their time thus:

> I unpacked quickly, showered, and put on a cool dress of black linen with touches of lime green. I slid my feet into high heeled black sandals and fixed gold star earrings in my ears (*Gabriella,* p. 14).

Or they note interior decor:

> It was a room of austere beauty, comfortably but sparsely furnished to effect that cool, uncluttered look so necessary in the tropics. The ceiling was lofty, giving one a sense of space and grandeur. From the center of an elaborate plaster rosette hung a crystal chandelier, while carved plaster cornices decorated the far reaches of the ceiling....Most of the furniture had that simplicity of design which belongs to the countries of Scandinavia, fluid of line and built of smooth, light woods...near the foot of the curving stairs in one corner of the

room hung a Chagall print of red poppies and green leaves in a tall vase...(p. 28, *Columbella*).

We went through regal double doors and into a beautifully furnished room. Soft blues and greens in brocade and silk glowed in the single light from a standard lamp near the dressing table. In the fine old four-poster...(p. 197, *Gabriella*).

I gasped involuntarily, barely noting the wide floor-boards, the sparsely utilitarian nature of the ancient furniture. My eyes went up the walls, from the simple panelled dado, about five feet in height, to plain plastered walls penetrated by stone mullioned windows that rose to a magnificently hammerbeam roof, enriched with elaborately scrolled Renaissance detail. (p. 14, *Evils*).[6]

...the big brick fireplace with the dead remnants of a fire, the low chairs and the large low settee covered with bright cushions, the pictures on the walls strategically placed to hide the discolored spots in the wallpaper, the large white rug in front of the fireplace, the gilt-framed mirror that gave back a dusky lamplit reflection of the room. The illusion of luxury...(P.9, *Lake*).

These novels are written for women who cook, who decorate their own houses, who shop for clothing for themselves and their children—in short, for housewives. But the Heroines—who toil not, neither do they spin—know and utilize (sometimes bizarrely) the occupation of their readers. "Occupation: Housewife" is simultaneously avoided, glamorized, and vindicated.

Modern Gothics are surprisingly conservative about sexuality, yet the sexuality that does appear in them is of a very prurient kind. Heroines are impeccably virginal (until married) and can even criticize a friend for being "mercenary" for accepting an expensive gift from a man she didn't intend to marry (*Lake*, p. 65). The Heroine who does so (this is in 1953) does not get beyond the "intense charm" (presumably erotic) of the moment when she buries her face against the Super-Male's tweed jacket, only a few pages from the end papers. The eighteen-year-old Heroine of *Nightingale*, whose family relationships are so complicated that it takes the reader 94 pages to unravel them nonetheless feels "a leap of nausea that left me sick and shivering" at a stranger's mention of her father's mistress, although "The discovery of Hugo's relationship with Dodie was years old" (p. 40). The mad villainess of *Columbella*, eventually revealed to be a jewel thief and smuggler, is criticized in the strongest terms possible; she has not only stolen a bracelet as a school-girl, but:

"I'm afraid she's merely graduated into taking more important property. Such as other women's husbands. And she's wildly extravagant" (p. 17).

When the villainess of this book actually threatens to run the Heroine over with her (the villainess's) car, it is clear that she has passed beyond the pale not only of good manners or decency but of simple sanity. It would be interesting to compare criminal acts in modern Gothics with criminal acts in modern crime stories and weigh the relative horribleness of the acts themselves in the two genres. The Heroine of *Shore* (1965) explains how she met the Super-Male:

> "...the next day he phoned and asked to take me out to a concert. I went. I shouldn't have because of Frank" [her escort] "but then...well, Frank and I weren't engaged, and I—I wanted to see Jon again" (p. 127).

Jon does not, however, as a Super-Male and an older, once-married man, impose such a stringent moral code upon himself:

> ...he...would have despised himself for having a woman within days of his coming marriage. It would have meant nothing, of course, but he would still have felt ashamed afterwards, full of guilt because he had done something which would hurt Sarah if she knew...(p. 41).

This is as far as the Gothic seems to go in spotting even a Super-Male's purity. But for the married Heroine sex becomes an entirely different matter. No longer bodiless and yet within the code of romance—the result is a very strange fusion of prurience and exaltation, i.e., the confusion of values described by Firestone (sex=personal worth) combines with the "religious" eroticism Greer notes in romance stories.[7] Thus the Super-Male's erection becomes the criterion of the Heroine's self-approval—and yet the whole business must somehow take place within the limits of the romantically sexless. As long as everything is kept vague, we are all right; thus in *Shore* the heroine's wedding night (blissful, by convention) is rendered thus:

> ...when he stooped his head to kiss her on the mouth at last, she was conscious first and foremost of the peace in her heart before her world whirled into the fire (p. 66).
> When he bent over her a moment later,[8] and she felt the love in every line of his frame flow into hers, she knew he would never again belong to anyone else except her (p. 159).

We are one stage away from the non-kiss at the end of *Lake*. Still romantic, though perhaps a little dithery about what turns out to be only necking, is this passage in *Nightingale:*

> His free hand was on my throat, his lips pressed on mine, hunger and passion in them. That was all I wanted. It was mine, and I took it greedily....When he pushed me from him, it was to demand in a voice that was harsh and breathless: "Melly...do you know what you're doing?" "Yes," I said (p. 115).

What she is doing is not clear, but the married are under no such constraint. The Heroine of *Evils,* who gasps, "horrified," when she thinks her young cousin may have been rolling in the hay with a boy friend (p. 100), nonetheless describes her own romantic interludes thus:

> And seeing Mark, wide-shouldered and narrow-hipped, standing back turned to me, I knew the past didn't matter....Only the present and the joyful future ahead of us, were real...he turned, our eyes met, and then he came to me swiftly, catching my hands up in his until finally we were close, one body, as our lips met...."You're cold, darling," Mark whispered. "I know how to warm you" (p. 34).
>
> He caught my shoulders, "Don't you know there have been lots of people killed in the tub?" he cried. *But his stern manner faded as his hands slipped.* A trio on my nearby portable radio sang of love and passion while my dripping arms held Mark close...(p. 49, italics mine).

The more sexuality gets into these scenes, the more discordant becomes the insisted-upon romantic aura. Quintessentially:

> He shoved his cup into my unoccupied hand...and solemnly untied my other shoulder strap. I sat giggling like a school girl, each hand burdened with a teacup, my nightgown rumpled about my waist....I didn't care about the unexpected trip. Not any more. *Only the moment mattered and the moment became increasingly beautiful and memorable* (*Evils,* p. 56, italics mine).

Of course the Heroine's husband in *Evils* is not a Super-Male but a Shadow-Male; perhaps something is wrong with his technique. The Heroine of *Gabriella* is married to a genuine Super-Male, a lean, dark, tigerish judo expert who snaps at her in brusque, masculine fashion throughout the book. He is as romantic as any, sometimes:

Then he lay, his arms around me, his body against mine. "Karen! Oh, Karen!" Above us, at last, a bird broke into song (p. 61).

Nick pulled me to my feet and drew me close. I could feel the hard beat of his heart as he kissed me; the strength that seemed to pour from his body into me. My blood raced, quivering, as he held me more tightly...it was the immediate passion of his love for me...There was [sic] just Nick and I caught up in our lovely desire for each other...(p. 136).

But there is always the possibility that desire is only desire:

I lay close against Nick, strengthened by contact with that hard body. He put an arm under my shoulder and turned to me. But the problem Maxine had set us still lay heavily on my mind. "Tomorrow," I began, "we must—" "Let's leave tomorrow." He was drawing me closer. "Tonight is a long time darling!" I lifted my head and saw his eyes in the semi-moonlight. They were alight and alive....Nick had raced through France for this—for *me* (*Gabriella*, p. 41)!

The birds had better sing like mad, or even a Gothic Heroine might wonder whether "this" and "me" are always identical.

Most striking about these novels is the combination of intrigue, crime, and danger with the Heroine's complete passivity. Unconscious foci of intrigue, passion, and crime, these young women (none of whom is over thirty) wander through all sorts of threatening forces of which they are intuitively, but never intellectually, aware. Most of all, *they are of extraordinary interest to everyone*—even though they are ill-educated, ordinary, characterless and usually very hazily delineated, being (as one might suspect) a stand-in for the reader. Sometimes Heroines are very beautiful (although they don't know it) or heiresses (which they don't know, either) or possess some piece of information about the Secret (which they are incapable of interpreting). Their connection with the action of the novel is always passive; they are focal points for tremendous emotion, and sometimes tremendous struggle, simply because they exist. At her most enterprising a Heroine may (like the Heroine of *Lake*, whose relation to the Super-Male is the nearest to equality of any shown in the books) recklessly toss about pieces of information that expose her to being drowned or pushed off a glacier. Alice (the Heroine) tries to solve the mystery of her school-friend's disappearance and does, in fact, unearth certain clues (which she misinterprets). But the Super-Male is the real detective of the piece. Even when faced with a miserably unhappy young girl, a Byronic Super-Male, and a mad, greedy, criminal Other Woman, the

Heroine of *Columbella* can only display her womanly goodness and try to win the young girl's confidence by appreciating her drawings and buying clothes for her. As the Super-Male declares to her:

> "Perhaps now I've found a new source of sanity—and honesty and decency. Things I thought I'd lost for good during the last few years. A source that isn't a place but a person—you!"
> (p. 125)

Here too the Heroine finds clues to a murder—after the important persons in the book have already done so. In the midst of family relationships that would baffle Oedipus, the Heroine of *Nightingale* does—nothing at all. The Heroine of *Evils* has amnesia—she also bungles about looking for clues which the Super-Male already knows. The detective in *Gabriella* is the Heroine's husband, whom she trails perpetually—again, there are several attempts of hers which either come to nothing or land both of them in trouble (which he fixes).

In the face of this really extraordinary passivity—for if the protagonist of a novel is not active in some way, what on earth is the novel about?—it is tempting to see these books as genuine family romances with the Heroine as the child who is trying desperately to understand what the grown-ups are up to, a description that fits *Nightingale* perfectly. At their best Heroines merely stand (passively) for love, goodness, redemption, and innocence. They are special and precious because they are Heroines. And that is that.

I have called the Gothics episodic, but that does not mean that the books have no central theme. The emotional center is that "handsome, magnetic suitor or husband who may or may not be a lunatic or murderer"[9]—i.e., it is the Heroine's ambivalence toward the Super-Male that provides the internal dramatic action of the book. The Heroine of *Lake*, for example, does not know if her former sweetheart is the murderer of her friend or not (two other men may be, one of whom—the Shadow-Male—starts out by being dependable and gentle and ends up with "tiger's" eyes and a collection of the clothing of the women he has killed). The Heroines of the Gothics are constantly reading men's expressions—in *Lake,* the Heroine's eyes meet the Shadow-Male's and:

> They gave an illusion of warmth because his mouth was tender. But really they were empty windows, waiting for that dark person to get out (p. 130).

Another Heroine reacts to the Super-Male she will eventually love in this way:

> I didn't like the man. He seemed to cast off vibrations that
> put the entire room in a subtle turmoil. And seeing how Priss
> looked at him, I was afraid for her....He looked as though he
> was gluttonous....He would ruthlessly take what he
> wanted...(*Evils*, p. 4).

Similarly the Heroine of *Dark* begins by mistrusting her
husband-to-be (things get worse):

> ...she felt the other familiar feeling of nervousness...She
> loved Jon and knew perfectly well that she wanted to marry him,
> but he remained an enigma to her at times and it was this
> strange unknown quality which made her nervous. She called it
> the Distant Mood (p. 58).

Even when the Super-Male is not a physical danger, sexuality
itself provides enough threat, (or that and the possibility of being
disliked or harshly judged). The Heroine of *Columbella* notes that
hero's "straight, rather harsh mouth," his "grim" smile, while his
"cold, judicial" comments about her outrage her. Even worse is his
"disturbing presence" and "alarming gentleness." As she finally
decides:

> I knew why I was uncomfortable with this man. It was
> because a current seemed to spring into being between us when
> we were together—a strangely disturbing current composed of a
> mixture of antagonism and attraction, perhaps in equal parts,
> so that I did not truly know which force was the stronger (p. 75).

We know, of course. But when the man the Heroine loves is
trying to pin a murder rap on her father, the conflict becomes much
worse; almost all of *Nightingale* is composed of tremendous
emotional oscillations undergone by the Heroine, at one moment
believing that the Super-Male loves her, at the next that he is only
using her as a source of information, at one moment that her father
(another Super-Male) is not a murderer, at the next moment that he
is:

> I couldn't be sure. I wasn't sure of anything: whether
> Charles Lewis was a sane man who, for four years, had been
> driven by a trigger-hot passion for revenge, or whether he was a
> madman obsessed with a phantom nightmare (p. 49).
> For a few seconds I was caught in a rush of hope that seemed
> as if it would bring me to the surface of the dark waters in which
> I'd been drowning....I felt the smile break on my face, and then
> I saw his eyes watching me, narrowed and fiercely intent. And
> suddenly the offer he'd made seemed machine-tooled in

treachery. I felt as sick as if I'd just escaped from stepping off a precipice (p. 152).

It is no wonder that after ten chapters of such ups-and-downs, the Heroine remarks, "I had the eerie sense that I'd lost the power to evaluate the simplest emotion" (p. 100). When the most important person in your life is your man, when you can't trust him (and can't trust anyone else) it becomes exceedingly important to "read" other people's faces and feelings. This is what most real women spend their time doing; therefore the novels not only portray them doing it, but glamorize and justify what in real life is usually necessary, but boring. In one way the Gothics are a kind of justified paranoia: people *are* planning awful things about you: you *can't* trust your husband (lover, fiance); everybody's motives *are* devious and complex, only the *most* severe vigilance will enable you to snatch any happiness from the jaws of destruction. In addition to hurricanes, madness, attempted murder, skeletons falling out of cupboards, diamond smuggling, theft, drug addiction, impersonation, and voodoo, the modern Gothics make extensive use of what I would like to call Over-Subtle Emotions, a "denseness" of interpersonal texture that is at its most complex, simply baffling, and at its simplest, pathetic. For example:

> It was a long, slow glance, guarded, half-apprehensive, half-exultant, that passed between Ariadne and Jager. In a way I couldn't understand, much less explain, it possessed an element of familiarity, as if they were not strangers...but in some ways allies. Vague, unresolved suspicions coursed through my mind and got nowhere. (*Nightingale,* P. 88)
> Suddenly my mind cleared and I knew. Something fell sharply and shockingly into place. "Last night, up by the chateau, Johnnie threatened me...From—from a distance it could have seemed that he and I—" "Were in the throes of a love affair? Well?" "And Goliath saw us. He can't have heard what we said...But don't you see?—if he thought I was having an affair with Johnnie and you had found out—?" "Sweet heaven. You mean Johnnie was killed because he probably knew the truth behind Maxine's impersonation? And we were sent down here to find the body—?" "And be implicated! If Goliath told the police what you had seen you could be regarded as the jealous husband." "Yes," he said slowly. "I see what you mean." (*Gabriella,* P. 142)
> For some reason his seemingly idle discussion made me as uncomfortable as did the shell. It was as if his talk of good and evil, his reference to flaws of beauty...the man spoke in symbols that carried a deeper significance—perhaps as a hint of warning, meant for me? Or was I being fanciful again?...Again

I had that uneasy sense of a deeper meaning and knew that he watched me intently with his pale, luminous eyes (*Columbella,* p. 49).

Where was Ada now? If she was downstairs...I would ask her. Plump and plain, I would ask her about Mr. Engleford. Ask her about the skeleton in the garden. Ask her what *really* happened to Mark's mother. Because somehow I knew Ada had the answers, if only she would divulge them (*Evils.* p. 125)[10]

It was curious how the pupils of his eyes expanded as she watched. Like a startled cat's, like a tiger's. Why should Katharine think his eyes were like a tiger's when the rest of his face was so bland and genial (*Lake,* p. 114)?

He was near Rivers now, but he could not see him properly. The man had not moved at all, and the odd half-light was such that Jon could not see the expression in his eyes. He was aware of a sharp pang of uneasiness, a violent twist of memory, which was so vivid that it hurt, and then an inexplicable wave of compassion (*Dark,* p. 35).[11]

The Heroine is such a virtuosa at this sacred version of everyday gossip that she knows even more than the mere fact that danger exists; she knows *it has all happened before.* The eeriest plot element in these books is the constant "doubling" of the Heroine— she is always in some fashion a "stand-in" for someone else, usually someone who has been killed. This someone is often the Other Woman (who is or was wicked) but it may be (as in *Columbella*) the Other Woman's daughter, who is being destroyed by her mother just as the Heroine's confidence has been undermined by *her* selfish, vain, attractive, irresponsible mother. In *Gabriella,* the Heroine's cousin is the double—she vanishes and in her turn impersonates a girl who has been killed. In *Evils* the Heroine has several predecessors, including her kind aunt, who was better to her than her own (bad) mother.[12] The Heroine of *Nightingale* has a younger half-sister, who suffers with her, and for whom she is very concerned, and a "mother" in the person of her father's mistress, irritable, aging, selfish, and vain, whom she starts out hating and learns—gradually—to pity. In two of the books, *The Dark Shore* and *The Brooding Lake,* the "doubling" is so explicit that the characters themselves comment on it. Sarah, the Heroine of *Dark,* has married a man whose first wife was murdered; not only does Sarah constantly compare her inadequate self to the dead Sophia (even their names are similar) but several characters remark the two women look alike. Eventually the doubling goes so far that Sarah is warned:

"It's all happening again, can't you realize that? It's all happening again—we're all here at Clougy...and you've been assigned Sophia's role" (p. 132).

In *Lake*, in order to resolve the mystery of a friend's disappearance, the Heroine begins to "impersonate" her friend, Camilla. She dresses like her, wears her "mantle—of trouble or danger, or whatever other complicated atmosphere it carried" (p. 46). She writes to the absent Camilla (who has in reality been murdered):

> Why were things getting dangerous? Seriously, you must tell me because it looks as if your mantle (and a troubled one) has fallen on me and I shall have to cope with these three indignant swains (p. 48).

So far does the doubling go that Alice is proposed to by the man who was going to marry Camilla. Alice accepts:

> The queer thing was that she didn't know whether she was being herself or Camilla as she answered, "You're so kind. How can one refuse you?" She was almost sure she would never have answered a proposal of marriage in those words. It was as if Camilla had spoken them (pp. 117-118).

The doubling goes even farther; the fiance (a Shadow-Male) almost drowns Alice as he drowned Camilla; then the theme escalates into the grotesque as Alice is trapped in a room containing two wax dummies dressed in wedding gowns belonging to the madman's earlier-murdered brides, while a minor character in wig and Camilla's squirrel coat impersonates the dead woman outside in order to terrify the madman into a confession.

What does this doubling mean? Is it that every woman fears the same man and undergoes the same fate? Is it an echo of the family romance in which Heroine plays daughter, the Super-Male is father, and the Other Woman/First Wife plays mother? Are the two identical?

The Super-Male may indeed be a disguised version of the Heroine's (wished-for) father. He is older than the Heroine, more intelligent, taller, stronger, cooler-headed, richer, and of higher social position. And the Heroine is certainly presented as a kind of child; she is precious to the Super-Male simply because she exists (like a child) and she is never independent. She has no profession in any of the books except for *Lake,* where there is some unconvincing background about her having been part of a traveling acting company. This particular Heroine is a bit snippy about her "independence," which soon collapses into an engagement with a madman and rescue by the Super-Male, who remarks:

"Little Alice!...Silly little lamb! You see, it took the sheep in wolf's clothing to rescue you" (p. 186).

The Gothics obviously envision the relationship between Super-Male and Heroine as neither abnormal nor unusual, but as the standard, even ideal, relation between men and women.

Independent women or women who have professions occur as follows:

> *Lake.* An (ugly) young girl who will be a doctor and a sympathetic but stereotyped spinster teacher (a minor character).
> *Gabriella.* A middle-aged woman, owner of a chateau in the French wine country who is a drug addict and dependent on her manager. She commits suicide.
> *Evils.* A deaf, ugly, deformed, middle-aged woman who makes an elaborate hobby of weaving. She finds happiness with a deaf, ugly, deformed, middle-aged man.
> *Dark.* The Super-Male's beautiful, brilliant, illegitimate half-sister, who loves music and plays the piano. She is in telepathic communion with the Super-Male, but unfortunately she depends on him (in this strange, telepathic way) while he can get along without her. She becomes promiscuous, then frigid, and goes into retreat in a convent, after taking upon herself the blame for the death of the Super-Male's first wife.

The Modern Gothics are neither love stories nor stories of women-as-victims. *They are adventure stories with passive protagonists.*

After all, what can a Heroine do?
1. She can be attached to a man.
2. She can be unknowingly involved in some family/criminal secret.
3. She can be threatened by murder.
4. She can be saved.
5. She can be uncertain of her man's real intentions toward her.
6. She can guess at his and other people's intentions or emotions.
And she can do all this within the confines of the feminine mystique.[13]

Since the Gothics are escape reading, they leave out women's real, tedious, everyday work—childbearing, child-rearing, and housekeeping. These have no place in the Gothics; only the prelude to them (the capture of, or relations with a man) is allowed, and that is very much glamorized.

The problem of the female protagonist in literature is still with us. If we assume that everything outside the domestic affections and the capture of a husband is masculine, we have a protagonist who cannot:

1. Solve an intellectual puzzle (whodunit or science fiction)
2. Build a career (the success story of the bright boy from the provinces)
3. Travel and have adventures (the adventurer has adventures; the adventur*ess* has sexual adventures only)
4. Carry out a political conspiracy
5. Head a religious movement
6. Grow up and form her character (the *bildungsroman* matters only if the protagonist is going to be someone in particular or do something; the Heroine's destiny is always the same—marriage. No matter what sort of character she has, she will not become a philospher, artist, general, or politician.)

The Love Story is—for women—*bildungsroman,* success, failure, education, and the only adventure possible, all in one.[14]

As I said before, the modern gothic is an accurate reflection of the feminine mystique and a glamorized version of the lives many women do live. The apparent sado-masochism of the genre is partly an artifact of the narrative premise—that the Heroine must remain passive (or incompetent) in situations that call overwhelmingly for activity and decision; therefore any connection the Heroine has with the situation must be that of Victim. Part may be "feminine masochism" but even where the sado-masochistic overtones are strongest (as in *Nightingale)* the Heroine's suffering is the principle action of the story *because it is the only action she can perform.* The Modern Gothic, as a genre, is a means of enabling a conventionally feminine heroine to have adventures at all. It may also be a way that conventionally feminine readers can see their own situation— dependent and limited as it is—validated, justified, and glamorized up to the hilt, without turning Heroines either into active persons or into sexually *adventurous* persons, both of whom violate the morality of conventional feminity.

APPENDIX (verbatim)

SUPERMALES
Lake. . . . his peculiar, mocking merriment (p.12). . . his tilted eyes narrowed with laughter (p.20). . . brows drawn down in one of their storms of impatience. . . Suddenly she knew what the three men were like: the squat, alert-eyed keas; and they, trembling Katherine, Margaretta in her hot childish dress, and herself, foolish and impulsive, and not very brave, were the defenseless lambs.
Gabriella. Nick could move swiftly as a tiger when he chose. (p.39). . . all my

expectations did not check Nick's anger with me. (p.106)...he had that whippy look of a healthy, disciplined man. His hair was very dark and his mouth long and mobile...(pp.6-7). I knew that light of determination on Nick's face only too well...(p.47).... Nick was a master of judo...(p.71).

Columbella...in his late thirties, forceful, tall, rather overwhelming. The sort of man who used to alarm me at first glance. (p.20) He was a ruggedly built man and I had to look up at him, for all that I am fairly tall. His eyes were a very dark brown, with heavy brows slashed above, emphasizing the angular, marked bone structure of his face. His hair was as dark as his eyes...there were deep creases running down each cheek...(p.21).

Evils...a great hulking fellow...stood there facing us belligerently, (p.39)....almost sneered now, looking down at his own huge feet in their dirty sneakers...he flexed a wicked looking hand.... He looked as though he was gluttonous in all his appetites. He would ruthlessly take what he wanted...(P.41)....his blatant masculine appeal...(p.85). Here was a man who could juggle women with bravado...(p.96)....brazen effrontery...(p.97). I could feel it. The sheer, unrestrained animal vitality...this brutal, stalking, almost savage man...this turbulent avalanche of raw sexuality (p.98).

Dark. Those eyes. You looked at those eyes and suddenly you forgot...tiresome things which might be bothering you...as soon as he touched those piano keys you had to listen. He moved or laughed or made some trivial gesture with his hands and you had to watch him (pp.17-18). Jon always got what he wanted.... He wanted a woman and he had only to crook his little finger; he wanted money and it flowed gently into his bank account; he wanted you to be a friend for some reason and you became a friend...(p.22). Jon ordered the meal, chose the wines, and tossed both menu and wine-list on one side (p.61).... Jon spent two hours making involved transatlantic telephone calls and dealing with urgent business commitments...(p.66).

Nightingale....arrogance, an aura of dark metaled pride...(p.12)....tall, dominating...(p.13). The same face, lean and dark under a high proud brow, from which near black hair rose in a thick crest. Grey eyes, cooly assured under vigorous brows. (p.34). Like lightning fury struck his face. His voice had the cutting quality of fine-honed steel. (p.39).

HEROINES

Columbella. Often enough my mother had told me that I was born to spinsterhood and the service of others (p.9)....all my natural instincts to aid, to support, to defend...(p.27)....an enveloping loneliness crept upon me...(p.34). His cheek was against my hair and I could hear without astonishment the words he was whispering. Soft endearments they were—words like "dearest" and "beloved"...(p.124).

Gabriella. I wear glasses....Heaven knew, when I first had to wear them I was plunged in gloom.... I have the large family mouth and short nose, like Maxine's only hers has beautiful, flaring nostrils that give her face a defiant, dramatic look. (p.13). "...they and their ancestors were born in captivity. Karen, dear, some things are better that way. *You* are!" (p.185). He suffered the same reaction as a mother who, fearful for her child's safety, slaps him when he comes home unharmed (p.106).

Evils. I was twenty-four. Until Mark came into my life, I'd never—not ever, not even once—had a date with anyone. "It's not that you're unattractive," ...my only close friend said to me once. "You've got a lovely, calm face and those nice neat features. Why, you've even got a goshdarn good figure, if you'd ever wear anything decent...you're so quiet and withdrawn no one ever gets a chance to know the real you...." (p.7)....when I was twelve, Mother sent me...to a summer camp (mostly, I realized even then, to get rid of me)...(p.8). "Yes, Tracy, you were bound to a selfish, bad-tempered woman.... She'd sent you to the basement for a bottle of wine.... You... dropped the bottle, and ... your mother struck you, turned on her heel, and left you to stumble and fall backwards down the basement steps" (p.87). "... I knew from the first minute I saw you that I'd never let anything happen to you, hurt you, ever. You're the sweetest little thing, so serious, so..." (p.118).

Lake. "...my father would have to sandwich me somewhere between the wing structure and the undercarriage of his new plane and I'd simply be an embarrassment to my mother..." (p.14) Obedience to his direction...had become a habit. (p.15) Alice felt immeasurably forlorn...(p.65). She felt so alone, so unwanted. (p.82)...his eyes had grown hard and contemptuous. (p.109) If one hadn't known him so well...one would not have been conscious of the subtle undertones of contempt...(p.123) "Oh, my darling! My poor little Alice! My wonderful crazy brave little fool!" (p.189).

Nightingale...my appalling innocence...(p.12). I'd outlived the stage of being embarrassed by our hermit life (p.17). I was as lonely as Emma. She begged money from strangers. I begged love! (p.44). I tried to imagine what it was like to be on a holiday, with gay outlandish clothes and money in your pocket. I couldn't (p.104). "Melly, don't you believe in your own beauty? Aren't you used to men appreciating it? I shook my head...(p.107).

Dark...her clear, unsophisticated view of life and the naive trust which he loved so much. (p.40) Sarah's voice, very clear and gentle...(p.45) Sarah, beneath her gay smile and excited eyes, felt very small and lost and nervous...she was caught in a violent wave of homesickness and the tears refused to be checked. (p.65) She felt ashamed, inadequate, tongue-tied. (p.72)...unwanted tears pricking at the back of her eyes...everything became blurred and she could no longer see. (p.73) "I love you" he said...and his voice was unsteady..."I love love love you and you're never never going to have to go through anything like this again." (p.159).

SHADOWMALES (all murderers)

Evils...gentleness...tender consideration of everything I did and said, the quiet humor...a composite of all the elegant English stars I've seen on the late night movies...the mild blue eyes were crinkled, the long lashes tangled, the handsome narrow face alight with amusement (p.13)....the gently sensual mouth...(p.35).

Lake....a round, fresh-colored, surprisingly young face beneath gray hair. The man's eyes were light-colored and smiling. He looked very pleasant...his solid figure and firm handshake...(p.19). He gave an impression of kindness and common sense and utter dependability (p.35)....his mild, old-fashioned way (p.37). He smelled pleasantly of shaving soap (p.102).

Dark....a tall man, unobtrusively good-looking, with quiet eyes and a strong mouth...as she echoed the greeting, the lawyer's cautious scrutiny faded into a more formal appraisal and there was warmth in his eyes and kindess in the set of his mouth (p.112). He could cope with the situation... He's spent his life dealing with other people's problems (p.126). He didn't hurry...calmly, with a slight air of irritability (p.134)....forced to fight back in self-defense (p.135).

THE OTHER WOMAN

Columbella. I had never seen anyone so arrestingly alive...(p.25)....she was a figure of such loveliness in her red and gold....(p.62). She was a dangerous woman...and evil—evil! (p.82). She could move like a panther...a spoiled child...(p.94)....her strange warped nature...(p.119)....the only man she had never owned...she would never stop until she destroyed him completely (p.138).

Nightingale....a sophisticated young woman who wore her model clothes as if she'd been born to them...her gestures were free and graceful like those of a princess in undisputed possession of every horizon in sight (p.84).

Lake. Camilla had thrived on emotional complications. To her they were the spice of life (p.15). "...she has the whole male population at her feet.... How does she do it?" (p.13). She was a scamp... One always ended by reluctantly forgiving her for her outrageous behavior....(p.117). Camilla's eyes had that sleepy adoring expression whenever she wished (p.24)....the flighty little witch...(p.26). She was attractive...but silly, easily flattered, unreliable, and ...extraordinarily deceitful (p.32).

Gabriella...rich russet hair swathed round a small, imperious head; greenish-bronze eyes that even in a "still" photograph seemed restless; a wayward mouth, full and a little pouting, and a figure so slim it fooled you into thinking she was fragile (p.8). She had been brought up to believe that what money could buy would always be hers. She was not trained for work and had an innate dislike for discipline...But her assets were enormous. Not only was she beautiful, but she had that female magnetism that is the strongest weapon any woman can have in life...(p.11)...always headstrong and impulsive...(p.198).

Dark....the voluptuous indolence, the languid movements, the dreadful stifled boredom never far below the lush surface...(p.23)....how much she loved life, even if life merely consisted of living...far from the glamor of London (p.62). She behaved like a spoiled child.... She flirted at her weekend parties and made Jon go through hell...with her tantrums and whims.... She flaunted her infidelity...(p.103). She wore skintight black slacks and...a halter—some kind of flimsy arrangement which left her midriff bare and exposed an indecent amount of cleavage (p.104).

NOTES

[1]In correspondence, November 18, 1970.

[2]I was attracted to the field by happening to pick up Fawcett's *Columbella* by Phyllis Whitney, 1966. The books provided by Ace are: *Nightingale at Noon* by Margaret Summerton, 1962; *The Least of All Evils* by Helen Arvonen, 1970; *The Dark Shore* by Susan Howatch, 1965: *I Am Gabriella!* by Anne Maybury, 1962; *The Brooding Lake* by Dorothy Eden, 1953 (by Macdonald & Co., Ltd.).

[3]In correspondence, November 18, 1970.

[4]*Journal of Popular Culture*, Fall 1970, IV, 2, "Love and Sex in the Romance Magazines," by David Sonenschein.

[5]Typically the word "oyster" here is a fashion-magazine word, not that of an artist or observer. The entire vocabulary is similar—"tomato silk," "chocolate-brown," "Lime green" "that cool, uncluttered look," and so on. The descriptions are magazine-ish set pieces, not part of the story. Typically, the "Chagall print" (above) does not lead to a discussion of art or the owner's taste or anything else.

[6]How ancient any of this can really be is in question, since the house—Engleford Court—is situated in Northern Ontario. The heroine asks no questions, however. Picturesqueness—not authenticity—is what counts.

[7]Shulamith Firestone, *The Dialectic of Sex,* Morrow, 1970, pp.167-170; Germaine Greer, *The Female Eunuch,* McGraw-Hill, 1970, pp.167-185.

[8]The Super-Male is *never* short.

[9]Terry Carr, q.v.

[10]There is no reason for the Heroine to believe this at this time. She turns out to be correct, however.

[11]This is not explained for almost 100 pages.

[12]She keeps having *deja vu* experiences—recollections *via* her aunt's letters which seem to be intended to warn her of her aunt's fate—in fact, she remembers the letters only in time to avoid being murdered by the same man (her own husband).

[13]Carol Carr, science-fiction writer, calls the helplessness of the Gothic Heroines, "the feminine version of conquering the environment." In conversation, Dec. 1970.

[14]Consider the recent film about Isadora Duncan, which concentrated on her sex life, not her dancing; or her Bolshevism, which the film managed to make merely silly. Even so, "Isadora" had to be re-titled, and became "The Loves of Isadora."

Discussing "Somebody's Trying to Kill Me and I Think It's My Husband: The Modern Gothic"

1) How does the gothic romance formula compare with another popular story formula favored by mostly women readers, the passionate romance novel?

2) Compare gothic romance novels with other famous horror fiction. Do modern gothics share anything in common with *Dracula,* for example?

3) The dark male hero Russ describes in her article has a long history, appearing in various guises in the nineteenth century novels of the Bronte sisters and even earlier in the novels and plays of Lord Byron. What is it about this kind of male stereotype that makes him so continuously fascinating to many women?

Monster Movies: A Sexual Theory

By Walter Evans

As has ever been the case, Dracula, Frankenstein, the Wolfman, King Kong and their peers remain shrouded in mystery. Why do American adolescents keep Dracula and his companion monsters of the 1930's and early 1940's alive yet largely ignore much better formula movies of the same period, Westerns (*Stagecoach*), gangster movies *(Little Caesar, Public Enemy)* and others?[1] What is the monster formula's "secret of life"? Is this yet another of the things which "man was not meant to know"?

The formula has inspired a plethora of imaginative theories, including several which attempt to explain the enduring popularity of these movies in terms of: contemporary social prosperity and order;[2] political decay;[3] the classic American compulsion "to translate and revalue the inherited burden of European culture;"[4] the public's need for "an acceptance of the natural order of things and an affirmation of man's ability to cope with and even prevail over the evil of life which he can never understand;"[5] the "ambiguities of repulsion and curiosity" regarding "what happens to flesh,...the fate of being a body;"[6] our "fear of the nonhuman;"[7] the social consequences of "deviance from the norm," particularly physical deviance;[8] and "mankind's hereditary fear of the dark."[9]

Dracula, Frankenstein's monster, King Kong and others have been fruitfully approached as cultural symbols, but their power and appeal are finally much more fundamental than class or political consciousness,[10] more basic than abstractions of revolt against societal restrictions, yet more specifically concerned with certain

From the *Journal of Popular Film,* 1975, 4(2), 124-142. Reprinted by permission of the editors and the author.

fundamental and identifiable features of human experience than such terms as "darkness" and "evil" seem to suggest. Their power, and that of the other movie monsters is, it seems to me, finally and essentially related to that dark fountainhead which psychically moves those masses in the American film and TV audiences who desperately struggle with the most universal, and in many ways the most horrible of personal trials: the sexual traumas of adolescence. Sex has a central role in many popular formulas,[11] but sexuality in horror movies is uniquely tailored to the psyches of troubled adolescents, whatever their age.

The adolescent finds himself trapped in an unwilled change from a comparatively comprehensible and secure childhood to some mysterious new state which he does not understand, cannot control, and has some reason to fear. Mysterious feelings and urges begin to develop and he finds himself strangely fascinated with disturbing new physical characteristics—emerging hair, budding breasts, and others—which, given the forbidding texture of the X-rated American mentality, he associates with mystery, darkness, secrecy, and evil. Similarly, stirred from a childishly perfect state of nature King Kong is forced into danger by his desire for a beautiful young woman, a dark desire which, like the ape himself, must finally be destroyed by a hostile civilization. And so, stirred from innocence and purity (see the Wolfman poem which appears below) by the full moon which has variously symbolized chastity, change, and romance for millennia, the wolfman guiltily wakes to the mystery of horrible alterations in his body, his mind, and his physical desires— alterations which are completely at odds with the formal structures of his society. The mysterious, horrible, physical and psychological change is equally a feature of Frankenstein, of Dracula's victims, the Mummy and his bride, and countless other standard monster movie characters.

The key to monster movies and the adolescents which understandably dote upon them is the theme of horrible and mysterious psychological and physical change; the most important of these is the monstrous transformation which is directly associated with secondary sexual characteristics and with the onset of aggressive erotic behavior. The Wolfman, for example, sprouts a heavy coat of hair, can hardly be contained within his clothing, and when wholly a wolf is, of course, wholly naked. Comparatively innocent and asexual females become, after contact with a vampire (his kiss redly marked on their necks) or werewolf (as in Cry of the Werewolf), quite sexy, aggressive, seductive—literally female "vamps" and "wolves."[12]

As adolescence is defined as "developing from childhood to maturity"[13] so the transformation is cinematically defined as

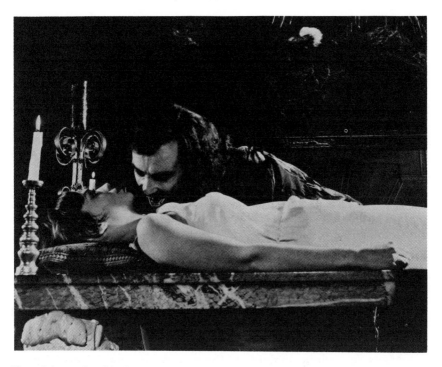

Vampirism, the black mass and the release of repressed sexuality in *The Deathmaster* (1972).

movement from a state of innocence and purity associated with whiteness and clarity to darkness and obscurity associated with evil and threatening physical aggression. In the words of *The Wolfman's* gypsy:

> Even a man who is pure at heart
>   And says his prayers by night
> May become a wolf when the wolfbane blooms
>   And the moon is full and bright.

The monsters are generally sympathetic, in large part because, as remarked earlier, they themselves suffer the change as unwilling victims, all peace destroyed by the horrible physical and psychological alterations thrust upon them. Even Dracula, in a rare moment of self-revelation, is driven to comment: "To die, to be really dead. That must be glorious... There are far worse things awaiting man, than death." Much suffering arises from the monster's overwhelming sense of alienation; totally an outcast, he painfully embodies the adolescent's nightmare of being hated and hunted by the society which he so desperately wishes to join.

Various aspects of the monster's attack are clearly sexual. The monster invariably prefers to attack individuals of the opposite sex, to attack them at night, and to attack them in their beds. The attack itself is specifically physical; Dracula, for instance, must be in immediate bodily contact with his victim to effect his perverted kiss; Frankenstein, the Wolfman, the Mummy, King Kong, have no weapons but their bodies. The aspect of the attack most disturbing to the monster, and perhaps most clearly sexual, is the choice of victim: "The werewolf instinctively seeks to kill the thing it loves best" (Dr. Yogami in *The Werewolf of London*). *Dracula's* Mina Seward must attack her fiance, John. The Mummy must physically possess the body of the woman in whom his spiritual bride has been reincarnated. Even more disturbing are the random threats to children scattered throughout the formula, more disturbing largely because the attacks are so perversely sexual and addressed to beings themselves soon destined for adolescence.

The effects of the attack may be directly related to adolescent sexual experimentation. The aggressor is riddled with shame, guilt, and anguish; the victim, once initiated, is generally transformed into another aggressor.[14] Regaining innocence before death seems, in the best films, almost as inconceivable as retrieving virginity.

Many formulaic elements of the monster movies have affinities with two central features of adolescent sexuality, masturbation and menstruation. From time immemorial underground lore has asserted that masturbation leads to feeblemindedness or mental derangement: the monster's transformation is generally associated with madness; scientists are generally secretive recluses whose private experiments on the human body have driven them mad. Masturbation is also widely (and, of course, fallaciously) associated with "weakness of the spine,"[15] a fact which helps explain not only Fritz of *Frankenstein* but the army of feebleminded hunchbacks which pervades the formula. The Wolfmen, and sometimes Dracula, are identifiable (as, according to underground lore, masturbating boys may be identified) by hairy palms.

Ernest Jones explains the vampire myth largely in terms of a mysterious physical and psychological development which startles many adolescents, nocturnal emissions: "A nightly visit from a beautiful or frightful being, who first exhausts the sleeper with passionate embraces and then withdraws from him a vital fluid: all this can point only to a natural and common process, namely to nocturnal emissions accompanied with dreams of a more or less erotic nature. In the unconscious mind blood is commonly an equivalent for semen,..." (p.59) The vampire's bloodletting of women who suddenly enter full sexuality, the werewolf's bloody attacks—which occur regularly every month—are certainly related

The symbolic sexual threat to the innocent bride. Boris Karloff and Mae Clarke in *Frankenstein*

to the menstrual cycle which suddenly and mysteriously commands the body of every adolescent girl.

Monster movies characteristically involve another highly significant feature which may initially seem irrelevant to the theme of sexual change: the faintly philosophical struggle between reason and the darker emotional truths. Gypsies, superstitious peasants, and others associated with the imagination eternally triumph over smugly conventional rationalists who ignorantly deny the possible existence of walking mummies, stalking vampires, and bloodthirsty werewolves. The audience clearly sympathizes with those who realize the limits of reason, of convention, of security; for the adolescent's experiences with irrational desires, fears, urges which are incomprehensible yet clearly stronger than the barriers erected by reason or by society, are deeper and more painful than adults are likely to realize. Stubborn reason vainly struggles to deny the adolescent's most private experiences, mysterious and dynamic conflicts between normal and abnormal, good and evil, known and unknown.

Two of the most important features normally associated with monster movies are the closely related searches for the "secret of life" and "that which man was not meant to know." Monster movies unconsciously exploit the fact that most adolescents already know the "secret of life" which is, indeed, the "forbidden knowledge" of sex. The driving need to master the "forbidden knowledge" of "the secret of life," a need which seems to increase in importance as the wedding day approaches, is closely related to a major theme of monster movies: Marriage.

For the adolescent audience the marriage which looms just beyond the last reel of the finer monster movies is much more than a mindless cliche wrap-up. As the monster's death necessarily precedes marriage and a happy ending, so the adolescent realizes that a kind of peace is to be obtained only with a second transformation. Only marriage can free Henry Frankenstein from his perverted compulsion for private experimentation on the human body; only marriage can save Mina Harker after her dalliance with the count. Only upon the death of adolescence, the mysterious madness which has possessed them, can they enter into a mature state where sexuality is tamed and santified by marriage.[16] The marriage theme, and the complex interrelationship of various other formulaic elements, may perhaps be best approached through a close analysis of two seminal classics, *Frankenstein* and *Dracula.*

Two events dominate the movie *Frankenstein* (1931), creation of the monster and celebration of the marriage of Henry Frankenstein and his fiance Elizabeth. The fact that the first endangers the second provides for most of the conflict throughout the movie, conflict much richer and more powerful, perhaps even profound, when the key thematic relationship between the two is made clear: creation of life. As Frankenstein's perverse nightly experiments on the monstrous body hidden beneath the sheets are centered on the creation of life, so is the marriage, as the old Baron twice makes clear in a toast (once immediately after the monster struggles out of the old mill and begins wandering toward an incredible meeting with Henry's fiance Elizabeth; again, after the monster is destroyed, in the last speech of the film): "Here's to a son to the House of Frankenstein!"[17]

Frankenstein's fatuous father, whose naive declarations are frequently frighteningly prescient (he predicts the dancing peasants will soon be fighting; on seeing a torch in the old mill he asks if Henry is trying to burn it down), declares, when hearing of the extent to which his son's experiments are taking precedence over his fiance: "I understand perfectly well. Must be another woman. Pretty sort of experiments they must be." Later, after receiving the burgomaster's beaming report on the village's preparations for celebration of the marriage, he again associates his son's experiments with forbidden sexuality: "There is another woman. And I'm going to find her."

There is, of course, no other woman. The movie's horror is

fundamentally based on the fact that the monster's life has come without benefit of a mother's womb. At one point Frankenstein madly and pointedly gloats over his solitary, specifically manual, achievements: "the brain of a dead man, ready to live again in a body I made with my own hands, my own hands!"

Significantly, a troubled search for the "secret of life" is what keeps Henry Frankenstein separated from his fiance; it literally proves impossible for Henry to provide for "a son to the House of Frankenstein" before he has discovered the "secret of life." Having discovered the "secret of life," he ironically discovers that its embodiment is a frightening monster horrible enough to threaten "normal" relations between himself and Elizabeth. Henry's attempt to lock the monster deep in the mill's nether regions are finally thwarted, and, in a wholly irrational and dramatically inexplicable (yet psychologically apt and profound) scene, the monster—a grotesque embodiment of Frankenstein's newly discovered sexuality—begins to move threateningly toward the innocent bride who is bedecked in the purest of white, then quite as irrationally, it withdraws. On his return Henry promises his wildly distracted fiance that there will be no wedding "while this horrible creation of mine is still alive."

The monster is, of course, finally, pitilessly, destroyed,[18] and Henry is only ready for marriage when his own body is horribly battered and weakened, when he is transformed from the vigorous, courageous, inspired hero he represented early in the film to an enervated figure approaching the impotent fatuity of his father and grandfather (there is plenty of fine wine for the wedding feast, Frankenstein's grandmother would never allow grandfather to drink any), prepared to renounce abnormal life as potent as the monster in favor of creating a more normal "son to the House of Frankenstein."

The message is clear. In order to lead a normal, healthy life, Henry Frankenstein must—and can—give up dangerous private experiments on the human body in dark rooms hidden away from family and friends. He must learn to deal safely and normally with "secret of life," however revolting, however evil, however it might seem to frighten and actually threaten pure, virgin womanhood; only then, in the enervated bosom of normality, is it possible to marry and to produce an acceptable "son to the House of Frankenstein."

Dracula's much more mature approach to womankind is clearly aimed at psyches which have overcome Henry Frankenstein's debilitating problem. Dracula (1931), obviously enough, is a seduction fantasy vitally concerned with the conditions and consequences of premarital indulgence in forbidden physical

The madness of maturation. Lon Chaney, Jr., as The Wolfman (1941).

relations with attractive members of the opposite sex.

Of all the movie monsters Dracula seems to be the most attractive to women, and his appeal is not difficult to understand, for he embodies the chief characteristics of the standard Gothic hero: tall, dark, handsome, titled, wealthy, cultured, attentive, mannered, with an air of command, an aura of sin and secret suffering; perhaps most important of all he is invariably impeccably dressed. With such a seductive and eligible male around it is certainly no wonder that somewhere in the translation from fiction to film Dr. Seward has become Mina's father and thus leaves Lucy, who also lost the two other suitors Bram Stoker allowed her, free to accept the Count's attentions. Certainly any woman can sympathize with Lucy's swift infatuation ("Laugh all you like, I think he's fascinating.") and Mina's easy acceptance of Dracula as her friend's suitor ("Countess, I'll leave you to your count, and your ruined abbey.").

Having left three wives behind in Transylvania, Dracula is obviously not one to be sated with his second English conquest (the first was an innocent flower girl, ravaged immediately before he meets Lucy and Mina), and he proceeds to seduce Mina, working a change in her which does not go unnoticed, or unappreciated, by her innocent fiance: "Mina, you're so—like a changed girl. So wonderful—" Mina agrees that indeed she is changed, and, on the romantic terrace, alone with her fiance beneath the moon and stars, begins, one is certain, the first physical aggression of their courtship. John is suitably impressed. "I'm so glad to see you like this!" Discovered and exposed by Professor Van Helsing, Mina can only admit that (having had relations with Dracula and thus become a Vamp) she has, indeed, suffered the proverbial fate worse than death, and shamefully alert her innocent, naive fiance: "John, you must go away from me."

Only when John and his older, respected helpmate foil the horrible mock elopement—Dracula and Mina are rushing to the abbey preparing to "sleep," he even carries her limp body across the abbey's threshold—only when the castrating stake destroys the seducer and with him the maid's dishonor, is Mina free to return to the honest, innocent, suitor who will accept her past, marry her in the public light of day, and make an honest woman of her.

Lucy, who has no selfless suitor to forgive her, marry her, and make an honest woman of her, is much less successful. When last seen she has become a child molester, a woman of the night who exchanges chocolate for horrible initiations.

The thematic importance of such innocent victims turned monster as Lucy and Mina, Dr. Frankenstein's creation, King Kong, the Wolfman and others points directly to one of the most commonly observed and perhaps least understood phenomena of monster movies, one which has been repeatedly noted in this paper: In those classics which are best loved and closest to true art the audience clearly identifies with the monster. Child, adult, or adolescent, in disembodied sympathetic fascination we all watch the first Karloff Frankenstein who stumbles with adolescent clumsiness, who suffers the savage misunderstanding and rejection of both society and the creator whose name he bears, and whose fumbling and innocent attempts at love with the little girl by the lakeside turn to terrible, bitter, and mysterious tragedy.

Clearly the monster offers the sexually confused adolescent a sympathetic, and at best a tragic, imitation of his life by representing a mysterious and irreversible change which forever isolates him from what he identifies as normality, security, and goodness, a change thrusting him into a world he does not understand, torturing him with desires he canot satisfy or even admit, a world in which dark psychological and strange physical changes seem to conspire with society to destroy him.

NOTES

[1]Though many critics focus on adult themes in monster movies, I believe that adolescents provide the bulk of the audience for such films, particularly the classic films shown on late night television all across America. Adolescents, of course, may be of any age.

[2]Curtis Harrington asserts that such movies are more popular in periods of depression and disorder. See "Ghoulies and Ghosties" in Roy Huss and T.J. Ross, eds. *Focus on the Horror Film* (Englewood Cliffs, New Jersey: Prentice Hall, 1972), pp.17-18. I should mention one of the finer essays in this fine collection, X.J. Kennedy's "Who Killed King Kong" (pp.106-109.

[3]Lawrence Alloway, "Monster Films" in *Focus on the Horror Film,* p.123.

[4]Frank McConnell, "Rough Beasts Slouching" in *Focus on the Horror Film,* p.26.

[5]R.H.W. Dillard, "The Pagentry of Death" in *Focus on the Horror Film,* p.26.

[6]Lawrence Alloway, p.124. He is speaking specifically of the effects of death and decay.

[7]John Thomas, "Gobble, Gobble...One of Us!" in *Focus on the Horror Film,* p.135.

[8]John D. Donne, "Society and the Monster" in *Focus on the Horror Film,* p.125.

[9]Drake Douglas, *Horror!* Collier Books (New York: Macmillan, 1966), p.11.

[10]I feel this is clearly true in spite of the more superficial importance of, for instance, the Nazi allusions in such a film as *Return of the Vampire* (1944). The classic monster movies deemphasize such non-essential material.

[11]According to Andrew Sarris, "There are no non-erotic genres any more." The statement was made on "Frame of Reference" following the "Film Odyssey" showing of *The Blue Angel.*

[12]The transformation is less obvious, and perhaps for this reason more powerful, in *King Kong* (1933). Kong himself is safe while hidden deep in the prehistoric depths of Skull Island, but an unappeasable sexual desire (made explicit in the cuts restored in the film's most recent release) turns him into an enemy of civilization until, trapped on the world's hugest phallic symbol, he is destroyed. The psychological transformation of Ann Darrow (Fay Wray) is much more subtle. While alone immediately after exchanging vows of love with a tough sailor she closes her eyes and, as in a dream vision, above her appears the hideously savage face of a black native who takes possession of her in preparation for the riotous wedding to the great hairy ape. Significantly, only when civilization destroys the fearful, grossly physical beast is she finally able to marry the newly tuxedoed sailor.

[13]*Webster's New World Dictionary of the American Language,* 2nd College Edition (Englewood Cliffs, N.J.: Prentice-Hall, 1970). Interesting, in view of the fiery death of Frankenstein's monster and others, is one of the earlier meanings of the root word: "be kindled, burn."

[14]It is interesting, and perhaps significant, that the taint of vampirism and lycanthropy have an aura of sin and shame not unlike that of VD. The good doctor who traces the taint, communicable only through direct physical contact, back to the original carrier is not unlike a physician fighting VD.

[15]See Ernest Jones, "On the Nightmare of Bloodsucking" in *Focus on the Horror Film,* p.59.

[16]In "The Child and the Book," *Only Connect,* ed. by Sheila Egoff, G.T. Stubbs, and L.F. Ashley (New York: Oxford University Press, 1969) noted psychiatrist Anthony Storr has discussed a precursor of monster movies, fairy tales, in a similar context.

Why is it that the stories which children enjoy are so often full of horrors? We know that from the very beginning of life the child possesses an inner world of fantasy and the fantasies of the child mind are by no means the pretty stories with which the prolific Miss Blyton regales us. They are both richer and more primitive, and the driving forces behind them are those of sexuality and the aggressive urge to power: the forces which ultimately determine the emergence of the individual as a separate entity. For, in the long process of development, the child has two main tasks to perform if he is to reach maturity. He has to prove his strength, and he has to win a mate; and in order to do this he has to overcome the obstacles of his infantile dependency upon, and his infantile erotic attachment to, his parents... The typical fairy story ends with the winning of the princess just as the typical Victorian novel ends with the marriage. It is only at this point that adult sexuality begins... It is not surprising that fairy stories should be both erotic and violent, or that they should appeal so powerfully to children. For the archetypal themes with which they deal mirror the contents of the childish psyche; and the same unconscious source gives origin to both the fairy tale and the fantasy life of the child" (p.93-4).

[17]The dialogue is followed by a close-up of a painfully embarrassed Henry Frankenstein.

[18]Significantly, the monster himself is pitifully sympathetic, suffering as adolescents believe only they can suffer, from unattractive physical appearance, bodies they don't understand, repulsed attempts at love, general misunderstanding. Though endowed by his single antagonistic parent with a "criminal brain," the monster is clearly guilty of little but ugliness and ignorance, and is by any terms less culpable than the normal human beings surrounding him. He does not so much murder Fritz as attempt to defend himself against completely unwarranted torchings and beatings; he kills Dr. Valdeman only after that worthy believes he has "painlessly destroyed" the monster (a euphemism for murder), and as the doctor is preparing to dissect him; the homicide which propels his destruction, the drowning of the little girl, is certainly the result of clumsiness and ignorance. She had taught him to sail flowers on the lake and, flowers failing, in a visual metaphor worthy of an Elizabethan courtier, the monster in his ignorant joy had certainly meant only for the girl, the only being who had ever shown him not only love, but even affection, to sail on the lake as had the flowers. His joyful lurch toward her after having sailed his flower is, beyond all doubt, the most pathetic and poignant lurch in the history of film.

Discussing "Monster Movies: A Sexual Theory"

1) Review the introduction to the chapter on popular rituals. Could adolescents going to horror movies be considered a rite of passage?
2) Make a list of your top ten favorite horror movies. What were they about? At what age did you see them? Do your own experiences with horror movies support or contradict Evans' ideas?
3.) Besides horror movies, what other elements of popular culture can you think of that reflect adolescents' fears about coming to sexual maturity?
4) During the 1970's horror movies such as the highly successful *The Exorcist* dwelt primarily with the occult and diabolical or, in films such as *Carrie*, centered on ESP. Do these movies support Evans' ideas or are they new directions in horror films which serve different psychological needs of their audience?

Love and Sex in the Romance Magazine

By David Sonenschein

It is fairly common to say that the mass media and popular culture contain suggestions as to many of our culture's values. There may be some disagreement as to the exact boundaries of these systems, but a general consensus among social scientists on this seems to exist. The anthropologist in particular is prone to examine textual material for value and symbolic content, for it is within this realm that he sees the very essence of culture. This area is our concern here.

Two major interests have motivated the present analysis: one in cultural conceptions of "pornography" and the other in forces of cultural socialization. A great deal of the mass media has been identified with, even defined as, "pornography," "obscenity," or "objectionable" material. Hard-core erotica (the sole, specific depiction of sexual action) has been referred to as "the mass media of sex," but now we find sex permeates much of the media around us; items readily available on the market that deal directly (girlie magazines) or indirectly (advertising) in erotica have been called "soft-core" pornography. Thus, the traditional and perennial question of obscenity—what are its effects?—is asked of a far wider range of material than before; in fact, many are asking that question of what they see to be no less than their total environment ("it's all around us!").

In addition, however, to the mere mention of acts, an extremely crucial aspect of erotica is the way in which sex is described with

From the *Journal of Popular Culture*, 1970, 4(2), 398-409. Reprinted by permission of the editor.

attendant values. It is the total configuration that becomes the major variable in socialization. Through this process of "social scripting,"[1] acts, contexts, and consequences are spelled out as behavioral alternatives in various interpersonal settings. It is this that determines for the observer or reader whether the sex is arousing or not, moral or immoral, and consequently, pornographic or not.

Beyond the immediate action in the stories, we find that sexual behaviors and attitudes are inseparably linked to broader cultural symbol systems, and it is within these that we begin to find and understand what it is that may be "wrong" with certain kinds of activities. We know that sexuality, previously thought of as a monolithic "drive" that motivates and determines a number of behaviors and dispositions, is in fact much more diffuse in human personalities and social systems.[2] We may gain a sense of this linkage in the ways sex is connected to non-sexual values and activities in the lives and thoughts of people in the magazine stories.

With regard to socialization interests, it is known that many of the readers of confession magazines are adults, usually younger married lower-middle or lower class housewives, living in the Midwestern United States.[3] On the other hand, there are indications from initial observations by this author that many readers of the magazines are of a different sort: younger girls of preteen years, usually from ages 9 to 12, are also attracted to the magazines. This population needs further definition in terms of its motivations and characteristics, but the need for socialization considerations for an age group younger than previously thought is established.

Eight different romance or confession magazines with a total of 73 fictional stories form the basis of the analysis. They were purchased from a downtown Austin newsstand and represent *all* of the magazines available on the stand at that time (one month's availability). While they are a "universe" of material at that point in time and space, they are a "sample" of a larger universe of published magazines. In 1966, there were 32 different confession magazines available; total readership was about 13½ million.[4]

The magazines used here were published by five different publishers, though there seems to be little difference among them with regard to editorial policies. Each magazine averaged about nine stories per issue.

An initial survey of their content was made by coding for aspects of format, characteristics of the narrator and main partner, sexual events and situations, and other factors that figure in the plots of the stories.

For those who have seen the magazines, it is clear that the most salient characteristic of them is sex. Throughout all of the format features, the themes of sex and the physical nature of people are heavily played upon. The immediate and initial appeal, however, is to the femininity of the potential buyer, an image with which she may most readily identify. For example, six of the eight magazines carry cover pictures of young females of a very wholesome sort; even those depicted in a "seductive" kind of pose (i.e., facial expressions, body postures, clothing arrangements and types suggesting eroticism) may still retain a look of innocence.

Surrounding the picture are the titles of the magazine itself and of the stories for that month, but, upon inspection, one is struck by the apparent incongruities of the two sets of images. The names of some of the magazines in the sample were such ones as *Real Confessions, Secrets, Intimate Story, Daring Romances,* and so on. The titles imply what is to be the nature of the stories. They promise to be stories of an intensely personal sort, the kind that one would confide only to one's closest friend. There is a strong element of wickedness and even sinfulness about the relationships to be described inside. Such large-type statements as

> One Night A Week We Were Wicked—We Were
> Single Girls on the Prowl For Men!
> I Lost My Virginity—And Reputation—In The
> Boys' Locker Room!
> He Left Sex Out Of Our Dates—If He Loved Me,
> Why Didn't He Show It!

all serve to heighten the anticipation for sex in a way that finds some correspondence with many popular judgments of what is seen to be "obscene:" *illicit* sex. Such activities as abortion, premarital sex, incest, and adultery are explicitly mentioned on the covers of the magazines.

In the table of contents, the stories are listed with a short statement of what is to be the basic theme, a kind of "abstract" of the story. Again, these statements serve to set up the reader for access to an illicit affair of the narrator. Some examples are:

> "When I Say It Baby, You Do It—Anything And Everything!"
> His Vile Commands Ring In My Ears, And There Is Nothing I
> Can Do To Escape His Ugly Desires!

> "My Stepfather Taught Me Sex!" It's My Wedding Night—I'm
> In My Bridal Bed. But The Arms That Hold Me, The Lips That
> Seek Mine, Belong To My Mother's Husband!

There begins to appear a message that the narrator seems to have little control over the situations she finds herself in. All in all, however, 77% of the story titles directly implied some sort of *sexual* activity as the *main* theme for the story.

For each story, there is an accompanying photograph supposedly depicting some main event in the story. These were coded in a broad way for the kind and style of posing in the picture. Photos of couples predominate, with 22% involving kissing (some with partial undress), and 15% depict the couple in a situation that can be described as "erotic," that is, there is a salient sexual intent between the two individuals. In most of these latter cases, the couple is touching or is in some kind of physical contact. Consequently, 37% of the format pictures involve a sexual or at least physical relationship. Thirty-three percent of the pictures represent some kind of fight, argument, or anguish, usually between a couple or in a family setting. This latter theme bcomes significant as we shall see in the content of the stories.

Advertising was also coded for simple content and kind of appeal. Ads selling material of a mail-order dime store variety comprised a large category, 37% of all ads. However, the general category of "improvement" was the largest and most significant. In this there were two varieties. One was labeled "appearance improvement," and included such things as bust development, weight losing aids, fashions, and beauty aids; this comprised 36% of all the ads. Other kinds of ads based on a direct appeal to the improvement of one's self and position, such as loans, medicine, and religion, comprised 27%. In total, "improvement" advertising amounted to 63%

The values of oneself as a physical being, more so as an appealing and in some ways a marketable physical being, are thus played upon heavily from the beginning. But we also start to get a sense of some of the risks that simply being a woman may entail. The relationships that await one, and the path through them that one must necessarily take, begins to seem more and more difficult. To what extent merely living life and being a woman means enduring punitive experiences are themes further elaborated upon in the texts of the stories.

Story types were classified into four general categories according to a classification set up by the editors of *True Story* magazine (one from 1958—not included in the sample) as a guide to potential authors. The resultant distribution on this basis was as follows:

Marriage story types...36%

Love story types...30%

Family story types...20%

Teenage story types...14%

It may be noted that the stories that deal with home life, marriage and family stories, total over half of the sample: 56%. The contextualization of the activities in the stories (recall the titles) are not as exotic, or erotic, as originally anticipated; they turn out to be settings that involve the basic values and symbols in our culture: the Home, Family, and Love.

Overwhelmingly, the narrator is female (90%), young in age (teenage, 36%, or in her twenties, 22%), fairly religious (34% of the narrators mentioned a Christian affiliation or a "general belief in God"), and usually a housewife, 41% (other occupations are secreterial/clerical/sales: 22%, or student, usually high school, at 16%). Race was, with one exception, unspecified but implied white. Fifty-one percent were married, 38% were single with no previous marriage. Married women usually had a small family of one or two children. The settings of the stories were usually in small towns, but if set in a large city, the narrator was mentioned as having come from a small town or rural area. The depiction of the narrator then is that she is just "average." Even her physical appearance is not especially gorgeous, but she is explicitly described many times as being "pretty." She is at the same time like all other girls, yet like all other girls want to be.

The life of the narrator is also "average," with problems that arise in any family which are not of a totally disabling sort. Money problems, for example, occur in 25% of the stories, housing problems in 21%, health difficulties in 16%, and occupational troubles in 14%. The complications in the lives of the narrators, however, derive not from aspects of a larger world or "society" (indeed, there is little that can be called social consciousness in the stories), but rather problems come from the people in life, especially those close to the narrator, and from within the narrator herself. Life is a series of personal involvements, the management of which constitutes "life" or "living," and the existence of which "makes life worthwhile." Satisfaction comes from having a loving mate and having a supportive environment of "people you can get along with."

To return to the characters of the stories, the main partner of the narrator usually had fewer specified qualities. The main "other" was usually a male (69%), older in age, either the narrator's spouse (34%) or a previously unmarried single male (25%). His religion and race are unspecified but he appeals less to religion or the name of God, and no question ever arises over miscegenation. His occupation is given in general terms but usually set in skilled jobs or middle class office work.

Given the anticipation for sex as set up by the format, the actual incidence of activities was not as frequent as expected. Coitus is the most frequently occurring singular activity (63% of all stories) but more diffuse in its setting, "scripting," and consequences. Kissing occurs in second place (60%) but with more partners than coitus. Heavy petting is mentioned least of all in its specifics but occurs in 18% of the stories. Other kinds of sexual activity are rare. Incest is mentioned in only a few of the stories, homosexuality hinted at only once, and oral-genital activity never considered. Extra-marital sex occurs in less than 5% of the married cases. It is of note that the partners with whom the narrator has sex are either the spouse (27% for coitus) or a single male (i.e., only one: 25%). In most of the cases, therefore, sex takes place within the boundaries of an emotional relationship with one male. Despite the lure of the titles, promiscuity in the sense of frequent and indiscriminate sexual behavior does not occur as a behavioral mode. In those few cases where it does happen, the punishments for indiscriminate sex are swift and severe; they are dealt out in an almost destructive fashion so as to indicate that those kinds of consequences were what was to be expected anyway.

The disruptive troubles that beset the stories are those that have personalistic references; that is, as we indicated before, "people" are the causes of trouble and the kinds we see in the stories are of a particularly damaging sort. Relationships are volatile, hostile, and even dangerous; in contrast to male-oriented erotica, it is trauma, rather than sex, which is "just around the corner." In those relationships where sex occurs, the results for the people involved were destructive. In relations where sex occurred, 54% of the relationships worsened because of the event. Much of this, of course, happened in cases of premarital sex, but even in many instances of marital sex the message was that when sex is attempted to be used as a solution for a problem, or the basis for forming a relationship, it became evident very quickly that it was not the answer. According to the stories then, guilt, anxiety, and personal difficulties for the narrator as well as damages to others are the costs of misusing or even just having sex.

Other themes of disruption occur significantly and regularly. Some are as follows:

> Fight or argument in stories...70%
> Mention of violence of any kind...53%
> Loss of partner...36%
> Guilt felt by narrator for coitus...34%
> Loss of virginity by narrator...33%

Each of these, of course, may be elaborated upon separately, but we may mention here only how they cumulatively contribute to the feeling of uneasiness underlying each story. In nearly all the stories, the narrator goes through some sort of crisis; the crux of each, and the attraction for the readers, seemingly, is the *consequences* of

events and their resolutions. This is in itself a separate topic for
investigation, but story endings give us a clue. Forty-eight percent
end on a note of the narrator having mixed feelings of guilt and
hope, punishment and salvation. This derives from the narrator
having gone through a basic and fundamental crisis that seems to
involve one's psychological self, particularly as felt through the
emotions of love and sex. Nineteen percent of the stories end on a
completely sad tone, where punishment has come about with the
tacit admittance by the narrator that she deserved what she got in
the end. Even though others are in the environment who will,
perhaps by their very nature, take advantage of the narrator, the
burden of villainy is assumed by her. She has misused or misapplied
her self and her sex in a way that brings not only punishment but
retribution.

We noted that the crucial and emotionally involving aspect of
the stories is not so much the sex itself but the "social scripting" of
the sex, the perception of the partner and the narrator as
"responsible" (as opposed to "responsive") beings, and the
consequences of interpersonal commitment. The emphasis in the
stories is that the purpose of life is the establishment of a series of
dependable and stable sets of interpersonal relations, ideally to be
founded upon that most stable and enduring of all forces, Love. To
this, sex is only secondary; sex can be generated by love but love
may be degenerated by sex. When we spoke of the "misuse" of sex,
we were referring to the settings in the stories where relationships
were attempted to be founded and sustained by sex. It couldn't be
done.

Forerunners of the modern romance magazines. More innocent "pulp" romance magazines 1925-
1945.

We spoke of sex as being "diffuse" in both personality and sociocultural systems. We wish to place particular emphasis upon the latter and suggest that in addition to sex being connected to such things as roles, preferences, and activities, sex is at least distributed through, and at most generated by, a broader system of values which contains views of the world and the social order.[5] It is this latter set of orientations that determines the place and propriety of sex. From the scriptings in the romance magazines, a very explicit sense of what that value and symbolic order is can be obtained.

The basic theme of each story is the stabilization of one's personal life. This may occur in a variety of settings (as with our story types on marriage, etc.) and with a variety of results (getting married, getting divorced, getting pregnant, etc.), but the essence of life is the search for continuity through dependable relationships. It is very obvious in the stories that the most desired manifestations of this essential quality for life are marriage, a family, and love. These are the stable blocks on which daily life, and hence our culture and society is built. These institutions are the resources for the relationships that allow for the expression of our "real nature." The crises in our stories all seem solvable by recourse only to love; love is the overriding context of sex and any use of sex beyond this is taboo and destructive.

Here are the links between the values of legitimate versus illegitimate behavior. The condemnation of sexual activities and relationships is discussed not so much in terms of themselves but in terms of their consequences. Thus, activities and attitudes that

Forerunners of the modern romance magazines. More innocent "pulp" romance magazines 1925-1945.

threaten or violate the symbols and values of love, marriage, and the family are acts which endanger their very existence. The stability of these institutions is threatened by the volatile nature of sex itself and the enduring values of the institutions are threatened by sexual and emotional exploitation, "taking" rather than "giving." Sex cannot occur without love; by itself it is immoral, illicit, and even "obscene." Outside the institutions of the family and marriage, it is even worse: it is "unnatural."

What we are led to is the conclusion that the condemnation and negative sanctioning of sex occurs when the continuity and stability of basic cultural institutions is perceived to be threatened or denied as valid and necessary. "Obscenity" and "pornography" in this sense are those acts and attitudes which violate fundamental and symbolic realms in our culture. We know historically the perception of this has varied with time and place, but we may explain the great variety of judgments that have occurred in the past on this basis.

The issues of obscenity and pornography are basically symbolic issues; they are connected to what is perceived to be the essential traditions of our society in its cultural values and social structures. Violations of these are what call forth the cries of the impending End of Civilization As We Now Know It. Judgments of obscenity and pornography can be applied to a wider variety of things and behaviors, many of them non-sexual in nature. It is believed that widespread and continued indulgence in "obscene" and illicit acts creates a "moral collapse" and social destruction. The family is the fundamental sociocultural unit and the institution of marriage through love is necessary for its origin and continuance. "When these go, what else is there?" ask the magazines.

Contrary to our initial expectations, then, the romance magazines really appear to be paragons of virtue, arguing with a traditional, cultural morality for the necessity of love and the family and the minimizing of sex if one is to survive personally or socially. The effects and consequences of acting outside these values are spelled out in a fashion that explicitly details the risk. For the reader, the result is not a pretty picture.

Contained in the romance magazines and their explicit treatments of sex is the argument for the continuity of the American mode of life. Obviously, one of the main ways of establishing cultural continuity is to define the borders of deviance and state the consequences for going over. This is done by imbuing specific areas of interpersonal relations with an aura of heavy negative sanctioning. If a young female reader acquires the language of sex in the punitive terms that are portrayed in the magazines, we may wonder what the cost is of maintaining cultural continuity. The alternatives are limited for us in the media and the penalties are severe for the wrong choices. Yet the social order continues to be questioned and challenged. The problem is one that is demanding attention by its very protestations.

NOTES

A revised version of a paper presented to a special session on "The Issue of Obscenity and Pornography in the Contemporary Media" for the American Association for Public Opinion Research (May, 1969). This paper is preparatory to a larger study of mass media erotica and popular culture funded by the Commission on Obscenity and Pornography. In operationalizing this, I am grateful to the following people who commented critically on earlier drafts: Eva Hunt, Hancy O. Lurie, Nancy L. Gonzalez, H.C. Dillingham, Brenda E.F. Beck, Alice Marriott, Carole Rachlin, Edward Sagarin, W.Cody Wilson, James L. Mathis, M.D., J. W. Mohr, Gunther Schmidt, and Roger Abrahams. Co-workers Mark J.M. Ross, Richard Bauman, and Morgan Malachlan join in colleagueship in the new project.

[1]William Simon and John Gagnon, "Pornography—Raging Menace or Paper Tiger?" *Trans*-action IV (1967), 41-48.

[2]William Simon and John Gagnon, "On Psychosexual Development," in D. Gloslin (ed.), *Handbook of Socialization Theory and Research* (Chicago: Rand McNally, 1969), 733-752; John Gagnon and William Simon, "Sex Education and Human Development," in P. Fink and V. Hammett (eds.) *Sexual Function and Dysfunction* (Philadelphia: Davis, 1969), 113-126.

[3]Fawcett Publications, Inc., *Reader Characteristics* (New York, 1953); Look Magazine, *The Audiences of Nine Magazines: A National Study* (New York: Politz Research, 1955).

[4]*Standard Periodical Directory* (2nd. ed., New York, 1967). A larger number of magazines for the new study has been obtained. However, due in part to the formalized nature of the stories, the present example sufficed in yielding significant themes in proper proportions. General agreement was also found in the present study with two earlier surveys. See George Gerbner, "The Social Role of the Confession Magazine," *Social Problems* V (1958), 29-40; and Wilbur Schramm, "Content Analysis of the World of Confession Magazines," in J.C. Nunnall (ed.), *Popular Conceptions of Mental Health* (New York: Holt, Rinehart & Winston, 1961), 297-307.

[5]David Sonenschein, "Pornography: A false Issue," *Psychiatric Opinion* VI (1969), 10-17; *ibid.*, "Pornography and Erotica in America," in E. Sagarin (ed.), *Sex and the Contemporary American Scene* (New York: Dell, 1970), in press.

Discussing "Love And Sex In The Romance Magazines"

1) Compare modern gothic novels as described in the essay by Joanna Russ with love magazines, Do they indicate similar or different ideas and fears?

2) Sonenschein describes how the love magazine formula is created for a specific audience. Examine the fiction in two or three different types of magazines. What are the formulas of the fiction in these magazines? What sort of audience would be drawn to these formulas?

3) Review the introduction to the chapter on stereotypes. Are the characters in love magazines mostly stereotypes? If so, do these stereotypes serve a useful or destructive purpose?